CAMBRIDGE STUDIES IN PHILOSOPHY

Moral realism and
the foundations of ethics

CAMBRIDGE STUDIES IN PHILOSOPHY

General editor SYDNEY SHOEMAKER

Advisory editors J. E. J. ALTHAM, SIMON BLACKBURN,
GILBERT HARMAN, MARTIN HOLLIS, FRANK JACKSON,
JONATHAN LEAR, WILLIAM LYCAN, JOHN PERRY, BARRY STROUD

Moral realism and the foundations of ethics

David O. Brink
Massachusetts Institute of Technology

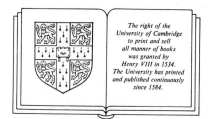

The right of the
University of Cambridge
to print and sell
all manner of books
was granted by
Henry VIII in 1534.
The University has printed
and published continuously
since 1584.

Cambridge University Press

Cambridge

New York   New Rochelle   Melbourne   Sydney

Published by the Press Syndicate of the University of Cambridge
The Pitt Building, Trumpington Street, Cambridge CB2 1RP
32 East 57th Street, New York, NY 10022, USA
10 Stamford Road, Oakleigh, Melbourne 3166, Australia

© Cambridge University Press 1989

First published 1989

Printed in the United States of America

Library of Congress Cataloging-in-Publication Data
Brink, David Owen, 1958–
Moral realism and the foundations of ethics / David O. Brink.
p.   cm. – (Cambridge studies in philosophy)
Bibliography: p.
Includes index.
ISBN 0-521-35080-8.   ISBN 0-521-35937-6 (pbk.)
1. Ethics.   2. Realism.   I. Title.   II. Series.
BJ1012.B676 1989
170–dc19   88–16179
CIP

British Library Cataloguing in Publication Data
Brink, David O.
Moral realism and the foundations of
ethics – (Cambridge studies in
philosophy)
1. Moral philosophy
I. Title
170

ISBN 0 521 35080 8 hard covers
ISBN 0 521 35937 6 paperback

Contents

v

vi

Preface

As the Introduction explains, this book concerns the foundations of ethics; it examines issues of metaethics, moral epistemology, moral psychology, value theory, and moral theory. I defend a number of positions on these issues; in particular, I argue that a realist metaethics, a coherentist moral epistemology, an externalist moral psychology, a nonreductive form of ethical naturalism, an objective theory of value, and an objective form of utilitarianism are individually plausible and mutually supporting. In the course of examining these issues and defending these claims, I discuss and assess both traditional and contemporary views. I have usually tried to introduce, explain, and motivate the issues and the positions that have been taken on them. To this extent, the book should be accessible to a fairly wide audience with varied interests and backgrounds. But it is not strictly introductory; nor is it in any way a survey of established terrain. I have generally assumed a certain threshold familiarity with traditional positions and disputes about the foundations of ethics and with traditional and contemporary issues in metaphysics and epistemology. Against this background, I argue for my own particular set of views about the foundations of ethics. So even if the book is accessible to a fairly wide audience, it speaks most directly to a somewhat narrower audience of more advanced students and specialists.

This book grew out of the doctoral dissertation I submitted to Cornell University in 1984; though recognizably related to the dissertation, the book is in many ways quite different. Its scope is considerably larger, in order to provide some defense of ideas and assumptions taken for granted in the thesis, and the organization and argument of the central project have changed in important ways.

I have tried to record in the body of the book my intellectual debts to authors of published writings. Here I'd like to mention more special debts. During the various stages of the book's gestation, I've been the fortunate beneficiary of a good deal of philosophical stimulus and moral support from a number of people. It is a pleasure to acknowledge these personal and intellectual debts and to express my gratitude to these people.

Because the book began as a doctoral thesis, I owe some of my greatest debts to members of my dissertation committee. Richard Boyd argued the merits of his own version of moral realism and helped me grapple with some of the metaphysical and epistemological parallels between ethics and science. I'm sure I'm still not quite the right sort of realist in his view, but the articulation of my own view owes much to stimulating discussions with him. David Lyons provided prompt and helpful comments on versions of each chapter of the thesis. His suggestions and complaints helped me avoid confusions and identify positions and arguments demanding articulation. I owe still greater debts to my two other readers, Nick Sturgeon and Terry Irwin. Nick provided detailed written and oral comments on each draft and has provided similar input on almost all of my subsequent work on these issues. I know that I've been profoundly influenced by Nick's views about moral realism, related metaethical issues, and consequentialism. Anyone familiar with his published work will notice the extent of my debt to him in my discussions of the significance of the realism–antirealism dispute in ethics (Chapter 4) and of the explanatory power of moral claims (Chapter 7, sec. 3). These are just the most salient features of a much larger intellectual debt I owe Nick. Perhaps my greatest debt is to Terry Irwin. Only those who know Terry, and perhaps only those who have been fortunate enough to work with him, will fully understand the nature of this debt. Terry provided copious, detailed, constructive comments and criticisms on every draft of every chapter of my thesis, comments we then often pursued in long and, for me, extremely fruitful discussions. He has provided similarly judicious comments and advice on much of my more recent work on these issues. Terry has made me rethink, reorganize, and reargue my position on almost every topic in this book. Perhaps most important, Terry's own work and his help with mine provided me with a model of philosophical integrity. Although my work does not approximate this model as closely as I would like, I know that Terry, especially, deserves credit for what is of value here, and I hope he finds some return on his investment in what follows.

Changing the thesis into a book proceeded in fits and starts. Teaching duties and work on shorter projects both interrupted and interacted with work on the book. A number of people read and commented on one or another version of the entire book during this period. Alan Sidelle read the thesis and a subsequent version of the book manuscript, as well as many of these shorter projects, and provided valuable suggestions. Perhaps more important, over the last seven years Alan has been both a constant source of philosophical ideas and advice and the best of friends. Jennifer Whiting read a version of the manuscript and provided several pages of very helpful written comments. Gilbert Harman was the reader for Cambridge University Press. In addition to influencing an earlier version of Chapter 3 (Brink 1986a), he gave me several pages of instructive comments on the penultimate version of the manuscript. Phil Gasper, David McNaughton, Julius Moravcsik, and Walter Sinnott-Armstrong each read a version of the manuscript and gave useful advice.

Two groups of graduate students, one at Stanford and one at MIT, helped sort through this material and its formulation. In this connection, I would especially like to thank Charles Dresser, Susan Dwyer, Richard Heck, Larry Kaye, Kwong-loi Shun, Eric Lormand, and Paul Pietroski. Others read or heard portions of this manuscript in one form or another and provided valuable input; they are John G. Bennett, Michael Bratman, Joshua Cohen, Norman Dahl, John McDowell, John Post, Geoffrey Sayre-McCord, Milton Wachsberg, and David Wong.

I'm sure that I've not taken full advantage of these people's comments, criticisms, and advice; there must be many places where I've ignored their worries or where the changes I've made still don't quite satisfy. But I've tried to answer (or avoid) what seemed to me to be their most serious worries and to take advantage of their good advice, and I know that the book is vastly better than it would have been without their careful and generous attention.

A final debt needs to be recorded. My wife, Bonny Sweeney, provided, during this long period, love and patient understanding without which work would have gone more slowly and painfully, and without which I certainly would have been much less happy.

The book has had a rather incestuous relationship with several shorter works written over the last five years or so: Papers formed the basis of chapters, whose revision sometimes suggested new papers, whose ultimate form sometimes required revision or reorganization of parts of the book. I would like to thank the following journals for permission to make use of material published in their pages: the *Australasian Journal of Philosophy* (1984), *The Southern Journal of Philosophy* (1986a), *The Journal of Philosophy* (1986b), and the *Canadian Journal of Philosophy* (1987).

1

Introduction

This book examines the foundations of ethics; it investigates a complex network of issues in the metaphysics of ethics, moral epistemology, moral psychology, and substantive moral theory. This agenda includes both what is usually called second-order issues and first-order issues about morality. It is worth pausing over this division within my agenda, since some attention to it should throw light upon the nature and scope of my project.

However difficult it is to state criteria for marking this distinction between first- and second-order levels of inquiry in ethics, it is an important distinction about whose application there is often a surprising amount of agreement. Second-order, or metaethical, issues are issues about, rather than within, morality and typically take the form of metaphysical, epistemological, semantic, or psychological issues about morality and our moral claims. In what sense, if any, is morality objective? Are there such things as moral facts or truths? Can we justify moral judgments? In what sense, if any, do moral considerations guide conduct? Is it irrational to be indifferent to moral considerations? If there are moral facts, how are they related to the natural features of agents, policies, and actions that those moral facts concern? These questions raise second-order issues and are my primary focus.

First-order, or normative, issues, by contrast, are issues within morality about what sorts of things are morally important (e.g., right and wrong). It is useful to mark a further distinction within normative ethics between issues of moral theory or principle and particular, substantive moral issues. Although this distinction is primarily between levels or degrees of abstraction among normative issues, it is an important distinction. Issues of moral theory or principle concern the theoretical structure of morality. How are goodness and rightness related? In what way should a moral theory be impartial among people? Does impartiality require us to maximize aggregate welfare, or would maximizing aggregate welfare

1

ignore important distributional considerations? What ideal of the person should we accept, and how does this decision affect the nature of the moral principles we adopt? Substantive moral questions, on the other hand, raise more specific moral issues. Is abortion ever justified and, if so, under what conditions? Should the death penalty be imposed as punishment for certain crimes? Should Vera keep the truth from Malcolm in order to spare him anguish? This book also examines issues of moral theory or principle, although it does not directly address substantive moral questions.

Since my project examines the foundations of ethics and conceives of them as including both first- and second-order inquiries, it is somewhat old-fashioned in scope. As those familiar with the history of ethical theory in this century will realize, the scope of my project somewhat resembles that of work at the beginning of this century, such as Henry Sidgwick's *The Methods of Ethics* (7th ed., 1907), G. E. Moore's *Principia Ethica* (1903) and *Ethics* (1912), and W. D. Ross's *The Right and the Good* (1930). Each of these works is concerned with both a variety of metaethical issues and issues of normative ethics (which in Sidgwick's and Ross's works includes substantive moral issues as well as moral theory). Although my discussion of the foundations of ethics does not range as widely as that of, say, Sidgwick or Ross, it resembles their work in scope more closely than it does much of the work within the noncognitivist tradition that followed such writers. The noncognitivists, by and large, viewed the foundations of ethics and the province of the moral philosopher more narrowly, as restricted to certain metaethical concerns. Happily, this trend is now changing; some of the most interesting recent work on the foundations of ethics (e.g., Harman 1977; Mackie 1977; Williams 1985; Nagel 1986) eschews this narrow scope. My views about the foundations of ethics differ from these most recent views more in content than in scope, although the differences are no less important for that reason, and here too my views may seem in some respects somewhat old-fashioned.

It may help to recall briefly some of this history, even if the recollection is rather crude and hackneyed. Moral philosophy during the first thirty years of this century was dominated by a position known as *intuitionism*. Intuitionists such as Sidgwick, Moore, Broad, and Ross, as I have noted, conceived of the foundations of ethics broadly, as including a wide range of metaethical and normative issues. Although the intuitionists differed quite a bit over normative issues, they displayed remarkable agreement on metaethical issues. In particular, most intuitionists accepted three metaethical claims: a realist or cognitivist commitment to the existence of moral facts and moral truths whose existence and nature are independent of our moral thinking, a foundationalist epistemology according to which our moral knowledge is based ultimately on self-evident moral truths, and a radically nonreductive metaphysics of moral facts and properties, known as nonnaturalism, according to which moral facts and properties are metaphysically independent of, for example, natural facts and properties and so are sui generis.

In part under the influence of then dominant metaphysical, epistemological, and semantic assumptions, moral philosophy in the 1930s, 1940s, and 1950s became highly critical of intuitionism and assumed an antirealist, *noncognitivist* form. I have in mind primarily the work of C. L. Stevenson (1944, 1963), A. J. Ayer (1946), R. M. Hare (1952, 1963a), and Patrick Nowell-Smith (1957). The noncognitivists found the metaphysical and epistemological commitments of intuitionism obscure and offered what they regarded as less extravagant metaphysical and epistemological claims. The various forms of noncognitivism asserted that moral claims and moral discourse could be seen, on analysis, to be fundamentally noncognitive in character. On this view, moral claims do not really make assertions of fact but, rather, express the moral agent's or appraiser's attitudes. Consequently, moral claims can be neither true nor false, there can be no moral facts or true moral claims, and moral knowledge is not possible. Not surprisingly, this trend in ethical theory drew a sharp line between metaethical and normative claims. Metaethical issues – in particular, "conceptual or logical analysis of fundamental moral concepts" – are cognitive issues, whereas normative issues are not. This sharp conceptual distinction between first- and second-order moral claims underwrote a sharp division of philosophical labor. Ethics or moral philosophy came for a while to be conceived of as including only metaethics; because normative ethics was fundamentally noncognitive, it was not the appropriate concern of the philosopher or something to which she could be expected to make any distinctive contribution.

Partly as a result of the dominance of this kind of noncognitivism, moral philosophy came to many, I think, to seem a fairly sterile and boring intellectual place. Perhaps for this reason, and

3

because of the pressing nature of substantive normative issues connected with social and political movements in the United States, philosophers began to return to first-order moral issues in the 1960s and 1970s. The resulting work in normative ethics has seemed to many to bear the marks of intellectual progress and to show that philosophers do have a distinctive contribution to make to these problems. Indeed, concern with normative ethics, including both moral theory and substantive moral problems, has dominated moral philosophy for the last two decades. With some exceptions and until quite recently, moral philosophers have not worried much about traditional metaethical concerns. They have seemed to assume, what the noncognitivist legacy claimed, that first- and second-order moral issues are independent of each other in a way that allows a person to pursue normative issues without worrying about metaethical ones. And many of those philosophers who have begun to address metaethical issues recently (e.g., Blackburn 1971, 1985; Harman 1977; Mackie 1977; Williams 1985) have embraced metaethical conclusions similar in important ways to those of noncognitivism. But, of course, it was precisely noncognitivism and its sharp distinction between levels of moral inquiry that led the turn away from normative ethics. It is puzzling, therefore, that there has not been a greater concern among these philosophers to reexamine the noncognitivist metaethical claims and the connections, if any, between metaethics and normative ethics.

Just such a reexamination is one of the main aims of this book. It is my view that the main features of the noncognitivist legacy are fundamentally flawed. The traditional noncognitivists, I shall argue, failed to see the issues that concerned them against the appropriate metaphysical and epistemological backdrops; either they failed to see the issues as continuous with general metaphysical and epistemological issues, or they relied on inappropriate (even if then dominant) metaphysical and epistemological assumptions. We should see traditional metaethical issues as continuous with general metaphysical and epistemological issues, and we now have better developed and more plausible metaphysical and epistemological principles to apply to our understanding of ethics. Applying this method to traditional metaethical issues, I shall argue, will support various metaethical theses; in particular, it will vindicate a form of cognitivism and objectivity about ethics that I call *moral realism*. Moral realism is at odds not only with traditional forms of

4

noncognitivism but also with much of the most recent work that has been done on these metaethical issues.

As I noted, the noncognitivists thought first- and second-order moral issues are completely independent of each other and, in particular, believed that whether one makes moral judgments and which moral judgments one makes are matters independent of the metaethical views one holds (see Hare 1957: 39–41, Mackie 1977: 16, Blackburn 1985: 11). My defense of moral realism will draw this independence into question. Although it is both possible and important to distinguish between metaethics and normative ethics, they are not completely independent. Metaethical claims can and do affect the moral theories and substantive moral judgments one is entitled to accept, or so I shall argue. It is in part because metaethics and normative ethics, especially moral theory, are interdependent in various ways that a study of the foundations of ethics should not be confined to metaethics but should include normative ethics, especially moral theory, as well.

1. OBJECTIVITY

In my view, the foundations of ethics include many topics in metaethics (including metaphysics, epistemology, semantics, and moral psychology) and issues of moral theory or principle. One traditional issue at the foundations of ethics concerns its objectivity. As a matter of philosophical and historical fact, issues about objectivity in ethics raise a number of these other issues of metaphysics, epistemology, semantics, and moral psychology. Because I want to discuss these issues and their bearing on our views about the objectivity of ethics, it may be helpful, before I sketch my views about the foundations of ethics, to distinguish in an introductory way some different views about the objectivity of ethics.

Most people writing about objectivity in ethics have (rightly, I think) focused on an important *comparative* issue: Is ethics or can it be objective in the way that other disciplines, such as the natural and social sciences, are, can be, or seem to be? This way of stating the comparative issue latent in the issue about objectivity in ethics may seem to raise as many issues as it sets aside (e.g., "What is to count as a natural or social science?" and "Are natural and social sciences equally objective disciplines?"). But let's try to table these questions, at least for the moment. The commonsense view of the

5

natural sciences (e.g., physics, chemistry, biology) and of the social sciences (e.g., psychology, history, economics) is that these disciplines study real objects and events whose existence and nature are largely independent of our theorizing about them, that they exhibit progress and convergence over time, and that they contain some at least approximate knowledge. This conception of objectivity is usually thought to be a realist view. Is this commonsense view of the natural and social sciences correct or reasonable, and if so, can such a view reasonably be maintained about ethics?

Although there are four possible general positions on this comparative issue, there seem to be only three worth serious consideration that can be found in the literature. Many traditional and contemporary metaethical views can be classified (if only crudely) in one of these three ways. (These metaethical positions will be explained and examined more fully in Chapter 2.)

1. Realism about science and antirealism about ethics: The commonsense view about the objectivity of the sciences is roughly right; ethics is not (and cannot be) objective in this way. There is a *special* problem about realism or objectivity in ethics. Traditional nihilists, noncognitivists (e.g., emotivists and prescriptivists), moral skeptics, and relativists can be viewed as holding this position on our comparative issue.

2. Realism about science and ethics: The commonsense view about the objectivity of the sciences is roughly right; ethics is or can be objective in much the same way. Although many traditional cognitivists found important disanalogies and discontinuities between ethics and the sciences, most of them, including the intuitionists (e.g., Richard Price, Thomas Reid, Sidgwick, Moore, Ross, Broad, and H. A. Prichard), believed that ethics does or can possess these marks of objectivity.

3. The third view is harder to label: Some will regard it as global subjectivism or antirealism, others as a sophisticated realism about both ethics and science. The idea is that, although ethics cannot fit the commonsense view of scientific objectivity, this establishes nothing interesting about the objectivity of ethics, since science itself does not satisfy the commonsense view of scientific objectivity. The commonsense view of scientific objectivity is naive; once we understand the objectivity obtainable in the sciences, we can see that ethics is or can be every bit as objective as the sciences. Although it is natural for sympathizers with view (1) or (2) to regard

6

(3) as global subjectivism or antirealism, proponents of (3) often regard their position as realist or objectivist. Presumably, they think it makes sense to call a position about the status of ethics or science antirealist only if there is some discipline whose status is more realistic or objective than that of ethics or science. Since they think that more realistic views are naive and that nothing actually possesses that kind of objectivity, they regard their views about ethics and science as realistic.

2. THE ELEMENTS

My own view or set of views about the foundations of ethics is best regarded as a version of (2). The main elements of my view are these: moral realism, an externalist moral psychology, a coherentist moral epistemology, a nonreductive form of ethical naturalism, and an objective conception of utilitarianism.

Moral realism is a thesis about the metaphysical status of moral claims. Realism about the external world asks us to take the claims of the natural sciences and commonsense physical theory literally, as claims that purport to describe more or less accurately a world whose existence and nature are independent of our theorizing about it. Realists about the external world who are not skeptics hold related epistemological and semantic claims; they think that the claims of the natural sciences and commonsense physical theory not only purport to describe but often succeed in describing such a world. Thus, scientific terms refer to real features of the world, and the sciences provide us with successively more and more accurate knowledge of the world.

In a similar way, moral realism asks us to take moral claims literally, as claims that purport to describe the moral properties of people, actions, and institutions – properties that obtain independently of our moral theorizing. Moral realism is roughly the view that there are moral facts and true moral claims whose existence and nature are independent of our beliefs about what is right and wrong. A moral realist who is not a skeptic holds related epistemological and semantic claims. The moral realist thinks that our moral claims not only purport to but often do state facts and refer to real properties, and that we can and do have at least some true moral beliefs and moral knowledge.

Although various sorts of considerations support moral realism,

7

its intuitive appeal derives, I think, from the way it explains the point and nature of moral inquiry. In moral argument and deliberation, it seems, we are trying to *discover* what sorts of things are valuable, praiseworthy, or obligatory. We *recognize* moral requirements, and if we are sensitive to moral requirements, they *constrain* our will and our conduct. We think people can be morally *mistaken* and some people are morally more *perceptive* than others. Whatever the intellectual aspects of moral inquiry, morality is also fundamentally practical. Moral deliberation aims at deciding what to do, and moral advice aims at influencing the conduct of others. We expect moral considerations to motivate people to act in certain ways or at least to provide them with reason to act in those ways. It is sometimes thought difficult for a realist to explain the practical character of morality. How can moral considerations influence conduct in the appropriate way if, as the realist seems to claim, they merely state facts?

This might be a problem for the realist if one had to represent the connections between morality and motivation and morality and rationality as internal, conceptual connections, since, it seems, purely cognitive states and objects can be motivationally inert. Moral antirealists, such as noncognitivists, are committed to this sort of internalist moral psychology. An externalist moral psychology, however, claims that whether moral considerations motivate or provide reason for action depends on factors external to the concept of morality, such as the content of morality, a substantive theory of reasons for action, and facts about the world, such as an agent's interests or desires. An externalist moral psychology not only allows the realist to avoid this objection, it is, I argue, preferable to its internalist rival on independent grounds. If so, then the fact that the realist can be an externalist but the traditional antirealist cannot is evidence for moral realism.

Suppose we accept moral realism. How could we have moral knowledge or justify our moral beliefs? Traditional moral realists (e.g., Price, Reid, Sidgwick, Moore, Broad, and Ross) were intuitionists; in particular, they combined moral realism with a kind of foundationalist epistemology. But intuitionism has seemed to many a mysterious and, hence, suspicious view. How could any moral claim be self-evident? Surely there is no special faculty of moral perception. Although I do not think that intuitionism deserves all of the scorn it has received, I do think that any kind of foundationalist epistemology faces general problems that force us to defend a coherence theory of justification. A coherentist moral epistemology claims that a moral belief is justified insofar as it coheres in the appropriate way with other beliefs, both moral and nonmoral, that we hold or might hold. But this sort of coherentist epistemology may not seem to sit very well with a realist understanding of ethics. Doesn't a coherentist epistemology require the rejection of realism? How can the coherence of a moral belief with other moral beliefs we hold be evidence of its objective truth? Although such worries about a coherentist moral epistemology are understandable, they can be answered. Coherence of the appropriate kind among our beliefs can be evidence of their objective truth.

But what are these moral facts like? And how are they related to the more familiar natural features of actions, policies, and personalities that such moral facts are supposed to concern? By itself, realism implies little about the nature of moral facts or their relation to other kinds of facts. But moral realism is most plausible, I think, if we accept a naturalistic view of these matters. According to the ethical naturalist, moral facts and properties *are* natural (i.e., natural and social scientific) facts and properties. Does this mean that we can deduce moral claims from natural claims, or that we can define moral terms in natural terms? If so, ethical naturalism seems committed to violating "Hume's law" that no 'ought' can be derived from an 'is'.

But ethical naturalism need not be understood in this reductive way. A nonreductive form of ethical naturalism claims that moral facts and properties are constituted by, and so supervene upon (or vary in a lawlike way with), natural and social scientific facts and properties even if moral terms are not definable by natural terms. Moreover, this sort of nonreductive ethical naturalism parallels the sort of nonreductive naturalism that we accept (or should accept) about a number of other, nonmoral disciplines in the natural and social sciences.

These metaethical views require the truth of no one moral theory; the metaphysical and epistemological commitments that I defend could be met by a wide variety of substantive moral theories. However, I do present, discuss, and defend a teleological moral theory (i.e., a theory that makes the proper moral assessment of such things as actions, motives, and policies a function of the value those things

9

bring about). This teleological theory can be regarded as a species of utilitarianism because it takes the good to be human (or sentient) welfare or happiness. This utilitarian theory is different from more familiar kinds of utilitarianism, though, because it incorporates a different view of happiness or welfare. Traditional forms of utilitarianism (e.g., hedonistic utilitarianism or desire-satisfaction utilitarianism) rely on subjective theories of value, according to which human happiness or welfare consists in, or depends importantly on, contingent psychological facts about an agent, such as what he desires or takes pleasure in. By contrast, objective theories of value construe happiness or welfare in largely nonsubjective terms; they claim that a valuable life consists in the possession of certain character traits, the development and exercise of certain capacities, and the possession of certain relationships to others and the world, and that the value of these things is independent of the pleasure they produce or of their being the object of desire. Despite their apparent appeal, subjective theories of value are, I argue, much less plausible than objective theories. Here, utilitarianism stands to learn something from the Greeks and from the British idealists. The form of utilitarianism that I favor incorporates one such objective theory of value.

This utilitarian theory is worth examining for two reasons. First, my defense of moral realism requires fairly abstract metaphysical and epistemological claims. By examining this utilitarian theory's implications for various metaethical issues, I can illustrate the kinds of specific metaphysical and epistemological commitments that substantive moral theories bring. Second, this utilitarian theory is a plausible as well as a possible account of morality. A coherentist epistemology creates a presumption in favor of moral theories that are unified in the way this utilitarian theory is. Moreover, standard objections to utilitarianism fail to undermine this theory, either because they depend on construing utilitarianism as a model of moral reasoning or because they depend on construing welfare as subjective versions of utilitarianism construe it. If we construe utilitarianism as providing a standard of rightness, rather than a decision procedure, and we provide an objective construal of the nature of welfare, we can respond persuasively to standard objections to utilitarianism. In particular, this objective version of utilitarianism promises to accommodate our beliefs about value, about the nature and extent of our obligations to others, and about rights and justice, and it violates neither personal integrity nor the separateness of persons. Objective utilitarianism may not be uniquely reasonable, but it does provide a plausible program for a realist view in ethics and deserves serious consideration.

3. STRATEGY

How one motivates and defends a philosophical view or set of views usually depends on whom one takes to be the relevant opposition. Not surprisingly, I take positions (1) and (3) concerning the objectivity of ethics to represent the relevant opposition, and this influences my discussion of many issues. Although I shall address (3) ("sophisticated realism" about both science and ethics, or global antirealism) and argue that the commonsense view of objectivity is *not* naive in the ways it is sometimes claimed to be, I will take (1) (commonsense realism about science and antirealism about ethics) to be the primary opposition. (1) claims that there are *special* problems with realism or objectivity about ethics. There are a number of reasons for this focus. First, although, as I say, I have some reasons for thinking that "naive realism" is preferable to "sophisticated realism," my main concern is with the *parity* of ethics and the sciences. And (3) respects this parity claim as much as (2) does. Indeed, it is this parity claim that joins (2) and (3) against (1). So, proponents of (3) should be able to accept a great deal, if not all, of my argument. This brings us to the second reason for focusing on (1): (1) is a common starting point for nonphilosophers (or nonprofessional philosophers), and, as I indicated, it is also pretty much the view with which twentieth-century metaethics – in particular, non-cognitivism – has left us.

I shall take 'realism' to refer to the commonsense view of objectivity I have described, unless I indicate otherwise. As I said, some people find realism about anything naive. Global antirealists often think that talk of a world that is independent of the way in which we conceive of it makes no sense. I will address some of these global antirealist worries; I will argue that there are general considerations about the nature of belief and justification that support a general realist metaphysical view.

But moral realism is also regarded as a black sheep within the realist metaphysical family. Doubts about moral realism remain even among those who accept a general realist metaphysical picture. These doubts are, broadly speaking, metaphysical or epistemo-

11

logical. What would moral facts be like? Would they be part of a plausible and explanatorily coherent naturalistic world view? How can we justify moral judgments, and is moral knowledge possible? Those who accept realism about nonmoral disciplines such as commonsense physical theory and the natural and social sciences but doubt that there are sensible answers to these metaphysical and epistemological questions about ethics conclude that ethics must be less objective than those recognizably realist disciplines. These doubts about moral realism will be my primary concern. I will argue that the metaphysical and epistemological commitments of moral realism are very similar to, and no less plausible than, those of realism about commonsense physical theory and the natural and social sciences.

It is possible to distinguish, at least in principle, between the negative task of defending a thesis against objections (removing grounds for disbelief) and the positive task of providing a case for a thesis (providing reasons for belief). Of course, these positive and negative tasks are often difficult to separate. My defense of moral realism will partake of both. Much of my argument will pursue the negative task. Moral realism is thought by many to succumb to a variety of devastating objections. I shall try to show why moral realism does not fall to standard metaphysical and epistemological objections. If this defense is successful, I shall have shown that the standard reasons for resisting moral realism are unfounded. Although this negative claim about moral realism is both interesting and important, I shall try also to establish the case for moral realism. Chapters 2 through 4 contain, among other things, fairly specific arguments for moral realism. But part of the case for moral realism must remain cumulative. In defending moral realism against objections, I shall stress the parallels between the metaphysical and epistemological commitments of ethics and those of other disciplines that we do or should regard as realist. If these parallels are as frequent and important as I claim, we have further reason for accepting moral realism.

Indeed, more generally, my arguments, both positive and negative, have an important cumulative character. Although I shall offer and, of course, endorse many specific arguments, both positive and negative, I recognize that few, if any, of them will literally refute or silence all opponents. But I assume that the argumentative standards here are those of systematic comparative plausibility. Even if none of my arguments is unanswerable, they pose problems and

12

puzzles for the moral antirealist and display the various virtues of moral realism. Taken collectively, my arguments should make the case for moral realism and the other claims about the foundations of ethics that I defend here plausible and worthy of serious consideration. Those who wish to reject these claims not only will have to respond to particular arguments but also will have to articulate an alternative set of views with comparable resources.

2

Moral realism and moral inquiry

I shall be defending moral realism against rival metaethical views. But before we examine the merits of moral realism and its rivals, we need to know what moral realism is and is not, what its rivals are, and whether, and if so why, it is of interest and worth defending.

1. WHAT IS MORAL REALISM?

Moral realism is a kind of metaphysical thesis about the nature and status of morality and moral claims. A realistic view about ethics presumably asserts the existence of moral facts and true moral propositions. But a moral relativist who thinks that moral facts are constituted by an individual's or social group's moral beliefs is able to agree with this. Moral realism, it seems, is committed to moral facts and truths that are *objective* in some way. But in what way?

We might employ either of two methods in characterizing moral realism. First, we might characterize it as a special case of a global realist metaphysical view. Second, we might characterize it in a way that is not topic-neutral, by contrasting it with metaethical views we already regard as antirealist or nonobjective. The interplay of these two methods, I believe, yields an interesting and important, if perhaps only partial, characterization of moral realism.

2. METAPHYSICAL REALISM

Metaethical views can be seen as special cases of more general metaphysical views. Thus, we might view moral realism as a special case of metaphysical realism. Realism about a discipline typically claims there are facts of a certain kind that are in some way mind-independent or independent of human thought. It is difficult, however, to make metaphysical realism both global (i.e., applicable to

14

all those disciplines about which we want to be able to formulate a realist thesis) and precise, since realism is contrasted with so many different metaphysical views (see Sober 1982). For example, we want to contrast realism with idealist theories claiming that facts about the world are constituted by facts about human or divine will, and with somewhat different idealist – or what I will call constructivist – theses claiming that facts about the world are constituted by our beliefs or evidence. With these constraints in mind, we might try to characterize realism by defining it simply as the claim that there are mind-independent facts of certain kinds.

But what kind of independence is involved in this claim? It cannot be causal independence, for surely realists about such things as artifacts will admit that the existence of things like tables and chairs is causally dependent on their creator's mental states, such as beliefs and desires. The realist must be asserting a different kind of independence, such as conceptual or metaphysical independence. The facts about the world are *not constituted* by the mental. But even if we construe 'dependence' as conceptual or metaphysical (rather than causal) dependence or constitution, this would seem to exclude too much. We want (I assume) to be able to formulate a realist theory about psychology, but surely psychological facts must be mind-dependent. We also want (I assume) to be able to construe hedonistic utilitarianism as a moral theory that might be objectively (realistically) true, but that moral theory makes moral facts consist in the existence or possession of certain qualitative mental states such as pleasure and pain.

There may be a single formulation of realism in terms of necessary and sufficient conditions that is both global and precise, or perhaps the various versions of realism form only a family or cluster of metaphysical theories, all of which assert some kind of mind-independence claim. I have sympathies with this second view, but I do not want to take a stand on the issue. Instead, I shall focus on an important kind of realist claim common to a number of disciplines. Whatever else realists might claim, they usually agree on the metaphysical claim that there are facts of a certain kind which are independent of our evidence for them. That is, realism claims there are facts of a certain kind that are metaphysically or conceptually independent of the beliefs or propositions which are our evidence that those facts obtain. I shall take this to be the central claim of meta-

15

physical realism.[1] This formulation of realism allows us to contrast it with two traditional, or at least familiar, forms of antirealism: nihilism and idealism, or constructivism. Nihilism about a certain subject matter denies the existence of facts of a certain kind; constructivism, or idealism, about that subject matter claims that there are facts of a certain kind but that these facts are constituted by some function of the evidence (i.e., the beliefs that are our evidence) for them.

The metaphysical theses of realism and constructivism allow us to distinguish realist and constructivist semantic theses.[2] Assume that truth is some kind of correspondence with, or conformity to, the facts. Because realism holds that the facts are evidence-independent, it will hold truth to be evidence-independent. Because constructivism holds the facts to be constituted by evidence, or evidence-dependent, it will hold truth to be evidence-dependent.

These claims allow us to represent realism as making two important metaphysical claims:

R: (1) There are facts or truths of kind x, or (2) these facts or truths are independent of the evidence for them.

Constructivism affirms R(1) and denies R(2).

C: (1) There are facts or truths of kind x, and (2) these facts or truths are constituted by the evidence for them.

Constructivism asserts and realism denies that the facts or truths in question are constituted by our evidence for them.[3]

---

1 In doing so, I do not mean to be assuming that facts − as opposed, say, to events or properties − form a, or the, basic or primitive ontological category. I intend my assumptions about metaphysical (and moral) realism to be compatible with any ontology that understands fact-talk.

2 The semantic theses that I take realism and constructivism to imply are theories of truth, not theories of meaning or language understanding. Cf. Dummett 1963: 145–6, 155; 1972; 1978: xxii, xxvii, xl; 1981: 464–70; and Putnam 1976: 125; 1978: 34–5; 1983: 84–5, 211, 238, 272.

3 C is meant to capture a number of similar antirealist views, which have sometimes gone under the name 'constructivism'. Compare: "Systematic coherence is not only the criterion we use for truth; it is what in the end we mean by truth" (Blanshard 1939: 304); "The opinion which is fated to be ultimately agreed to by all who investigate, is what we mean by the truth, and the object represented in this opinion is the real" (Peirce 1934: 268); "A statement is true, in my view, if it would be justified under epistemically ideal conditions for many sorts of statements" (Putnam 1983: 84–5). Cf. Joachim 1906; James 1907: 97; Bradley 1914: 111, 113–14; Peirce 1934: 186–7, 189, 268, 391, 394–6; Blanshard 1939: 260–301; Dummett 1963: 162f.; 1972; 1978: xxii; Quine 1968; Kuhn 1970: 110–11, 135, 150, 206; Putnam 1976: 132; 1981: 55; 1983: xvii, 84–5, 231, 272; Goodman 1978: 120–5; and Rorty 1980: 279–81, 295–311. Intuitionists about mathematics are also

16

R may not state sufficient as well as necessary conditions of metaphysical realism; there may be some purposes for which R will not be a fully adequate characterization of realism.[4] But R is a central tenet of metaphysical realism. Nihilism and constructivism (C) are important and traditional kinds of antirealism, and a central thesis of metaphysical realism denies nihilism and constructivism. In assessing the relative merits of moral realism and its rivals, one version of constructivism will be more important to consider than others. Although the reasons for this will not be completely clear until Chapter 5, it is important to focus on constructivist views that incorporate a coherence theory of justification. A coherence theory of justification, as we shall see, claims that a belief is justified if it is part of an explanatorily coherent system of beliefs. Constructivists who accept a coherence theory of evidence or justification will claim that the facts are constituted by coherent beliefs and so will accept a coherence theory of truth.

3. MORAL REALISM, NONCOGNITIVISM, AND CONSTRUCTIVISM

We might try to formulate moral realism as a special case of this formulation of metaphysical realism. 'Moral' is simply substituted for the variable x.

MR: (1) There are moral facts or truths, and (2) these facts or truths are independent of the evidence for them.

called 'constructivists'. "For this reason, in mathematics an antirealist (i.e., constructivist) position involves holding that a mathematical statement can be true only in virtue of *actual* evidence, that is, of our actually possessing a proof" (Dummett 1963: 163). Cf. Dummett 1977: v, ix, 4, 6–7, 372–5, 382–3, and Benacerraf and Putnam 1983: 18, 23–7, 30–1. I suppose, however, that it is not entirely clear that intuitionism in mathematics satisfies C. For, while intuitionism is usually formulated as the claim that mathematical truth is evidence-dependent, it is not clear that 'evidence' should here be understood, as C understands it, epistemically. Intuitionism, at least as some understand it, may make mathematical truth consist in the existence of a proof (i.e., physical tokens of certain formulas arranged in certain ways) or in the existence of an ability to produce a proof. Understood in either of these ways, mathematical intuitionism probably does not satisfy C. I don't take this to be a defect in C or R, however. Those concerned to reveal the antirealist character of mathematical intuitionism can try to formulate further necessary conditions of realism, beyond those contained in R.

4 For instance, idealist theories that make facts about the external world consist in facts about divine or absolute will satisfy R. But see Mackie (1982: 64–80), who treats Berkeley's idealism as a form of immaterial realism.

17

I do not claim that MR states necessary and sufficient conditions of moral realism (although I do think it states important necessary conditions) or that it is the only way of stating the moral realist's claim. In fact, it seems clear to me that MR does not state sufficient conditions for moral realism, since there are some metaethical views I am prepared to regard as antirealist, that satisfy MR. But I can identify no further conditions to add to MR, so as to exclude those views, that do not seem ad hoc.[5] Therefore, I shall treat MR as a fairly clear core element in moral realism. MR possesses the virtues of making moral realism parallel to an important and common formulation of metaphysical realism (R) and of allowing us to distinguish metaethical theories in an intuitively attractive way. The opponents of moral realism are of two main kinds: (a) nihilists, emotivists, prescriptivists, and other noncognitivists who deny that there are moral facts or truths[6] and (b) constructivists or idealists in ethics who are cognitivists because they recognize the existence of moral facts and true moral propositions but who claim that these moral facts are constituted by some function of our moral beliefs. Noncognitivism denies MR(1), while constructivism in ethics de-

5 Thus, for instance, in Chapter 3 I discuss an argument that purports to show, among other things, that moral obligations are desire-dependent in the sense that one can be under a moral obligation to do x only if there is some desire or purpose that one has that x would fulfill. Now this theory seems to be some kind of antirealist, relativist thesis about ethics. Yet it satisfies MR. If we were looking for necessary and sufficient conditions for moral realism, then either we would have to supplement MR in some way so as to exclude this view, or we would have to accept this view as a kind, perhaps a rather peculiar kind, of moral realism. But I don't know how to supplement MR in a way that is not ad hoc (i.e., other than by adding a clause to MR that would eliminate only this particular view as antirealist), and the second alternative is not entirely happy either (i.e., this would be a rather peculiar form of moral realism). Perhaps we should simply note the respects in which this theory is realistic (e.g., it recognizes the existence of moral facts that are independent of people's beliefs about what is right or wrong) and those in which it is antirealist (e.g., it makes people's moral obligations depend on, and vary with, their desires), and let others draw the lines where they like. Later in this section I discuss another classificatory issue – whether the debate between objectivism and subjectivism about value is part of the debate between moral realism and antirealism.

6 I construe cognitivism in ethics as the claim that we possess or could possess moral knowledge; so construed, cognitivism implies that there are moral facts and true moral propositions, and so implies nonnihilism. But this is not the only way of construing noncognitivism; for instance, we could understand it as the claim that we can hold some cognitive attitude, such as belief, toward moral claims. (For example, Mackie [1977] is a noncognitivist by the first construal and a cognitivist by the second, because he believes that we have moral beliefs but that, since there are no moral facts, these beliefs are all false.)

18

nies MR(2). Because of these virtues, I shall treat MR as the core element in moral realism, and treat other possible features of moral realism on an ad hoc basis as they seem relevant or seem to arise. If this makes for a somewhat fuzzy account of moral realism, it is, I submit, unavoidable fuzziness, or at least it is fuzziness I do not know how to avoid.

The traditional opponent of moral realism is the nihilist or non-cognitivist who denies that there are moral facts or true moral propositions or, as a result, any moral knowledge. Nihilists and noncognitivists must, therefore, be moral skeptics. The nihilist thinks that moral predicates such as 'good', 'fair', and 'wrong' fail to refer to real properties. Noncognitivism is the most familiar form of antirealism, and it is the metaethical view with which twentieth-century thinking has left us. Traditional forms of noncognitivism claim not only that moral terms and phrases are non-referring but also that their meaning is primarily expressive or prescriptive rather than descriptive.[7] Emotivists such as Stevenson claim that moral judgments are not primarily fact-stating but, rather, express approval and invite others to join in the appraiser's attitudes (1937, 1944). Prescriptivists such as Hare claim that moral judgments are not primarily fact-stating but, rather, express universal prescriptions or recommendations (1952, 1963a, 1981).

Constructivism in ethics is in some ways the less traditional opponent of moral realism. Constructivism agrees with moral realism that there are moral facts and true moral propositions but disagrees with realism about the nature or status of these moral facts and truths. A constructivist in ethics claims that moral facts or truths are *constituted by* some function of those beliefs that are our evidence in

---

7 This is a bit oversimplified. Noncognitivists typically claim that moral terms or phrases have a primary emotive or prescriptive sense and a secondary descriptive sense. It is in this primary sense that the noncognitivist claims that moral language is nonreferring. In its secondary, descriptive sense, however, moral language can refer in a certain way. Moral language can, secondarily, refer to those nonmoral facts on the basis of which individual speakers express their attitudes or make their prescriptions. In this view, not only is the reference of moral language secondary, the referent of a moral term or phrase is a matter of brute psychological fact that can vary from speaker to speaker and from utterance to utterance. Although non-cognitivists can perhaps claim that moral language refers in this way, their claim should be distinguished from the way in which moral realists think moral terms refer and the way in which most people (moral realists or not) think that most natural and social scientific terms refer, that is, independently of the speaker's beliefs or attitudes.

ethics. Indeed, constructivism in ethics can be formulated as a special case of constructivism.

MC: (1) There are moral facts or truths, and (2) these facts or truths are constituted by the evidence for them.

We can distinguish between relativist and nonrelativist forms of constructivism. Relativist constructivism (relativism) is true just in case there are a plurality of sets of moral facts each constituted by different moral beliefs or different bodies of moral beliefs. According to moral relativism, a moral claim x (e.g., that abortion is wrong) states a moral fact for S (x is true for S) just in case S believes x, S would believe x upon reflection, S is part of a social group the majority of whom believe x, or some such thing (e.g., Westermarck 1932; Benedict 1934; Sumner 1940; Herskovits 1948). Nonrelativist constructivism holds that there is a single set of moral facts that are constituted by some function of our beliefs, often by our moral beliefs in some favorable or idealized epistemic conditions (cf. Peirce 1934: 395; Dworkin 1973; Rawls 1980; 5.9 and Appendix 4 in this book).

This way of characterizing moral realism helps explain the sense in which a realist thinks that ethics is objective and helps distinguish moral realism from rival metaethical views. A moral realist thinks that moral claims should be construed literally; there are moral facts and true moral propositions, and moral judgments purport to state these facts and express these propositions. Ethics is objective, then, insofar as it concerns matters of fact and insofar as moral claims can be true or false (some of them being true). But moral realism claims that ethics is objective in another sense, which is not always distinguished from this first kind of objectivity. Not only does ethics concern matters of fact; it concerns facts that hold independently of anyone's beliefs about what is right or wrong. This first kind of objectivity distinguishes moral realism and other cognitivist theories from nihilism and noncognitivism; the second kind of objectivity distinguishes moral realism from constructivist versions of cognitivism.

We might say, oversimplifying somewhat, that this way of reconstructing the debate between realism and antirealism over the objectivity of ethics takes the main issue to be moral *truth* and its nature and takes the main antirealists to be the nihilist or noncognitivist, who denies truth, and the relativist or constructivist, who makes truth belief- or evidence-dependent. It is perhaps worth pointing out that this way of characterizing moral realism cuts across a de-

20

bate some people associate with the debate between realism and antirealism. Moral realism, so construed, is itself neutral between what are sometimes called *subjectivism* and *objectivism about value*. Subjectivism about value is the view that value consists in, or depends importantly on, an individual's contingent psychological states. Thus, hedonism is a form of subjectivism because it says that the one and only thing of intrinsic value is a certain qualitative mental state, namely, pleasure. A desire-satisfaction theory of value is also subjective, because it says that an activity is valuable just in case, and insofar as, it is the object of people's desire. By contrast, objectivism about value denies that value consists in, or depends importantly on, people's mental states; in particular, it claims that things, say, certain activities and relationships, are valuable independently of the pleasure they produce or their being the object of desire. Some people (e.g., Platts 1980) seem to associate moral realism with objectivism about value and antirealism with subjectivism about value, but I do not. There may well be some interesting connections between realism and objectivism and between antirealism and subjectivism. Moreover, I shall discuss the differences between subjectivism and objectivism about value and defend a theory of value incorporating important objective components (8.2). But this dispute seems to be more a dispute *within* ethics, between competing theories of value, than a dispute *about* ethics and its status, as the debate between realism and antirealism should primarily be. Although I reject the noncognitivist claim that metaethics and normative ethics are completely independent of each other (see Chapters 4 and 8.9), I assume that the truth of a metaethical view is not tied in this way to the truth or defensibility of a particular kind of moral theory or theory of value. I assume that we want to be able to give a realist construal of hedonistic and desire-satisfaction forms of utilitarianism. Certainly, traditional antirealists, such as the noncognitivists, could not admit that subjective theories of value might be literally true. At any event, I shall be understanding moral realism to be neutral as between subjectivism and objectivism; those who think that a realist must also be an objectivist may take consolation in the fact that I do defend objectivism, even if I do not take this to be a *part* of defending realism.

Construed in this way, the debate between moral realism and moral antirealism is parallel to the general debate between metaphysical realism and antirealism, and often the grounds for accept-

21

ing moral realism or moral antirealism are perfectly general. But the debate between realism and antirealism in ethics is nonetheless logically independent of the debate between realism and antirealism about other disciplines such as commonsense physical theory and the natural and social sciences; it is possible to be a metaphysical realist about such nonmoral disciplines but a moral antirealist. Indeed, the most influential opponents of moral realism and my principal concern are those who accept metaphysical realism about these other disciplines but reject moral realism.

4. MORAL REALISM, NATURALISM, AND
NONNATURALISM

Suppose, for the moment, that moral realism is true. There are moral facts. What are these moral facts like? My characterization of moral realism is in important respects metaphysically neutral; it does not itself place any constraints on the nature of these evidence-independent moral facts. In particular, moral realism is compatible with a wide variety of views about the relationship between moral and various nonmoral facts and properties.

Naturalism, supernaturalism, and nonnaturalism are traditional, competing views about the nature of this relationship. We can, for present purposes, give the following highly simplified account of the debate among these views. First, we must distinguish within the class of nonmoral facts and properties between natural and supernatural facts and properties (see Moore 1903: chaps. 1, 2, 4). This distinction is supposed to be one of which we have an intuitive grasp. Natural facts and properties are presumably something like those facts and properties as picked out and studied by the natural and social sciences (broadly conceived); whereas supernatural facts and properties are studied in other ways (e.g., by religion). (Of course, this distinction will not always be easy to draw and may be, on certain cosmological views, impossible to draw.) Ethical naturalism is the claim that moral facts and properties just are natural facts and properties, whereas ethical supernaturalism claims that moral facts and properties just are supernatural facts and properties (e.g., facts about and properties of the will of a divine being). Nonnaturalists such as Moore (1903), Broad (1930), Ross (1930), and Prichard (1949), however, claim that moral facts and properties are neither natural nor supernatural facts and properties; they are sui generis.

22

A full and proper discussion of moral realism and its rivals must address the debate among these three views, in part because anti-realists have pressed specific metaphysical and epistemological objections to each of these three views and defended their own position by appealing to the implausibility of each of these three views. But the proper formulation and the assessment of these views raise large philosophical and exegetical issues that I shall return to in Chapters 6 and 7. The important point, for present purposes, is that naturalism, supernaturalism, and nonnaturalism are all equally realist theories; each is a theory about the nature of evidence-independent moral facts.

5. MORAL REALISM AND MORAL INQUIRY

The preceding section has given us some idea of what moral realism is, what it is not, and what its main rivals are. But what interest do these metaethical views hold, and is there any reason to believe one rather than another?

In many areas of dispute between realism and antirealism, realism is the natural metaphysical position. We begin as realists about the external world or the unobservable entities mentioned in well-confirmed scientific theories. Generally, people *become* antirealists about these things (if they do) because they become convinced that realism is in some way naive and must be abandoned in the face of compelling metaphysical and epistemological objections. So too, I think, in ethics. We begin as (tacit) cognitivists and realists about ethics. Moral claims make assertions, which can be true or false; some people are morally more perceptive than others; and people's moral views have not only changed over time but have improved in many cases (e.g., as regards slavery). We are *led to* some form of antirealism (if we are) only because we come to regard the moral realist's commitments as untenable, say, because of the apparently occult nature of moral facts or because of the apparent lack of a well developed and respectable methodology in ethics.[8]

I think there is more to this dialectical picture than just a sugges-

8 Of course, not everyone accepts this dialectical picture in either the moral or nonmoral cases. Berkeley denies that his idealism (or immaterialism) is revisionist in this way, and Hare (1981: 85–6) holds what seems a similar position about the nonrevisionist character of his antirealism. But I shall defend this dialectical picture of both the moral and nonmoral cases in the rest of this chapter.

tive thumbnail sketch of the history of twentieth-century metaethics. Moral realism should be our metaethical starting point, and we should give it up only if it does involve unacceptable metaphysical and epistemological commitments. What follows is a defense of this dialectical position. In the rest of this chapter I shall explain and defend our commitment to moral realism. In subsequent chapters I shall argue that we do not need to, and should not, abandon this commitment; indeed, many of the appropriate metaphysical and epistemological claims about ethics actually strengthen the case for moral realism.

Our commitment to moral realism is sometimes defended on phenomenological grounds. Various writers have noted that certain phenomenological aspects of moral life reflect our belief in, or commitment to, the objectivity of ethics (e.g., Mackie 1977: chap. 1). Moral judgments are typically expressed in language employing the declarative mood; we engage in moral argument and deliberation; we regard people as capable both of making moral mistakes and of correcting their moral views; we often feel constrained by what we take to be moral requirements that are in some sense imposed from without and independent of us. These phenomena are held to demonstrate the realist or cognitivist character of commonsense morality; morality seems to concern matters of fact that people can and sometimes do recognize and debate about. I think that these phenomenological claims are correct and important, in part on their face and in larger part because they reflect, and are confirmed by, various philosophical presuppositions of inquiry in general, and moral inquiry in particular. Before trying to substantiate this claim, however, I should forestall two misinterpretations of it.

First, this thesis is not the transcendental thesis that moral inquiry is possible only on realist assumptions. Perhaps this is true, but my claim is somewhat more modest: It is that features of actual and possible moral inquiry are hard to understand on antirealist assumptions and much easier to understand on realist assumptions. Realism, and realism alone, provides a *natural* explanation or justification of the way in which we do and can conduct ourselves in moral thought and inquiry. Of course, even so, moral realism could still be false; moral inquiry might be confused or misguided in some fundamental way. But if this claim about the realist nature of moral inquiry is right, we have reason to accept moral realism that can be overturned only if there are powerful objections to moral realism.

24

Second, I want to avoid a possible misunderstanding about the nature of my argument and its appeal to commonsense morality and moral thought. I do not claim that moral realism is a common belief. I am willing to admit that, about moral realism, common belief is silent, divided, or even antagonistic. My concern, however, is not with unreflective and untutored metaphysical or meta-ethical views. My appeal to commonsense moral thinking is not a prediction about the likely results of a Gallup poll on the issue of moral realism. Rather, my concern is with the philosophical implications or presuppositions of moral thought and practice. (Compare the way in which philosophers of science take the practices of working scientists as an important methodological constraint but largely discount scientists' philosophical views about the status of their research.) I claim that cognitivism seems to be presupposed by common normative practices of moral judgment, argument, and deliberation and that reflection on the nature of moral theorizing seems to support a realist view about these moral facts and truths. This claim may be false, but this is not shown by an appeal to common metaethical beliefs (or the lack thereof).

6. THE FORM AND CONTENT OF MORAL JUDGMENTS

Moral realism and other cognitivist theories derive support from the form and content of our moral judgments. As many have observed, moral discourse is typically declarative or assertive in form. We say things like 'The government's tax plan is unfair', 'Waldo is just', 'It would be wrong to work for that cause', and 'My obligation to Maurice is greater than my obligation to Malcolm'. This language is putatively fact-stating (because it is declarative in form) and certainly seems to ascribe moral properties to persons, actions, policies, and so forth.

Our moral judgments not only have fact-stating and property-ascribing *form;* they have cognitivist *content* as well. Many common moral judgments themselves make reference to moral properties, moral facts, or moral knowledge (cf. Sturgeon 1986a: 125–6). For instance, it is often claimed that one should not be held responsible for actions one could not have *known were wrong,* that *goodness* deserves reward, that the *turpitude* of a crime should determine the severity of punishment, and that *good* intentions do not always excuse. In making such moral judgments, we (or at least those who

25

make them) certainly seem to presuppose the existence of moral facts and properties and the possibility of moral knowledge. The form and content of our moral judgments, therefore, presuppose cognitivism.

The form and content of our moral judgments also tell against those versions of moral relativism that claim that moral truth for someone is constituted by something like her sincere moral beliefs. We do not say that murder is wrong for Spike, unless by this we mean to imply only the nonrelativistic claim that Spike believes murder is wrong or the equally nonrelativistic claim that it is wrong for someone in Spike's circumstances to commit murder. Nor do we say that Spike should be held responsible only for those actions he could have known were wrong for him, unless, again, we mean by this only the nonrelativistic claim that Spike should be held responsible only for those actions he could have known were wrong for someone in his circumstances.

If we reject moral realism (or any other antinoncognitivist and antirelativist metaethical view), it seems we must regard the form of our moral judgments as misleading and inappropriate. We can retain the declarative form of moral judgments only by treating these putative assertions of moral fact as something like disguised imperatives, prescriptions, or expressions of approval. We must treat putative assertions of moral fact, such as 'x is wrong', as disguised expressions of the appraiser's disapproval of x or as disguised prescriptions to avoid x.

But it seems an open question whether the noncognitivist can account for the form and content of our moral judgments in this way. First, it seems that one can make moral judgments with no intention of expressing one's feelings and with no intention or even hope of influencing others' conduct (cf. Warnock 1967: 25–6). If asked about my own moral views, for example, I can reveal them by expressing moral judgments without, it seems, necessarily intending to express my approval or influence others. Someone might reply that if I really only intend to inform others what my moral views are in saying 'x is wrong', then my claim reports only a nonmoral fact about what my moral views are and does not express a genuine moral judgment. But this seems to confuse what J. L. Austin distinguished as illocutionary and perlocutionary speech acts (1962: chap. 10); the fact that I may hope to inform you of my moral views (and succeed in so informing you) by asserting

26

'x is wrong' does not show that my assertion fails to express a moral judgment. Also, it seems we can conceive of the amoralist, that is, someone who recognizes certain considerations as moral considerations and yet remains unmoved by them and sees no reason to act on them.[9] An amoralist makes moral judgments with no intention of expressing his attitudes or of influencing the conduct of others. These noncognitivist paraphrases, therefore, seem inadequate to these actual and possible contexts in which people make moral judgments.

Second, it is still more difficult to see how the noncognitivist is going to account for the references to moral facts, moral properties, and moral knowledge embedded within many of our moral judgments. Can someone who denies the existence of moral properties, moral facts, and hence the possibility of moral knowledge continue to assert or even understand moral claims such as 'One can be held responsible only for actions one could have *known were wrong*' or 'The *turpitude* of a crime should determine the severity of punishment'? The noncognitivist might conclude that no one is ever responsible for her actions and that it is impossible to determine the severity of punishment appropriate to different crimes. I assume, however, that the noncognitivist will instead attempt to paraphrase or reconstruct these common moral judgments. But I have doubts about the adequacy, or at least the equivalence, of the reconstructions the noncognitivist can offer.

The noncognitivist might suggest that she who judges that the turpitude of a crime should determine the severity of punishment is, say, prescribing to others that the severity of punishment for a certain activity should be determined by the intensity with which she prescribes against engaging in that activity. But I am not sure how to gauge the intensity of a prescription, and I doubt that the intensity with which we prescribe against a particular kind of conduct should determine how severely we punish that conduct, if for no other reason than that we think that our own moral views might be mistaken and we think that punishment should track the actual turpitude of the crime and not our beliefs or attitudes to the crime (should these diverge).

Concerning our other example, deriving from the M'Naghten

9 Noncognitivists deny, explicitly or implicitly, the existence of the amoralist. But as we shall see (3.3, 3.8, 4.1), this is a defect, not a defense, of noncognitivism.

Rule, the noncognitivist may suggest that because moral knowledge is, strictly speaking, impossible, she who judges that one can be held responsible only for actions one could have known were wrong is really doing something like prescribing that people be held accountable only for actions against which they could have sincerely prescribed. (The relevant sense of 'possibility' or 'capacity' in both the original and reconstructed claims is, of course, a kind of psychological possibility or capacity.) But I doubt that the capacity to prescribe against an action is, as I do think the cognitive capacity to know that an action is wrong is, a necessary condition for responsibility or culpability, if only because this reconstruction would allow amoralists to avoid responsibility. At any rate, the original claim and reconstructed claim are not equivalent, as the case of the amoralist shows. Or suppose the noncognitivist suggests we reinterpret the original claim as the claim that we should not hold people responsible for actions unless they could have known that their actions had those nonmoral characteristics by virtue of which we think such actions wrong. But this won't do either. Consider Zenobia's case. The actions Zenobia thinks are wrong (i.e., prescribes against) all have nonmoral characteristic C, and she thinks them wrong because they have C. Can Zenobia's claim that people should be held responsible only for things they could have known were wrong really be analyzed as the claim that people should be held responsible only for actions that they could have seen possessed C? One reason this won't do is that people might be able to recognize C but not (be able to) recognize C as a wrong-making characteristic (this is true of certain psychopaths), and although the original claim absolves them of responsibility (although they may still require detention and treatment), the reconstructed claim does not. The noncognitivist might avoid this inequivalence by understanding Zenobia's claim as follows: People are to be held responsible only for actions that they could have seen were C *and* that they could or would have prescribed against. But this reintroduces the inequivalence between the original and reconstructed claims that the amoralist's case demonstrates. Moreover, there is still the problem that this ties the content of the reconstructed principle to Zenobia's criteria of wrong-making in a way in which the original claim does not. Zenobia would want to allow that her moral views might be mistaken and that there are wrong-making characteristics different from, or in addition to, C and that people

28

should be held responsible only if they could have known that their actions were in fact wrong and not merely believed by Zenobia to be wrong (should these diverge). In this way the reconstructed claim will absolve some people whom the original claim would not have absolved (i.e., those who hold correct moral views, contrary to those of the person holding or asserting the reconstructed moral claim).

Hence I find it hard to believe in the adequacy of noncognitivist reconstructions of the apparent cognitive character of the form and content of moral judgments; they seem unable to capture the actual content of our moral judgments. If so, then it is not clear that noncognitivists can make (all of) the moral judgments contained in commonsense moral thinking and available to the moral realist. Perhaps the form and content of our moral judgments are systematically misleading in some way, but this claim should be accepted only as the conclusion of a compelling philosophical argument.

7. THE EXISTENCE OF RIGHT ANSWERS IN ETHICS

Commonsense moral thinking also supports moral realism insofar as we act as if there are moral facts. This is true in both intrapersonal and interpersonal contexts. We often *recognize* the existence of moral requirements that constrain our conduct in certain ways. And when we are uncertain about moral issues, we often *deliberate* as if there were a right answer to the issue before us. At other times, we disagree and argue with others as if there were right answers to the moral issues about which we disagree. About some moral issues, of course, we are unsure what to think, and sometimes, when we do have moral views, we do not hold them all that confidently. But about many moral issues we have fairly firm views. We can and do argue with others about these issues. We examine the moral and nonmoral beliefs that underlie our disagreement. If our dispute is genuine and we see no reason to give up our position, we regard the other parties to the dispute as mistaken. If our dispute is not the result of nonmoral disagreement, we regard our opponents as *morally mistaken*. Indeed, the possibility of moral mistakes is explained by a thesis often taken to have antirealist implications, namely, the is/ought thesis. I shall discuss the is/ought thesis at greater length in Chapter 6. But one of the ideas originally behind it is that there can be disagreement between per-

29

sons and the possibility of error even once all the nonmoral facts are in or agreed on (cf. Sturgeon 1986a: 128).

If moral mistakes are possible, then moral argument and deliberation are intellectual activities that, at least in principle, always make sense. This is so even if there are good reasons for terminating argument or deliberation, say, because we regard further argument as unprofitable or unfriendly.

Noncognitivist theories such as emotivism or prescriptivism underplay the possibilities for moral mistakes and so for moral argument and deliberation. Of course, noncognitivist theories allow room for deliberation about moral issues. According to the noncognitivist, we can argue about those nonmoral matters upon which, as a matter of psychological fact, our moral attitudes and commitments depend, and we can deliberate about the logical consistency and coherence of our attitudes and commitments. But the point of *moral* argument, as opposed to argument about what is sometimes called "logic or the (nonmoral) facts," according to these views, is to change the attitudes or commitments of one's interlocutor, not to establish truth. No sense can be made of being wrong in one's consistent and informed attitudes or commitments.

Noncognitivists do sometimes try to allow for the possibility of mistaken attitudes (e.g., Hare 1981: chaps. 2, 3; Blackburn 1985: 5). The suggestion is usually that an individual's attitude or set of attitudes, say, the set consisting of an aversion to poetry and an affinity for push-pin, is mistaken (1) if the individual actually possesses a second-order attitude, say, the desire to cultivate intellectual attitudes, which conflicts with this set of first-order attitudes, or (2) if the individual would come to possess such a second-order attitude were she to acquire more nonmoral information (e.g., more experience reading difficult poetry). We might wonder why either condition should be taken to show that the first-order attitude or set of attitudes is *mistaken*. Why doesn't (1) simply establish conflict within the individual's attitudes, and, if it must be taken to reveal mistaken attitudes, why not conclude that the second-order attitude is the mistaken one? Does (2) establish anything more than that the individual's first-order attitudes are revisable? In any case, neither condition (1) nor condition (2) adds anything to the picture of mistaken attitudes that I have not already conceded; (1) reveals inconsistent attitudes, and (2) reveals insufficiently informed attitudes. The noncognitivist still has no explanation of how fully

30

informed and consistent, yet mistaken (perhaps monstrously mistaken), attitudes are possible. If one's moral judgments express a consistent and well informed set of attitudes or commitments, then, according to the noncognitivist, the question of the correctness of those attitudes or commitments does not arise and no sense can be attached to moral deliberation. But we do think that some actual and possible sets of attitudes are fully informed (as to the nonmoral facts) and consistent, yet wrong, and we do sometimes want to know which attitude or commitment of those we could (in consistency) have is the correct one or the one worth having.

8. REALISM ABOUT RIGHT ANSWERS

Moral argument and deliberation presuppose not only correct answers to moral questions but also answers whose correctness is independent of our moral beliefs. In moral deliberation and argument we try and hope to *arrive* at the correct answer, that is, at the answer that is correct prior to, and independently of, our coming upon it (cf. Nagel 1980: 100). And the correctness of our moral beliefs appears to be independent not only of our actual justification for holding them but even of ideal justification. We may not be able to doubt that beliefs that are ideally justified are reasonable to hold, but we can sensibly ask whether such beliefs are true. There may be no answer for us to make short of rehearsing our justification for holding these beliefs, but the question of their correctness is coherent.

Indeed, this is the chief objection to any form of constructivism; its identification of truth and justified belief seems implausible. Truth and justification appear to be distinct properties of beliefs. About nonmoral fact-stating disciplines metaphysical realism seems immensely plausible. Commonsense physical theories, the natural sciences, and the social sciences seem to be concerned with facts about the world whose existence and nature are independent of our evidence about them. The truth of claims in these areas appears to be evidence-independent. Indeed, not only do truth and justification appear distinct; justification does not even provide a guarantee of truth. Knowledge implies truth, but justification does not; justified beliefs might nonetheless be false. Of course, justification must provide evidence of truth, but it should not guarantee truth.

Because we have seen reasons to regard moral claims as fact-stating, these general grounds for distinguishing justification and

31

truth, as realism does and constructivism does not, are grounds for preferring moral realism to constructivism in ethics.

The constructivist might reply that our concepts of justification and truth tell only against the identification of partial or everyday justification and truth and so only against unsophisticated versions of constructivism (cf. Putnam 1981, 1983). True, there are beliefs that are currently or synchronically justified that may turn out to be false, but a suitably idealized diachronic account of justification could perhaps reveal such synchronically justified beliefs to be less than fully justified. Wouldn't false beliefs that are justified on the basis of currently available evidence be shown to be false "in the limit of rational inquiry"? Why not, then, identify truth with suitably idealized justification, as sophisticated constructivism does?

But familiar skeptical possibilities demonstrate why we should not identify truth even with idealized justification. Because they do not want to impoverish the scope of our knowledge by restricting it to sense data or observational reports, these sophisticated constructivists must admit that, even in the limit of rational inquiry, we are and will be justified in holding beliefs about an external world. But then the possibilities that we might be brains in vats or the playthings of Cartesian demons show that even idealized diachronic justified beliefs do not guarantee truth.[10] Indeed, so long as ideal, diachronic justification includes nondeductive inference patterns, even ideal, diachronic justification or pursuit of rational methods of inquiry in the limit will not guarantee the falsity of these skeptical possibilities or the truth of justified beliefs. (In fact, it would seem that for the sophisticated constructivist idealized justification can contain no nondeductive inference patterns, since no inferences that are part of idealized justification could fail to be truth-preserving.)

Indeed, our ability to represent these skeptical possibilities is evidence for realism.[11] If justification were to constitute or even guarantee truth, we would not be able to represent the skeptical possibility

---

10 I assume that these skeptical possibilities are genuine possibilities. Putnam (1981, chap. 1), of course, denies this. I cannot here assess Putnam's intriguing argument. When his argument is not just part of a skeptical solution to epistemological skepticism (discussed later in this section), it depends on a theory of reference that, I suspect, presupposes successful reference and so begs the question against the possibility of the skeptical scenarios. Cf. Nagel 1986: 71–4.
11 I take Nagel (1986: 9–10, 67–74, 90) to be making a similar point.

that our beliefs, though ideally coherent, might nonetheless be false. In this way, constructivism offers a kind of solution to epistemological skepticism, but it is a "skeptical solution," not a "straight solution." A straight solution to a skeptical problem recognizes the skeptic's challenge as legitimate and attempts to answer it in some way; a skeptical solution attempts to dissolve the skeptical problem as misconceived (cf. Kripke 1982: 66–7). Constructivism's solution to epistemological skepticism is a skeptical solution, since it purports to show not that the skeptic's demands can be met or safely disregarded but that the skeptical possibilities are really spurious and, thus, that skepticism is really misconceived. The skeptical possibilities are spurious because the constructivist interprets truth in such a way (i.e., as ideally justified belief) that justified belief is infallible. The skeptic's worry, according to the constructivist, rests on a misunderstanding about the nature of truth; once the constructivist corrects this misunderstanding, our skeptical worries must disappear.

But skeptical solutions to skeptical problems are in general not very satisfying resolutions of these problems; skeptical solutions dispose of disturbing challenges too easily and so fail to do justice to the worries that give rise to the skeptical problems. At least, we should accept skeptical solutions to skeptical problems only if we have an independently satisfying account of how the skeptical worry is, and must be, misconceived or if we have good reason to believe that no straight solution to the skeptical problem can possibly succeed. Until one of these things is shown, we should (continue to) explore straight solutions. This seems true of epistemological skepticism, which requires us to take these skeptical possibilities seriously and attempt to show why they are not realized or why we need not worry about whether they are realized. A commitment to taking skepticism seriously requires that we not identify truth even with idealized justification, and so this commitment is evidence for realism and against constructivism.

Moreover, even if, contrary to fact, ideally justified beliefs were infallible, this would not show that justification *constitutes* truth. (I shall return to some of these issues about the independence of justification and truth at 5.7.)

Perhaps these skeptical possibilities force us to distinguish between the truth and justification of nonmoral beliefs, say, about the existence of an external world. But are there any comparable skepti-

33

cal stories explaining how our justified moral beliefs might nonetheless be false? If not, perhaps we have reason to be constructivists about ethics even if we must be realists about commonsense physical theory and the natural and social sciences.

In the nonmoral case, the skeptical possibilities depend on the possibility of systematic error that infects our theorizing to such an extent as to be uncorrectable. Because our observational beliefs contain a commitment to external objects and are an important part of theory confirmation, our most coherent scientific theories seem likely to remain theories about an independently existing external world. But because our observational beliefs are fallible, our best scientific theories could be systematically mistaken. (See 5.7.)

Similarly, as we shall see (5.8–5.9), our considered moral beliefs about the morality of, say, particular actions or kinds of actions play a central role in constructing and testing moral theories. When conjoined with considered moral beliefs, moral theories have implications for our observational beliefs; when conjoined with nonmoral beliefs, moral theories have implications for our considered moral beliefs. Theory construction and confirmation in ethics can correct for more or less isolated mistakes among our considered moral beliefs and produce a coherent body of moral and nonmoral beliefs. But, like its scientific counterpart, moral theorizing cannot guarantee against *systematic* error among our considered moral beliefs. This possibility of systematic error among our moral beliefs could be realized in different ways. As in the nonmoral case, the cause could be a Cartesian demon who induces in us considered moral beliefs that, when conjoined with nonmoral beliefs, form a coherent system. Or it could be some more familiar source of distortion such as excessive self-concern or gross imaginative limitations; but, of course, in order to be the source of uncorrectable error, these more familiar sources of distortion would have to be much more widespread and more opaque to us than we believe they are.

These possibilities illustrate how justified moral belief, no matter how coherent, fails to guarantee truth, and thus give us reason to distinguish the truth and justification of moral beliefs as we have reason to distinguish the truth and justification of nonmoral beliefs. These possibilities, therefore, illustrate why we should prefer moral realism to constructivism in ethics.

There is also a further ground for resisting constructivism's identification of truth and justification. According to constructivism, there are facts or truths of kind *x*, and these facts or truths are constituted by the evidence for them; truth is evidence-dependent. But evidence must be evidence *for something;* evidence is evidence for believing that such and such is the case. First-order beliefs are beliefs that the world is such and such a way; they are not second-order beliefs about our evidence or beliefs that the world is such and such a way. First-order beliefs are beliefs that the world is such and such a way (period), that is, whatever people's second-order beliefs about these first-order beliefs are. The same is true about first-order beliefs about morality (moral beliefs). They are beliefs that a certain action is wrong or praiseworthy, that a certain person is wicked, admirable, or the like. They are not beliefs that we have evidence for certain moral beliefs (this would make them nonmoral second-order beliefs about morality). This means that our evidence that certain facts obtain must be understood as evidence that these facts obtain independently of our evidence.

We also say that evidence is evidence for believing that some claim or proposition is true. If so, then, for similar reasons, we must analyze this occurrence of 'true' as evidence-independent. Otherwise, we turn our first-order beliefs into second-order beliefs. Or perhaps it would be more accurate to say that we are committed to analyzing some occurrence of 'true' as evidence-independent on pain of infinite regress. The constructivist may construe evidence that *p* is true as evidence of evidence that *p* is true, but then this must be construed as evidence of evidence of evidence that *p* is true, and so on. To avoid such a regress, the constructivist must admit the existence of genuinely first-order beliefs – belief that *p* is true (period, full stop).

Now perhaps the constructivist can admit this consistently. He can claim that although our evidence is evidence for evidence-independent truth, the truth of the beliefs that are our evidence actually consists only in their being held coherently with other beliefs, as self-evident, or whatever. This may be a consistent view, but it forces the constructivist to concede the need for a concept of realist truth. Once this concession is made, the realist can fairly ask why truth isn't, as we must conceive it to be, evidence-independent. Perhaps there is an answer to this question, but the onus is on the constructivist to provide it.

9. CONCLUSION

If my argument has been correct, general considerations about the nature of inquiry and considerations about moral inquiry in particular are most easily explained on the assumption that moral inquiry is directed at discovering moral facts that obtain independently of our moral beliefs and at arriving at evidence-independent true moral beliefs. I take this conclusion to establish a presumptive case in favor of moral realism and to shift the burden of proof to the moral antirealist. That is, the burden of proof is on the antirealist to explain why the apparent realist presuppositions of commonsense morality are mistaken. We shall see whether the antirealist can meet this burden of proof and rebut this presumption.

3

Externalist moral realism

We might, perhaps a little misleadingly, represent my claims about realism and moral inquiry by saying that moral realism is presupposed or supported by certain features of commonsense moral thinking. Now, both those who accept this kind of argument for moral realism and those who do not will often identify another important feature in commonsense moral thinking, namely, the practical or action-guiding character of morality. The practical character of morality is often thought to call for an antirealist, especially noncognitivist, construal of moral claims. If moral judgments merely purported to state facts, it is claimed, they could not fulfill the action-guiding function they do. To fulfill this function, moral judgments must concern or express affective, fundamentally noncognitive, features of people's psychology.[1] It is this sort of antirealist argument that I wish to consider here. I shall argue that, properly understood, the practical or action-guiding character of morality not only fails to undermine the case for moral realism but actually strengthens it.

1. INTERNALISM AND EXTERNALISM

Moral considerations are practical in some very important sense. Agents engage in moral deliberation in order to decide what to do and give moral advice with the aim of influencing others' conduct in certain ways. We expect people who accept moral claims or make moral judgments to act in certain ways. We would regard it as odd for people who accepted moral claims about an issue to be completely indifferent about that issue. For these reasons, we expect moral considerations to motivate people to act in certain ways, or at least to provide them with reason to act in those ways. We

---

1 Cf. Hume 1739: III, i, 1/pp. 457–63; Stevenson 1937; Hare 1952: chap. 5; Nowell-Smith 1957: 36–43; Harman 1975; Mackie 1977: chap. 1.

should hesitate to accept any metaethical or normative theories according to which moral considerations are considerations to which well informed, reasonable people might always be completely indifferent.

Internalism is one way of representing these beliefs about the nature of morality. Broadly speaking, internalism is the view that there is an internal or conceptual connection between moral considerations and action or the sources of action. However, we need a more precise statement of internalism than this. But this is not so easy, since writers have asserted so many internal connections between morality and action.

Sometimes, internalism has been formulated as a thesis about the connection between morality and motivation. As Richard Price puts it, "When we are conscious that an action is *fit* to be done, or that it *ought* to be done, it is not conceivable that we can remain *uninfluenced*, or want a *motive* to action."[2] In part because internalists have not always distinguished clearly between having a motive or desire to do something and having a reason to do that thing, they have not always distinguished their thesis about the connection between morality and motivation from what seems, upon reflection, to be a different, if related, thesis about the connection between morality and reasons for action. W. D. Falk, who often formulates internalism as the thesis about motivation, here formulates it as a thesis about reasons for action: "But, in fact, we believe that morality needs no external sanction: the very thought that we morally ought to do some act is sufficient without reference to any ulterior motive to provide us with a reason for doing it."[3] Bearing

2 Price 1787: 194. Compare: " 'Goodness' must have, so to speak, a magnetism. A person who recognizes X to be 'good' must ipso facto acquire a stronger tendency to act in its favor than he otherwise would have had" (Stevenson 1937: 13); "Somehow the very fact of a duty entails all the motive required for doing the act" (Falk 1947: 499); "To think that you ought to do something is to be motivated to do it. To think that it would be wrong to do something is to be motivated not to do it" (Harman 1977: 33); "But it is also held that just knowing them [objective values] or 'seeing' them will not merely tell men what to do but will ensure that they do it, overruling any contrary inclinations" (Mackie 1977: 23); "It seems to be a conceptual truth that to regard something as good is to feel a pull towards promoting or choosing it, or towards wanting other people to feel the pull towards promoting or choosing it" (Blackburn 1984: 188).

3 Falk 1947: 494. Compare: "If S says that (morally) A ought to do D, S implies that A has reasons to do D which S endorses" (Harman 1975: 9); "Objective wrongness, if there is such a thing, is intrinsically prescriptive or action-guiding, it in itself gives or constitutes a reason for not doing the wrong action" (Mackie 1982: 115).

these two possibilities in mind, we can, as a first approximation, formulate internalism as the claim that it is a part of the concept of a moral consideration that such considerations motivate the agent to perform the moral action or provide the agent with reason to perform the moral action.[4] But this still conceals a number of different theses. First, there is the distinction, already alluded to, between internalism about *motives* and internalism about *reasons*. This distinction requires another distinction, between two different senses of 'reason for action'. We often speak of an agent's reasons for action in explaining her behavior; here we use 'reason for action' to refer to the considerations that *motivate* the agent and so *explain* her actions. But we often think that an agent can have explanatory reasons for action without having *good* or *justifying* reasons (cf. Baier 1958: 100, 149; Nielsen 1963: 539; Frankena 1973: 114). Thus, if I am a light-bulb eater, my belief that light bulbs are nutritious and my desire to be healthy constitute my reason, in this first explanatory sense, for eating light bulbs, although presumably I do not have reason, in this second justificatory sense, to eat light bulbs.

Of course, there are some connections between explanatory and justifying reasons. First, good or justifying reasons for action will presumably explain an agent's actions *insofar as she is fully rational* and so will constitute explanatory reasons for action for a fully rational agent, since one is rational, in this sense, simply insofar as one recognizes and acts on good or justifying reasons for action. And perhaps an attribution of some minimal amount of rationality is a precondition of our attributing intentional states (e.g., beliefs and desires) to individuals and so to our seeing them as possessing explanatory reasons for action (cf. Davidson 1980: 237). But this threshold amount of rationality necessary for the ascription of in-

---

4 Cf. Price 1787: 167–8, 194; Prichard 1912 (but see Falk 1947); Stevenson 1937: 13; Falk 1947: 494–5, 499–501; Nowell-Smith 1957: 88–9, 174; Medlin 1957: 59; Hare 1952: 20, 31, 169, 197; 1963a: 71; 1981: 21, 23–4, 83–6; Baier 1958: v, 171; Foot 1958a: 101; 1958b: 111, 125, 128; Grice 1967: 3–4, 27, 29; Murdoch 1970: 42, 66; Harman 1975: 191, 193, 195; 1977: 33, 66, 91; Mackie 1977: 23, 26–7, 29, 40, 42, 49; 1982: 102, 104, 115–16; McDowell 1978: 26; 1979: 335; 1985: 111, 120; Blackburn 1984: 187–8.

This kind of internalism about morality should be distinguished from internalism as a thesis about the nature of rationality, although, as we shall see, some writers think these two theses are connected. Internalism about rationality assumes that all reasons for action depend on actual or counterfactual desires of the agent; see, for example, B. Williams 1980 and Darwall 1983: chap. 5.

tentional states is far short of full rationality (cf. Føllesdall 1982). Second, it might be that there is some deeper, counterfactual connection between being motivated and having a reason. For instance, it might turn out that one has reason to do *x* just in case a perfectly rational being under suitably idealized conditions would desire *x* and so be motivated to do *x* (cf. Brandt 1979; Darwall 1983: 20, 41–2, 79–80, 86; Gauthier 1986: chap. 2). However, neither of these possible connections between explanatory and justifying reasons threatens the distinction between them or its importance.

Some of the confusion between internalism about motives and internalism about reasons may be due to a confusion between the two different senses of 'reason for action'. For if motives are taken to supply explanatory reasons for action, then internalism about motives would establish what we might call 'internalism about explanatory reasons'. But this is not what many have meant by internalism and not how I shall understand internalism about reasons; internalism about reasons concerns the connection between moral considerations and good or justifying reasons for action. Internalism about motives holds that it is a conceptual truth that moral considerations motivate, while internalism about reasons claims that it is a conceptual truth that moral considerations provide agents with reason for action.

Second, we should distinguish among agent internalism, appraiser internalism, and hybrid internalism. *Agent internalism* claims it is in virtue of the concept of morality that *moral obligations* motivate, or provide reason for, the agent to do the moral thing. Thus, it is a conceptual truth about morality, according to agent internalism, that agents have reason or motive to comply with their moral obligations. *Appraiser internalism* claims it is in virtue of the concept of morality that *moral belief* or *moral judgment* provides the appraiser with motivation or reason for action. Thus, it is a conceptual truth about morality, according to appraiser internalism, that someone who holds a moral belief or makes a moral judgment is motivated to, or has reason to, perform the action judged favorably. (Of course, the person who is the appraiser is very often the person who is the moral agent.) Agent internalism is objective in the sense that it ties motivation or reasons for action to moral obligations, independently of anyone's recognition of these obligations. By contrast, appraiser internalism is subjective in the sense

40

that it ties the appraiser's motivation or reasons for action to the appraiser's beliefs or judgments, independently of whether these beliefs or judgments are correct or justifiable. These features of agent and appraiser internalism allow us to construct a hybrid version of internalism that is both objective and subjective. *Hybrid internalism* claims it is a conceptual truth about morality that the *recognition of a moral obligation* motivates or provides the agent (the person who recognizes his obligation) with reason for action.

Unfortunately, internalists often fail to mark the distinctions between motives and reasons and among agent, appraiser, and hybrid internalisms. Indeed, once we make these distinctions and identify and distinguish different possible internalist theses, some of these theses begin to look more plausible than others. In particular, appraiser and hybrid internalism about motives may seem more plausible than agent internalism about motives. It may be impossible to accept a moral judgment or recognize a moral obligation without being correspondingly motivated, but it seems all too possible to have a moral obligation and remain unmoved if only because one does not recognize the obligation as an obligation. And agent internalism or hybrid internalism about reasons seems more plausible than appraiser internalism about reasons. Moral obligations may in themselves supply agents with reasons for action, and if so, recognition of a moral obligation will supply reasons for action. But because one's moral beliefs or judgments might be mistaken or unwarranted for various reasons, it seems implausible to suppose that mere moral belief or mere acceptance of a moral judgment could supply the appraiser with a (good or justifying) reason for action.

For some purposes, these distinctions are not important. In such situations, I shall not distinguish among them but shall speak merely about the motivational force or rationality of moral considerations. In other situations, however, the distinctions are important. Here, I shall distinguish among them or allow context to do so.

One final distinction should be made here; it is between *weak* and *strong* internalism. Weak internalism about motives claims it is a conceptual truth that moral considerations provide *some* motivation, while strong internalism about motives claims it is a conceptual truth that moral considerations provide *sufficient* motive for action. Weak internalism about reasons claims it is a conceptual truth that moral considerations provide *a* reason for action, while

41

strong internalism about reasons claims it is a conceptual truth that moral considerations provide the agent with *conclusive, overriding,* or *sufficient* reason for action. Although some internalists have been strong internalists (e.g., Mackie 1977: 23; Hare 1981: 60–1; Harman 1984: 34), many internalists accept some form of weak internalism. I shall understand internalism as weak internalism unless I indicate otherwise.

With this battery of distinctions under our belts, we can begin to put internalism into some perspective. Internalism (of any form) has at least three distinguishable components. The first claim is that moral considerations *necessarily* motivate or provide reason for action. The second and third claims come out of the internalist thesis that it is the concept of morality that establishes this. Since it is the *concept* of morality that shows that moral considerations necessarily motivate or provide reasons for action, this claim about the motivational power or rationality of morality must be a priori. Since it is the *concept of morality* that determines this fact, the rationality or motivational power of moral considerations cannot depend on substantive considerations such as what the content of morality turns out to be, facts about agents, or the content of the correct theory of rationality. Internalism, so construed, is a very narrow and strong claim, but it is this claim that underlies and explains traditional internalist claims and the internalist antirealist arguments I am considering here. (Traditional defenders of internalism are, I believe, committed, explicitly or implicitly, to all three of these claims. But it might be that some of those who subscribe to 'internalism' accept only the first or second component of what I call 'internalism'. I have no immediate quarrel with such people; my present concern is only to explain why a realist can and should resist all three claims.)

Externalism is the denial of internalism; externalism claims that the motivational force and rationality of moral considerations depend on factors external to the moral considerations themselves. One can be an externalist by denying any one of the three claims internalism involves. The externalist can claim, first, that moral considerations only *contingently* motivate or justify; second, that the motivational power or rationality of morality, whether necessary or contingent, can be known only a posteriori; or third, that the motivational power or rationality of morality, whether necessary or contingent, a priori or a posteriori, depends on things other than the concept of morality, such as what the content of morality turns

42

out to be, a substantive theory of reasons for action, or facts about agents such as their interests or desires.[5]

Like internalism, externalism admits of many possible versions. We can distinguish externalism about motives and externalism about reasons for action and agent, appraiser, and hybrid versions of either. Again, I shall observe or mark these distinctions only where this affects the course of the argument.

2. INTERNALISM AND REALISM

What is the bearing of all this on moral realism? To many people internalism seems the only way to represent adequately the practical or action-guiding character of morality. Externalism seems unable to account for the "dynamic" or motivational aspects of morality and for the authority or rationality of moral considerations. By contrast, internalism about morality and motivation seems to account for the effect morality has on the will, and internalism about morality and reasons for action seems to account for the authority of moral considerations.

If we must recognize the practical character of morality, and if internalism is the appropriate way to represent this practical character, then moral realism must be compatible with internalism. In particular, the moral realist must claim it is a conceptual truth about morality that moral considerations motivate or provide reason for action. On this view, it must be inconceivable that someone could recognize a moral fact and remain unmoved or fail to have reason to act. Some moral realists accept these claims; they combine moral realism and internalism (e.g., Price 1787; Falk 1947; Foot 1958a, 1958b; Nagel 1970; McDowell 1978, 1979, 1985). But many others regard realism and internalism as uneasy, indeed incompatible, bedfellows. Internalism is a premise in many arguments for noncognitivism. Some claim that no set of facts or cognitive states (e.g., beliefs) could necessitate any affective or motivational attitude, in particular the kind of pro-attitude that people take their moral obligations to entail (e.g., Hare 1957: chap. 5; Nowell-Smith 1957: 36–43; Mackie 1977: chap. 1). It seems possible to be indifferent to any

5 Thus, I take the following to be externalists or provide externalist arguments: Plato *Republic* II–IV, VIII–IX, and Aristotle *EN* (cf. Irwin 1977: chap. 8, and 1981); Sidgwick 1907: 498–503 (cf. Brink 1988a); Frankena 1958, 1973: 114–15; Nielsen 1963; Gauthier 1967; Foot 1972a, 1972b.

set of facts, but this cannot be true of moral facts if internalism is true. This is the antirealist argument from internalism about motives. Others assume that moral facts must provide reasons for action but find "queer" the idea of facts that provide agents with reasons for action, regardless of the agents' interests or attitudes (e.g., Harman 1975: 4–11, 1977: chaps. 8–9; Mackie 1977: chap. 1). This is the antirealist argument from internalism about reasons. If reflection on commonsense morality supports internalism, and if these philosophers are right about the incompatibility of realism and internalism, then some general features of common moral beliefs and practices provide an argument against moral realism.

These considerations are thought not only to undermine moral realism but also to support noncognitivist antirealism.[6] For although realism and internalism are thought to be incompatible, traditional noncognitivist theories are internalist. Although there are differences between emotivism and prescriptivism, both claim it is an essential part of the meaning of moral judgments to express the appraiser's attitudes or commitments. Emotivists claim moral judgments express the appraiser's approval and invite others to join in the appraiser's attitudes; prescriptivists claim moral judgments express (universal) prescriptions or recommendations. On both forms of noncognitivism, therefore, it is part of the meaning of moral judgments, and so a conceptual truth, that the appraiser holds a pro-attitude to things judged moral and a negative attitude to things judged immoral. The noncognitivist is, therefore, an internalist about motives and so can easily explain the dynamic character of moral judgments and attitudes. Moreover, the noncognitivist can explain how an agent's moral commitments, resting as they do on the agent's attitudes, give him reasons for action that are anchored in his interests or desires and so can apparently explain the authority of moral demands.

I don't think we should accept this antirealist argument. One realist reply would be to question the incompatibility of realism and internalism. A realist might argue that moral belief can itself be motivational and that moral facts can themselves be reason giving (e.g., Nagel 1970; McDowell 1978, 1985). However, this is not my preferred strategy; I think we should reject the internalist premises

---

6 Harman's argument (1975, 1977: chaps. 8–9) is meant to support a version of moral relativism that relativizes moral requirements to agents' motivations and attitudes.

of these antirealist arguments. (At least, given my understanding of internalism, this is how I would describe my strategy.) If so, then the implausibility of conjoining realism and internalism in this way derives from internalism and not from moral realism. Morality is practical, as our moral beliefs and practices assume, and so we should expect to find important connections between morality and both motivation and reasons for action. But externalism, not internalism, is the correct way to represent these connections, and there is no difficulty reconciling externalism and moral realism.

Let us look more closely at these forms of internalism and the antirealist arguments that rely on them.

3. MORALITY AND MOTIVATION

Internalists often assume that externalism threatens morality's dynamic character. If the motivational force of moral considerations is not part of those considerations but depends on factors external to those considerations, don't we lose our assurance that moral considerations will motivate? Yet moral considerations certainly do motivate.

Now, agent internalism itself threatens morality. We have some initial idea about what people's moral obligations are; call the actions we think we are morally obligated to perform x, y, and z. We also believe that even if most people have a desire to perform x, y, and z, some people do not have this desire. If this second belief is correct, then agent internalism forces us to revise our first belief about the moral obligations of those who are indifferent to x, y, and z. If agent internalism is true, it would seem that our views about people's moral obligations would have to be restricted or tailored to actions people already have a desire to perform (cf. Frankena 1958: 73). Although our initial moral beliefs are revisable, it does not seem they should be revised for this reason. It is no vindication of the practical importance of moral demands if, in order to ensure their motivational force, we must compromise the moral demands themselves.

At this point, the internalist about motives may insist on representing internalism as appraiser or hybrid internalism. Motivation follows, the internalist might insist, only from recognition of a moral obligation (hybrid internalism) or moral belief or judgment (appraiser internalism); there must be motivation to perform x, y, and z *only if x, y,* and z are *regarded as moral obligations.* And this is just what appraiser and hybrid internalism claim.

But internalism, so construed, seems just false to both actual and possible psychological facts. Although indifference to what is regarded as moral considerations may be fairly rare, it does seem to exist. Some people (e.g., certain sociopaths) do not care about what they regard as moral considerations. Moreover, the internalist cannot rest content with the extensional claim that everyone is, in fact, motivated by moral considerations. Externalists could claim this. The (appraiser or hybrid) internalist about motives claims it is a conceptual truth about morality that moral judgment or belief motivates. According to the internalist, then, it must be conceptually impossible for someone to recognize a moral consideration or assert a moral judgment and remain unmoved. This fact raises a problem for internalism; internalism makes *the amoralist* conceptually impossible.

Even if everyone is, as a matter of fact, motivated by moral considerations, we still regard it as possible to ask for a justification for this concern. Much moral skepticism is skepticism about the objectivity of morality, that is, skepticism about the existence of moral facts or the possibility of moral knowledge. But another traditional kind of skepticism accepts the existence of moral facts and concedes that we have moral knowledge, and asks why we should care about these facts. Call this *amoralist skepticism.* Amoralists are the traditional way of representing this second kind of skepticism; the amoralist is someone who recognizes the existence of moral considerations and remains unmoved.

The appraiser internalist must dismiss the amoralist as inconceivable. The standard internalist reply is that we may think the amoralist is conceivable, but this can only be because we confuse moral senses of terms and "inverted-commas" senses of those same terms (e.g., Hare 1952: 124–6, 163–5). We use terms that have a moral sense (e.g., 'good', 'bad', 'right', 'wrong') in a nonmoral, inverted-commas sense when we use these terms, not to express our own moral views but to convey the moral views of others with whom we do not agree. The internalist relies on the possibility of inverted-commas usage of moral language, and replies that people can be unmoved by considerations that are only *conventionally regarded* as moral, but insists that a genuine amoralist is inconceivable. Thus, according to the internalist, apparent amoralists such as

Plato's Thrasymachus, Hobbes's Fool,[7] and Mike, the conman in David Mamet's film *House of Games,* remain unmoved not by what they regard as moral considerations but only by what *others* regard as moral considerations; their own views about morality are really completely different from conventional views.

The hybrid internalist, by contrast, could concede the conceivability of this kind of amoralist but would have to insist that the amoralist is necessarily mistaken in thinking that morality does require the action to which she sincerely professes indifference. (Although it is not clear how a form of hybrid internalism that insisted on moral *mistakes* could be a premise in an antirealist argument.)

The problem for internalism is that it does not take the amoralist's challenge seriously enough. Amoralist skepticism is a familiar philosophical and popular form of skepticism. Reflection on the stringent character of many apparent moral demands can make us wonder whether we do have good reason to be moral. We may even come to wonder whether we have good reason to become amoralists. All of this seems to assume that the amoralist is an intelligible figure. Whatever the merits of these internalist gambits as interpretations of particular, putative amoralists (real or fictional), the amoralist certainly seems conceivable. It is simply unclear why we should assume that the person who professes indifference to what she insists are moral requirements is confusedly using moral language in inverted commas or mistaken about what moral-

---

7 Hobbes's precise attitude to amoralism and the amoralist is a little unclear. Hobbes defines injustice as the breaching of covenants and justice as whatever is not unjust, by which he must intend the keeping of covenants (1651: chap. XV, p. 71). He then goes on to describe the Fool's attitude toward justice; the Fool wonders whether keeping covenants is always in his interest. What makes the Fool seem to raise the amoralist challenge is that "he questioneth, whether Injustice, taking away the feare of God, (for the same Foole hath said in his heart there is no God,) may not sometimes stand with that Reason, which dictateth to every man his own good" (1651: XV, 72). The amoralist reading of the Fool, however, is somewhat undercut by the way Hobbes introduces him: "The Foole hath sayd in his heart, that there is no such thing as Justice" (1651: XV, 72). This description of the Fool, although apparently inconsistent with the later description (which I quoted first), seems to be a kind of internalist reading. Later, Hobbes says "And [1] if it be not against Reason, it is not against Justice: or [2] else Justice is not to be approved for good" (1651: XV, 72). Here Hobbes seems to offer us a choice between (1) internalism and (2) amoralism. For these reasons, I would not want to be committed to defending the amoralist (or any single) interpretation of Hobbes's Fool; although some of his claims support this interpretation, not all of them do. I hope it is clear, however, that my argument against internalism commits me to no such exegetical claim.

47

ity requires. We can imagine someone who regards what we take to be moral demands as moral demands – and not simply as conventional moral demands – and yet remains unmoved. We may think that such a person is being irrational and that she can be shown to be irrational. We may even think that such a person is merely possible and has never existed and will never exist (although I think this thought is wrong). But we do think that such a person is possible, and if we are to take the amoralist challenge seriously, we must attempt to explain why the amoralist should care about morality.

The real or fictional figure of the amoralist – one who is indifferent to what he concedes are moral considerations – is the traditional way of raising what I have called amoralist skepticism – skepticism about the justification or rationality of moral demands. I suppose, however, that it is possible to formulate amoralist skepticism without assuming the actual or possible existence of the amoralist. Even if it is a conceptual truth about morality that recognition of moral considerations motivates, we may still ask whether such motivation or concern is justified. Thus, someone might claim, internalism about motives is committed to dismissing not amoralist skepticism but only the amoralist. Even so, it seems a defect in internalism about motives that it must dismiss as inconceivable something that surely seems conceivable, namely, the amoralist.

Now, the internalist might try to defend his position here by distinguishing between *strong* and *weak* amoralisms and amoralists. Weak amoralism denies that agents have *sufficient* reason to be moral, while strong amoralism denies that agents have *reason* (i.e., any reason) to be moral. Similarly, the weak amoralist is someone who is *insufficiently* motivated to do what he recognizes to be morally required, while the strong amoralist is someone who is *completely indifferent* to what he recognizes to be morally required. Internalism, as we have been understanding it, is weak internalism. So the internalist might claim that internalism about motives rules out only the strong amoralist and so need not dismiss the weak amoralist. Thus, the internalist might claim, we don't need to reject (weak) internalism in order to take one kind of amoralist seriously. I agree, but I do not think that this constitutes a good defense of internalism. For even if the weak amoralist is in some sense a more probable character than the strong amoralist (this, after all, is what it means to call him weak), the strong amoralist is still *coherent,* and it is evidence against (even weak) internalism that it rules out the strong amoralist as incoherent.

These are reasons for rejecting internalism about motives as the correct account of the connection between morality and motivation. Internalism overstates the connection between morality and motivation; agent internalism holds our moral theories hostage to agents' desires, and appraiser and hybrid internalism prevent us from recognizing the amoralist and, thus, from in this way taking the amoralist challenge seriously.

Externalism provides a more plausible account of the connection between morality and motivation; it makes the motivational force of moral considerations a matter of contingent psychological fact, depending on the beliefs and desires agents happen to have. First, because it does not make the motivational force of moral obligations a conceptual feature of morality, externalism does not hold the scope and stringency of moral obligations hostage to people's actual desires (as agent internalism does). Second, externalism also makes the motivational force of moral judgment and moral belief a matter of contingent psychological fact, depending on both the content of people's moral views and their attitudes and desires. Nonetheless, externalism can base this motivation on "deep" or widely shared psychological facts. Let's think about common moral views that recognize the other-regarding character of many moral demands. If, for example, sympathy is, as Hume held, a deeply seated and widely shared psychological trait, then, as a matter of contingent (but "deep") psychological fact, the vast majority of people will have at least *some* desire to comply with what they perceive to be their moral obligations, even with those other-regarding moral obligations. Moral motivation, on such a view, can be widespread and predictable, even if it is neither necessary, nor universal, nor overriding. These are limitations in the actual motivational force of moral considerations that, I think, reflection on commonsense morality recognizes. At least, these externalist claims recognize familiar limits to moral motivation while explaining why well informed, reasonable people will not always be indifferent to moral considerations.

Finally, externalism allows us to take amoralism and the amoralist challenge seriously. Because externalism does not try to find the motivational force within moral considerations themselves, it recognizes that we can imagine someone who recognizes moral considerations and remains unmoved. But the fact that externalism about motives allows us to conceive the amoralist does not make the amoralist challenge unanswerable. There is nothing about externalism about motives that prevents us from showing that an amoralist is irrational not to care about moral considerations. Whether the amoralist is irrational depends on the rationality, not the motivational force, of moral considerations. This is the issue to which we shall turn in the next section.

Since externalism provides a better account of the connection between morality and motivation than internalism does, the connection between morality and motivation that reflection on common-sense morality recognizes does not support antirealist arguments. The moral realist could concede that belief itself never entails an attitude, or that intrinsically motivational facts are queer; neither claim, if true, would undermine a realistic construal of moral claims.

4. MORALITY AND REASONS FOR ACTION

What about the antirealist argument that relies on internalism about reasons? This antirealist argument is sometimes formulated in the same abstract way as the previous argument, which relied on internalism about motives. Just as proponents of that argument claimed (against a realist account of moral judgment and moral requirements) that mere cognitive states (e.g., beliefs) and objects (e.g., facts) cannot themselves be motivational, as moral attitudes and considerations are, so, too, proponents of this argument sometimes reject as indefensible the idea that moral obligations could provide agents with reasons for action, independently of the agents' interests or desires, as internalism requires. But this quick, abstract way of stating the alleged incompatibility of moral realism and internalism about reasons conceals a much more complex antirealist argument with a great deal of argumentative structure. We need to examine this argument and the role it assigns to internalism.

5. BACKGROUND TO THE ANTIREALIST ARGUMENT

Kant is well known for defending the objectivity of ethics and the rationality of moral requirements and moral concern. He seems to think both that moral requirements *apply* to agents independently of their particular and variable desires and inclinations and that it is *rational* for agents to act on or fulfill these requirements independently of whether such actions fulfill the desires and inclinations that agents happen to have.

In *The Possibility of Altruism,* Thomas Nagel defends a Kantian position that he claims involves both realism, or objectivity, and internalism. Although Nagel does not distinguish very clearly between the motivational influence of moral considerations and their rationality, I think his position is best construed as concerning the rationality and not the motivational force of moral considerations.[8] "It will in any case not do to rest the motivational influence [rationality] of ethical considerations on fortuitous or escapable inclinations. Their hold on us must be deep, and it must be essentially tied to the ethical principles themselves, and to the conditions of their truth. The alternative is to abandon the objectivity of ethics" (1970: 6). Here Nagel draws on our second Kantian theme and associates it with realism; he assumes that the realist must claim that moral requirements provide any agent to whom they apply with reason for action, independently of the agent's desires, and that the externalist cannot do this because she must tie the rationality of moral requirements to agents' contingent and variable inclinations. His defense of the second Kantian theme leads him to accept the first.

In *Ethics: Inventing Right and Wrong,* J. L. Mackie also assumes that the realist must be an internalist and takes Kant as his model. At one point, Mackie focuses on the first Kantian theme: "[The objectivism or realism implicit in commonsense morality] involves a call for action or for the refraining from action, and one that is absolute, not contingent upon any desire or preference or policy or choice, his [the appraiser's] own or anyone else's" (1977: 33). Here Mackie assumes that the realist thinks moral requirements apply to everyone, regardless of her desires or inclinations. Because he assumes that moral obligations must provide reasons for action and because he thinks that a person's reasons for action are based on her desires, Mackie rejects moral realism. He begins by rejecting the second Kantian theme and is led to reject the first as well.

8 Internalism about motives and internalism about reasons are often confused in this way. Moral considerations are said to be motivational, even if they do not actually motivate, so long as they have the *capacity* to motivate. But what these writers usually mean when they say that *x* has the capacity to motivate is that a *rational* person would be motivated to do *x* or that an agent would be motivated to do *x if she were rational,* and this is just to say that one *has reason* to do *x.* For this reason, these claims about the motivational capacity or content of moral considerations are, I submit, best construed as claims about the rationality of moral considerations.

51

Finally, there is Gilbert Harman, who in a number of places (1975: 4–11, 1977: chaps. 8–9, 1984: 34–41) rejects moral realism and defends moral relativism, in part on internalist grounds. Like Mackie, Harman assumes that moral requirements must provide reasons for action and that a person's reasons for action depend on her desires or aims and concludes that moral obligation must be relativized to people's desires or aims and, hence, that moral relativism is true. Harman also begins by rejecting the second Kantian theme and is led to reject the first as well.

Even brief reflection on these various positions raises a host of questions. Mackie and Harman seem to be in some kind of agreement against Nagel and Kant. Are these the only positions available? Is the antirealist argument simply that Nagel and Kant hold occult views about rationality? Are their theories of rationality occult? Must the realist hold such theories of rationality? How, exactly, are these two Kantian themes related to each other, and how, if at all, is either related to moral realism? What role, exactly, does internalism play in this debate?

6. THE ANTIREALIST ARGUMENT

I think we can offer answers to these questions only by providing a careful reconstruction of this antirealist argument. I suggest the following reconstruction.[9]

1. To be under a moral obligation to do x, one must have reason to do x.
2. One has a reason to do x just in case x would contribute to the satisfaction of one's desires.
3. Hence, one can have a moral obligation to do x only if doing x would contribute to the satisfaction of one's desires.
4. Not everyone has the same desires.
5. Hence, there is no single set of moral requirements that applies to everyone; there will be different moral requirements that apply to different people in virtue of their different motivational sets.

How plausible is this argument? Does it undermine our commitment to moral realism? I don't think that it should. A number of difficulties with the argument allow the realist to resist it and thereby preserve our commitment to moral realism.

---

9 Gasper (1987: 255–8) advances a similar argument; it was reflection on his argument, among other things, that helped me see the antirealist arguments of Mackie and Harman this way.

Before examining the details of this argument, we might notice some of the ways in which it reconstructs and explains the positions we have been looking at. The first two premises are, of course, crucial. (1) typically, and certainly in Mackie's and Harman's cases, rests on internalist assumptions. (2) is the familiar Humean idea that all reasons for action are desire-dependent; it contradicts the second Kantian theme, which Nagel accepts, that the rationality of moral requirements is independent of agents' contingent and variable desires. Thus, the argument proceeds from a denial of the second Kantian theme. (3) follows from (1) and (2), and seems to deny the first Kantian theme that moral requirements apply to agents independently of their contingent and variable desires. If moral realism is indeed committed to this first Kantian theme, then (3) seems sufficient to undermine moral realism. As we shall see, however, this is not entirely clear. Moral realism may require only the somewhat weaker claim that there is a single true morality that applies to all agents. But this claim also seems undermined if we add to (3) an uncontroversial premise about the diversity of desire [(4)]. For then we seem to get (5) which does deny the existence of a single true morality.

7. REALISM, RELATIVISM, AND THE DIVERSITY OF DESIRE

This argument certainly has the flavor of an antirealist argument; it also seems to support a certain kind of moral relativism, as Harman explicitly claims. But exactly what part of the argument makes it antirealist and relativist? There is a way of understanding moral relativism that does not require (5). (3) asserts only the relational thesis that moral requirements must be relative to the agent's desires or motivational set. If everyone were to share all the relevant desires, then there could still be a single true morality. If moral relativism involves the denial of a single true morality that applies to all agents, then the argument for moral relativism must establish (5), and not just (3) (cf. Harman 1984: 27, 34–41). [10] If, however, we

10 Could we treat even (5) as compatible with moral realism? I have claimed that we ought to treat subjective versions of utilitarianism as possible versions of what the moral facts are. If so, should we treat (5) also as a substantive moral claim that a realist could accept? In particular, we might treat the claim that Z is under a moral obligation to do x only if x would contribute to the satisfaction of

construe relativism as only the relational thesis that moral requirements are relative to agents' desires, then, of course, (3) is sufficient to establish moral relativism.

It is not entirely clear what to say here. For instance, (3) seems to contradict the first Kantian theme that moral requirements apply to agents independently of their desires or inclinations, which both Mackie (the antirealist) and Nagel (the realist) associate with moral realism. And (3) seems to satisfy Harman's understanding of moral relativism in his original paper "Moral Relativism Defended"; he construes it as a "soberly logical thesis" that relativizes an agent's moral obligations to her motivational set (1975: 3, 10). If we think of moral relativism and moral realism in these ways, then (3) is all that is needed to refute moral realism and establish moral relativism.

However, this is not the only way of thinking of realism and relativism. Our initial formulation of the first Kantian theme held that moral requirements apply to agents independently of contingent *and variable* desires. If this is how we understand that theme, then it is compatible with the claim that moral requirements depend on uniform, and what Nagel might call "deep," desires. *This* Kantian claim is compatible with (3) and inconsistent only with (5). Moreover, the *interest* in the debate between moral realism and

some desire or purpose of Z as just a different, nonimpartial, function from desire-satisfaction into rightness. Thus, we might treat it as a kind of crude relative of ethical egoism or of Scheffler's agent-centered prerogatives (1982; cf. 8.17).

In assessing this suggestion, it may be useful to consider Harman's attitude toward (5). One problem with this suggestion is that Harman, as I construe him, suggests that contribution to the satisfaction of one's desires is only a necessary condition for one's being under an obligation. So it is not clear that we can construe (5) as a moral theory rather than a metaethical claim with antirealist implications. But perhaps this just shows that (5) is only *part* of a moral theory.

Notice also, however, that Harman thinks of his view in traditionally metaethical terms: he calls it "relativism" and takes it to constitute a denial of the claim that there is a single true morality. Moreover, if my reconstruction of this argument is right, then Harman's position rests primarily on metaethical (or at least not first-order moral) claims, namely, internalism and a desire-based view of rationality. Although I am willing to concede that metaethical views have normative implications (indeed, I shall argue this in Chapter 4), all this dependence gives Harman's conclusion a certain metaethical air. And, of course, if the line between metaethics and normatives ethics is not sharp (as, again, I am willing to allow), then at least some normative views can have metaethical implications; and thus the fact, if it is a fact, that (5) can be construed as part of a moral theory does not show that it does not have antirealist implications. So, with these qualifications, I shall continue to regard (5) as a challenge to moral realism.

54

moral relativism often depends on thinking of the realist as embracing, and of the relativist as denying, the existence of a single true morality that applies to all moral agents. Indeed, this seems to be how Harman thinks of the debate in his later writings (1984: 27, 34–41). If we rely on this conception of the debate between realism and relativism, we should examine the argument for (5) as well as that for (3).

We have just distinguished (3) from (5); (3) is weaker than (5). But the difference between them may not seem significant, since the only premise on which the argument from (3) to (5) relies is the uncontroversial premise of the diversity of desire [(4)].

But a closer look shows that the argument here is not so straightforward; (5) does not in fact follow from (3) and (4). A given action can satisfy any of a large number of different desires the action's agent might have. In particular, even if there are some descriptions of an action under which an agent does not desire to perform it, there may nonetheless be other descriptions of the action that show the action to satisfy desires the agent has. Thus, in one sense, I may not desire to forgo my Sunday afternoon nap in order to help you proofread your paper, but it may nonetheless be true that proofreading your paper would contribute to the satisfaction of desires that I have – say, my desire that you think well of me. So the indisputable fact that people have different desires does not establish that there is no single set of moral requirements that everyone has reason to comply with, since it may be true that there is a set of (otherwise plausible) moral requirements whose fulfillment would satisfy at least one desire of every agent.

Consider Harman's claims about Hitler. Harman implies that Hitler was someone to whom obligations of a certain sort, for instance, of fairness, decency, or respect for human life, did not apply, because he (Hitler) lacked the relevant attitudes necessary for him to have reasons to be fair, to be decent, or to respect human life (1975: 7–11). But although it is true that Hitler sought, and so desired, to exterminate the Jews, it also seems certain that the extermination of Jews frustrated desires Hitler had, and therefore that he also had reasons, by virtue of the assumptions about rationality embodied in (2), not to exterminate Jews. For instance, I suspect (though cannot prove) that Hitler was immoral, not amoral; that is, he wanted to do the right thing and sought to do the right thing but had terrifyingly (and culpably) mistaken moral views. If so, then

55

his extermination of Jews frustrated his desire to do the right thing, and his desires gave him reason not to exterminate Jews. Of course, this claim assumes that we can have reasons for action of which we are not aware, but I take this assumption to be uncontroversially true. Moreover (and less controversially), Hitler undoubtedly had desires to be popular, both during his lifetime and posthumously, which his extermination of Jews obviously frustrated. In this way also, his desires gave him reason not to exterminate Jews.

Of course, even if this is true, it does not establish that Hitler had *sufficient* or *conclusive* reason not to exterminate Jews. What Hitler had most reason to do, on this view of rationality, would presumably depend on the number and intensity of the desires that alternative courses of action available to him would have satisfied. To establish that moral requirements always give people, including Hitler, conclusive reasons for action would require stronger and perhaps less plausible psychological assumptions. But (1) does not make this strong claim that moral obligations provide sufficient or conclusive reason for action; it makes only the weaker claim that moral obligations provide *some* reason for action (but see Harman 1984: 34). The stronger reading of (1) would, therefore, make the case for (5) more compelling. But this is not what (1) in fact says, and, as we shall see, the stronger reading would make (1) (even) more dubious than it is on the actual, weaker reading.

Of course, a plausible set of moral requirements will demand more than refraining from genocide; it will presumably include obligations to help and benefit others in appropriate circumstances. But, as this discussion suggests, it is plausible to suppose that, whatever our psychological differences, we all have some desires that will be satisfied by the fulfillment of even these more strenuous moral requirements. If so, then, even by the assumptions about rationality embodied in (2), we will all have (at least some) reason to comply with any (plausible) unique set of moral requirements. So, if we take moral relativism to be committed to (5), then the case for moral relativism has not yet been established.

However, this might seem to be a rather weak objection. The relativist might claim that the crucial issue is not whether there is a set of moral requirements whose fulfillment would satisfy desires of all actual persons, but, rather, whether there *could* be agents, perhaps beings with psychologies completely different from ours, for whom fulfillment of these requirements satisfied no desires whatsoever. If so, then they could not have reasons to comply with these requirements, and so these requirements could not apply to them. (This may be Harman's reason for discussing the case of extraterrestrials with completely different psychologies [1975: 5].) If this is even possible, isn't it enough to show that there is no single true morality?

It is hard to know how to reply here. On the one hand, it is not clear that even the realist expects moral requirements to apply to beings *completely* different from us psychologically. On the other hand, there is the first Kantian theme that moral requirements must apply independently of the desires and attitudes that agents happen to have; Kant thought that they apply to all *rational* beings, as such. This Kantian theme captures one way in which moral requirements seem *external* to us and seem to *constrain* us. This is a kind of objectivity we might expect the moral realist to defend.

Fortunately, we need not decide this issue; the argument from (3) to (5), though interesting, is not the most important part of the antirealist argument. Realists, I think, should at least be troubled by (3). However, (3) depends upon the assumptions about the connection between morality and rationality in (1) and about the nature of rationality in (2). Both sets of assumptions deserve careful scrutiny, and it is to them that we now turn.

8. THE JUSTIFIABILITY OF MORALITY

Premise (1) claims that moral obligations entail reasons for action. Is this true? Although (1) may seem to be supported by our reflections on the practical character of morality (3.1), this depends on how we construe the conclusion of those reflections. Does the practical character of morality require that moral obligations necessarily give rise to reasons for action, or just that they typically do? Won't moral considerations still play an important practical role even if they do not provide every agent on every occasion with reason for action? Isn't it possible for there to be people to whom moral obligations apply who nonetheless sometimes fail to have good reason to comply with these obligations? Certainly, moral requirements can still be considerations to which well informed, reasonable persons could not always be completely indifferent, even if they do not provide everyone with reason for action on every occasion to which they apply.

Premise (1) can be, and is, defended by Mackie and Harman on internalist grounds. In particular, it can be defended by appeal to internalism about reasons. This form of internalism claims that it is a conceptual truth about morality that moral considerations provide agents with reason for action. Here, it is agent internalism that is important. The claim that one has reason to do x is the claim that one has good reason to do x or is justified in doing x. But, as noted earlier (3.1), no one thinks that merely believing or judging that one has a moral obligation to do x gives one (good or justifying) reason to do x; one's moral belief or judgment may be wrong or in some way unwarranted. And false or unwarranted moral beliefs or judgments need not provide good reasons to act. Internalism, therefore, must be construed here as the agent internalist claim that it is a conceptual truth about morality that moral obligations or requirements provide reason for action.

It is important to be clear that internalism, as I am understanding it, and (1) are *not* equivalent; rather, internalism is one possible *ground* for asserting (1). Recall that internalism, as I defined it, asserts (in this context) not only that moral obligations necessarily provide reason for action but also that this fact is known a priori and by virtue of the concept of morality or the concept of a moral obligation. Although perhaps not all those who have called themselves internalists or who would so regard themselves subscribe to all three of these claims,[11] many within the internalist tradition have made all three claims, and certainly those, like Mackie and Harman, who offer internalist arguments against moral realism accept all three claims. This can be seen from the fact that most of those in the internalist tradition, and those like Mackie and Harman who offer internalist antirealist arguments, accept (1) without, or prior to, discussing and assessing competing theories about the content of morality and our moral obligations and competing substantive theories of rationality or reasons for action. An externalist, as I under-

11 Thus, Nagel (1970), although he calls himself an internalist (1970: 7), will not count as an internalist about reasons, given my understanding of internalism. For he reaches (1) only as the result of a sustained defense of a particular substantive theory about the nature of reasons for action that depends on contingent (even if "deep") facts about agents and the world. This explains how I can, or at least could, agree with most of Nagel's project despite the fact that he associates realism and internalism, since internalism about reasons, in his view, seems to assert no more than (1). As I shall argue, however, even (1) is more than we should insist that the realist accept.

stand externalism, might actually accept (1), but he could do so only *after* or *as the result of* defending, or at least accepting, certain claims about the nature of morality and rationality. I'll return to this point in sections 12 and 13.

Thus, internalism about reasons is sufficient for (1). But internalism about reasons, like internalism about motives, comes at a high price. The internalist about motives, as we noted, cannot represent the possibility of the amoralist and so cannot even consider the challenge of amoralist skepticism in the usual way. Unlike the internalist about motives, the internalist about reasons can conceive of the amoralist – someone who is not motivated by moral considerations. But she cannot regard as coherent the amoralist challenge '*Why* should I care about moral demands?'. The figure of the amoralist is someone who is unmoved by moral considerations, but the point of her challenge is to ask for a justification of the rationality of concern with moral demands. The internalist must regard the amoralist challenge as conceptually confused. According to the internalist, the amoral skeptic must have made either a conceptual or a moral mistake. In asking why she should be moral, the skeptic may be using moral language in "inverted commas." Thus, she can ask if she has reason to do things that are *regarded by others* as morally obligatory, but she cannot ask this about something she correctly regards as obligatory. Or if she is not using moral language in inverted commas, she can ask whether there is reason to be moral, but then she must simply be mistaken in thinking that morality does require the action whose rationality she questions.

But, again, this seems to be a rather facile solution to a traditional philosophical and popular problem. Why should we assume that the person who asks 'Why should I be moral?' is using moral language in inverted commas or is mistaken about what morality requires? Why can't someone have correctly identified his moral obligations and still wonder whether these obligations give him good reason for action? The thought that someone might possibly not have good reason to act on his moral obligations need not force us to withdraw our ascription of obligation. The amoralist challenge seems to be intelligible and, therefore, deserves to be taken seriously.

There are various replies available to the internalist. She can try to allow for the possibility of amoralism, or she can claim there are compelling reasons to accept internalism, even if it does make amoralism inconceivable.

59

The internalist might try to allow for amoralism in a way very similar to the way in which the internalist about motives tried to accommodate the amoralist. She might distinguish between strong and weak versions of both internalism and amoralism. As we have seen, weak internalism claims it is a conceptual truth about morality that moral requirements provide the agent with *a* reason for action, whereas strong internalism claims it is a conceptual truth about morality that moral requirements provide the agent with *conclusive, overriding,* or *sufficient* reason for action. Weak amoralism denies that agents have *sufficient* reason to be moral, while strong amoralism denies that agents have *reason* (i.e., *any* reason) to be moral. As long as we stick to the kind of weak internalism, which we have been operating with and which is sufficient for (1), we can still take a form of amoralism seriously. Weak internalism need treat only strong amoralism as incoherent; the weak internalist can still take seriously weak amoralism. So we do not need to reject internalism in order to take one form of amoralism seriously. As before, I agree, but I do not think that this point makes the (weak) internalist defense of (1) plausible. Although weak internalism may be more plausible than strong internalism, it is still implausible. For even if strong amoralism is less plausible than weak amoralism (after all, this is what makes it strong amoralism), it is still *coherent,* and it is evidence against (weak) internalism that it makes strong amoralism incoherent.

Of course, taking either form of amoralism seriously does not require conceding that (that form of) amoralism is true. We can take amoralism seriously and still claim that people do have reason to be moral. One can attempt to show that on plausible views about the nature of rationality and the demands of morality, people either always or at least typically do have reason (perhaps conclusive reason) to be moral. But this requires admitting that it is coherent to claim that moral requirements do not provide reasons for action.

Harman or Mackie might defend (weak) internalism and (1) by claiming that moral considerations supply moral reasons and that moral reasons are reasons for action. This reasoning seems natural, but it confuses different senses of 'reason'. It's uncontroversial that moral requirements supply reasons in the sense that they are norms of a certain kind that apply to people in certain situations (recall our first Kantian theme) and that these moral norms or reasons will provide explanatory reasons for those agents who adopt them. But neither of these ways in which moral requirements do or can supply reasons constitutes internalism or implies the interpretation of (1) that Harman and Mackie require, namely, that moral considerations provide agents with good or justifying reasons for action (recall our second Kantian theme). The facts that certain norms apply to one's situation and that, if adopted, they would supply one's explanatory reasons for action do not themselves establish that one has good or justifying reason to act on them (cf. Foot 1972a).

Or Harman or Mackie might reply that internalism and (1) are true because of an inner or conceptual connection between reasons for action and correct application of moral terms such as 'ought' and 'should'. The idea would be that it is incoherent to say, as the amoralist must, 'I ought to do *x*, but do I have reason to do *x*?' (cf. Nesbitt 1977). But this question is not incoherent if we distinguish two senses of 'ought': a moral 'ought' and an 'ought' of rationality. We might admit that it is part of the meaning of the 'ought' of rationality that if we ought (in this sense) to do something, we thereby have (good) reason to do it, and still deny that it is part of the meaning of the moral 'ought' that if we ought (in this sense) to do something, we thereby have (good) reason to do that thing. This second claim is supported by the fact that what should be an equivalent question, 'I have a moral obligation to do *x*, but do I have good reason to do *x*?'; does not, we have seen, seem incoherent. We could then claim that (1) seems to be a conceptual truth only by failing to distinguish these two senses of 'ought'.

Finally, Harman or Mackie might reply by *stipulating* that what he means by an 'ought' statement is one whose correct application implies the existence of reasons for action and that this argument for moral relativism is not intended to apply to moral claims that are not expressed by such statements.[12] On this suggestion, the phrase "'ought' statement" becomes a highly technical phrase, and normal ascriptions of obligation using 'ought' may turn out not to be 'ought' statements after all, with the result that the antirealist argument does not apply to them. But this reply threatens to make the argument for moral relativism vacuous; it may fail to apply to anything about which the moral realist makes claims. The argument seemed interesting, because it purported to show that we must relativize *moral obligations* to people's attitudes and desires. If

12 See Harman's discussion of "inner judgments" (1975: 8–11) and his claims about what he means by a "single true morality which applies to everyone" (1984: 34). I discuss these features of Harman's argument in more detail in Brink 1988b.

the argument applies not to moral obligations but only to claims – whichever, if any, they are – expressed by 'ought' statements, it has lost most, if not all, of its interest.

The denial of (1), therefore, is coherent. Whether it is plausible is more difficult to say. This will depend on our views about the demands of morality, the nature of rationality, and the role of moral considerations in practical reasoning. Since premise (2) in the argument for moral relativism incorporates certain assumptions about rationality, we might pursue these issues by examining it.

9. THE NATURE OF RATIONALITY

(2) claims that reasons for action are desire-dependent; one has a reason to do x just in case x would contribute to the satisfaction of one's desires. This is a familiar idea about reasons for action. Mackie seems simply to assume that it is correct (but see 1977: 77–80), and Harman is quite candid that his argument relies on, without defending, this claim about reasons for action (1975: 9). And this claim is by no means idiosyncratic. But we should not accept this argument for moral relativism without examining all of the claims on which it rests.

Why should we accept (2)? Can't some considerations provide me with reasons for action, whether or not they contribute to the satisfaction of my desires?

10. REASONS FOR ACTION AND MOTIVATION

(2) might be defended by appeal to the need for a connection between an agent's reasons for action and motivational states of the agent, such as her desires. We appeal to an agent's reasons for action in explaining her behavior. Because actions are produced as the result of the interaction of the agent's beliefs and desires and the explanation of behavior is causal, reasons for action must entail desires; an agent can have reason to do x only if she desires x or has desires that x would satisfy (cf. B. Williams 1980: 102, 106–7).

But this defense of (2) confuses explanatory and justifying reasons. (1) links obligation with good or justifying reasons for action. If there is to be no equivocation on 'reason for action', (2) must be construed as a thesis about the conditions under which one has good or justifying reasons. So construed, (2) cannot be defended by appeal to the fact, if it is a fact, that explanatory or motivating reasons are desire-dependent.

11. A PURELY INSTRUMENTAL THEORY OF RATIONALITY?

However, neither Harman nor Mackie need be making this mistake. (2) can stand as a claim about good or justifying reasons for action. *Instrumental rationality* is the very familiar kind of means-ends rationality; it tells agents how best to satisfy their existing desires. Insofar as rationality is instrumental, agents have reason to do things that contribute to the satisfaction of their desires or ends. We would be committed to (2)'s claim that an agent has reason to do x just in case x contributes to the satisfaction of his desires if rationality were *purely* instrumental, that is, if instrumental rationality were the *only* kind of rationality. Indeed, this seems to be Harman's view, for he tells us that he accepts a broadly Humean account of rationality and rejects Kantian claims about rationality (1975: 9). And Mackie's own views about ethics and practical reasoning are, of course, broadly Humean as well (1977: 40, 79–80; 1980).

Hume claims that reason can only be "the slave of the passions" and that passions themselves can be neither reasonable nor unreasonable (1739: II, iii, 3/esp. 415). These claims are usually taken to imply that we can only reason about how best to satisfy existing desires or ends and that, in particular, we cannot reason about these desires or ends themselves. Of course, some desires – we might call them *extrinsic* desires (e.g., the desire to eat at a particular restaurant) – depend on the agent's beliefs (e.g., that that restaurant is nearby and serves good food at an affordable price), and insofar as we can reason about these beliefs, we can reason about these desires. But extrinsic desires also depend on *intrinsic* desires (e.g., the desire to eat) that do not themselves depend on the agent's beliefs, and we cannot reason about these desires (1739: II, iii, 3/414, 416; cf. 1751: app. 1, v/87–8). Kant, of course, denies these claims; he believes that some ends and desires are contrary to reason and that agents have reasons for action independently of whether the action contributes to the satisfaction of their desires; this view of rationality underlies our second Kantian theme that an agent's reasons to be moral do not depend on her existing desires.

If this kind of Humean account is right, only facts about what would promote the agent's actual or existing (intrinsic) desires can provide him with reason for action, and this establishes (2). Some version of the Humean account is often assumed to be true, because alternative views – in particular, Kantian views – seem mysterious or even unintelligible (cf. Brandt 1979; B. Williams 1980: 108–10). But we can raise questions about this Humean defense of (2) without defending Kant or engaging in Kant scholarship. The Humean defense of (2) assumes that all rationality is instrumental rationality and, hence, that we cannot deliberate about the ends or desires that figure as the starting points for instrumental reasoning. These assumptions seem mistaken, because we can reason about which ends and desires are *valuable* or *worth pursuing*.

We all begin with certain ends and desires; we are attached to, and have desires for, particular people, activities, and states of affairs more than others. Now these ends and desires reflect *evaluative judgments*. In the case of most things we desire, we desire them *because we think these things valuable*. This is true of our preferences for many activities and relationships as well as for states of the world. This sort of value-laden explanation may not be required for all desires. For instance, gustatory preferences do not seem to presuppose the greater value of the preferred smell or taste. But even if there is no need for value-laden explanations of gustatory preferences, this is not the case with many desires; they require value-laden explanations. At least part of the explanation of the fact that I want to be a professional philosopher involves my belief that philosophy is a valuable activity; I would not have this desire if I did not think that philosophy was a valuable activity. Part of the explanation of my wanting to relieve my neighbor's suffering is that I think pain and suffering are bad; if I were somehow to come to think that there was nothing objectionable about pain and suffering, I would probably have very little concern about my neighbor's situation.

So our particular desires and ends reflect assumptions about the value of particular things. But we need not and should not remain content with a mere collection of particular evaluative judgments. There are various reasons to consider and adopt more general, theoretical evaluative claims about what kinds of ends are valuable and why (cf. Sidgwick 1907: 99–100). One reason is an *intellectual* need. Even if we could somehow muddle through life relying only on our particular evaluative judgments that x is good, y is bad, and so forth, an intellectual puzzle would remain: *Why* are all the various things that we think valuable (or disvaluable) valuable (or disvaluable)? To answer this question we would naturally appeal to more general evaluative principles or theories that try to systematize and bring order to our various views about value and that seek to explain what makes valuable things valuable and bad things bad. However, there is also a more pressing, *practical* need for evaluative theory. No mere collection of discrete evaluative claims would be adequate to meet the various practical difficulties we often face. Sometimes we are *uncertain*. This is true when we face choices between things not covered by our collection of evaluative views. Which of various activities or courses of action available to us is the one most worth pursuing? Here, an appeal to more general evaluative principles or theories may *provide guidance* in cases that our previous particular judgments do not cover. At other times our evaluative views are *in conflict*. Perhaps we think it is important to develop one's talents, and we also think that family relations and commitments are important. But, like Gauguin, we face (or think we face) a choice between pursuing our artistic talents to their fullest and maintaining our family life and commitments. What do we do? Here, appeal to a theory that explains and ranks various constituents of value might help *resolve intrapersonal conflict*. And, of course, even when our own evaluative views seem reasonably clear and fairly consistent, they are subject to *challenge from others*. Others, concerned about us or our actions, may express evaluative disagreement with us or ask us for justification for our evaluative views. Thus, I may appeal to the principle that one should develop one's talents as a justification, which I expect or hope my son will recognize, for telling him to limit his television watching in certain ways. Here we may hope to *resolve interpersonal conflict* by appealing to more theoretical evaluative claims that subsume and explain our actions and our particular evaluative views.

But how do we go about constructing and assessing theories and principles of value? A full discussion of these issues will come in Chapter 5, but I can sketch the relevant details here. Our method must rely on the interplay between theory and particular judgments. We try to identify theoretical claims about value that will explain and support a number of our firmly held evaluative beliefs. We then (further) assess these theories by comparing their implications about the value of real and imaginary states of affairs, lives, activities, and actions with our own independent assessments of the value of those states of affairs, lives, activities, and actions. If a theory has counterintuitive implications, then this is prima facie evidence against the theory. If the counterintuitive implications of the theory are fairly common, then this is reason to abandon the theory for another or at least to modify it in significant ways. But if we decide that this counterintuitive implication of the theory is a more or less isolated phenomenon and that the theory accounts for many of our particular value judgments, and especially if it seems to explain more of our value judgments better than alternative theories, then this initial evidence against the theory will be overridden and we should revise the particular value judgment that conflicted with the theory. Ideally, we should make trade-offs between the levels of theory and particular judgments in response to conflicts between the two, making adjustments here at one level and there at the other, until we have a theory that is, to borrow John Rawls's useful phrase, in "reflective equilibrium" with our considered evaluative beliefs (1971: 19–21, 46–51, 579–81).

These are necessarily abstract claims about how we can and should reason about value. But they explain, if only in outline, how we can reason about the value or worth of our actual desires and ends. So (2) cannot be defended by maintaining a purely instrumental theory of rationality. A fact will not provide an agent with a good or justifying reason for action by contributing to the satisfaction of her desires if those desires reflect value judgments that would not survive the process of reflective equilibrium. Moreover, we can appeal to these noninstrumental claims about rationality and maintain that a fact can provide an agent with reason for action if it would help secure values that the process of reflective equilibrium would vindicate. This means that whether moral requirements provide reasons for action need not depend upon whether fulfillment of those requirements would promote the agent's existing desires.

12. A DESIRE-SATISFACTION VERSION OF RATIONAL EGOISM?

Of course, it would be possible to defend (2) as the proper form for a *noninstrumental* account of rationality. One might claim that the outcome of the process of reflective equilibrium would be a *desire-*

satisfaction theory of value according to which something is valuable just in case, because, and insofar as it contributes to the satisfaction of someone's desire. Such a theory, he might claim, provides the best overall account of our views about value and supports (2)'s claims about rationality.

Now, of course, this would not be enough to establish (2), since (2) makes the agent's reason for action a function only of what would satisfy *his* desires. Harman or Mackie would have to combine a desire-satisfaction theory of value with an *egoist* theory of reasons for action. Rational egoism is a theory about the grounds of reason for action; it says that an agent has reason to do *x* just in case, and insofar as, *x* would contribute to *his own* interest, welfare, or happiness.[13] (As such, *rational* egoism should be contrasted with *psychological* egoism – the view that agents act only so as to promote their own real or perceived interests – and *ethical* egoism - the view that an agent's one and only moral obligation is to promote his own interest.) Different versions of rational egoism result from incorporating different conceptions of value or welfare into an egoist theory of rationality. If we combine rational egoism with a desire-satisfaction theory of value, we get a desire-satisfaction version of rational egoism, which claims that an agent has reason to do *x* just in case, and insofar as, *x* would contribute to the satisfaction of his desires. (Notice that a desire-satisfaction version of rational egoism, so construed, places no constraints on the *content* of the agent's desires; in particular, it allows that an agent might have other-directed desires and that these desires provide the basis for his reasons for action. If Zach desires Zenobia's welfare, then, according to a desire-satisfaction version of rational egoism, he has reason to do those things that would promote her welfare, even if he does not otherwise benefit from her benefit.) (2) could thus be defended as part of a desire-satisfaction version of rational egoism.

Such an account of individual rationality is often assumed in formal and informal discussions of rational decision theory and in large bodies of literature in economics and political science. In all these discussions it is assumed that what the agent has most reason

13 It is possible to regard Harman's argument as resting on a desire-satisfaction version of rational egoism, despite his criticism of egoism in 1977: chap. 12. First, Harman does not distinguish there between rational and psychological egoism. And, second, insofar as he discusses rational egoism at all, he has in mind a much more restricted view than the one I here suggest he could hold.

to do is a direct function of which course of action would most contribute to the satisfaction of his desires.

If we understand (2), in this way, as part of a desire-satisfaction version of rational egoism, the antirealist argument commits no equivocation, does not depend on a purely instrumental theory of rationality, and relies, in fact, on familiar assumptions about the nature of individual rationality. But (2), on this reading, is only as plausible as a desire-satisfaction version of rational egoism, and a desire-satisfaction version of rational egoism is only as plausible as rational egoism *and* a desire-satisfaction theory of value. Although a fully satisfying discussion of the merits of a desire-satisfaction version of rational egoism is not possible here, we can raise some serious questions about both rational egoism and a desire-satisfaction theory of value.

To assess the plausibility of desire-satisfaction versions of rational egoism, we need to be able to compare them with alternative accounts of rationality and value.

Rational egoism is an *agent relative* theory of rationality, because it makes an agent's reasons for action depend only upon how her actions might affect *her* welfare, interest, or happiness. An *agent neutral* theory denies this; it takes an agent's reasons for action to be a direct function of the value her actions would produce, whether this value accrues to the agent or not.

We have already observed the distinction between subjective and objective theories of value. Subjective theories of value claim that the constituents of a valuable life consist in or depend importantly upon subjective states of the person whose life it is. A desire-satisfaction theory of value is a form of subjectivism, because it makes the value of things depend on whether people happen to desire those things. A desire-satisfaction theory claims that value consists in the satisfaction of desires and that disvalue consists in the frustration of desires. It is worth distinguishing between two different forms of the desire-satisfaction theory. An *actual* desire-satisfaction theory claims that what is valuable is what would satisfy one's actual desires. But our desires can be inconsistent, misinformed (i.e., based on false beliefs), or incompletely informed. For this reason, proponents of a desire-satisfaction theory may wish to adopt a *counterfactual* desire-satisfaction theory. A counterfactual desire-satisfaction theory claims that what is valuable is what would satisfy the desires one would have were one to occupy some preferred epistemic state (e.g., if one's beliefs and desires were consistent and based on full nonevaluative information). By contrast with these various forms of subjectivism, objective theories claim that what is valuable neither consists in nor depends importantly upon anyone's psychological states. There are many different possible objective theories, but most will claim that the main constituents of value are things that contribute to a valuable *life*. Such theories claim that a valuable life consists in things such as the possession of certain character traits, the exercise of certain capacities, and the development of certain relations with others and to the world, and that the value of such a life is independent of the pleasure it contains and whether or not this sort of life is desired (cf. Kraut 1979). A theory of value is *purely* subjective, as the desire-satisfaction theory is, if it contains only subjective components; a theory of value is *purely* objective if it contains only objective components. And, of course, theories of value can be *mixed*, containing both subjective and objective components.

The first thing to notice in assessing premise (2) and its role in the antirealist argument is that, insofar as (2) does or might depend on a desire-satisfaction version of rational egoism, it would seem to depend on an actual desire-satisfaction version of rational egoism. For insofar as the argument is intended to establish (5), and not just (3), it requires the assumption that people are or can be psychologically so different that there could be no plausible set of moral requirements fulfillment of which would satisfy some desires of everyone. This modified version of (4) may be called (4a). Now, while something like (4a) may be plausible with respect to people's actual desires, it is not clear that it is true of people's *counterfactual* desires. The fact, which troubles Nagel, that some people might actually lack motivation to do as morality requires does not show that these people would not have the appropriate desires in some preferred epistemic state. If they would and if we accept a counterfactual desire-satisfaction version of rational egoism, rather than an actual desire-satisfaction version, then we might accept (4a) as applied to actual desires and still resist (5). Of course, the *applicability* of moral requirements would still depend on, or be relativized to, counterfactual desire. Thus, (3) would still be true, even if we read 'desires' as 'counterfactual desires'. But (3), so construed, need not

69

violate the Kantian (or Nagelian) theme that moral requirements must apply to agents independently of their variable, escapable, and idiosyncratic sentiments and motivations, because counterfactual desires will arguably be fairly uniform and, in Nagel's sense, "deep." Now this may not satisfy all Kantian claims, but it arguably satisfies those Kantian claims with which we may fairly saddle the moral realist.[14] Thus, a counterfactual desire-satisfaction theory of rationality, not that different from the actual desire-satisfaction theory of rationality that might be used to support (2), offers one possible response to this antirealist argument. Whether such a theory is fully adequate, even as a response to this objection, will depend on the details of the idealized conditions in its specification of counterfactual desire. (I shall undertake a discussion of some of these issues in 8.2.)

Although this is a possible response, it is not the only one or even the best one; the realist might defend either an objective version of rational egoism or an agent neutral theory of rationality. Let us consider the plausibility of rational egoism. Does an egoist theory account for our considered judgments about rationality? Certainly, an egoist theory can account for our beliefs about *prudential* reasons for action, because an agent's prudential reasons for action just are determined by what is most in the agent's interest. But are all reasons for action prudential reasons for action?

It may seem as if the answer should clearly be no. People have and act on all sorts of reasons (e.g., moral reasons, reasons of etiquette, reasons of state), and this shows that prudential reasons are merely one kind of reason for action. But this opposition to rational egoism may rest on a confusion between different senses of 'reason for action'. There undoubtedly are many different kinds of

14 Because Kant insisted on both the rationality of morality and the independence of duty from *all* empirical motives, he would probably not be satisfied with the dependence of duty on even this sort of counterfactual desire. See Kant 1785: 388–9, 391, 394, 398, 405, 408, 426–7, 432, 442. But his opposition to this sort of theory depends upon further Kantian assumptions and is not established by the more modest assumption that the rationality of moral demands cannot depend upon the variable sentiments of agents. And although I shall myself argue against even counterfactual desire-satisfaction theories of value and rationality (8.2), I don't think that such a position should be seen as a commitment of moral realism or as necessary to resisting this antirealist argument.

behavioral norms which, if adopted, would supply an agent with explanatory reasons for action. But theories of rationality are theories about the conditions under which an agent has good or justifying reason to do something, and it is less clear that there are multiple kinds of good or justifying reasons for action (cf. 3.8).

However, we can, without confusion or equivocation, ask whether all (good or justifying) reasons for action are agent relative. Agent relative theories of rationality seem to assume that *sacrifice requires compensation* (SRC), that is, that an agent has reason to make a sacrifice, say, to benefit another, if, and only if, the agent receives some (sufficient) benefit in return. Is SRC plausible?

In support of SRC we might note that it seems to explain some intuitions about the rationality of sacrifice. There seem to be a number of cases where the possible benefits I could bestow on others do not seem to give me reason for action. The fact that Bonny could confer a benefit upon an applicant to her firm by resigning her position does not seem to give Bonny reason to resign her position. One explanation of this intuition is that Bonny's resignation would be an uncompensated sacrifice, which she does not have reason to perform. Now, of course, we do want to distinguish between having a reason to do something and having sufficient or conclusive reason to do that thing. And the critic of SRC might claim that the applicant's interests give Bonny *a* reason to resign her position, even if it is a reason that can be outweighed. But there is a problem with this reply to SRC. It does not seem to be true, as an agent neutral theory would imply, that our decision about whether Bonny has (sufficient) reason to resign her position to benefit the applicant to her firm awaits some showing that the job is more important to her than it is to the applicant; the reasonableness of Bonny's retaining her position does not seem to be hostage to the outcome of this sort of calculation. If so, this fact weakens alternative, agent neutral accounts of Bonny's case and so provides some support for SRC's explanation of our intuitions here.

More generally, we might defend SRC by appeal to the separateness of persons. Because I am a separately existing person, with only one life to live, it is unreasonable to expect me to make uncompensated sacrifices (cf. Nozick 1974: 33). Of course, it is equally true of others that they "only go around once," but SRC acknowledges this fact by insisting that they too must be compensated if

71

sacrifices are to be reasonably demanded of them. Indeed, a general willingness to make completely uncompensated sacrifices may be incompatible with genuine commitments to personal goals and projects – commitments that seem terribly important and that, in some views about personal identity, are themselves at least partially constitutive of my being a particular, metaphysically distinct being who is the bearer of reasons for action (cf. Williams 1973a: 116; Whiting 1986).

Finally, we might note that SRC provides a natural explanation of those popular and philosophical worries about the justifiability of morality that, we have seen, support externalism. It is true that most of us expect moral considerations to turn out to be important practical considerations. But it is also true, as we have noted, that we think an important part of morality requires agents to benefit or respect others in ways that seem to constrain the pursuit of their own interest or happiness. This observation makes many wonder whether we really have good reason to comply with some of these other-regarding moral demands. In formulating this worry we seem to be relying on agent relative, rather than agent neutral, assumptions about rationality. For there is no difficulty in justifying other-regarding demands on agent neutral assumptions, since the agent neutral theory denies that the rationality of sacrifice requires compensation; it is only if we assume that the rationality of sacrifice requires compensation, as the agent relative theory claims, that we can explain why it should seem hard to explain why I have reason to sacrifice my own interests to benefit others, as morality seems to require. This is not to rule out agent neutral responses to the amoralist challenge. But it does seem to show that our worries about the justifiability of morality rest on agent relative assumptions about rationality such as SRC and that, as a result, the burden will be on the defender of the agent neutral theory to *argue us out of* these assumptions.

Even if these intuitions support or can be made to support SRC and agent relativity, SRC may seem to justify a very limited amount of sacrifice, and this may make rational egoism look implausible. Surely, we might think, we have good reason to help others in distress if we can do so at little cost to ourselves, even if we do not derive any benefit from helping them. If so, this will be evidence against SRC and agent relativity and will be evidence for an agent neutral theory of the sort Nagel defends in *The Possibility of Altruism*. This is a legitimate worry about SRC and agent relativity. But the egoist can defend SRC by claiming that the force of this worry is somewhat hard to assess, since our judgments about the rationality of particular sacrifices can reflect our assumptions about value as much as they reflect our assumptions about rationality. SRC places few, if any, constraints on the forms compensation may take. SRC implies that if I am to have reason to benefit you, then I must myself benefit from your benefit. If we accept a desire-satisfaction theory of value, the connection between your benefit and my benefit can be at most contingent. I can have reason to do something that will satisfy your desires only because doing so will, in fact, satisfy desires of mine, either because, as a matter of contingent psychological fact, I desire that your desires be satisfied or because, as a matter of contingent psychological fact, you will reciprocate. Since the relevant contingent psychological facts do not always obtain, SRC will justify limited sacrifice on (actual) desire-satisfaction assumptions. But SRC will have quite different implications about the scope of justified sacrifice on different evaluative assumptions. Many objective conceptions of welfare recognize a variety of social or other-regarding components in a person's good. Family relations, friendships, and social relations involving mutual concern and respect make our lives more valuable than they would otherwise be. By having friends and cooperating with others on a footing of mutual concern and commitment, we are able to exercise new capacities, secure ourselves against a variety of misfortunes, and generally extend our interests in new ways. On such views, the good of others is *part of* my good, and so I will benefit *directly* and *necessarily* by benefiting them (cf. 8.2 and 8.6). This observation about the connection between SRC and the admissible forms of compensation should assuage some immediate worries about SRC, agent relativity, and rational egoism.

Nor are objective theories of value just abstract possibilities; there are, as we shall see later (8.2), additional, independent reasons to reject desire-satisfaction theories of value in favor of objective theories. There are character traits and activities that are valuable and whose value is independent of their being desired. And as long as there are important social or other-regarding components among these objective constituents of a valuable life, agents will typically,

73

perhaps always, have reason to comply with moral demands – even when these demands are other-regarding.

Of course, neither Harman nor Mackie could appeal to objective conceptions of value in order to defend rational egoism in this way, since premise (2), on this reading, requires a subjective, desire-satisfaction version of rational egoism. So objective versions of rational egoism provide one basis for rejecting (2) and this anti-realist argument.

Someone might worry that a defense of moral realism that relies on an appeal to objectivism about value begs the question against moral relativism. But this is not true. The argument for moral relativism purports to show why everyone, even the person who began as a moral realist, say, for the reasons discussed in Chapter 2, must accept moral relativism. So if objectivism is plausible, if only to someone not yet committed to moral relativism or even if only to the person who is already a moral realist, and if a theory of rationality incorporating objectivism blocks the inference from (1) to (3), this argument for moral relativism fails.

Therefore, whatever the merits of other forms of rational egoism, we should reject desire-satisfaction versions of rational egoism. If so, we must reject this last defense of (2). If reasons for action are not (entirely) dependent on the desires or attitudes of the agent, then moral requirements need not be relativized to the desires or attitudes of agents, even if moral requirements necessarily provide reasons for action. If, for example, objective versions of rational egoism are true, then agents will have reason to comply with moral requirements, even if they have no desire to, so long as compliance promotes some objective constituents of their good. In discussing the plausibility of SRC, we saw that many plausible objective conceptions of welfare will recognize important social or other-regarding components in an individual's good. Such objective conceptions of rational egoism will imply that agents typically, perhaps always, have at least some reason (though not necessarily a conclusive reason) to comply with even the more other-regarding moral requirements. And, of course, agent neutral theories of rationality can provide an even stronger vindication of the rationality of such other-regarding moral requirements; according to these theories, agents have reason to comply with moral requirements as long as such compliance promotes value, for the agent or others (cf. Nagel 1970).

74

13. THE JUSTIFIABILITY OF MORALITY AND THE NATURE OF RATIONALITY

We have been considering the individual plausibility of premises (1) and (2). I have argued that both (1) and (2) are questionable. But in discussing (1), I also noted that our views about the justifiability of morality and about the nature of rationality are interdependent in a certain way. Once we reject internalist, conceptual defenses of the justifiability of morality, we must accept the fact that the justifiability of morality depends on the nature of morality, the nature of individual rationality, and the constituents of human welfare. But once we concede the interdependence of (1) and (2), we can see another very important objection to this argument for moral relativism.

Not only are the assumptions about the justifiability of morality in (1) and about the nature of rationality in (2) individually problematic; they are *mutually implausible*. If we begin by accepting the first Kantian idea – which might seem to be a commitment of moral realism – that moral requirements are not up to us (i.e., that they do not fail to apply to us just because we are not disposed to act on them), then we should conclude that the plausibility of (1) varies inversely with the plausibility of (2).

For then the more plausible we find the claim that an agent's reasons for action depend on his desires, the more plausible we should find the claim that moral obligations do not always provide reasons for action. I think (2) is an implausible view about the nature of individual rationality. (Although I have provided some argument for this claim here, more of the argument appears in 8.2.) But if we were nonetheless to accept it, the independence of duty and inclination should lead us to deny that moral requirements are rational for everyone to follow in all circumstances. This would require us to reject the second Kantian theme, but not the first: Moral requirements would still apply to agents independently of their contingent and variable desires, even if they would not provide agents with reasons for action independently of their desires. Thus, we could still charge people who violate their moral obligations with immorality, even if we could not always charge them with irrationality. And the fact, if it is a fact, that some people sometimes fail to have reason to be moral does not show that moral considerations are not important practical considerations; in particular, it does not show that moral considerations are considerations to which normal, well informed people might always be completely indifferent (cf. Foot 1972a).

And, of course, the less plausible we find the desire-dependence of reasons for action and the more plausible we find objective versions of rational egoism or agent neutral theories of rationality, the more plausible it will seem that moral obligations provide agents with reason for action. This is not to say that mere rejection of (2) is sufficient to vindicate the rationality or justifiability of morality. The justifiability of morality will depend on what theories of rationality, value, and morality are correct. And even on favorable assumptions about these issues it may be that moral requirements do not always give every agent conclusive reasons to be moral. But on plausible objective views about value that recognize important social components in a person's good, on either agent relative or agent neutral theories of rationality, and on common views about the content of moral requirements (i.e., about what morality requires of agents), everyone will typically, perhaps always, have at least some reason to fulfill these moral requirements and will frequently have conclusive reason to do so.

This relationship between (1) and (2), of course, is very important and spells serious trouble for the argument for moral relativism, since that argument requires the plausibility of *both* (1) and (2).

Someone might object to this line of argument by claiming that, of course, if we reject (3) we will find (1) and (2) inversely plausible – this is just what it means to claim that (1) and (2) imply (3). Because the inverse plausibility argument (perhaps tacitly) denies (3), it simply begs the question against proponents of the antirealist argument. But this objection to the inverse plausibility argument mistakes our dialectical situation. Of course, if we begin with no views about (3)'s plausibility and if (1) and (2) are taken as given or at least as very firm starting points, then the inverse plausibility argument will seem to beg the question. But this is not our situation; rather, the situation is: The Kantian idea, which resembles the denial of (3), seems initially plausible (partly because of moral phenomenology and partly because of the kind of arguments I offered in Chapter 2). The antirealist is supposed to offer arguments that force us to give up this commitment. To do this, the cases for (1) and (2) must each be more compelling than our initial commitment to the Kantian idea and, hence, to the denial of (3). Now the arguments against (1) and (2) are meant to show that neither is obviously true or compelling. And, in particular, once we give up the internalist justification of (1), (1)'s plausibility can be seen to rest on a complex set of views about the nature of morality (e.g., the sorts of things morality requires), the nature of rationality, and, in all likelihood, facts about agents and their world. In this situation, I claim, we will think that the more plausible we find (1), the less plausible we will find (2), and vice versa. For instance, given common views about what morality requires, acceptance of a desire-based theory of rationality should lead us to doubt that moral considerations necessarily do give rise to reasons for action, because morality seems to require us to do things we might not (i.e., that it is possible not to) have any desire to do. Similarly, given common views about what morality requires, if we assume that moral considerations necessarily provide reasons for action, we shall be inclined to expect that not all reasons for action can be desire-dependent, precisely because morality seems to require us to do things we might not have any desire to do. Of course, I rely on common moral views here, including the Kantian idea that morality requires us to do things we might not have any desire to do. This is quite close to denying (3). But it is dialectically proper to rely on such views, insofar as they are common views or views that our previous argument has supported, since the proponents of the argument were supposed to be arguing us *out of* them.

This completes a long and complicated examination of an antirealist argument that is important both for its influence and for the number of important foundational issues it raises. It might be helpful to summarize briefly the results of this examination. Both the unconverted and the moral realist can and should resist this argument for moral relativism. Even if we concede the assumptions about the desire-dependency of rationality and the relationship between morality and rationality on which the argument rests, it is still not clear that the argument succeeds in undermining a single true morality. Moreover, and more importantly, these two assumptions are individually problematic and mutually implausible. Internalism is implausible, and this makes the rationality of moral requirements an open question whose answer depends on, among other things, the correct theory of rationality. Which theory of reasons for action we accept will affect the extent to which morality can be justified. But

77

no theory of rationality, not even the one on which the antirealist argument is based, threatens the status of moral considerations as important practical considerations.

14. A REALIST EXPLANATION OF THE ACTION-GUIDING CHARACTER OF MORALITY

Indeed, not only does the practical character of morality not undermine moral realism; moral realism is able to *explain* the action-guiding character of morality in a way that traditional antirealist theories cannot. As we have seen, it is noncognitivists who like to stress the practical or dynamic character of morality. It is a fundamental feature of moral judgments, in their view, that they have emotive or prescriptive force. But it seems we can explain the emotive or prescriptive force that moral judgments have most easily on the assumption that our moral judgments are, or at least purport to be, true (cf. Carson 1984: 21–4).

As we have seen, the emotive force of a moral judgment consists in part in an invitation to others to share the appraiser's attitude; the prescriptive force of a moral judgment consists in recommending to others things the appraiser judges favorably and recommending against things he judges unfavorably. The noncognitivist seems unable to explain not only the possibility of making moral judgments with no emotive or prescriptive force (in contexts in which we have no intention to express attitudes or influence others' conduct [2.6]) but also such emotive or prescriptive force as moral judgments have. For it is hard to see *why* anyone should be so keen on getting others to share his attitude, or on recommending a course of action, unless he thought the attitude he was expressing or the course of action he was recommending was correct or valuable.

The noncognitivist may remind us that our attitudes can be very important to us and can reflect fundamental concerns. But the question is precisely why these attitudes should matter so and why some things should cause us so much concern, unless we think that the objects of our attitudes and concern *possess value*. As we noted in our discussion of purely instrumental theories of rationality, most of our attitudes and desires require this sort of value-laden explanation. And we typically invite others to share our attitudes and prescribe courses of action because we hold the (defeasible) belief that these attitudes and courses of action are correct or valuable.

78

Nor would an appraiser's audience have much reason to share his attitude or heed his recommendation if it had no reason to regard the attitude he was expressing or the course of action he was recommending as correct or valuable. But people do seek and heed moral advice. For these reasons, realistic assumptions about morality provide a natural explanation of the emotive or prescriptive force of moral judgments; it is not clear how the noncognitivist can explain these facts about moral judgments of which his theory makes so much.

Perhaps the noncognitivist will tell us that we can invite others to share our attitudes or prescribe courses of action without believing those attitudes or courses of action are objectively valuable so long as we share enough closely related attitudes and preferences with our audience. But this reply not only leaves our attitudes unexplained; it makes our moral practices look too much like the practices of some exclusive club. The fact is that we address our moral judgments to audiences whose psychology we are not familiar with or whom we fear hold preferences and attitudes different from our own. Moreover, people seek and sometimes even heed moral advice from others with unknown or even quite different psychological makeup. The natural explanation of why we bother to invite others to share our moral attitudes or prescribe to them some course of action, and the natural explanation of why they have reason to listen to us, is that, on various grounds, we purport to hold correct (or nearly correct) attitudes or to prescribe right (or nearly right) actions. If we reject moral realism, there seems to be no ground or explanation for the emotive or prescriptive force our moral judgments carry.

15. CONCLUSION

Some think that internalism is the correct way to represent the practical character of morality and, therefore, that the practical character of morality tells against moral realism. But moral realism is perfectly compatible with the practical character of morality. This is because externalism, rather than internalism, is the appropriate way to represent the practical or action-guiding character of morality. The rationality and motivational force of moral considerations depend, as the externalist claims, not simply on the concept of morality but (also) on the content of morality, facts about agents, and a substantive theory of reasons for action. Not only can moral realism accommodate the action-guiding character of morality, properly understood; it can do so better than its traditional opponents can. The realist, but not the noncognitivist, can take amoralist skepticism seriously, and the realist, but not the noncognitivist, can explain the action-guiding character of morality.[15] Consideration of the action-guiding character of morality, therefore, supports, rather than undermines, moral realism.

15 Moral realism will have these advantages over certain forms of constructivism in ethics as well. Some forms of constructivism rely heavily on a publicity constraint, according to which a "true" moral principle must be a standard that is taught and that serves as a public justification of actions, policies, institutions, and so on. Cf. Rawls 1971: 133, 177–82, 582, and 1980: 517, 537–8, 555. This publicity constraint is often defended on internalist grounds; cf. Medlin 1957 and 4.3. If the argument here is correct, externalist moral realism is preferable to internalist constructivism as well as to internalist noncognitivism.

4

Does moral realism matter?

So far, I have argued that reflection on commonsense morality supports moral realism. Reflection on moral inquiry supports a realist form of cognitivism. And this case for moral realism is strengthened, not defeated, by appeal to the practical or action-guiding character of moral considerations.

The moral antirealist might concede these points about the realist presuppositions of our normative practices but deny their significance. Rejection of moral realism and acceptance of some form of antirealism, such as noncognitivism, the antirealist might claim, would make no difference to our normative practices (Hare 1957: 39–41; Mackie 1977: 16; Blackburn 1985: 11). The alleged impotence of moral realism and other metaethical views is sometimes thought to constitute an argument against moral realism (Blackburn 1980, 1981: 185–6, 1984: chap. 6). This antirealist inference can seem puzzling. One would have thought that if metaethical views made no practical difference, then this would at most be reason to avoid, or be unconcerned with, metaethics, not to prefer one metaethical view to another. Not only would the impotence of metaethical views seem to be neutral among metaethical views, it would also seem to leave unaffected the presumption in favor of moral realism for which I argued in the two preceding chapters. That is, if the choice between moral realism and antirealism makes no practical difference, then this fact would seem neither to add to nor detract from the arguments for moral realism that we have been considering.

But there are two ways in which the impotence of metaethical views might be thought to be a feather in the antirealist's cap. First, it might be thought that there are serious worries about the metaphysical and epistemological commitments of moral realism; the metaphysical and epistemological commitments of the moral antirealist might be thought preferable. As I noted (2.5), this is the usual reason for accepting antirealism. The antirealist might then try to establish his view further by arguing that his position not only is preferable on metaphysical and epistemological grounds but also contains no practical liabilities. Thus, the moral antirealist might claim, there are no practical costs to accepting the antirealist's metaethics. (See Sturgeon 1986a: 115.)

But there seem to be two problems with this way of understanding the antirealist's claim about the impotence of metaethics. First, as we shall see, moral antirealism is not preferable to realism on metaphysical and epistemological grounds; standard worries about the metaphysical and epistemological commitments of moral realism can be answered. So the fact, if it is a fact, that there are no practical differences between realism and antirealism cannot be part of an overall defense of antirealism. Second, even if the alleged impotence of moral realism could be part of a defense of antirealism, this would not alter the evidence in favor of moral realism that we found in the two preceding chapters.

This suggests the second way in which the alleged impotence of metaethical views might be thought to be a feather in the antirealist's cap. The antirealist might claim that all that matters in deciding between realism and antirealism is what practical differences either would make. If it were a fact that the choice between realism and antirealism made no difference, then this fact would, on this assumption, erase the presumption in favor of moral realism that I tried to establish in Chapters 2 and 3.

We need consider only noncognitivist versions of this argument, because if there are moral facts and truths, as the cognitivist claims, the sort of intellectual considerations in favor of realism (as against constructivism) adduced earlier are clearly evidential.

This antirealist response to our defense of moral realism is objectionable on several grounds. First, even if we assume that there are no practical differences between moral realism and antirealism and we assume that only practical differences matter to the truth of a metaethical theory, this would still not constitute an argument in favor of antirealism. At most it would erase the presumption in favor of moral realism that I tried to establish; it would not actually establish any case for antirealism.

Second, it probably begs the question against a realist view of ethics to assume that only practical implications could be evidence for a metaethical view. Only if we assumed that morality was essentially a system of practices, *rather than,* say, a set of beliefs or a body of knowledge, would the practical implications of a metaethical theory be all that mattered to its truth. But this seems to characterize morality in a noncognitive way from the start. I do not deny that practical implications of metaethical views, if any, can be evidential; I deny only that this is the *only* evidence for a metaethical view. If, as I argued, reflection on moral inquiry and the practical character of morality supports moral realism, then this is evidence for the truth of moral realism. And the fact, if it is a fact, that the choice between realism and noncognitivism makes no practical difference cannot overturn the presumption in favor of moral realism.

Finally, the realist need not and should not concede the claim that her view makes no difference. The truth of moral realism does seem to matter: It matters to the way in which moralists can and should respond to actual or potential amoralists; it matters to the moral judgments we can accept; it matters to the way in which we can defend certain kinds of moral theories (e.g., utilitarianism); and it matters to the appropriateness of certain sorts of attitudes to our own moral beliefs and those of others. Nor should this be surprising if a realist form of cognitivism does underlie our moral theorizing.

Not all of the issues to which I claim moral realism matters are straightforwardly normative or first-order issues. But I do not think this admission much affects my claim that moral realism does have practical implications, in part because I do not think it is possible to draw a perfectly happy distinction between metaethics, or second-order issues, and normative ethics, or first-order issues (cf. Chapter 6), and also in part because I do not think first-order issues exhaust the significant practical issues connected with morality. At least, whether the implications of moral realism are practically significant is best determined after I draw them out.

1. THE TREATMENT OF AMORALISM

As we saw in Chapter 3, realism and many forms of antirealism imply different responses to the amoralist. Although some realists have been internalists, we saw that realists can and should be externalists. But traditional noncognitivists, we saw, must be (appraiser) internalists (about motives). Whatever the differences between emotivism and prescriptivism, both claim that it is an essential part of the meaning of moral judgments to express the appraiser's attitudes or commitments. On both forms of noncognitivism, therefore, it is

83

part of the meaning of moral judgments, and thus a conceptual truth, that the appraiser holds a pro-attitude to things judged moral and a negative attitude to things judged immoral. This builds motivation into the concept of a moral judgment or belief and so commits non-cognitivism to internalism about motives.

Because of this commitment to internalism, noncognitivists must dismiss the possibility of a genuine amoralist – one who is indifferent to moral considerations – as incoherent. The noncognitivist must insist that these putative amoralists are only using the terms with which they express moral judgments in inverted commas; sincere moral judgments reflect motivation in the appraiser.

The noncognitivist is forced to dismiss what seems to be a genuine philosophical challenge by accusing the amoralist of conceptual or semantic confusion. Indeed, the noncognitivist reply to the amoralist resembles other skeptical solutions to skeptical problems. (See 2.8; cf. Sturgeon 1986a: 121.) Phenomenalism offers a skeptical solution to epistemological skepticism about our knowledge of an external world. According to the phenomenalist, "material-object language" expresses only claims about actual or possible sensory experiences. As a result, the skeptic's problem about how sensory experience could be evidence about an external world of material objects is, according to the phenomenalist, really incoherent. Similarly, since the very meaning of moral judgments ensures motivation, the skeptical problem posed by the amoralist is, according to the noncognitivist, really misconceived.

But, again, skeptical solutions are in general not very satisfying responses to skeptical problems; they dispose of disturbing challenges too easily. The noncognitivist's victory over the amoralist also seems to be won too easily. We can imagine someone who sincerely thinks that some action, say, is wrong – and not simply that it is conventionally regarded as wrong – and yet remains unmoved. If so, the amoralist is conceivable and we should not simply dismiss amoral skepticism as incoherent. At the very least, we should accept a skeptical solution to this skeptical problem only when all straight solutions have failed.

The moral realist can attempt a straight solution to amoral skepticism. The realist can and should be an externalist. As an externalist, the realist can recognize the amoralist as intelligible and so can take the amoralist challenge seriously. The realist can attempt to show that an amoralist is irrational not to care about moral considerations.

A defense of the rationality of morality will depend on a conception of the nature of moral demands, a substantive theory of rationality (such as a counterfactual desire-satisfaction theory, an objective version of rational egoism, or an agent neutral theory of rationality), and facts about agents and the world. Although different theories about these issues will support defenses of different strengths, all such theories promise to vindicate the commonsense view that moral considerations are important practical considerations.

So there is a difference between moral realism and standard forms of antirealism in how they may reply to the amoralist and amoralist skepticism. And, given the persistence in philosophical and popular thought of the worry about the justifiability of moral demands, this seems to be a difference that works to the credit of moral realism. It is a virtue of moral realism that it allows us to take amoralist skepticism seriously and attempt to answer it, and it is a vice of noncognitivism and other internalist theories that they are committed to a facile treatment of amoralist skepticism.

Moreover, as Nicholas Sturgeon points out, the case of the amoralist illustrates another difference between realism and noncognitivism: the realist and noncognitivist must count disputes differently (Sturgeon 1986a: 120–4). It is part of noncognitivist semantics to identify moral agreement with agreement in attitude and moral disagreement with disagreement in attitude (Stevenson 1937, 1948a, 1948b; Hare 1952: chaps. 6, 7). Now, these claims give rise to a general problem of representing the disagreement among interlocutors with different moral views. It was precisely the problem of explaining how people with different moral views might nonetheless use moral language univocally that led to the formulation of noncognitivist semantic views that make "emotive or prescriptive meaning primary" (cf. Hare 1952: chap. 7). But if emotive or prescriptive meaning is primary, then there is a question about how individuals who take the same attitude to an action they judge to be good could nonetheless be disagreeing morally, as are interlocutors who hold different views about what features of that action make it good. One natural response is not available to the noncognitivist. A realist might claim that the interlocutors use moral terms (e.g., 'good') with the same meaning or reference but hold different beliefs about the proper extension of these terms. But the noncognitivist cannot make quite these claims, because she thinks that moral terms are nonreferring, or at least primarily nonreferring. The noncognitivist does appeal to a "secondary, descriptive meaning" of moral language that reflects particular users' criteria for applying these terms and thus reflects their differing moral views. She can then try to represent the disagreement between the two moralists by saying that they associate different descriptive meanings with their moral terms; they avoid simply talking past each other (i.e., using terms in completely different senses) by associating the same emotive or prescriptive meanings with their use of 'good'. But it is not clear that we can represent the disagreement between two such interlocutors while maintaining the primacy of emotive or prescriptive meaning. Moreover, even if these claims allow the noncognitivist to represent the disagreement among moralists with different moral views, they are of no help in representing the disagreement between the moralist and the amoralist. It would seem to follow from the noncognitivist semantic claims that the amoralist and the moralist must be in *moral disagreement,* because they hold different attitudes toward the same actions, for example. But although there may be an important dispute between the moralist and the amoralist (i.e., the amoralist thinks moral concern irrational while the moralist does not), their dispute is not a moral one. For the genuine amoralist is precisely someone who shares the moralist's moral views yet remains unmoved. And this explains in part why the noncognitivist gets no help by appeal to descriptive meaning. For even if the moralist and amoralist associated different descriptive meanings with their use of moral language, this would at most help to show that they have a moral disagreement, and this, as was just noted, is precisely not the nature of their disagreement. Moreover, there is absolutely no need for the moralist and amoralist to hold different criteria for their shared moral judgments. Not only does the amoralist share in the moralist's assessment of various actions; she may also share the moralist's moral views about what makes good or right actions good or right. What distinguishes the moralist and amoralist is that the latter is indifferent to what the former is not.

Of course, we won't worry about how to represent the disagreement between the moralist and the amoralist unless we have already accepted the antinoncognitivist claim that there are or can be amoralists. But I have already argued that we should accept this claim. It is a further difference between the noncognitivist and the realist, which also redounds to the credit of the realist, that the realist can represent this disagreement properly, as the noncognitivist cannot.

2. REVISIONARY SEMANTICS AND NORMATIVE REVISION

In Chapter 2 I argued that the form and content of our moral judgments are typically cognitivist. In moral discourse we use sentences that are declarative in form and that appear to ascribe moral properties to persons, actions, and so on. Moreover, many of our moral judgments refer to moral facts and properties and the possibility of moral knowledge. There will be a normative or practical difference between cognitivist and noncognitivist semantics here if, and only if, the noncognitivist cannot adequately reconstruct the apparently cognitivist form and content of moral judgments. And, as I indicated in 2.6, it is doubtful that the noncognitivist can do this. Not only must the noncognitivist regard the factual form of our moral judgments as misleading; she must provide an account of the true structure of these judgments (e.g., moral judgments are disguised imperatives, expressions of the appraiser's approval or disapproval, or recommendations to the appraiser's audience) that is faithful to the contexts in which moral judgments are made. Moreover, she must attempt to provide noncognitivist reconstructions of those moral judgments that themselves make reference to moral facts, properties, and knowledge whose content is equivalent to the cognitivist originals. And the noncognitivist, I argued, seems unable to perform either task; the noncognitivist account of the true structure of moral discourse seems unable to account for moral discourse in "nondynamic contexts," and the reconstructions that the noncognitivist can offer of those moral judgments with cognitivist content are not equivalent in content to the originals. If so, then noncognitivists cannot make (all of) the moral judgments contained in commonsense moral thinking and available to the moral realist. This surely would be a practical difference between realism and noncognitivism, and unless there is some reason for regarding our common moral judgments as mistaken in ways this sort of noncognitivist revision corrects, this practical difference works to the credit of realism.

3. COULD THERE BE AN ESOTERIC MORALITY?

It is a common belief about nonmoral matters that we can distinguish between the truth of a claim and the desirability or value of accepting or publicizing that claim. Although we typically assume that acceptance and publicity of true claims is a good thing, this is not always so, and more important, the acceptance or publicity value of a claim is distinct from its truth. This commonsense distinction is relatively straightforward for the metaphysical realist. Some claims are true, and their truth is independent of their acceptance or publicity value. It is harder for antirealists to draw this distinction. Nihilists cannot draw it, because they recognize no claims as true. And constructivists, who identify the truth of a claim with its acceptance value, cannot draw it.

The application of this distinction to ethics can be important. Can't we, in a similar way, distinguish between the truth of a moral theory and the desirability or value of accepting or publicizing that theory? Isn't it at least conceivable that there should be circumstances in which the general acceptance or publicity of a true moral theory would be undesirable or disvaluable? Couldn't there be circumstances in which an "esoteric morality" would be a good thing (cf. Sidgwick 1907: 489–90)?

The idea of an esoteric morality might strike us as strange. Why would we ever want to suppress a true moral theory? Doesn't belief in a moral theory commit us to using that theory in moral deliberation, moral argument, and moral education? But the idea of an esoteric morality is not so strange; indeed, a very traditional way of articulating and defending teleological or consequentialist moral theories assumes that an esoteric morality is possible (i.e., that there are possible circumstances in which a correct moral theory can and should be esoteric). Consider utilitarian moral theories. As we shall see in Chapter 8, it is a traditional utilitarian claim, to be found in both Mill and Sidgwick, that agents are likely to satisfy best the utilitarian standard of right conduct (do that action which maximizes human or sentient welfare) not by using the principle of utility as a principle of deliberation or by acting solely on disinterestedly benevolent motives but by using a number of rules of conduct that make no reference to the principle of utility and by acting from a diverse set of motives (say, the moral rules and motives of what is sometimes called "commonsense morality"). If utilitarianism is true, we might conclude, people should not always reason by appeal to the principle of utility. This does not yet make utilitarianism an esoteric morality. The utilitarian can reject the idea that the principle of utility should always figure in moral deliberation without embracing the claim that it never should or that no one should accept or communicate the truth of utilitarianism. To what extent agents should adopt "utilitarian" reasoning and motivation is an open and partly empirical question. The utilitarian must, however, recognize the *possibility* of an esoteric morality. That is, the utilitarian must admit there are possible circumstances in which satisfaction of the utilitarian standard would require complete or near complete suppression of the utilitarian doctrine. If there were circumstances in which human welfare could be maximized if, and only if, it was generally believed, say, that Kantianism is true, then utilitarianism would in these circumstances be an esoteric morality.

As we shall see, some people take this to be a reductio of utilitarianism (e.g., B. Williams 1972: 107). In Chapter 8, I shall argue that this is not an implausible implication of utilitarianism. But I am not here concerned with the merits of utilitarianism. Instead, I want to point out a connection between metaethics and moral theory. The realist can easily accept this implication of utilitarianism, but it is not clear that the antirealist can (cf. Parfit 1984: 43; Sturgeon 1986a: 129–34). The realist can easily explain how utilitarianism could require its own suppression: the truth of a moral theory is distinct from its acceptance or publicity value. According to the realist, someone can think a moral theory is true and yet not want to act on that theory, perhaps even want to forget the theory, and not want others to act on or believe in that theory. But many antirealists cannot admit these claims. If, as the noncognitivist claims, there are no moral truths, or if, as certain constructivists claim, the truth of a moral claim is to be identified with its publicity or acceptance value, then we cannot explain the possibility of utilitarianism's being an esoteric morality by distinguishing between the truth and acceptance value of utilitarianism. Perhaps there is some way to explain the possibility of an esoteric morality without distinguishing between a moral theory's truth and acceptance value. If so, then some antirealists may be able to accommodate this feature of utilitarianism. But there is a problem for the traditional noncognitivist in recognizing the possibility of an esoteric morality at all and not in any particular explanation of this possibility. For, according to the noncognitivist, to accept a moral judgment *is* to be motivated to act on that judgment and to desire that others act on that judgment as well. If so, the noncognitivist cannot accept utilitarianism, since there are possible circumstances in which utilitarianism would require its own suppression (cf. Medlin 1957).

If this is right, then the realist – but not the noncognitivist – can be a utilitarian. At least the realist has an easy time accommodating this feature of utilitarianism, while the noncognitivist does not. But now notice two things. First, this fact seems to establish a practical, in particular, a normative difference between moral realism and non-cognitivism. Second, if we assume that whatever the ultimate merits of utilitarianism, it should not be ruled out from the start on conceptual grounds, then the fact that there is this practical difference between realism and noncognitivism (that the realist can be a utilitarian, but the noncognitivist cannot) is evidence for moral realism.

4. EMBARRASSING DIFFERENCES?

In discussing the practical implications of moral realism, it is perhaps worthwhile to examine another class of possible differences between moral realism and antirealism. For although some people see no practical differences between realism and antirealism, it is a popular belief that there are indeed practical differences between the realist and the antirealist – differences that should embarrass the realist and support the antirealist. It is sometimes thought or claimed that the moral realist must be, but that the antirealist need not be, a moral "absolutist;" that the moral realist, unlike the antirealist, will or should be dogmatic in the way he holds his own beliefs and intolerant of those who hold contrary beliefs; and that the moral realist, unlike the antirealist, is committed, implausibly, to the existence of moral experts. Although these claims are less popular with professional philosophers (at least, they are seldom defended in print) than they are with philosophy students, they are worth examining because they raise issues about which realists and noncognitivists can and will say different things. Here, too, I shall often focus discussion on noncognitivist versions of antirealism, either because the arguments purport to support specifically noncog-nitivist forms of antirealism or because similar arguments apply mutatis mutandis to other forms of antirealism.

5. MORAL REALISM AND ABSOLUTISM

Moral relativists often say that what is right or wrong depends on, and can vary with, the circumstances. This claim is often contrasted with "moral absolutism," which presumably claims that moral requirements are not relative to, and do not vary with, the circumstances. This may seem a natural way to distinguish moral realism and moral relativism, especially if we see the dispute between these positions as a dispute over the existence of a single true morality (cf. 3.7). But if the moral absolutist thinks that moral requirements do not vary with circumstances, then she must think that there is some set of coarse-grained moral rules, such as 'don't lie' and 'don't cause suffering', that apply to everyone in all circumstances. And this, at least on reflection, is likely to seem harsh and insensitive to certain people in certain circumstances; surely what is right for you in your circumstances is not necessarily going to be right for someone else situated differently. Here we seem to have a moral difference between the realist and the relativist in which the realist's moral commitments seem rather unattractive.

But the realist is not committed to being this sort of moral absolutist. No moral realist should deny that what is right or wrong can and will vary with circumstances. The realist can insist that moral facts must vary as morally relevant circumstances vary. The ethical naturalist will claim that moral facts will vary as certain natural facts change, and the ethical supernaturalist will claim that moral facts will vary as certain supernatural facts (e.g., facts about divine will) vary (cf. 2.4 and Chapters 6 and 7). The moral realist insists only or at least principally that moral facts not vary as people's moral beliefs and attitudes vary. Thus, it is only a very special class of circumstances with respect to which the realist holds the moral facts fixed. So, too, the relativist is saying that the moral facts vary not with just any circumstances but in relation to people's moral beliefs and attitudes.

This means that the moral realist's facts and moral rules can be as complicated as you like. There is no commitment to this sort of moral absolutism. Moreover, denial of this sort of absolutism is compatible with the existence of a single true morality. If the moral realist were omniscient and had sufficient time, he could presumably list all the obligations people would have in different sorts of circumstances and could then formulate extremely complicated moral rules specifying all of these obligations. Then one set of moral rules would apply to everyone, although, of course, they would tell people in different circumstances to do quite different things. This set of rules would state (at least a large part of) the one

91

single true morality. We can even say that these realist claims amount to a form of moral absolutism; but this form of absolutism is no embarrassment to the moral realist.

6. TOLERANCE AND FALLIBILISM

It is sometimes thought that moral realism would underwrite a kind of dogmatism about one's own moral beliefs and intolerance toward those who hold different moral beliefs. I suppose the reasoning is something like this: If I am a moral realist, I must think that moral beliefs are objectively true or false. If so, I must think that no more than one party to any genuine moral dispute can be right and that at least one party is mistaken. But in my disagreements with others, I must think that my moral belief is objectively true (otherwise I would not hold it) and, consequently, that my interlocutors are mistaken. If I think my interlocutors' moral beliefs are wrong, I must try to change their beliefs or prevent them from acting on them. But surely it is dogmatism to think that only my own moral beliefs can be right and intolerance to try to change people's moral beliefs or interfere with their actions. Moreover, these commitments are objectionable; dogmatism and intolerance are wrong.

A proponent of this argument might find the implications of noncognitivism or moral relativism more reassuring. If I am a noncognitivist, I think that moral judgments express attitudes or decisions of principle. Because attitudes and decisions of principle can vary and are not criticizable (although they may be based on nonmoral reasoning that is criticizable), I cannot regard different moral judgments as objectively true or false (2.7). Nor, if I am a moral relativist, can I regard moral attitudes different from mine as mistaken, provided those attitudes reflect the moral beliefs of those who hold them or, perhaps, the moral beliefs of the group of which those who hold them are members. In either view, I cannot regard people who make moral judgments that differ from mine as mistaken. Since I cannot assume that my moral judgments are any truer than other judgments, I should not be dogmatic about mine. Since different moral judgments are no less true than mine, I should be tolerant of others who make different moral judgments and should not seek to change their judgments or interfere with their conduct.

But there are a number of parallel errors in both arguments. Consider the claim about intolerance. (I shall discuss the claim about dogmatism later in this section.) First, it is simply wrong to think that the realist must be intolerant. We can distinguish two principles of tolerance. A weak principle of tolerance claims only that it is sometimes wrong to try to change others' beliefs or interfere with their conduct; the rightness or wrongness of such interference will depend on, among other things, the nature of the conduct or beliefs being interfered with and the nature of the interference. By contrast, a strong principle of tolerance claims it is always wrong to try to change others' beliefs or interfere with their conduct. A realist could accept either moral claim as true. But once we distinguish these two principles, I think it is clear that the weaker principle is more plausible, since we think there are some moral beliefs or actions that should not be tolerated (e.g., certain racist moral beliefs or actions). Now, the realist can claim that it is precisely because a weak principle of tolerance is true that it is usually wrong to be intolerant – even if one's interlocutors are mistaken. An agent's moral beliefs may be false and she may act on them and do wrong, but it does not follow that anyone else should try to change her beliefs or interfere with her actions. This is especially clear regarding interference with others' actions. The rightness or wrongness of some action x is one thing; the rightness or wrongness of another action y – which constitutes interference with x – is another thing. It is a matter of substantive moral theory whether and when we should attempt to interfere with others' conduct. The moral realist, therefore, can recognize the moral importance of tolerance and tolerate moral beliefs that she believes are mistaken (cf. B. Williams 1972: 19–26).

Moreover, neither noncognitivism nor relativism seems to have any special commitment to tolerance. If no one moral judgment is any more correct than another, how can it be that I should be tolerant? Someone with well informed and consistent attitudes might be intolerant, and neither the noncognitivist nor the relativist can complain that his attitude is mistaken (although, of course, many noncognitivists and relativists will hold different attitudes and may express their attitudes in his presence). Thus, one person's intolerance is no less justified than the tolerance of others, on these antirealist claims, and acceptance of these antirealist claims provides no reason for the intolerant person to change his attitude.

Finally, the argument seems to assume that tolerance is appropriate and intolerance is inappropriate; otherwise, the fact, if it were a fact, that realism implies intolerance and antirealism implies tolerance would be no reason to accept antirealism. But the assumption here must be that tolerance is right and intolerance wrong, period, that is, whatever one's moral beliefs or attitudes. But then it is not clear how the antirealist can avail himself of this presupposition about the moral importance of tolerance, because it is just such claims that the antirealist is supposed to deny. Of course, we can understand how particular noncognitivists or relativists, given the appropriate psychology, might make moral judgments expressing tolerant attitudes and so might make judgments condemning intolerance and those who are intolerant. But this does not explain the appropriateness of these attitudes. Nor does it explain how the antirealist could claim, as he surely wants to claim, that someone who accepted realism even though it was committed to intolerance was making a mistake (he could only say that he and such a realist fail to have the same attitudes).

So there is no special affinity between realism and intolerance or antirealism and tolerance. If anything, the appropriate sort of commitment to tolerance seems to presuppose the truth of moral realism.

What about dogmatism? Whether or not the realist is tolerant, mustn't she assume that her moral beliefs are true and that the moral beliefs of those who disagree with her are mistaken? Doesn't this make realism dogmatic?

A realist need not have an opinion on every moral issue about which she thinks there is a fact of the matter. On these issues, of course, she will not be dogmatic. On issues about which a realist does have moral beliefs, she must think that she is right and that those who disagree with her are wrong. To believe a proposition is to believe that it is true and that contradictory propositions are false. A moral realist, therefore, must regard those who disagree with her as mistaken. But this does not imply that she must hold her moral beliefs dogmatically. She can and should keep an open mind about moral issues, engage the opposition in dialogue, and reassess her evidence from time to time. For, as a realist, she can also be a *fallibilist* (cf. Sturgeon 1986a: 127–9).

If Waldo holds a moral belief p, he must think that p is true and that contradictory moral beliefs are false. Belief p is a first-order belief. But Waldo can also hold a second-order belief (that is, a belief about his first-order beliefs) that some of his moral beliefs, possibly including p, are mistaken. Fallibilism is a possible and typically rational form of epistemological modesty or caution. There are various reasons for this kind of modesty. Our justification in holding beliefs typically does not guarantee the truth of those beliefs; there are degrees of justification in holding beliefs; and we can acquire new evidence that may either further support or undermine beliefs we previously held with justification.

Indeed, it seems that a moral realist can be *more* modest than the traditional antirealist. The realist can eschew a dogmatic attitude because he can recognize that his moral judgments can be mistaken. But because the noncognitivist claims that moral judgments are neither true nor false, there is nothing for a noncognitivist to be mistaken about. Of course, the noncognitivist can be a fallibilist about those nonmoral claims on which, as a matter of psychological fact, his moral judgments depend; he can be mistaken about these nonmoral judgments. But the noncognitivist cannot be mistaken in the moral judgments he makes on their basis. Once he is clear about what the nonmoral facts are, there is no room for error. There is no such thing as distinctively moral error for the noncognitivist (cf. 2.7). But the moral realist will disagree. He thinks moral error is possible. It is possible to be in error about the moral conclusions one draws from nonmoral facts.

7. MORAL EXPERTISE

Even if moral realism does not imply dogmatism, doesn't it have the implausible implication that there are moral experts or authorities? Where there is knowledge, it is usually distributed unequally: Some people are experts, and others are mere laymen. Moral realism, we noted, does not sit well with skepticism; if there are moral facts, there had better be moral knowledge too. If there is moral knowledge, there should be moral experts. But who could possibly lay claim to expertise or special authority in moral matters?

Expertise is comparative; there can be experts only if there are others who know comparatively less. There can fail to be moral experts if we are all equally ignorant or equally knowledgeable about morality. On the assumption that moral realism is true, universal moral ignorance, though possible, is implausible. We could simply have no cognitive access to moral facts. But if there was good reason for thinking that no one has or could have moral knowledge, this would be reason for rejecting moral realism. So the moral realist cannot deny moral expertise in this way.

Alternatively, there might fail to be moral experts, because everyone is roughly equally knowledgeable about the moral facts. This possibility deserves to be taken more seriously, and I think there is at least a grain of truth in it. But the truth in it is quite compatible with moral realism.

One reason for the existence of experts in the natural and social sciences is that these disciplines study issues that are, in some sense, optional and do not, or at least need not, concern everyone. As a result, only those who set themselves to study these disciplines acquire significant knowledge of these issues. There is a division of intellectual labor here that in large part produces expertise. Whereas, someone might claim, moral issues (at least on most conceptions of morality) *do* concern everyone, since they concern, at least among other things, the appropriate distribution of the benefits and burdens of personal and social interaction, and these issues concern everyone. Since everyone has to think about moral issues some of the time, there is no comparable division of intellectual labor in ethics. Everyone must, indeed, perhaps has a duty to, think about morality, and this will improve people's grasp of the subject. In this way, morality may seem more like commonsense physical theory or folk psychology than quantum physics or neuropsychology. If true, this claim would explain why we do not expect to find the kind of expertise in ethics that we find in some of the sciences. But such claims, even if true, are all perfectly compatible with moral realism and its commitment to the existence of moral knowledge.

Moreover, the fact that we all do some moral thinking does not mean we are all equally good moral thinkers. Here an analogy with folk psychology may be more apt than an analogy with commonsense physical theory. Perhaps we are all roughly equally good commonsense physicists, but there is not the same intellectual equality in folk psychology or ethics. Just as there are people who have more psychological insight and have thought more about psychological problems and so are psychologically more perceptive, so, too, there are people who have more moral insight and experience and have thought more about complex moral problems and so are morally more sensitive. In both the psychological and moral case, we often appeal to such people for advice and might reasonably regard them as experts or people with some degree of expertise.

In fact, the role for ethical *theory* in systematic thinking about moral issues makes possible the development of a significant division of labor in moral thinking and the recognition of moral expertise akin to the expertise we do find in the special sciences. The fact that moral thinking begins with common concerns does not mean that systematic reflection on those concerns will not transform common beliefs. As we shall see (5.8; cf. 3.11), systematic reflection on our moral beliefs calls for the introduction of moral principle and theory and the integration of these principles and theories with other philosophical, psychological, economic, and social claims. Not everyone, not even all those with strong moral concerns, can or will pursue such theoretical inquiries. Those who do – ethicists or moral theorists – are likely to develop moral views that go well beyond popular moral thought and that may contradict it at points. Insofar as these theories originate from common moral views and cohere with reasonable claims of other sorts, they deserve to be taken seriously as the most systematic accounts of the moral matters with which they deal, and their authors can reasonably claim to possess some degree of moral expertise. In this way, the sort of moral expertise we might expect to find among moral theorists (if only when moral theory has flourished longer) bears comparison, after all, with the situation in the special sciences.

So who are these moral experts? Expertise comes in degrees, and there will likely be greater moral expertise the longer and more fully systematic moral thought flourishes (cf. 7.4). Insofar as there has been moral expertise, moral philosophers (or at least some among them) must be *among* the moral experts; moral philosophy just is the systematic study of morality, and the history of moral philosophy contains a number of distinguished attempts to systematize our moral thought. But expertise need not be limited to those with professional philosophical training, since such training is not a necessary condition for having thought fairly systematically about morality. Academic training may sometimes actually be a liability in acquiring moral expertise, since it may remove people from many of the situations in which they acquire the relevant experience with certain kinds of ongoing moral problems. (But the fact that systematic moral thinking does not presuppose academic training in philosophy and so can be done by those who are not professional philosophers does not show that it is anything other than a philosophical activity.) Generally, we should expect intelligent, well in-

97

formed people who deal on a regular basis with complex moral problems, and who have thought about these problems in a systematic way, to be among the most reliable people on moral issues. It would be rational to listen to such people's moral advice, to rethink one's own views should they conflict with such advice, and perhaps in some circumstances to defer to moral views that command a consensus among such people – at least in ways consistent with fulfilling one's responsibilities as a competent moral agent. We have reason, I think, to recognize this kind of moral expertise.

Indeed, it seems that only the moral realist can recognize this kind of moral expertise. The noncognitivist cannot. Since the noncognitivist denies the existence of true moral propositions, she must deny the possibility of moral knowledge. If there can be no moral knowledge, there can be no moral expertise. The noncognitivist can recognize only nonmoral expertise. But we think that some people can be very knowledgeable about the nonmoral facts and yet not know how to draw the right sort of moral conclusions.

8. CONCLUSION

Practical implications are not the only evidence for a metaethical view. So a defense of moral realism does not depend on the existence of such differences or the superiority of realism's practical implications. But there are some significant differences between moral realism and its rivals, and where this is true, realism's implications seem more plausible. First, realism and noncognitivism have different implications for the treatment of amoral skepticism. The noncognitivist must dismiss this skeptical challenge as incoherent, while realism can take this challenge seriously. Second, realism can respect the cognitive form and content of ordinary moral judgments; the noncognitivist must try to reconstruct these in a way that does not change ordinary moral views. Third, the realist can readily accommodate certain commitments of utilitarianism, while the noncognitivist cannot. Finally, realism does not have embarrassing practical commitments, as some think. Realism has no commitment to any objectionable form of absolutism. And its implications for possible and proper attitudes to one's own moral judgments and those of others are more plausible than those of the antirealist. Whether these differences between realism and its rivals can all be regarded as normative differences is perhaps doubtful, but they are all practical differences in that they matter to the way we think about morality and its role in our reasoning and behavior. Moral realism, therefore, does seem to matter in ways that contribute to the presumption in its favor.

5

A coherentist moral epistemology

The kind of moral realism that I have been defending asserts the existence of moral facts and true moral claims. But how could we come to know these facts, and how could we justify moral claims? Many of those who are skeptical of moral realism are skeptical on epistemological grounds. They doubt whether we can have knowledge of objective moral facts, and, in particular, they doubt whether we can justify our moral beliefs. This is another point at which metaethics and general metaphysical and epistemological concerns intertwine.

There are influential general arguments that claim to demonstrate that foundationalism rather than coherentism must be the correct account of justification and that realism requires that foundationalism be true. Traditional defenders of moral realism, such as Clarke (1728), Price (1787), Reid (1788), Sidgwick (1879, 1907), Moore (1903), Broad (1930), Ross (1930), and Prichard (1949), seem to accept these arguments; they combine moral realism with a version of foundationalism to form a metaethical position known as "intuitionism." (As we saw in Chapter 1, many intuitionists are also nonnaturalists, but this metaphysical claim is not part of intuitionism as I shall understand it here.) But contemporary writers, many of whom accept foundationalism and metaphysical realism, reject the epistemological claims of intuitionism as mysterious or implausible.[1] They conclude that moral realism is false and embrace some form of antirealism. I believe these writers have mislocated objections to intuitionism; intuitionism is no less plausible than foundationalism is generally. Nonetheless, there are serious objections to any form of foundationalism; there can be no genuine foundational beliefs (i.e., beliefs that are noninferentially justified). This conclusion would be disastrous both generally and for moral realism if we had to accept the argument for the necessity of foundationalism and

1 Cf. Nowell-Smith 1957: 39–42; Baier 1958: 22–3, 240; Brandt 1959: 189–201; Hudson 1967: 51–3; Warnock 1967: 15; Mackie 1977: 38–9, 41; 1980: 146; Smart 1984: 4, 23, 38, 49.

the argument connecting realism and foundationalism. Neither argument is compelling, however. Coherentism can be defended and is compatible with realism. Moreover, coherentism can be applied to the justification of our moral beliefs; it provides us with an account of justification in ethics that is compatible with our commitment to moral realism.

1. FOUNDATIONALISM AND COHERENTISM

Theories of justification offer accounts of when cognizers are warranted in believing claims or propositions to be true. Foundationalism and coherentism represent the historically most influential alternative theories of justification. Here is a brief, largely structural, account of these two theories.

Foundationalism holds that one's belief p is justified just in case p is either (a) foundational (i.e., noninferentially justified or self-justifying) or (b) based on the appropriate kind of inference from foundational beliefs.[2] Versions of foundationalism vary according to their views about the nature and content of foundational beliefs and about the appropriate kind of inferences linking foundational and nonfoundationally justified beliefs. First, some take a conservative view of the appropriate kind of inference, restricting it to deductive inference, while others take a more liberal view, countenancing various kinds of nondeductive inferences. Indeed, some inferential liberals claim that some, if not all, nonfoundational beliefs are to be justified on the basis of their coherence with foundational beliefs (e.g., Russell 1912: 22–6). It is important to notice, however, that despite its appeal to coherence, this liberal version of foundationalism is still quite distinct from coherentism. For even liberal foundationalism claims that certain beliefs – indeed, by far the most important class of beliefs, namely, foundational beliefs – are self-justifying. But as we shall see, coherentism denies that any beliefs are self-justifying. Second, some read the contents of foundational beliefs phenomenally (e.g., as beliefs reporting sense data), while others read them realistically (e.g., as beliefs about external objects and their properties). Finally, some construe foundational beliefs subjectively as beliefs that make strong doxastic claims on cognizers

2 Cf. Aristotle *APo* bk. A, chaps. 2–3; Descartes 1642; Russell 1912; Schlick 1934; Ayer 1940; Lewis 1946; Chisholm 1977, 1982; Quinton 1973: pt. 3.

101

(in the limit, on this view, foundational beliefs are indubitable or incorrigible), while others construe the nature of foundational beliefs objectively as beliefs that have a high probability of being true (in the limit, on this view, foundational beliefs are infallible). Moral foundationalism represents the application of foundationalism to the justification of moral beliefs. It holds that one's moral belief p is justified just in case p is either (a) foundational or (b) based on the appropriate kind of inference from foundational beliefs. Almost all defenders of moral foundationalism have been intuitionists.[3] Intuitionism is that version of moral foundationalism which holds that one's moral belief p is justified just in case p is either (a) foundational or (b) based on the appropriate kind of inference from foundational *moral* beliefs. The intuitionist requires of every justified moral belief that it be foundational or that the termini of its justification include foundational moral beliefs. A moral belief about a particular action or situation can be justified in part by reference to another, often more general, moral belief. But, the intuitionist claims, at some point this process of justification must come to a stop with moral beliefs whose justification does not rest on other beliefs; these moral beliefs are foundational. Moreover, intuitionism is nonskeptical; it claims that there are foundational moral beliefs and that we have knowledge of evidence-independent moral facts.[4] Because in-

3 The defender of moral foundationalism does not commit himself, as the intuitionist does, to the existence or even the need of any foundational moral beliefs. It might be that every justified moral belief was nonfoundational and that its justification terminated in foundational nonmoral beliefs. Locke (1700: I, iii, 1–4, and IV, iii, 18) and Chisholm (1977: 123–6) seem to hold such a view; Lewis (1946) may hold such a view.

Historically, intuitionism has been motivated by acceptance of foundationalism and the existence of an is/ought gap (see, e.g., Frankena 1939: 52). I postpone assessment of this motivation until Appendix 3, but roughly the line of argument is as follows: Because of the existence of an is/ought gap, the inferential justification of a moral belief must always involve another moral belief (the latter belief must be a more general moral belief under which the former may be subsumed). By foundationalism, however, all justification must terminate in foundational beliefs. Therefore, the justification of any moral belief must terminate in a foundational moral belief.

4 Cf. Clarke 1728; Price 1787; Reid 1788; Sidgwick 1879, 1907: xvi, 36, 97–8, 200–1, 304, 338–42, 382, 391, 497, 505; Moore 1903: vii–x; Prichard 1949: 8, 16; Ross 1930: 21n, 23, 29–30, 146. Intuitionism in ethics should, of course, be contrasted with intuitionism in mathematics. The former combines a foundationalist epistemology with a realist metaethics; the latter is an antirealist, constructivist view about mathematics. Cf. Dummett 1977: v, ix, 4, 6–7, 372–5, 382–3; Benacerraf and Putnam 1983: 18, 23–7, 30–1.

tuitionism has been by far the most influential version of moral foundationalism, my discussion of moral foundationalism focuses on it.

Coherentism, by contrast, holds that no beliefs are noninferentially justified. One's belief p is justified, according to coherentism, insofar as p is part of a coherent system of beliefs and p's coherence at least partially explains why one holds p.[5] The degree of one's justification in holding p varies directly with the degree of coherence exhibited by the belief set of which p is a member. Moreover, coherence is not simply a matter of logical consistency (cf. Joachim 1906: 76; Bradley 1914: 202–3). The degree of a belief system's coherence is a function of the comprehensiveness of the system and of the logical, probabilistic, and explanatory relations obtaining among members of the belief system. In particular, explanatory relations are an especially important aspect of coherence. But I will not attempt to characterize further the property of coherence, much less offer a decision procedure for identifying coherent beliefs. Nor should this come as a surprise, since there is no reason to expect there to be an abstract or mechanical decision procedure for determining the comprehensiveness and explanatory power of our beliefs. The relative coherence of competing beliefs is often difficult to determine, especially where the issue involved is interesting. But we are all familiar (I assume) with the greater explanatory coherence that some bodies of belief exhibit when compared with others and that we seek to achieve in our own beliefs.[6]

Moral coherentism or a coherence theory of justification in ethics represents the application of coherentism to the justification of moral beliefs. It holds that one's moral belief p is justified insofar as p is part of a coherent system of beliefs, both moral and nonmoral, and p's coherence at least partially explains why one holds p.[7] A

5 Cf. Plato *Republic* 511b, 53e–533e; Joachim 1906; Bradley 1914: 202–18; Duhem 1914: 183–8; Neurath 1932; Blanshard 1939: 212–59, 263–6; Quine 1951, 1960: chap. 1, 1969b, 1975; Sellars 1956; Harman 1965, 1973: 155–72; Lehrer 1974: 154–214; Bonjour 1976, 1986; M. Williams 1977, 1980.

6 One illustration of these claims about coherence is the work of good detectives in good detective stories. The conclusions of good detectives represent not "deductions," as Sherlock Holmes would have us believe, but inferences to the most coherent explanatory account. Kitcher 1982: 46–50 contains a useful account of some of the marks of explanatory coherence.

7 Cf. Aristotle *EN* 1098b9–12, 1145b2–7 (my reading of Aristotle follows Irwin 1981; contrast Hardie 1980: 37–45); I. Scheffler 1954; Rawls 1951: 56, 61, 1971: 19–21, 46–51, 589–81, 1980: 534; Sartorius 1975: 31–3; Daniels 1979a, 1980; White 1981.

103

coherence theory of justification in ethics is essentially John Rawls's method of wide reflective equilibrium. In explaining the justification of his theory of justice, Rawls writes:

> Here the test is that of general and wide reflective equilibrium, that is, how well the view as a whole meshes with and articulates our more firm considered convictions, at all levels of generality, after due examination, once all adjustments and revisions that seem compelling have been made. A doctrine that meets this criterion is the doctrine that, so far as we can now ascertain, is the most reasonable for us. (1980: 534)

We all have or entertain moral beliefs of various levels of generality, concerning particular actions and policies and action types as well as quite abstract moral principles. Many of these moral beliefs depend on other moral beliefs. For instance, beliefs about the value of a particular activity depend, among other things, on ideals of the person (i.e., moral beliefs about what kind of persons we ought to be). Moral beliefs also depend upon nonmoral beliefs. For instance, beliefs about the moral or political legitimacy of a welfare state depend on nonmoral beliefs about such things as human nature, social theory, and economics. A coherence theory of justification in ethics demands that these and other beliefs be made into a maximally coherent system of beliefs.

These are very abstract claims about epistemological *structure*. I shall describe intuitionist and coherentist moral epistemologies in somewhat more detail later in this chapter; I shall be concerned first with the structural features of foundationalism and coherentism.

2. ARGUMENTS FOR FOUNDATIONALISM

Two general epistemological arguments seem to provide strong support for foundationalism and, hence, an intuitionist moral epistemology. The first argument is sometimes referred to as the *regress argument,* and we might represent the second argument as an *antiskeptical argument.* Because these arguments are perfectly general, I present and examine them in their general form, discussing their application to ethics where this deserves separate treatment.

The first argument is based on the plausible epistemological requirement that justifying beliefs themselves be justified.[8] I might

---

8 Cf. Aristotle *APo* 72a36–73a20; Russell 1912: 111–12, 132–3; Lewis 1946: 186–7; Armstrong 1968: 188, 1973: 150–61; Quinton 1973: 119–23; Chisholm 1977: 19.

base my belief p on other beliefs q and r. But unless I am justified in holding q and r, it seems that these beliefs cannot justify me in holding p. This requirement implies that for any case of inferentially justified belief, if belief q is to justify belief p, then q must itself be justified.[9] Of course, any belief that one might adduce to justify q must itself be justified. And so on.

There appear to be three ways of incorporating this epistemological requirement: We can claim (1) all justification is both linear and inferential; (2) although all justification is inferential, it is not all linear; or (3) although all justification is linear, it is not all inferential. The regress argument claims that (1) and (2) are unacceptable alternatives and that (3) alone adequately incorporates the epistemological requirement that justifying beliefs themselves be justified.

The regress argument claims that (1) involves a vicious regress. If all justification is linear and inferential, then the requirement that justifying beliefs be justified implies that for one to be justified in holding any belief, one must be justified in holding an infinite number of inferentially linked beliefs. But since we do not, and cannot, possess an infinite number of beliefs, we are not, and cannot be, justified in holding any beliefs. The infinite regress that (1) implies is vicious, the regress argument claims, because it leads to skepticism.

Coherentism represents the most important version of (2). It claims that all justification is inferential but denies that justification is linear. Although all justification is inferential, coherentism avoids a regress because it allows justificatory chains to loop back upon themselves. One's belief p is justified by one's belief q, which is justified by one's belief r, which is justified ultimately, at least in part, by one's belief p. The regress argument claims that coherentism succeeds only in trading the vicious regress in (1) for vicious circularity. Circular reasoning allows one to prove anything; it is never an acceptable form of justification. We do not count a belief p as justified if it rests on belief q, which, in turn, rests on p. Why should larger belief circles confer any more justification?

Claim (3) represents foundationalism, which promises to avoid both the regress in (1) and the circularity in (2). Foundationalism maintains that all justification is linear, thus avoiding circularity,

9 As we shall see (Appendix 1), this formulation of the epistemological requirement may be too strong. This possibility does not affect my claims, and the present formulation better represents the premise of the regress argument.

105

but denies that all justification is inferential, thus avoiding the regress. Few of our beliefs need be foundational; many of our beliefs will be justified inferentially, indeed, by quite long inferential chains. But foundationalism insists that all justifications terminate in beliefs that are self-justifying or noninferentially justified. It is these foundational beliefs that stop the regress while providing evidential support for our justified beliefs.

It is perhaps a little misleading to call this argument the regress argument. The name would be justified if (1) was the only alternative to (3). But, of course, (2) is also a possibility. We do no harm by calling it the regress argument, as long as we see that the argument must defend (3) as the proper reaction to both the threat of a regress and of the threat of circularity.

The second argument for foundationalism has two premises. The first premise is realism: Truth is belief- or evidence-independent. Typically, a realist metaphysics is simply taken for granted; it could be defended on the strength of considerations of the sort adduced in 2.8. The second premise represents a certain assumption about justification. Justification for believing p is justification for believing p to be true. If so, and if an account of justification is to provide an answer to epistemological skepticism, then justification must ensure or guarantee truth. Call this principle *objectivism about justification*. Now realism and objectivism about justification provide an antiskeptical argument for foundationalism. For only an account of justification that includes noninferential justification can possibly guarantee that our justified beliefs accurately describe a world whose existence and nature are independent of our beliefs about it. Foundationalism promises to base the justification of our beliefs on direct, noninferential access to the world and so promises to satisfy objectivism about justification compatibly with realism. Similarly, intuitionism promises to base the justification of our moral beliefs on direct, noninferential access to objective moral facts. Coherentism, by contrast, makes justification purely a matter of relations among beliefs and so cannot satisfy objectivism about justification compatibly with realism. This point is sometimes put metaphorically by claiming that coherentism provides no guarantee of "contact with reality," no assurance that a coherent system of beliefs will not be free-floating with no moorings attaching it to the world. Coherentism could guarantee truth, and so satisfy objectivism about justification, only if some version of constructivism, in particular, a coherence theory of truth were true. Similarly, a coherence theory of justification in ethics could satisfy objectivism about justification only if a coherence theory of moral truth were true. (Similar remarks would presumably apply mutatis mutandis to any purely inferential account of justification, including the regress of justification [(1)].) Objectivism about justification seems to imply the dependence of realism on foundationalism and, hence, of moral realism on intuitionism.

3. INTUITIONISM

It is not clear to what extent intuitionists have relied on the antiskeptical argument for foundationalism, but they have often relied on a particular form of the regress argument. Let's begin by distinguishing three different levels of generality or abstraction among moral claims: particular moral judgments (i.e., moral claims that concern specific actions or action tokens), moral rules (i.e., moral claims that concern classes of action or action types), and moral principles or first principles (i.e., moral claims that apply to many or all action types and purport to systematize and explain particular moral judgments and moral rules). Of course, we can also distinguish moral beliefs at these three levels of generality. Now we can imagine an intuitionist claiming that belief in moral rules or particular moral judgments is or can be foundational.[10] Indeed, many particular moral judgments and moral rules (e.g., that genocide is wrong) express moral beliefs that seem more fixed and less revisable than almost any other beliefs, moral or nonmoral, that we hold. But justification in ethics seems to have a definite *structure,* and this structure seems to support a form of intuitionism that restricts foundational status to moral beliefs at the more general levels.

We can and do justify particular moral judgments inferentially; we

10 Sidgwick (1907: 97–102) distinguishes three kinds of intuitionism: perceptual, dogmatic, and philosophical. Perceptual intuitionism allows foundational moral beliefs about action tokens as well as action types and first principles. Dogmatic intuitionism denies the existence of foundational moral beliefs about action tokens but allows them about action types as well as first principles. Philosophical intuitionism allows foundational moral beliefs about, and only about, ethical first principles. Perceptual intuitionism implies that little if any of our moral knowledge is nonfoundational. Prichard may be the only perceptual intuitionist. Reid, Sidgwick, Moore, and Ross all deny perceptual intuitionism. Sidgwick, of course, defends philosophical intuitionism (1907: 98–104, 200–1, 337–407).

107

justify a particular moral judgment (e.g., that it would be wrong to punish Spot after the fact for his indiscretions) by appeal to moral rules (e.g., that it is wrong to punish animals if they won't understand what they are being punished for). We might justify such moral rules by appeal to moral principles (e.g., that it is wrong to cause pointless suffering). There may be a kind of hierarchy of moral principles (e.g., we might try to justify the wrongness of pointless cruelty and other moral principles by appeal to a utilitarian moral theory). But this process of inferential justification must, on pain of infinite regress or circularity, come to a stop with general moral claims that do not depend on other moral claims for their justification. This is the view that Sidgwick calls *philosophical intuitionism*.[11]

However, intuitionism seems implausible even to many who accept foundationalism. There seem to be two principal objections to intuitionism. First, it is claimed that intuitionism is committed to the implausible claim that cognizers possess a special faculty for the perception of moral facts and properties.[12] Second, it is claimed that intuitionism must be embarrassed by the existence of conflicting moral beliefs.[13]

In order to assess objections to foundationalism or intuitionism, we must distinguish different versions of foundationalism and intuitionism. If foundational beliefs are to be self-justifying, they must have some special features that give them this character. Different versions of foundationalism result from different specifications of the nature of foundational beliefs. Although defenders of foundationalism have not always been careful to separate alternative versions of foundationalism, *subjective* and *objective* conceptions of

11 See the preceding note. Sidgwick also claims that first principles are self-justifying if they meet four tests: They must be (1) clear and precise, (2) evident upon reflection, (3) mutually consistent, and (4) generally accepted (1907: 338–42).
12 See Baier 1958: 22–3, 240; Brandt 1959: 189; Mackie 1977: 38–9, 41; 1980: 146; Smart 1984: 4, 23.
13 Nowell-Smith 1957: 39–42; Brandt 1959: 192–6; Hudson 1967: 52–3; Warnock 1967: 15; Smart 1984: 38, 49. As we saw in Chapter 1, many intuitionists are also nonnaturalists; they claim that moral facts and properties must be sui generis - that is, ontologically independent of other kinds of facts and properties. A third objection to intuitionism is that it is committed to the metaphysically queer doctrine of nonnaturalism. I consider this objection in Chapters 6 and 7, and argue that either (1) the standard arguments for nonnaturalism fail, in which case intuitionists are not committed to nonnaturalism, or (2) the standard arguments for nonnaturalism succeed, in which case nonnaturalism is not queer and therefore is no weakness in intuitionism.

foundationalism, as well as *strong* and *weak* versions of each, can be distinguished. On a subjective conception, foundational beliefs are beliefs that make a strong doxastic claim on cognizers. The doxastic claim that beliefs exert must be construed as something like the psychological force with which cognizers hold those beliefs. A strong subjective conception makes foundational beliefs indubitable or incorrigible,[14] while a weak subjective conception makes foundational beliefs prima facie indubitable or incorrigible. Thus, the doxastic claim of strong subjective foundational beliefs is nondefeasible, while that of weak subjective foundational beliefs is strong but defeasible. By contrast, objective conceptions of foundationalism connect the justification of foundational beliefs with their truth implication. A strong objective conception makes foundational beliefs infallible, while a weak objective conception makes foundational beliefs probable or (as a class) reliably true. Of course, intuitionism, as well as foundationalism, admits of these different conceptions.

We can now examine these standard objections to intuitionism; I shall argue that neither objection is compelling, as it stands.

On the face of it, it is difficult to understand the motivation for the belief that intuitionism is committed to the existence of a special faculty of moral perception. Neither subjective nor objective versions of intuitionism make any reference to such a faculty. Indeed, it is a principal claim of one of the traditional intuitionists, Richard Price, that our "moral intuitions" (i.e., our foundational moral beliefs) are not the result of any sensory faculties analogous to perceptual faculties (1787: 131–3, 142–3, 151). The motivation for the belief that intuitionism requires special faculties of moral perception derives, I suspect, from a comparison with foundationalism about our nonmoral beliefs. Because the most plausible candidates for nonmoral foundational beliefs are perceptual beliefs, critics of intuitionism have assumed that foundational moral beliefs would have to be perceptual as well. Like other perceptual beliefs, then, foundational moral beliefs might seem to require their own perceptual faculty.

But what exactly is supposed to be objectionable about the existence of a special faculty of moral perception? Intuitionism's critics

14 Cf. Frankfurt's (1970) interpretation of Descartes (1642); Moore (1925, 1939, 1959a).

109

usually claim that we have good a posteriori evidence that there are no special faculties of moral perception. They must be assuming that a special faculty of moral perception requires something like the existence of a special sensory organ (perhaps a pink, fleshy lobe), and not just a distinctive way of seeing the world or a distinct set of conceptual categories. For surely it is only the former sort of commitment that we can brusquely dismiss on a posteriori grounds.

But is intuitionism committed to either the perceptual status of moral intuitions or their derivation from such special sensory faculties? I think that this argument misconstrues the status of perception in foundationalism about nonmoral beliefs and the relation of sensory organs to perception. What is essential to foundational beliefs, according to foundationalism, is their relative incorrigibility (subjective conceptions) or their relative reliability (objective conceptions). Now, it so happens that the most plausible candidates for foundational status in the nonmoral case are perceptual beliefs of some kind, and these perceptual beliefs, we might concede, result from the operation of particular sensory faculties. But this does not show that foundationalism is essentially committed to the foundational status of perceptual beliefs, much less that foundational moral beliefs must be perceptual. We might even concede that foundational moral beliefs were perceptual in the sense that, like nonmoral perceptual beliefs, they concern the properties of particular people and particular events and do not result from any conscious inference (though this kind of intuitionism would not be philosophical intuitionism). This concession would not force us to conclude that our moral intuitions were based on the operation of some special sense organ. The intuitionist need only claim that these moral intuitions possess the appropriate kind of incorrigibility or reliability.

Why should the existence of moral disagreement embarrass the intuitionist? Perhaps it is thought that moral disagreement would threaten the principle of noncontradiction if intuitionism were true. If foundational moral beliefs guarantee truth, then conflicting moral intuitions imply that certain moral propositions are both true and not true.

But the intuitionist can respond that the existence of conflicting moral beliefs either fails to show the existence of conflicting foundational moral beliefs or fails to threaten breach of the principle of noncontradiction. Because strong objective foundational beliefs are infallible, they do guarantee truth, and the existence of conflicting moral beliefs *of this kind* would threaten the principle of noncontradiction. But we need to distinguish between the loose or popular and technical, philosophical senses of 'intuition'; the existence of conflicting moral beliefs does not demonstrate the existence of conflicting strong objective foundational moral beliefs. Indeed, the strong objective intuitionist will appeal to the principle of noncontradiction to deny the existence of conflicting moral intuitions. People may hold conflicting moral views quite firmly, but these moral views need not be foundational. The other versions of intuitionism do not guarantee the truth of moral intuitions, and so even the existence of conflicting moral views that were genuine moral intuitions would not threaten the principle of noncontradiction.[15] Weak objective intuitionism claims only that foundational moral beliefs are as a class reliable and so does not guarantee the truth of any particular foundational moral belief. Since neither indubitability nor incorrigibility is the same as infallibility (i.e., indubitable or incorrigible beliefs could be false), neither version of subjective intuitionism implies the truth of foundational moral beliefs. Therefore, on none of these three versions of intuitionism would the existence of conflicting moral intuitions threaten the principle of noncontradiction.

The critic of intuitionism might respond that it is not the principle of noncontradiction that the existence of conflicting moral beliefs threatens. The problem for intuitionism, she might claim, is that the existence of conflicting moral intuitions would *justify* cognizers in believing contradictory propositions, and this seems a counterintuitive implication of a theory of justification.

But here the intuitionist might dig in her heels and insist, again, on the distinction between the popular and technical senses of 'intuition'. The objection requires not just the existence of conflicting moral beliefs but the existence of conflicting moral intuitions or foundational moral beliefs. Intuitionists, in particular, objective intuitionists and strong subjective intuitionists, should concede the existence of conflicting moral beliefs but deny the existence of con-

---

15 Of course, it could be argued that any version of intuitionism that does not ensure that foundational moral beliefs are true is unacceptable because it violates objectivism about justification. But although this kind of intuitionist could not avoid the objection to intuitionism based on the existence of moral disagreement consistently with acceptance of the antiskeptical argument for foundationalism, this is a poor ground for criticism, because, as I shall argue (5.7), objectivism about justification is implausible.

flicting moral intuitions. Few of our moral beliefs are indubitable and still fewer are infallible. The strong subjective intuitionist, for example, can claim that commonly held moral beliefs are always possible to doubt and that we must subject them to dialectical investigation in order to identify the moral principles that underlie them. Only after such a dialectical investigation of moral beliefs and first principles can one isolate a moral principle whose truth will be self-evident. This is Sidgwick's position.[16] On this view, coherentist reasoning about morality serves as a heuristic device *to identify, not to justify,* moral principles. Only after a principle has been dialectically identified can it appear self-evident, and about its self-evidence there can at this point be no disagreement.

There may well be problems with this form of philosophical intuitionism. First, one may doubt whether moral disagreement is impossible even after full and systematic dialectical investigation of morality. Although, even if this doubt is well founded, this may not constitute an objection to intuitionism, since there is some question whether the intuitionist need claim that *no* disagreement is *possible* after full and systematic dialectical investigation of our moral beliefs. A strong subjective intuitionist might claim that disagreement need not be impossible even at this point, as long as people all in fact agree, and the strong objective intuitionist might claim that moral disagreement at this point simply shows that some people's dialectically tested moral beliefs are still not genuine moral intuitions. Second, if these first principles are or can be self-evident, why should this dialectical investigation of common moral beliefs be *necessary* to the justification of these first principles? We might concede that to understand fully the content of a first principle it is necessary to see its implications for various cases. But this point does not explain the role of the comparison of the first principle's implications for particular cases with our own or common assessments of those cases which is part of dialectical inquiry. This fact raises the following question: Can Sidgwick defend the necessity of dialectical investigation of common moral beliefs without making it evidential? Third, we might wonder why we can't ask for a justification of first principles. Of course, a coherence theory claims that we can and that the answer lies in the way in which (correct)

16 See Sidgwick 1879: 106, and 1907: xvi, 36, 97–8, 200–1, 304, 337–61, 373–4, 382, 391, 497, 505; Schneewind 1977: 264, 268, 284, 287; Irwin 1981: 203.

112

first principles support various features of our moral beliefs. But the philosophical intuitionist denies that this question can be coherently asked about self-evident first principles. Is this denial plausible? Are there any principles whose justification we cannot ask for?

These are serious questions about the adequacy of philosophical intuitionism, questions connected with more general worries about foundationalism that I shall pursue shortly. But the intuitionist position here is not absurd, as some have claimed; the standard dismissal of intuitionism by appeal to moral disagreement should not be accepted so lightly.

Neither the worry that intuitionism is committed to the existence of a special faculty of moral perception nor the worry that intuitionism threatens the principle of noncontradiction is well conceived. The worry that intuitionism might justify competing moral beliefs, though well conceived, is not compelling, at least as it stands. If these criticisms of intuitionism were the most serious ones, then one might well try to answer the questions I have raised for Sidgwick in order to defend intuitionism as supplying an appropriate epistemology for moral realism.[17]

4. THE ANTISKEPTICAL ARGUMENT FOR FOUNDATIONALISM RECONSIDERED

However, the standard objections to intuitionism are not the most serious objections to it. Intuitionism suffers from defects inherent in any form of foundationalism. Despite their initial appeal, both of our arguments for foundationalism fail. Foundationalism does not successfully incorporate the epistemological requirement that justifying beliefs themselves be justified, and realism requires neither acceptance of foundationalism nor rejection of coherentism. Because some people have been attracted by the antiskeptical argument for foundationalism, its failure is dialectically interesting and important. Because I ultimately reject the objectivist principle of justification on which that argument relies, however, its failure has only ad hominem force. My case against foundationalism, therefore, must rest on the failure of the regress argument.

Let's consider the antiskeptical argument first. This argument

17 Also see Appendix 3 for further defense of the claim that intuitionism is no less plausible than foundationalism is elsewhere.

assumes both realism and objectivism about justification. Objectivism about justification claims that justification must guarantee truth, and this claim may seem necessary in any attempt to answer skepticism. If we cannot guarantee against the possibility of error, how can we answer the skeptic? And objectivism about justification and realism require the rejection of coherentism. For coherentism makes justification a matter of relations among beliefs and so provides no guarantee that any beliefs justified by their coherence correspond to the objective or evidence-independent facts. Coherentism could guarantee truth only if truth were constituted by coherent belief, that is, only if a coherence theory of truth were true. Foundationalism, by contrast, does not make all justification inferential and so promises to guarantee objective truth; it claims to base justification on direct, noninferential access to the world and so appears to guarantee truth. These claims can be formulated in terms of the "contact with reality" that foundationalism and coherentism afford. Purely inferential accounts of justification, like coherentism, only establish relations among a cognizer's beliefs and so do not guarantee contact with (evidence-independent) reality; whereas accounts of justification based on noninferential justification, like foundationalism, promise to provide this direct contact with reality. Thus, realism and objectivism about justification seem to require acceptance of foundationalism and rejection of coherentism.

For present purposes, I shall leave objectivism about justification unquestioned and argue only that this argument for foundationalism fails because, like coherentism, foundationalism fails to satisfy objectivism about justification compatibly with realism. No acceptable version of foundationalism can provide a guarantee of objective truth.

It is easy to see that subjective versions of foundationalism fail to satisfy objectivism about justification compatibly with realism. For the justification of subjective foundational beliefs consists in the kind of doxastic claim they make upon cognizers, and no amount of doxastic claim can ensure objective truth. Weak subjective foundationalism makes foundational beliefs only prima facie indubitable or incorrigible and so cannot guarantee their objective truth, much less the objective truth of nonfoundational beliefs justified on the basis of weak subjective foundational beliefs. The justification of strong subjective foundational beliefs consists in their indubitability or incorrigibility. But neither indubitability nor incorrigibility is the same as infallibility; beliefs that we can neither doubt nor revise might yet be false.

So neither strong subjective foundational beliefs nor beliefs based on them guarantee objective truth. Subjective foundationalism could guarantee truth only if noninferential beliefs making strong doxastic claims were constitutive of truth. But this would be to abandon realism.

It should be no great surprise that objective foundationalism satisfies objectivism about justification better than subjective foundationalism does; objective versions of foundationalism define foundational beliefs in terms of their truth implication. But even if objective foundationalism fares better here, it does not fare well enough. Weak objective foundational beliefs are only probable or (as a class) reliable, so weak objective foundationalism does not guarantee the truth of all foundational beliefs. Therefore, neither weak objective foundational beliefs nor nonfoundational beliefs based on them are guaranteed to be true. Strong objective foundationalism, on the other hand, does guarantee the truth of *foundational* beliefs, because strong objective foundational beliefs are infallible. But objectivism about justification requires more than this. Because *all* justification is justification in believing true, objectivism about justification requires that *all* justification guarantee truth. But inferentially justified beliefs can satisfy this demand only if (a) strong objective foundationalism is true, *and* (b) warranted inferences from foundational beliefs to nonfoundational beliefs are restricted to deductive inferences. For only then will all justification guarantee truth. This version of foundationalism is possible, but it threatens to introduce a kind of skepticism, namely, solipsism of the present moment. For if our justified beliefs are restricted to infallible beliefs and their deductive consequences, we are unlikely to be justified in most of our beliefs. Certainly we will be justified in none of our beliefs about the existence and nature of the external world (cf. Russell 1912: 22–6, 140; Armstrong 1973: 156–7). As long as there is inferential justification based on nondeductive forms of inference, objectivism about justification cannot be satisfied compatibly with realism.

So, foundationalism can satisfy objectivism about justification compatibly with realism no better than coherentism could. If objectivism about justification is required to avoid skepticism, then we must either accept skepticism or abandon realism. In this way, we might come to reject realism and accept some form of constructivism.[18]

5. FOUNDATIONALISM RECONSIDERED

But is foundationalism necessary? The regress argument claims that foundationalism, and foundationalism alone, successfully incorporates the epistemological requirement that justifying beliefs themselves be justified. In section 6 of this chapter and Appendix 1, I shall address the claim that foundationalism's rivals cannot successfully incorporate the epistemological requirement. Here I want to argue that foundationalism fails because there are no foundational beliefs to stop the regress while avoiding circularity; there are no beliefs that are *self*-justifying.

Recall the three strategies for incorporating the epistemological requirement that justifying beliefs themselves be justified: (1) All justification is both inferential and linear; (2) although all justification is inferential, it is not all linear; and (3) although all justification is linear, it is not all inferential. Besides claiming that (1) involves a vicious regress and (2) involves vicious circularity, the regress argument claims that (3) succeeds. Foundationalism succeeds in avoiding the regress in (1) without the circularity in (2) by making all justificatory chains terminate in beliefs which are self-justifying or noninferentially justified.

But can there be such beliefs? Justification is justification in believing true. In order to be justified in holding one's belief *p*, one must have reason to hold *p* to be true. But *p* is a first-order belief that such and such is the case and, as such, cannot contain the reason for thinking *p* is true. Indeed, self-justification can be regarded as the limiting case of circular reasoning – that is, self-justification is the smallest justificatory circle imaginable. And everyone – even the coherentist – regards such small circles of justification as nonexplanatory and, hence, as nonjustifying. Thus, it seems, foundationalism

---

18 If objectivism about justification forced us to give up realism, we might have reason to reject the regress argument. For if realism is rejected, then it is no longer clear that the ban on circular reasoning imposed by the regress argument can be maintained. Because I shall reject objectivism about justification, this point can only be urged ad hominem against defenders of objectivism about justification and the regress argument.

116

is not an alternative to (2); instead, it is the limiting and least plausible case of (2).

We can put the point another way. To be justified in holding p, one must have reason to hold p. If p is a first-order belief, this would seem to imply that one must base p on beliefs about p, in particular, on second-order beliefs about what kind of belief p is (e.g., under what conditions p was formed) and why p-type beliefs are likely to be true. But this shows that one's belief p cannot be *self*-justifying.

These claims may seem to beg the question against foundationalism by simply assuming that justification must always be inferential. But however quick and abstract these claims are, they do not just beg the question. I am making the structural observation that foundationalism's commitment to self-justifying beliefs is actually the limiting case of circular reasoning and claiming that *this* kind of circularity is vicious, since no belief about the world can also be the reason for thinking that that belief is true.

Although this argument against the existence of foundational beliefs applies to all versions of foundationalism, it may be useful to consider how it applies to the particular versions we have discussed.

Consider subjective versions of foundationalism first. Subjective foundational beliefs are beliefs that make a strong doxastic claim on cognizers. The doxastic claim that beliefs exert is to be construed as the psychological force with which cognizers hold those beliefs. Weak subjective foundational beliefs are beliefs that are prima facie indubitable or incorrigible, that is, that make a strong but defeasible doxastic claim. But one cannot be justified in holding prima facie indubitable or incorrigible beliefs to be true independently of any beliefs whatsoever about why these prima facie indubitable or incorrigible beliefs should be true. The mere fact that one holds these beliefs with a certain psychological force does not justify one in holding them to be true. This is especially clear because weak subjective foundational beliefs are neither unrevisable nor infallible. So if one is to be justified in holding one of them, one must have some reason for thinking that it is true. One must base these prima facie indubitable or incorrigible beliefs on some second-order beliefs about why these prima facie indubitable or incorrigible beliefs are likely to be true. But this shows that prima facie indubitable or incorrigible beliefs cannot be *self*-justifying.

The same considerations apply to strong subjective foundationalism. Strong subjective foundational beliefs are beliefs that are indubitable or incorrigible. But one cannot be justified in holding indubitable or incorrigible beliefs to be true independently of any beliefs whatsoever about why indubitable or incorrigible beliefs should be true. The mere fact that certain beliefs hold one with irresistible psychological force does not justify one in holding them. We have already noticed that incorrigible beliefs are not infallible; we could be incapable of doubting or revising beliefs that are nonetheless false. To be justified in holding indubitable or incorrigible beliefs, one must base these beliefs on second-order beliefs about why particular indubitable or incorrigible beliefs are likely to be true. Indeed, indubitability and incorrigibility may themselves be inferential notions, since it is not clear that the psychological notion of the revisability of a belief is independent of the psychological effects (e.g., in terms of the effects on other beliefs) that giving up the belief would have on the rest of the cognizer's mental life. If so, having strong subjective "foundational" beliefs already implicates other beliefs. In any case, indubitable or incorrigible beliefs cannot be *self*-justifying.

Now, consider objective versions of foundationalism. Weak objective foundational beliefs are beliefs that are probable or (as a class) reliable. But one cannot be justified in holding beliefs that *are* probable or reliable independently of any beliefs that, and why, the beliefs in question are probable or reliable. The mere fact that certain beliefs are reliable does not justify one in holding them. To be justified in holding some belief p that is in this sense reliable, one must base p on reasons for thinking p is true, that is, on second-order beliefs about what kind of belief p is and why p-type beliefs should be reliable. This would require, among other things, that one believe that p is reliable and that p be based on or sustained by this second-order belief. But this shows that probable or reliable beliefs are not *self*-justifying. (This explains what is wrong with externalism about justification; see Appendix 2 for details.)

Since infallible beliefs are just the limiting case of probable beliefs, it should be no surprise that the same objections tell against strong objective foundationalism. Some philosophers doubt the existence of infallible beliefs (e.g., Armstrong 1968: 100–112). But even if there are infallible beliefs, they cannot be self-justifying. One cannot be justified in holding a belief p, even if p *is in fact* infallible, independently of any beliefs whatsoever about why p should be true (e.g., independently of belief that p is infallible). The mere fact that p must be true does not justify one in holding p. To be justified in holding p, one must base p on second-order beliefs about what kind of belief p is and why p-type beliefs should be true. But this shows that infallible beliefs are not *self*-justifying.

The role of second-order beliefs in justification demonstrates the inferential character of justification and so undermines any form of foundationalism. But two possible variations on foundationalism may be worth considering. The first variation results from combining subjective and objective conceptions of foundationalism, while the second, although retaining foundationalism's structure, treats the termini of justification as being incapable of justification.

We might think that the difficulties faced by subjective conceptions of foundationalism, on the one hand, and by objective conceptions, on the other hand, could be overcome by combining those conceptions into a *hybrid* form of foundationalism. Hybrid foundationalism would construe foundational beliefs as beliefs that make a strong doxastic claim *and* are highly probable. Of course, weak and strong versions of hybrid foundationalism could be distinguished.

Hybrid foundationalism would be an attractive alternative to subjective and objective versions of foundationalism if the difficulties faced by subjective foundationalism, on the one hand, and by objective foundationalism, on the other, were complementary. But their difficulties are not complementary; they are identical. Both subjective and objective versions of foundationalism fail to acknowledge the need for second-order beliefs in justification. Hybrid foundationalism fails here too.

Consider just two versions of hybrid foundationalism (the same remarks apply, mutatis mutandis, to the other two possible versions of hybrid foundationalism). Weak hybrid foundationalism makes foundational beliefs prima facie indubitable or incorrigible and probable. But the facts that one's belief p exerts a strong psychological hold upon one and that p is probable do not justify one in holding p independently of any beliefs about why p should be true. To be justified in holding p, one must base p on second-order beliefs about what kind of belief p is and why p-type beliefs are likely to be true.

Strong hybrid foundationalism makes foundational beliefs both indubitable and infallible.[19] Suppose both that one cannot doubt one's belief p and that p is, in fact, infallible. We have already

19 This is a fairly traditional form of foundationalism; for example, Descartes (1642) and Lewis (1946) fairly clearly hold such a view.

suggested that the indubitability of a belief essentially implicates other beliefs, and this would seem to threaten the foundational status of strong hybrid "foundational" beliefs. Even if this is wrong, these facts alone do not justify one in holding p. One must have some reason for thinking p is true, and this requires that one base p on second-order beliefs about what kind of belief p is and why p-type beliefs should be true (at least, e.g., second-order beliefs that p is indubitable or that p is infallible).

The need for second-order beliefs in justification demonstrates that no belief can be *self*-justifying. All justification must be inferential. This shows that no version of foundationalism can successfully incorporate the epistemological requirement that justifying beliefs themselves be justified.[20]

Despairing of ever finding genuine foundational beliefs, someone might reconstrue foundational beliefs as noninferential beliefs that are neither justified nor unjustified.[21] This proposal, call it *groundless foundationalism,* retains the justificatory structure of foundationalism insofar as it maintains that all justification is linear and that all justificatory chains terminate in beliefs that are not themselves inferentially justified. But unlike foundationalism, groundless foundationalism claims that the termini of justification are not themselves capable of justification. We could, of course, formulate *groundless intuitionism* as a special case of groundless foundationalism according to which the justification of a moral belief must terminate in a moral belief that is not itself capable of justification.[22]

Although groundless foundationalism retains the structure of foundationalism, it abandons the traditional characterization of foundational beliefs and the central premise of the regress argu-

---

20 Pastin (1975) and others have claimed that the distinction between weak and strong versions of foundationalism is important, because weak versions are more plausible than strong versions. Weak versions of foundationalism may be more plausible insofar as they are more likely to avoid skepticism. But the argument of this section shows that weak foundationalism fails for the same reasons strong foundationalism does.

21 Cf. Chisholm 1982: 80, 128, 137–8; and Wittgenstein 1969: secs. 205, 253. (This interpretation of Wittgenstein is controversial; some would regard him as a defender of a coherence theory or as what we might call "a contextualist" [see 5.6]. But this does seem to be a possible interpretation.)

22 Cf. Price 1787: 160; Reid 1788: 303; Mill 1861: chap. 4, par. 1; Sidgwick 1879: 106; Moore 1903: x. In most cases, these writers do not distinguish the position I am calling 'groundless intuitionism' from other epistemological views. For instance, neither Price, Reid, Sidgwick, nor Moore distinguishes groundless intuitionism from his own preferred endorsement of subjective intuitionism.

ment. The traditional formulation of foundationalism construes foundational beliefs as beliefs that are noninferentially *justified* or *self-justifying*. The central premise of the regress argument is the epistemological requirement that justifying beliefs *themselves be justified*. By contrast, the termini of justification, according to groundless foundationalism, are incapable of justification. Although the epistemological requirement may be formulated too strongly (see Appendix 1), some such requirement is surely plausible. How can beliefs provide the justification for other beliefs and not themselves be even capable of justification? More basically, how can there be beliefs about which the question of their justification cannot even arise? Of course, there may be beliefs about whose justification we do not inquire or whose justification we would be unsure how to reconstruct. Indeed, a willingness to hold certain beliefs unquestioned may be a necessary condition of progress in any discipline (cf. Kuhn 1970: 13, 19–20, 163–4). But the fact that we hold certain beliefs *unquestioned* does not show that these beliefs are *unquestionable*. The appearance that we can intelligibly question any belief is prima facie evidence against groundless foundationalism.

The defender of groundless foundationalism might reply that there must be some beliefs that are unjustifiable justifiers, because some principles $p_1 \ldots p_n$ appear as premises in the justification of all other claims. Because of the ban on circular reasoning, there can be no justification of $p_1 \ldots p_n$ (immediate appeal to $p_1 \ldots p_n$ would be immediately circular, and appeal to some other principle would, by hypothesis, have to refer to $p_1 \ldots p_n$ and so be circular). $p_1 \ldots p_n$, therefore, are unjustifiable justifiers or groundless beliefs.

There are two objections to this reply. First, it is simply not clear that there are any principles that figure as premises in the justification of *all* other claims but that themselves admit of no (noncircular) justification; indeed, this is just what the regress [(1)] denies. Of course, the regress argument claims that a regress here is a vicious regress. But I shall raise some questions about this claim (Appendix 1), which, moreover, rests on the epistemological requirement that justifying beliefs be justified, which groundless foundationalism rejects. Second, the reply of groundless foundationalism depends on the rejection of coherentism. The next section will argue that the rejection of coherentism contained in the regress argument is premature and that coherentism can incorporate the epistemological requirement that justifying beliefs be justified. But if coherentism is defensible, we do not need to deny our ability to question any belief, as groundless foundationalism does, in order to have a theory of justification. Moreover, the ban on circular reasoning derives from the regress argument, which, in turn, depends on the epistemological requirement that justifying beliefs be justifiable. Since groundless foundationalism abandons this requirement, it is not clear that groundless foundationalism is entitled to defend itself by invoking the ban on circular reasoning.

This concludes my case against foundationalism and, hence, intuitionism. The antiskeptical argument for foundationalism fails, because no acceptable version of foundationalism can satisfy objectivism about justification compatibly with realism. The regress argument fails, because foundationalism cannot incorporate the epistemological requirement that justifying beliefs be justified. There are no foundational beliefs, because justification in holding a belief p requires that one base p on second-order beliefs about what kind of belief p is (e.g., under what conditions p was formed) and why p-type beliefs should be true. A fortiori, there are no foundational moral beliefs as intuitionism claims. Justification in holding a moral belief p requires that one base p on second-order beliefs about what kind of belief p is and why p-type beliefs should be true.

6. A DEFENSE OF COHERENTISM

The regress argument claims (i) foundationalism can successfully incorporate the epistemological requirement that justifying beliefs be justified and (ii) no other theory of justification can incorporate this requirement. A corollary of (ii) is that coherentism cannot incorporate the epistemological requirement. If (ii) is correct, then our demonstration in section 5 that (i) is false implies that there is no acceptable theory of justification. This result would imply general and not just moral skepticism.

Fortunately, we are not forced to this skeptical conclusion. (ii) is no more compelling than (i). In particular, coherentism promises to incorporate successfully the epistemological requirement. (Appendix 1 will reconsider the case against the claim that all justification is inferential and linear. I shall argue that this claim also represents a plausible strategy for incorporating the epistemological requirement and compare this strategy with the strategy represented by coherentism.)

Recall that coherentism claims that although all justification is inferential, it is not all linear. It avoids a regress because it allows justificatory chains to loop back on themselves. Against coherentism, the regress argument claims that circularity is vicious because one can prove anything by circular reasoning. Small justificatory circles are vicious, and larger ones are no better.

The coherentist needs to distinguish between two different kinds of justification: *systematic* and *contextualist*. Systematic justification is absolute or complete justification and results from consistently applying the epistemological requirement that justifying beliefs be justified. Contextualist justification, by contrast, is partial or incomplete justification and results from refusing to apply the epistemological requirement consistently. In the contextualist justification of some belief *p,* certain background beliefs are treated as justified that would actually have to be justified if *p* were being systematically justified. We satisfy ourselves with some degree or other of contextualist justification, both because we believe our background beliefs can be justified, and because pursuit of systematic justification would prevent us from getting on with our inquiries. But the demand for systematic justification is an intelligible one that we must answer if we are to take skepticism seriously.

The linear view of justification maintained by foundationalism seems so natural, and coherentism seems so implausible, as a result of focusing on the kind of contextualist justification involved in our normal practices of justifying beliefs. In normal contexts of justification, we do not consistently apply the epistemological requirement that justifying beliefs be justified. Although we recognize that the justification of any particular belief could be demanded, we in fact hold certain beliefs to be true without demanding their justification (and, as I have indicated, with good reason). Because in these contexts a large number of beliefs are simply held to be true, most of the justificatory chains we actually produce are quite short and linear. If the belief for which justification was initially asked were to appear as a premise in one of *these* justificatory chains, the resulting justification would be spurious and not merely incomplete. But if we accept the epistemological requirement and take the demand for systematic justification seriously, then not all justification can be like contextualist justification.

And the coherentist can claim that this difference between systematic and contextualist justification makes all the difference. The coherentist can claim that there is no clear reason to suppose that linearity can or need be preserved when the epistemological requirement is consistently observed and the demand for justification (as a result) becomes systematic and not merely contextualist. This allows her to deny that systematic justification can or need be linear as contextualist justification can be. Because contextualist justification is only partial it can also be local, involving only those beliefs contiguous with the belief whose justification is in question. As a result, contextualist justification can be more or less linear. But as contextualist justification gives way to systematic justification, and those beliefs that formed the background for contextualist justification are themselves brought into question along with the beliefs originally in question, justification must become more and more a matter of mutual support and less and less a matter of linear support. Contextualist justification could be linear without the conclusion appearing in the premises *only because* a great many background beliefs were not brought into question. But once the epistemological requirement is enforced and the background beliefs of contextualist justification are brought into question, the systematic justification of any belief can only be explained as a function of its relation to the totality of other beliefs one does or might hold. Coherentism meets this demand for systematic justification by claiming that one's belief p is fully or systematically justified insofar as p is part of a maximally coherent system of beliefs and p's coherence at least partially explains why one holds p. In this way, coherentism can explain and defend the importance we attach to linearity and the inadmissibility of circular reasoning in contextualist justification, while offering a nonlinear account of systematic justification, and so can distinguish the probative values of small and large circles in reasoning.

Section 5 argued that justification cannot be noninferential. To be justified in holding a belief p to be true, one must base p upon some second-order beliefs about what kind of belief p is and why p-type beliefs should be true. Of course, by the epistemological requirement, if these second-order beliefs are to help in the justification of p, then they must not merely be held but reasonably or justifiably held. Thus, justified beliefs must be inferentially connected with, among other things, second-order beliefs that are themselves well supported. Coherentism takes account of these facts by making the justification of a belief depend on its coherence with a total system

124

of beliefs – including second-order beliefs of various kinds. The coherence of a belief p with, among other things, second-order beliefs about p, which themselves form part of a coherent system of beliefs, is evidence of p's truth.

Having rejected foundationalism, coherentism seems our best hope for avoiding skepticism; it can explain and yet resist our worries about circularity and can accommodate the importance of second-order beliefs in justification. This is enough for us to take seriously a coherence theory of justification, develop it, and try to apply it to ethics.

7. COHERENCE AND REALISM

The regress argument is mistaken not only in claiming that foundationalism can incorporate the epistemological requirement but also in claiming that coherentism cannot. Foundationalism's failure does not imply skepticism, because coherentism can be defended. But, if the second premise of the antiskeptical argument – objectivism about justification – is accepted, then this defense of coherentism requires rejection of realism. Coherentism cannot guarantee objective truth, because it makes all justification inferential; it does not guarantee "contact with [evidence-independent] reality." It could guarantee truth only if constructivism, in particular, a coherence theory of truth were true. A fortiori, a coherence theory of justification in ethics would require rejection of moral realism and acceptance of constructivism in ethics, in particular, a coherence theory of moral truth.

This line of argument has been very influential. Many philosophers have accepted the inference from coherentism to constructivism[23] and, in particular, from a coherence theory of justification in ethics to constructivism in ethics.[24] But this argument depends on or

23 Compare: "Now if we accept coherence as the test of truth, does that commit us to any conclusions about the nature of truth or reality? I think it does. . . . It is past belief that the fidelity of our thought to reality should be rightly measured by coherence if reality itself were not coherent. To say that the nature of things may be *in*coherent, but we shall approach the truth about it precisely so far as our thoughts become coherent sounds very much like nonsense" (Blanshard 1939: 266–7). Also see Joachim 1906; Blanshard 1939: 266–9; Quine 1968; Kuhn 1970; Putnam 1976, 1981, 1983 (cf. Horwich 1982b, and M. Williams 1984); Horwich 1982a: 185–6.
24 See, for example, Hare 1973, 1978, 1981: 12, 40, 75–6; Dworkin 1973; Singer 1974; Lyons 1975; Brandt 1979: 16–23. Cf. Rawls 1980. See 5.9 below.

presupposes objectivism about justification. Our commitments to realism and moral realism should make this concession to objectivism about justification disturbing. Fortunately, we can and should reject objectivism about justification. We can defend coherentism compatibly with realism because, first, objectivism about justification overstates the connection between justification and truth, and, second, purely epistemic theories of justification, such as coherentism, can provide evidence of objective truth.

Coherentism requires the rejection of realism only if objectivism about justification is true. Objectivism about justification starts from the simple and uncontroversial claim that justification in holding a belief is justification in holding that belief to be true and construes this as requiring that justification must ensure or guarantee truth ("contact with reality"). But objectivism about justification fails precisely because it overstates the connection between justification and truth. Knowledge implies truth, but justification does not. It is possible to be completely justified in holding beliefs that turn out to be false. Objectivism about justification, therefore, threatens to collapse the distinction between justification and knowledge. Like constructivism, objectivism about justification prevents us from representing the skeptical possibility that our justified beliefs might be false (cf. 2.8). A commitment to taking epistemological skepticism seriously does not mean accepting skepticism; we can try to show that these skeptical possibilities are not in fact realized and that belief that they are not realized is reasonable, or we can try to explain why we should not be concerned about whether these skeptical possibilities are realized. But showing such things requires that we at least be able to represent these skeptical possibilities, and this, in turn, requires that we reject objectivism about justification. And if justification does not guarantee truth, no reason has been given for inferring the falsity of realism from the truth of coherentism.

Nor can the objectivist about justification claim that these objections depend only on our need to distinguish truth and partial, ordinary, or synchronic justification. For, as we have seen (2.8), even a suitably idealized or diachronic account of justification should not be taken to guarantee truth. Familiar skeptical possibilities apply to ideally justified beliefs too. So long as ideal justification includes nondeductive inference patterns, even ideal, diachronic justification cannot guarantee truth.

But even if objectivism about justification overstates the connection between justification and truth, isn't there a real worry it was trying to express? We may not want justification to imply truth, but we do want justification to provide evidence of truth. But if, as coherentism insists, all our evidence is inferential and, hence, epistemic, how can we have evidence about a world whose existence and nature are independent of our beliefs?

The answer lies in the important role that second-order beliefs play in coherentism (cf. Blanshard 1939: 285–6; Bonjour 1976: 294; M. Williams 1980: 248–50). First-order beliefs are about features of the world external to us; second-order beliefs, by contrast, are about our first-order beliefs, typically about the relationship between first-order beliefs and the world. Second-order beliefs include beliefs at various levels of generality about the nature and reliability of our belief-formation mechanisms. As we saw in the criticism of foundationalism, second-order beliefs are essential to justification; one cannot be justified in holding a belief p independently of second-order beliefs about what kind of belief p is and why p-type beliefs should be true. Without second-order beliefs our belief system would be insufficiently coherent and explanatorily weak. Our beliefs can be neither comprehensive nor explanatory if we have no theories explaining our belief-formation mechanisms and their reliability. The second-order beliefs we accept are *realist* second-order beliefs. They are realist beliefs because they are beliefs about our relation to a world that though causally dependent on us in some ways, is metaphysically or conceptually independent of our evidence about it. Our realist second-order beliefs include beliefs about our psychological makeup, our cognitive and perceptual equipment, and their hookup to the world. We combine these second-order beliefs with belief in (other) scientific theories, such as evolutionary theory, and form still other realist second-order beliefs about the nature and reliability of various belief-formation mechanisms that we possess (cf. Quine 1969b, 1975). The result is a theory of the world and our place in it that identifies certain features of the world that we reliably detect and explains why this should be so. This theory tells us, for instance, that certain introspective beliefs are highly reliable; that at close range and in good lighting we are reliable detectors of medium-sized dry goods; that the reliability of memory beliefs varies with such factors as length of time since the occurrence of the events recalled, age of the cognizer, and so on; and that palm reading is not a reliable guide to future events.

127

And, of course, the epistemological requirement demands that these second-order beliefs be justified. The justification of this theory and the second-order beliefs it represents depends, of course, on its coherence. Such a theory is justified insofar as it provides part of a unified explanatory account of all of our beliefs, including, importantly, our observational beliefs. Justification of these second-order beliefs must be *diachronic* as well as *synchronic*. Synchronic justification is possible but must be relative to a body of evidence available at the time. Partly as the result of nearly continuous perceptual input, our stock of observational beliefs is nearly always expanding. Although these observational beliefs are revisable, their addition to our belief systems can affect the coherence of particular second-order beliefs. We can acquire further confirmation for second-order beliefs; we can acquire anomalous beliefs that may lead us to reject previously accepted second-order beliefs; or we can acquire grounds for deciding the reliability of belief-formation mechanisms for which our evidence had been conflicting and indeterminate. Coherentism meets the demand for diachronic justification by requiring that justified beliefs cohere with, among other things, observational beliefs over time.

The role of second-order beliefs in coherentism allows us to reconcile realism and coherentism. The coherence of a belief p with, among other things, realist second-order beliefs is evidence of p's truth. Before we extend this defense of realism and coherentism to ethics, however, we must consider a perfectly general objection to this reconciliation of realism and coherentism. Someone might object that the realist second-order beliefs, coherence with which is supposed to be evidential, are just more beliefs, and their support consists in their coherence with still other beliefs. Because this sort of epistemic theory of justification cannot guarantee truth, even ideally coherent second-order beliefs might nonetheless all be "wildly false." Doesn't the dependence of coherentism on beliefs that might all be wildly false commit coherentism to skepticism?

In response, it is important to distinguish two senses of 'wildly false'. In one sense the claim that our second-order beliefs might all be wildly false is true, and in another sense the claim is false. Once these two senses are properly distinguished, the charge that coherentism is based on beliefs that might all be wildly false loses its sting.

'Wildly false' can mean either 'crazy and unreasonable' or 'false and not even approximately true'. On the second interpretation, but not the first, it is true that realist second-order beliefs, even though ideally coherent, might nonetheless all be wildly false. We might not be reliable detectors of an external world; we might be brains in vats or the playthings of Cartesian demons induced to have beliefs with which realist second-order beliefs cohere. Although we have rejected objectivism about justification, there is a weaker objectivist principle of justification that these skeptical possibilities would violate. According to this weaker principle, genuine justified belief must be based on at least *some* beliefs that could not be false. These skeptical possibilities show that coherentism bases justification on beliefs all of which could be false. According to this weak objectivist principle of justification, therefore, coherentism implies skepticism.

But as we shall see, this weak objectivist principle of justification is not the only way, or even the best way, of dealing with such skeptical possibilities. The motivation for this objectivist principle, therefore, is unclear. What may provide a false motivation for this principle is a slide from the genuine possibility that our realist second-order beliefs might all be wildly false, because false and not even approximately true, to the spurious possibility that they might all be wildly false, because crazy and unreasonable. Since the realist second-order beliefs in question are, ex hypothesi, maximally coherent, there is the best kind of reason we can have for holding them to be true. Our assumption is that certain realist second-order beliefs provide the best explanatory account of a wide range of observational beliefs consistently with other theoretical beliefs we hold. Such beliefs might turn out to be false, but it is surely neither crazy nor unreasonable for us to hold them.

If coherentism can provide us with the best of reasons for holding realist second-order beliefs, then the fallibility in coherent beliefs that these skeptical possibilities expose does not threaten our defense of realism and coherentism. These skeptical possibilities are real, but they bear on our knowledge claims, not our justification claims. Skeptical possibilities make the truth of our knowledge claims (or at least those subject to skeptical doubt) contingent. If we are brains in vats or the playthings of Cartesian demons induced to have beliefs with which realist second-order beliefs cohere, then we cannot have knowledge, because knowledge implies true belief. But we can nonetheless have justified beliefs. This means that whether our justified beliefs count as knowledge depends (is contingent) on whether these skeptical possibilities are realized. If we are deceived, then we can have no knowledge; but if we are not deceived, then we can have knowledge. Deceived or not, so long as all of our beliefs, including our second-order beliefs, cohere in the appropriate way, we will be justified in our beliefs and their coherence will be evidence of their objective truth.[25]

8. COHERENCE AND REALISM IN ETHICS

We can now extend the defense of realism and coherentism to moral realism and a coherence theory of justification in ethics. A coherence theory in ethics claims that one's moral beliefs are justified insofar as they cohere together in the appropriate way. This is a version of strategy (2), since it claims that the justification for a moral belief p depends on, among other things, another moral belief q, whose justification consists in part in the fact that it is appropriately related to p. Given the importance of a coherentist moral epistemology to my project, I should offer a fuller characterization of its demands.

Most people's moral beliefs largely concern particular people, particular actions, or kinds of actions. But it is unlikely that these beliefs are consistent, much less maximally coherent. As we might infer from the discussion of evaluative method (3.11), explanatory coherence demands that we introduce more general, theoretical moral claims into our moral views in order to extend our moral views to new cases, to try to resolve internal inconsistencies in our moral views, to try to resolve disagreements with others over particular moral issues, and to unify and explain the more particular moral views we already hold. Coherence asks us to try to identify theoretical moral claims that will explain and support a number of our more firmly held moral views and to assess (further) these theories by comparing their implications for real or imaginary particular cases with our own existing or reflective moral views about these cases. If

25 The interested reader might wish to compare my discussion of these epistemological issues – in particular, my defense of realism and coherentism – with the more systematic treatment of many of the same issues in Bonjour (1986), who develops them more fully than I do, or could do, here. I'm sure there are some issues about which we disagree. But overall our concerns and positions seem pretty similar, and anyone who wanted to see how my claims might be developed still further could begin by consulting Bonjour 1986.

a theory has counterintuitive implications, then this is evidence against the theory. If the counterintuitive implications of the theory are fairly common and widespread, especially if the apparent counterexamples share important features, then this is reason to abandon the theory for another, or at least to modify the theory in significant ways. But if this counterintuitive implication of the theory is a more or less isolated phenomenon and the theory explains more of our moral views better than alternative theories, then we should override this initial evidence against the theory and revise the particular moral views that conflicted with the theory. Ideally, we should make trade-offs among the various levels of moral belief in response to conflicts among them, making adjustments here at one level and there at the other, as coherence seems to require, until we achieve maximum coherence among all our beliefs. At this point, our beliefs are in the state Rawls calls "reflective equilibrium" (1971: 20). Any moral belief that is part of reflective equilibrium is justified according to a coherence theory of justification in ethics. Because the process of reflective equilibrium is one we can (only) approximate to a greater or lesser extent, our moral views can exhibit coherence to different degrees, and the degree of justification with which we hold our moral views will vary accordingly.

According to our reconciliation of realism and coherentism in the nonmoral case, the coherence of a belief p with, among other things, realist second-order beliefs about p is evidence of p's objective truth. If p is a moral belief, then there should be realist second-order beliefs about morality with which p may cohere. The distinction between moral beliefs and second-order beliefs about morality is just a special case of the distinction between first- and second-order beliefs. Moral beliefs are beliefs about moral properties and their instances (e.g., beliefs about what moral principles are true and about which actions are right). Second-order beliefs about morality, by contrast, are nonmoral beliefs about the relation between our moral beliefs and the world. Realist second-order beliefs about morality are nonmoral beliefs about our moral beliefs. If coherence with realist second-order beliefs about morality is to provide evidence of objective moral truth, then there must be realist second-order beliefs about morality that cohere with our other beliefs, both moral and nonmoral.

Realist second-order beliefs about morality are of various levels of generality. They include belief in moral realism. Chapters 6 and

131

7 will provide sustained defense of moral realism, and Chapters 2 through 4 already established a presumption in favor of moral realism. Just as the realist second-order beliefs of 5.7 included beliefs about the reliability of various belief-formation mechanisms, realist second-order beliefs about morality also include beliefs about the reliability of certain kinds of moral beliefs. These realist second-order beliefs about morality form quite an important part of a coherence theory of justification in ethics, for the coherence of a moral belief p with other moral beliefs that there is reason to think are reliable is an important part of p's justification.

Determination of reliable moral belief must itself be guided by considerations of coherence. To begin with, moral beliefs formed under conditions generally conducive to the formation of true belief will be more reliable than moral beliefs not formed under these conditions. A belief that is based on available (nonmoral) evidence and is thus well informed, that results from good inference patterns, that is not distorted by obvious forms of prejudice or self-interest, that is held with some confidence, and that is relatively stable over time is formed under conditions conducive to truth. These conditions of general cognitive reliability confer some reliability on moral beliefs so formed. A yet more reliable class of moral beliefs is picked out by the addition of certain morally motivated conditions. Of course, if coherence with a morally motivated class of beliefs is being used as a test for competing moral theories, then this class of moral beliefs had better not be picked out by only one of the competitor theories (cf. Rawls 1951: 52; Daniels 1979a: 259, 1980: 86–100). The conditions for membership in the class of reliable moral beliefs can be morally motivated as long as that motivation has general plausibility, not peculiar to one of the competitors. Because of the importance of impartiality in making moral decisions and the connection between morality and human good and harm, we are likely to obtain a more reliable class of moral beliefs by focusing on moral beliefs that have been formed not only under conditions of general cognitive reliability but also on the basis of an impartial and imaginative consideration of the interests of the relevant parties. We might call beliefs formed under such conditions *considered moral beliefs* (cf. Rawls 1951: 53–5, 1971: 47–8).

Considered moral beliefs are hardly infallible, and, because it is coherence with these beliefs, *among others,* that a coherence theory of justification in ethics demands, considered moral beliefs are certainly revisable. But considered moral beliefs do play an important role in the justification of our moral beliefs. Because there is reason to treat considered moral beliefs as generally reliable, coherence with, among other things, considered moral beliefs can be evidence of objective moral truth.

9. OBJECTIONS TO COHERENCE AND REALISM IN ETHICS

Some, however, will find this defense of realism and coherentism in ethics unacceptable. Whatever the merits of realism and coherentism for the nonmoral case, how can coherence with moral beliefs one already holds be evidence of objective moral truth? This objection takes various forms, most of which focus on the role of considered moral beliefs. Moral realism and a coherence theory of justification in ethics are incompatible, it is claimed, because coherence with considered moral beliefs cannot be evidential, or could be evidential only if moral facts are in some way constituted by our moral beliefs.

As I have already noted, in *A Theory of Justice,* Rawls defends a coherence theory of justification in ethics that emphasizes the evidential role of considered moral beliefs. Many reviewers were critical of Rawls's reliance on considered moral beliefs, and even those who were not critical of Rawls's method nonetheless shared important assumptions with his critics.[26] We can identify and distinguish a number of possible objections that reviewers seemed to voice.

The first objection, raised by R. M. Hare, Ronald Dworkin, David Lyons, and Richard Brandt, is that moral coherentism's reliance on considered moral beliefs makes it intuitionist.[27] These critics identify moral coherentism's considered moral beliefs with intuitionism's foundational moral beliefs or moral intuitions. But it is often left unclear why this claim, if true, should constitute an objection to a coherence theory of justification in ethics. We have seen

26 Thus, Dworkin (1973), not himself a critic of Rawls's method, claims, in effect, that coherentism undermines realism and requires constructivism. This puts Dworkin and me at odds. Whether it puts Dworkin and Rawls at odds depends on whether Rawls 1971 should be interpreted as a form of moral realism.
27 Hare 1973: 83, 1978: 121, 124, 1981: 75; Dworkin 1973: 28–32; Lyons 1975: 147; Brandt 1979: 16–23. Dworkin and Lyons offer this as one reading of Rawls's methodological claims; Dworkin ultimately embraces a different, constructivist reading, while Lyons despairs of finding a plausible reading of Rawls's claims.

that although the standard objections to intuitionism are weak (5.3), intuitionism is undermined by epistemological objections to any version of foundationalism (5.5). So *we* can explain why if moral coherentism's reliance on considered moral beliefs is intuitionist, as these critics claim, a coherence theory of justification is unacceptable.

But if we construe 'intuitionism', as I have been construing it, to refer to the traditional foundationalist version of moral realism, then it would be surprising if a coherence theory of justification in ethics turned out to be intuitionist, because I have been contrasting the epistemological claims of coherentism and intuitionism. In fact, a coherence theory of justification in ethics is not intuitionist, and because there has been some confusion about this, it is worth pointing out why.

Defenders of a coherence theory of justification in ethics have replied to the charge of intuitionism by pointing out that considered moral beliefs are revisable (e.g., Daniels 1979a: 264–6). But since at least some versions of intuitionism (e.g., weak subjective intuitionism and weak hybrid intuitionism) treat foundational moral beliefs as revisable (e.g., Ross 1930: 41–2), the revisability of considered moral beliefs does not establish that a coherence theory of justification in ethics is not intuitionist. Another consideration, however, does show that it is not intuitionist. If considered moral beliefs were the foundational moral beliefs of intuitionism, as the objection alleges, considered moral beliefs would have to be self-justifying. But according to coherentism, considered moral beliefs are not self-justifying; they are justified by their coherence with both moral and nonmoral beliefs. In particular, reliance on considered moral beliefs is justified, a coherence theory of justification in ethics claims, because considered moral beliefs are made under conditions whose selection is motivated by theories of general cognitive reliability and by a wide variety of plausible moral theories. Considered moral beliefs, therefore, are not *self*-justifying and so cannot be construed as the foundational moral beliefs of intuitionism.

Perhaps those who raise the intuitionism charge are using 'intuitionism' in a nonstandard way and so do not intend to saddle coherentism with a foundationalist epistemology. Hare suggests that moral coherentism's intuitionism makes it subjectivist and, therefore, without probative force (1981: 12, 75–6). It is true that a coherence theory of justification in ethics makes the justification of any moral belief depend, in part, on moral beliefs we already hold, and this may tempt one to think that coherence with other moral beliefs cannot be evidential. Brandt puts this, the second, objection as follows:

> There is a problem here which is quite similar to that which faces the traditional coherence theory of justification of belief: that the theory claims that a more coherent system of beliefs is better justified than a less coherent one, but there is no reason to think that this claim is true unless some of the beliefs are initially credible – for some reason other than coherence, say, because they state facts of observation. (1979: 20; cf. Brandt 1979: 236; and Lewis 1946: 339)

There are at least two different ways of taking this objection. First, the demand that some moral beliefs be initially credible may be the demand that some moral beliefs be noninferentially justified. This way of construing the second objection makes it not so much accuse coherentism of intuitionism as insist that intuitionism *rather than* coherentism is true. I won't rehearse the arguments against foundationalism at this point (the reader may refer to 5.5).

Second, the demand that some moral beliefs be initially credible may be the demand that some moral beliefs be initially credible before reflective equilibrium, that is, before the end point of coherentism. This demand sounds reasonable, and a coherence theory of justification in ethics can meet a reasonable interpretation of it. Considered moral beliefs are initially credible; we have seen reason to regard the class of considered moral beliefs as generally, or at least significantly, reliable. Thus, although the systematic justification of any moral belief is reached only at the end point of coherentism, the reliability of considered moral beliefs can be contextually established before reflective equilibrium.

It is interesting that Brandt should contrast the moral and scientific cases, because they seem to be on a par in this respect. Experimental testing is an important part of theory confirmation in science. Scientific theories are tested by their coherence with, among other things, observational beliefs (e.g., beliefs that substances are precipitating out of solution, that a certain chemical reaction produces a certain smell, and that meter readings of a certain kind are registering). The reliability of these observational beliefs is explained by scientific (e.g., physical, chemical, and optical) theories whose credibility is more or less independent of the particular test situation and the scientific principles being tested. Observational beliefs, though revisable, have initial credibility. Although the systematic justification of any particular observational belief is reached only at the end point of coherentism (we may conclude on the strength of theoretical considerations that an observational belief is mistaken), the credibility of observational beliefs can be established by appeal to certain scientific theories before a determination of which perceptual beliefs are part of a maximally coherent system of beliefs.

Similarly, reliance on considered moral beliefs is an important part of moral justification. Moral theories are tested by their coherence with, among other things, considered moral beliefs (e.g., beliefs that slavery is unjust, that avoidable suffering is wrong, and that promises should in general be kept). The reliability of these considered moral beliefs is explained by psychological theories about cognitive reliability and generally plausible moral theories whose credibility is more or less independent of the particular moral theories being tested. Considered moral beliefs, though revisable, have initial credibility. Although the systematic justification of any moral belief is reached only at the end point of coherentism (reflective equilibrium), the credibility of considered moral beliefs can be established by appeal to psychological and moral theories before determining which moral beliefs are part of a maximally coherent system of beliefs. Thus, considered moral beliefs do have initial credibility and are not just initially believed.

I should emphasize two things that I am not claiming in my defense of the initial credibility of considered moral beliefs. First, I am not claiming that considered moral beliefs *replace* nonmoral observational beliefs when we turn from coherentism about nonmoral matters to a coherence theory of justification in ethics. It is not that coherentism and a coherence theory of justification in ethics concern different systems of belief, containing different kinds of belief. Rather, we hold both moral and nonmoral beliefs, and coherentism represents the demand that we systematize all of our beliefs. A coherence theory of justification in ethics simply represents coherentism's claim about the justification of our moral beliefs. It follows that a coherence theory of justification in ethics will demand coherence with, among other things, observational beliefs.

Moreover, a coherence theory of justification in ethics implies that moral beliefs can be tested against observational beliefs in the same holistic way in which nonmoral beliefs get tested against observational beliefs. Scientific theories are not testable in isolation;

they have no observational consequences themselves (cf. Duhem 1914: 183–8; Quine 1951; Putnam 1974). A scientific theory has observational consequences only when conjoined with other scientific principles ("auxiliary hypotheses"). Thus, only in conjunction with other scientific beliefs can a particular scientific belief have its coherence with our observational beliefs tested. Of course, in testing a particular hypothesis, one tries to rely as much as possible on auxiliary claims that are independently well supported, but the role of auxiliary hypotheses in theory confirmation means that confirmation is not a simple matter of the success or failure of observational predictions we make on the basis of our theory. Predictive failure need not undermine the theory in question, since the fault may lie with express or tacit auxiliary hypotheses; and predictive success may be due entirely to auxiliary hypotheses, with the main hypothesis doing no explanatory or predictive work. To determine at whose door we should lay the blame for predictive failure, we must ascertain the independent plausibility of each of the contributing hypotheses, and because hypotheses can be tested only in bundles, we must judge the independent support of contributing hypotheses by testing them and varying the bundles in which we test them (cf. Kitcher 1982: 46).

Similarly, moral principles have observational consequences but are not testable in isolation. Only in conjunction with other moral beliefs can we test a particular moral belief's coherence with our observational beliefs. My moral belief that good people keep their promises when doing so involves great personal sacrifice has no observational consequences when taken in isolation. But when I conjoin it with my independently supported moral belief that Zenobia is a good person (i.e., my evidence not including Zenobia's promise-keeping behavior), I can obtain the observational consequence that Zenobia will keep her promise to Zelda, even though doing so will involve great personal sacrifice on Zenobia's part. If Zenobia does keep her promise to Zelda, then this will tend to support my moral principle about promise-keeping, provided that I can safely rule out alternative explanations of Zenobia's actions. If Zenobia fails to keep her promise, then, other things being equal, this tells me something either about my principle or about my assessment of Zenobia. To decide where to lay the blame for predictive failure, I should see if others whom I regard as good people keep their promises under adverse circumstances, and I should go over my independent evidence about Zenobia's moral character. If my independent evidence about Zenobia seems strong, and if other people for whom I have high regard also sometimes fail to keep their promises when doing so involves significant cost, then I shall conclude that my original principle was wrong or at least too simple. But if others whom I think are good do keep their promises, even in the face of significant hardship, and especially if my independent evidence about Zenobia's character is sparse or somewhat conflicting, then I may decide that Zenobia is something less than thoroughly good. It is in this way that we can test both moral principles and character assessments against our observational beliefs, and that our moral views and assessments of others' characters evolve.

So my claim is not that considered moral beliefs, rather than observational beliefs, have a role to play in moral justification; it is only that considered moral beliefs have an important role to play in a coherence theory of justification in ethics. Indeed, my claims about how we can test moral beliefs against nonmoral beliefs illustrates the need to rely on considered moral beliefs; to test the observational consequences of any one moral belief, we must rely on other considered moral beliefs as auxiliary hypotheses.

Second, I am not claiming that considered moral beliefs have the *same degree* of credibility that observational beliefs have. Noncommittal observational beliefs – such as belief that the stuff in this test tube that made a piece of paper turn red made a similar-looking piece of paper turn blue after that stuff in the other test tube was added to it – may be more credible and more reliable than considered moral beliefs. But this is so not because the credibility of such noncommittal observational beliefs is not theory-dependent (it is), but because their credibility is dependent on theories that are even more reliable and better confirmed than those theories on which the credibility of considered moral beliefs depends. Notice also that the credibility of noncommittal observational beliefs will compare in a similar way with the credibility of more committal (or theoretical) observational beliefs, such as belief that addition of a base solution to an acid solution neutralized the acid solution (to take the more committal, or theoretical, version of the noncommittal observational belief just mentioned). The degree of credibility of considered moral beliefs probably corresponds more closely to the credibility of these and other more committal or theoretical beliefs that figure in our testing of the plausibility of various social and natural scientific theories.

All I claim is that considered moral beliefs have initial credibility. I do not claim they enjoy maximum initial credibility; such a claim is not necessary in order to claim that coherence with considered moral beliefs is evidential. If we can show that moral beliefs with some initial credibility cohere with other beliefs, including beliefs of still greater initial credibility, we have reason to accept those moral beliefs and others that they support.

This reply to the second objection may lead to a third objection commonly brought against a coherence theory of justification in ethics. Someone who thought that a coherence theory of justification in ethics was somehow subjectivist might argue that if the credibility of considered moral beliefs is itself established by coherence with other beliefs, including other moral beliefs, then moral coherentism must fail to provide evidence of objective moral truth. Moral coherentism requires rejection of moral realism and acceptance of what I have called 'constructivism in ethics', because coherence could provide evidence of moral truth only if the truth of a moral belief consists in its coherence with other beliefs.[28] Peter Singer raises this objection in the course of his discussion of Rawls and Sidgwick:

Most importantly: is the fact that a moral theory matches a set of considered moral judgments in reflective equilibrium, to be regarded merely as *evidence* of the validity [substitute 'truth' for 'validity' and 'true' for 'valid'] of the moral theory, or is it then valid *by definition* – in other words, is the achievement of a stable reflective equilibrium what Rawls means by 'valid', as applied to moral theories, or would he allow that there is a meaningful sense of 'valid' that goes beyond this? My belief is that Rawls has left no room for any idea of validity that is independent of achieving reflective equilibrium. (1974: 493)[29]

28 Rawls may encourage this criticism by comparing a coherence theory of justification in ethics with what he takes to be a similar method in linguistics (Rawls 1971: 47). Someone might reasonably claim that grammaticality is *constituted by* the systematization of our linguistic judgments. If a coherence theory of justification in ethics followed linguistic method in *this,* it would seem to imply constructivism in ethics. But we can interpret the analogy with linguistics as a claim about similarity of methods rather than as a claim about similarity in the status of the results of the two methods. On this interpretation, coherence theories of justification in ethics and linguistics need share only the methodological commitment to the systematization of people's moral and linguistic judgments.
29 See also Singer 1974: 494, 500, 508; Dworkin 1973: 31–2; Hare 1973, 1978, 1981: pt. 1; Lyons 1975: 147; Brandt 1979: 16–23.

Singer clearly takes what he regards as moral coherentism's *identification* of moral truth and coherent moral belief to be an objection to it. This is a little hard to understand because Singer himself professes to be a moral antirealist (1979: chap. 1). Such an identification, however, would threaten our project because it would mean the rejection of moral realism.

Although I think Rawls's defense of a coherentist moral epistemology in *A Theory of Justice* is compatible with a belief in moral realism, I do not want to defend Rawls's acceptance of moral realism, because he has recently made a number of second-order claims about his work, at least some of which appear to endorse a form of moral antirealism. (See Appendix 4.) However, I do want to claim that a coherence theory of justification in ethics can provide evidence of moral truth without identifying moral truth and coherent moral belief. Most of the argument for this has already been given in 2.8, 5.7, 5.8, as well as this section.

I can conceive of two reasons for thinking that a coherence theory of justification in ethics implies constructivism in ethics. The first is that the credibility of considered moral beliefs consists in their coherence with other beliefs we hold. If a coherence theory of justification in ethics identifies the credibility of considered moral beliefs with their coherence, it might be claimed, it must identify the truth of a moral belief with its coherence. But the credibility of considered moral beliefs refers to our justification in holding them and not to their truth. To claim that moral coherentism's identification of credibility and coherence implies the identification of moral truth and coherent moral belief, therefore, just begs the question of whether a coherence theory of justification in ethics requires the rejection of moral realism.

A second reason for thinking that a coherence theory of justification in ethics implies an antirealist, constructivist metaethics is objectivism about justification. If justification must guarantee truth, as objectivism about justification claims, then a coherence theory of justification in ethics could provide evidence of moral truth only if the truth of a moral belief *consisted in* its coherence. But as I have argued (5.7), objectivism about justification is false; it overstates the connection between justification and truth. Justification need only provide evidence of truth, and a coherence theory of justification in ethics provides evidence of truth by requiring that moral beliefs cohere with, among other things, second-order beliefs about morality. Coherence provides evidence of objective moral truth, and so is compatible with moral realism, as long as there are realist second-order beliefs about morality, which themselves form part of a coherent system of beliefs, with which our moral beliefs may cohere. Moreover, there are good grounds for holding realist second-order beliefs about morality. There is reason to believe moral realism, and theories of cognitive reliability and a wide variety of plausible moral theories support belief in the general reliability of considered moral beliefs. Of course, however well supported, these realist second-order beliefs about morality might be mistaken. But this skeptical possibility, like the one that applies to coherent nonmoral beliefs, threatens our claims to knowledge, not our claims to justification.

Fourth, we might interpret the charge that coherentism's reliance on considered moral beliefs is subjectivist as the charge that a coherence method of justification is essentially *conservative*. In particular, reliance on considered moral beliefs might seem conservative in the sense that it allows people who employ this method no objective or external vantage point from which to criticize their existing moral beliefs.[30]

I doubt that it is either desirable or even possible to start from a vantage point completely external to one's own moral beliefs and commitments. Moreover, and perhaps more importantly, such a vantage point is not necessary to assuming a critical attitude to one's own moral views and, hence, to avoiding conservatism. As we have noted, no one brings to the dialectical process of reflective equilibrium a consistent, much less maximally coherent, system of beliefs. Explanatory coherence demands that we introduce theory and principle into our moral views, and theory will require revision among our existing moral views, including our considered moral judgments. Another analogy with the scientific case may be helpful here. Although scientific theories (e.g., physical and optical theories) draw support from the way in which they explain observations, empirically well supported theories may force us to revise some of our

---

30 Cf. Brandt 1979: 21–2; Hare 1981: 76; and Copp 1984. Copp actually distinguishes between coherentism and conservatism; he takes as his target only conservatism. So perhaps he wouldn't think that his worries apply to my view. He does think, however, that the coherentism of Rawls and Daniels is conservative, and I think of my own epsitemological views as similar to those of Rawls and Daniels. But it seems to me that Copp is wrong to find (what he calls) conservatism in the coherentism of either Rawls or Daniels; not even *considered* moral judgments are unrevisable or self-justifying.

141

original observational beliefs (e.g., that the stick in the water is bent). In a similar way, the theory that best accounts for all of our moral views may force us to revise some of the firmly held moral views with which we began the dialectical process. Indeed, the stepwise character of the adjustments involved in the dialectical process makes it possible, at least in principle, that people would emerge from the process with *none* of the (precise) moral views with which they began. Moreover, assessment of our moral views is, as we have noted, essentially comparative. In deciding which moral views to retain and which to abandon or revise, we must consider the "overall fit" of different possible moral theories, rules, and particular judgments. This will require us, at least in principle, to consider and explore the appeal of quite different moral views and traditions, and to examine the basis of our allegiance to the moral views we brought to the dialectical process. These demands of systematic coherence are rigorous and not easily met. The ideal of maximal coherence is clearly only an ideal to which we can try to approximate more or less closely. The fact that we begin the dialectical process with certain views, therefore, by no means dooms those views to vindication.

Finally, someone might suppose that coherentism's reliance on considered moral beliefs commits us to regarding moral disagreement as unresolvable, because coherentism treats considered moral beliefs as a constraint on theory choice in ethics, and, of course, people can hold and do hold quite different considered beliefs about the morality of particular actions, policies, and practices. If so, then the only kind of "truth" we could assign to the results of the dialectical process would be a kind of antirealist truth that made the truth of one's moral beliefs relative to the moral beliefs with which one started the dialectical process. (This sort of argument may capture the reasoning behind Rawls's recent defense of a "constructivist" view that claims moral truth must be relativized to our ideals of the person. For a discussion of Rawls's constructivism, see Appendix 4.)

Although I postpone a full discussion of what moral realism should say about the existence of moral disagreement until later (7.4), our response to the worry about coherentism's conservatism indicates the outline of a response to this worry. Because the dialectical process of the coherence theory can produce fundamental changes in the beliefs with which people begin the process, the fact that people begin the process with significant differences is no evidence that their disagreement would persist to the end of the dialectical process. Because the dialectical process is one we can at best approximate, even the existence of reflective moral disagreement fails to show that moral disagreement is in principle inevitable. As long as interlocutors share some moral beliefs at the beginning of the dialectical process, there is no reason to assume that their disagreement is in principle unresolvable. Indeed, even though there will always be some agreement among interlocutors, this is not a necessary condition for dispute resolution. For, as we have seen, the moral beliefs with which people might emerge from the dialectical process need not overlap at all with the beliefs with which they started the process. This makes it possible, at least in principle, for those who enter the process with completely different moral beliefs to emerge with the same moral beliefs.

Thus, none of these common or possible objections to a coherentist moral epistemology reveals any problems either for the coherence theory or for its combination with moral realism. A coherentist moral epistemology, like a coherentist epistemology for nonmoral beliefs, is defensible; and realism and coherence are compatible in ethics, as well as in the nonmoral case.

10. CONCLUSION

One reason for skepticism about moral realism is the belief that there is no acceptable theory of justification for our moral beliefs. Traditional arguments for foundationalism seem to tie moral realism to an intuitionist moral epistemology. Although traditional worries about intuitionism are weak, there are perfectly general reasons for rejecting any kind of foundationalist epistemology. There cannot be the sort of self-justifying beliefs to which foundationalism is committed. Fortunately, this does not commit us to skepticism; coherentism can be defended against the traditional foundationalist arguments. Moreover, despite appearances to the contrary, a coherentist epistemology is compatible with a realist metaphysics. These claims allow us to combine a coherentist moral epistemology with our commitment to moral realism. Coherence with, among other things, considered moral beliefs provides evidence of objective moral truth. The individual plausibility and joint compatibility of moral realism and a coherence theory of justification add to the case for moral realism. Perhaps this case can still be defeated, but this requires compelling argument.

6

Moral realism and the is/ought thesis

Chapters 2 through 5 present a strong case for the individual plausibility and joint compatibility of moral realism and a coherentist moral epistemology. In this chapter I shall examine possible rebuttals based on arguments for and from the existence of an is/ought gap.

Most discussions of the is/ought gap concern its existence, not its implications or importance. Although nonnaturalists were happy to concede the existence of an is/ought gap, nonnaturalism is no longer thought respectable; most contemporary parties to the discussion seem to assume that the existence of an is/ought gap would in some way undermine the objectivity of ethics. One reason for thinking that an is/ought thesis would be inimical to moral realism has been quite influential: Noncognitivists have argued that the existence of an is/ought gap would undermine ethical naturalism and commit moral realism to an absurd kind of nonnaturalism, leaving noncognitivism as the only sane response to the existence of an is/ought gap. There are other, less well articulated worries about the compatibililty of moral realism with an is/ought gap, which I shall try to reconstruct: An is/ought gap can be thought to support both nihilism and skepticism. If any of these claims were true, the existence of an is/ought gap would undermine the metaethical views I have been defending.

I shall argue that these claims are false; the existence of an is/ought gap would undermine neither moral realism nor a coherence theory of justification in ethics. Although I shall present and critically discuss the arguments for the existence of an is/ought gap, my main concern is not with the soundness of these arguments. I shall not attempt a conclusive resolution of the issue concerning the existence of an is/ought gap. If there is no such gap, so much the better for moral realism. My main concern is to explain why – even if there is an is/ought gap – no antirealist or anticoherentist consequences follow. (Appendix 3 explains why a standard argument against moral realism based on foundationalism and an is/ought gap fails.)

1. THE IS/OUGHT THESIS

At least since Hume, many philosophers have defended the existence of an inferential gap between moral and nonmoral claims commonly known as the is/ought gap.[1] Historically, the is/ought thesis has taken two forms, both of which probably derive some support from Hume.

One form the is/ought thesis takes is based on internalist assumptions about the motivational properties of moral considerations. As we have seen, it is an assumption of commonsense views about morality that normal people will not be indifferent to moral considerations. Internalists about motives account for this belief by claiming that it is part of the very concept of morality that moral considerations motivate. Certain noncognitivists, such as Hare and Nowell-Smith, have built a version of the is/ought thesis on this internalist claim. They claim that no statement of nonmoral fact itself entails a pro-attitude; it is always possible to be indifferent to any set of nonmoral facts.[2] This internalist is/ought thesis is then used to argue

1 Cf. "I cannot forbear adding to these reasonings an observation, which may, perhaps, be found of some importance. In every system of morality, which I have hitherto met with, I have always remark'd, that the author proceeds for some time in the ordinary way of reasoning, and establishes the being of a God, or makes observations concerning human affairs; when of a sudden I am surpriz'd to find, that instead of the usual copulation of propositions, *is,* and *is not,* I meet with no proposition that is not connected with an *ought,* or an *ought not.* This change is imperceptible but is, however, of the last consequence. For as this *ought* or *ought not,* expresses some new relation or affirmation, 'tis necessary that it shou'd be observ'd and explain'd; and at the same time that a reason should be given, for what seems altogether inconceivable, how this new relation can be a deduction from others, which are entirely different from it. But as authors do not commonly use this precaution, I shall presume to recommend it to the readers; and am persuaded, that this small attention wou'd subvert all the vulgar systems of morality, and let us see, that the distinction of vice and virtue is not founded merely on the relations of objects, nor is perceiv'd by reason" (Hume 1739: III, i, 1/469–70). For some of the controversy over how to interpret Hume on this issue, see Hudson 1969 and Sturgeon 1987.

2 Hare 1952: 85–93; Nowell-Smith 1957: 35–8. Cf. "Since morals, therefore, have an influence on the actions and affections, it follows, that they cannot be deriv'd from reason; and that because reason alone, as we have already prov'd, can never have any such influence. Morals excite passions, and produce or prevent actions. Reason of itself is utterly impotent in this particular. The rules of morality, therefore, are not conclusions of our reason" (Hume 1739: III, i, 1/457).

that moral claims cannot be fact-stating and that, as a result, non-cognitivism is true.

I will not evaluate the consequences of this is/ought thesis, because I already argued in Chapter 3 that its internalist assumptions should be rejected. Agent internalism threatens to compromise the authority of morality by tailoring the scope of moral demands to people's motivations, and appraiser and hybrid internalism are unable to represent the possibility of the amoralist (one who is indifferent to moral considerations). The internalist's is/ought thesis does not threaten moral realism, because it is, as the externalist about motives claims, a matter of contingent psychological fact whether moral considerations actually motivate.

But another, more traditional, version of the is/ought thesis makes no internalist assumptions. It is a claim about the inferential relations between moral and nonmoral statements. This is/ought gap is typically defended with respect to deductive inference only (although I shall consider it as a claim about nondeductive inference in 6.8). We may formulate this thesis as the claim that no moral statement can be validly derived from a consistent set of premises whose members are all nonmoral statements (and vice versa). A moral conclusion, the thesis maintains, can be derived only from premises containing at least one moral statement.[3]

This formulation of the is/ought thesis does not depend on any internalist assumptions about the essentially or intrinsically prescriptive nature of moral considerations; it depends instead, as we shall see, primarily on the semantic claim, embedded in G. E. Moore's discussion of the so-called naturalistic fallacy, that moral and nonmoral terms are not interdefinable. This version of the is/ought thesis descends from Hume through Moore, Prichard, Broad, Ross, Prior, and Blackburn. A virtue of this formulation of the is/ought thesis, as we shall see, is that it explains the division that the is/ought thesis created between nonnaturalists and noncognitivists. It is this externalist version of the is/ought thesis and its alleged implications with which I shall be concerned in the rest of this chapter.

So formulated, the is/ought thesis presupposes a distinction between moral terms/senses/statements and nonmoral terms/senses/

3 See Prichard 1912: 4; Broad 1930: 112, 181; Prior 1949: esp. 26–7, 36; 1960: 88–90; Hare 1963a: 2; Mackie 1977: 68, 72.

statements. I know of no *criterion* for making this distinction. Any criterion of the moral is likely either to appeal to moral notions itself or to beg the question against the moral status of certain, possibly eccentric, moral claims. Nor does this situation seem peculiar to the moral. I know of no criterion for marking in an entirely happy way the distinction between, say, the social and the nonsocial.

It is not incumbent on the realist, however, to provide a criterion for distinguishing the moral and the nonmoral. It is a presupposition of the is/ought thesis, not of moral realism, that an important distinction can be clearly marked between the moral and the nonmoral. Proponents of the is/ought thesis unfortunately tend to assume this distinction rather than explain it. They may perhaps reply that whatever the difficulties in formulating the distinction, it is one we all recognize and apply. We even tend to agree about hard cases. For present purposes, I shall go along with defenders of the is/ought thesis and simply rely on our ability to distinguish the moral and the nonmoral. In particular, I shall rely on our ability to distinguish moral and nonmoral senses of terms.

If we rely on this ability to distinguish moral and nonmoral senses of terms, we can distinguish between moral and nonmoral statements in a way that is important to the formulation and assessment of the is/ought thesis. Proponents of the is/ought thesis claim or assume that a statement is a moral statement just in case it is a *synthetic* statement expressed by a sentence in which at least one term is used (and not merely mentioned) in its moral sense. Only synthetic statements count as moral, on their view, because analytic statements are held to be linguistic or semantic and, hence, not moral statements.[4] A statement is a nonmoral statement when it is not a moral statement in the sense just defined.

This account of the distinction between moral and nonmoral statements and, in particular, the claim that analytic statements using terms in their moral senses are not moral statements is open to a certain objection, namely, that it confuses the *ground of a statement's truth* with its *content*. Although we shall appreciate this better in a moment, the rejection of this claim and the consequent construal of such analytic statements as moral statements would make the is/ought thesis much easier to establish. For then there would be

4 See, for example, Frankena 1939: 53; Hare 1952: 41, 44; 1963a: 30–3, 35; 1981: 17; Searle 1969: 132, 135–6, 178–9, 181.

no need to assert the semantic claim that moral and nonmoral terms are not interdefinable in order to maintain that moral statements cannot be derived from nonmoral ones (and vice versa). But proponents of the is/ought thesis have typically not thought it this easy to establish their conclusion; they have linked the is/ought thesis with this semantic thesis; and a number of them have clearly endorsed the claim that analytic statements using terms in their moral senses would not count as moral statements. For these reasons, I shall concede this claim, if only for the sake of argument. (Those who are unwilling to concede this claim can prize apart my discussion of the is/ought thesis and this semantic claim and interpret my claims and arguments mutatis mutandis.)

This account of the distinction between moral and nonmoral statements presupposes a distinction between analytic and synthetic statements. Traditional defenders of the is/ought thesis rely on this distinction (although, as we shall see, the is/ought thesis may be formulated without this presupposition). For purposes of argument, I propose that we understand the analytic–synthetic distinction in the following way: A statement is analytic just in case its truth is determined solely by virtue of the meanings of the words used to express that statement (cf. Ayer 1946: 78–9; Lewis 1946: 35–7; Hare 1952: 42; Carnap 1956: 222). For example, the statement that bachelors are unmarried is analytic, because its truth owes to the fact that it is part of the meaning of the word 'bachelor' that bachelors are unmarried men. A statement is synthetic just in case it is not analytic in this sense. The traditional theory of meaning, also held by defenders of the is/ought thesis, maintains that the meaning of a term is the set of properties that any competent speaker (i.e., a speaker who knows how to use the term) associates with that term (cf. Frege 1892: 57–8; Lewis 1946: 133, 168; Carnap 1956: 234, 242–3, 246). In this view, the criteria that all speakers use to determine the application of a word constitute the meaning of that word. For example, our criterion for application of the word 'bachelor' is a man who has never been married, and it is this criterion that is the meaning of the word 'bachelor'. Two terms are synonymous just in case they are both associated with the same criteria or set of properties. There is a meaning implication from one term to another just in case the set of properties conventionally associated with the second term is a proper subset of the set of properties conventionally associated with the first term.

Having explained some of the philosophical presuppositions of the is/ought thesis, we are now in a position to offer a more perspicuous, if less simple, formulation of that thesis. Because nonmoral statements consist of (i) synthetic statements expressed by sentences using no term in its moral sense, and (ii) analytic statements, the is/ought thesis claims that no moral statement can be deduced from a consistent set of premises made up entirely of statements of types (i) and (ii). This formulation allows us to distinguish two subtheses in the is/ought thesis. The *logical thesis* claims that no moral statement can be deduced from statements exclusively of type (i). The *semantic thesis* claims that there are no type (ii) statements which by themselves, or in conjunction with type (i) statements, would entail a moral statement. In particular, the semantic thesis claims that there are no statements asserting relations of implication between the possession of moral properties and the possession of nonmoral properties – moral *bridge premises* – that are analytic.

(If we were to deny the existence of analytic statements, we could construe the is/ought thesis as the claim that no moral statement can be deduced from a consistent set of premises consisting entirely of statements of type (i), and the is/ought thesis would depend only on the truth of the logical thesis.)

2. THE PLAUSIBILITY OF THE IS/OUGHT THESIS

Many arguments conform to the is/ought thesis so formulated. For example:

A. 1. Spike could maximize pleasure by breaking his promise to Malcolm.
   2. One has an obligation to do that action which would maximize pleasure.
   3. Therefore, Spike has an obligation to break his promise to Malcolm.

As the logical thesis claims, the moral conclusion (3) cannot be derived from the synthetic, nonmoral statement (1) alone. (3) is deducible from (1) only by the addition of a moral bridge premise such as (2). (2) is a substantive moral claim and is not analytic. In particular, it is not part of the meaning of the word 'obligation' that one must maximize pleasure, as it is part of the meaning of the word 'bachelor' that bachelors are men who have never been married. Being such as to maximize pleasure is not the criterion by which every speaker applies the word 'obligation'. (3), therefore, cannot be derived from exclusively nonmoral premises.

But, of course, the is/ought thesis states a universal claim: *No moral conclusion can be derived from exclusively nonmoral premises* (and vice versa). So, even if argument A conforms to the is/ought thesis, it does not establish that thesis. The is/ought thesis requires that both the logical and semantic theses be true.

The logical thesis appears to be true because it seems a reasonable logical principle that no term can occur (with a particular sense) in the conclusion of an argument that does not occur (with the same sense) in the premises of the argument. A. N. Prior, however, has argued that the logical thesis is strictly false (1960). He presents two kinds of counterexamples.

B. 1. Tea drinking is common in England.
    2. Therefore, either tea drinking is common in England or all New Zealanders ought to be shot.
C. 1. Undertakers are church officers.
    2. Therefore, undertakers ought to do whatever all church officers ought to do.

Prior himself takes these cases to undermine only the letter and not the spirit of the logical thesis. Unfortunately, although he promises to diagnose the failure of the logical thesis and to explain just what thesis can be defended, he never really fulfills this promise.

The defender of the is/ought thesis might make one of two responses: He might claim that B and C are not genuine counterexamples, or he might reformulate the logical thesis in light of B and C. First, one might deny that either B or C is a counterexample by questioning whether either B2 or C2 is a moral statement. Prior warns us that we should not conclude from the fact that neither makes an all-things-considered moral claim that neither makes a moral claim (1960: 96). This is surely good advice. But one may wonder whether B2 or C2 makes even a prima facie moral claim. B2 does not require the truth of any moral claim, and although C2 provides information that together with moral claims about church officers may yield moral statements, it is not clear that C2 itself makes any moral claim. If we deny that the conclusions of B and C make moral statements, it seems we must recast our distinction between moral and nonmoral statements, for, by our criteria, both B2 and C2 should be moral. One suggestion for revising our distinction comes from Prior himself. He suggests that in B2 the occurrence of 'ought to be shot' is nonessential or "contingently vacuous" (1960: 89, 93). That is, for the moral expression in question any expression of the same grammatical type could be substituted without changing the truth value of the statement that the sentence containing that expression expresses. (Indeed, in B2 the entire second independent clause could be replaced by any other independent clause without affecting B2's truth value or the validity of B.) Now, Prior denies that this strategy can be successfully applied to C2 (1960: 94). But he does admit that the *two* 'oughts' in C2 – *taken together* – are vacuous or nonessential, and this seems to be all that we need. We might define moral statements as synthetic statements expressed by sentences in which terms are used in their moral senses *essentially*. Neither B2 nor C2 is a moral statement according to this criterion of moral statements, and so neither B nor C offends the logical thesis.

Alternatively, the defender of the is/ought thesis might rely on our unmodified criterion for moral statements and modify the logical thesis. If it be conceded that B2 and C2 are moral statements, the defender of the is/ought thesis can reconstrue the logical thesis as the claim that no nonvacuous moral statements can be derived from type (i) statements. Since this modified logical thesis is really equivalent to the first strategy, it too is immune to counterexample.[5] In what follows, therefore, I shall assume that the logical thesis (or some modification of it) is defensible.

(I hope it is clear that this defense of the logical thesis, or some modification of it, would be sufficient to establish the is/ought thesis if we were to insist that analytic statements using terms in their moral senses were moral statements. For this defense shows that we need moral bridge premises to derive moral conclusions from otherwise nonmoral premises, and if moral bridge premises are moral statements, whether they are analytic or synthetic, then the is/ought thesis is true.)

Defense of the semantic thesis is more complicated and problematic. Moore's open-question argument represents, among other

5 It is interesting here and elsewhere in this chapter to compare issues about the is/ought thesis with analogous issues about intertheoretic reduction in the sciences. Nagel (1949 and 1961: 343, 353–4) embraces the reductionist analogue of our original logical thesis. Kemeny and Oppenheim (1956: 13) argue from B-type putative counterexamples to the reductionist logical thesis to the reductionist analogue of our modified logical thesis.

things, the standard defense of the semantic thesis (1903: 7, 16–7; cf. Ayer 1946: 104–5). The semantic thesis requires that there be no relations of synonymy or meaning implication between moral and nonmoral terms. As we shall see, Moore thinks, and many concur, that the open-question argument shows more than this, but it is designed to show at least this. Moore writes:

> But whoever will attentively consider with himself what is actually before his mind when he asks the question 'Is pleasure (or whatever it may be) after all good?' can easily satisfy himself that he is not merely wondering whether pleasure is pleasant. And if he will try this experiment with each suggested definition in succession, he may become expert enough to recognize that in every case he has before his mind a unique object, with regard to the connection of which with any other object, a distinct question may be asked. Everyone does in fact understand the question 'Is this good?' When he thinks of it, his state of mind is different from what it would be were he asked 'Is this pleasant, desired, or approved?' It has a distinct meaning for him. (1903: 16–17)

As we shall see, Moore uses this argument in an attempt to show the impossibility of identities between moral and nonmoral properties. Part of the argument is intended to show that moral and nonmoral terms cannot be synonymous. It is this part of the open-question argument that bears on the semantic thesis.

Roughly, Moore's argument against the possibility of synonymy between moral and nonmoral terms is this: If two terms are synonymous, then, by the traditional theory of meaning, any speaker competent with both must associate the same criteria or set of properties with both. Then, if two terms are synonymous and a speaker is competent with both, she cannot sensibly doubt whether their meaning is the same. But whereas it is never possible to doubt whether F is F, it is always possible to doubt whether F is G. So, 'F' and 'G' cannot be synonymous. Therefore, moral and nonmoral terms cannot be synonymous. We might set this argument out more carefully as the *synonymy argument*.

1. If two general terms are synonymous, then the substitution of one term for the other in a sentence-form should not alter the question asked.
2. If two sentence-tokens ask the same question, then it cannot be the case for any speaker competent with the terms in both that the one sentence-token asks an open question (i.e., one to which it is possible to doubt an affirmative answer) and the other sentence-token asks a closed question (i.e., one to which it is not possible to doubt an affirmative answer).
3. Where 'F' is any general moral term and 'G' is any general nonmoral

term, some speaker competent with both 'F' and 'G' will always find the question asked by the sentence-type 'Are G things G just insofar as they are G?' closed and the question asked by the sentence-type 'Are F things F just insofar as they are G?' open.

4. Therefore, moral and nonmoral terms may never be substituted for one another in a sentence-form so as to ask the same question.
5. Therefore, no moral term is synonymous with any nonmoral term.

As a number of people have recognized, an argument similar to the synonymy argument can be constructed against the possibility of meaning implications between moral and nonmoral terms.[6] The *meaning implication argument* claims that if it were part of the meaning of 'F' that what is F is necessarily G or vice versa, then the questions asked by the sentence-types 'Are all F things G?' and 'Are all G things F?' should be closed. It is claimed, however, that some speaker competent with both 'F' and 'G' will always find them open. It is concluded that there can be no meaning implications between moral and nonmoral terms.

Critics of the semantic thesis will want to raise doubts about both synonymy and meaning implication arguments. Premise (1) of the synonymy argument is based on a reasonable view about the connection between meaning and propositional content according to which sameness of meaning (synonymy) of expressions implies sameness of proposition expressed or question asked. Premise (2), however, is more problematic: It appears to be a consequence of the traditional theory of meaning according to which the meaning of a term is the set of properties that any speaker competent with the term associates with it. It seems hard to believe, on this theory of meaning, that one could doubt that two terms were synonymous if the properties one associated with them were the same. But this means that knowledge of synonyms implies ability to recognize synonymy. Some find this claim acceptable (e.g., Dummett 1975: 100). But it precludes the possibility of "covert" or "opaque" synonymy. In particular, it seems to rule out the possibility that we could discover by semantic analysis new facts about concepts with which

6 See, for example, Blackburn 1971: 105–16; 1984: 182–7, 221. Although Hare's claim is often the internalist claim that moral terms have prescriptive meaning and no prescription is part of the meaning of a nonmoral statement (cf. 6.1), he is often willing to assert the corresponding claim about meaning implication without any internalist assumptions (i.e., there are no meaning implications between moral and nonmoral terms). See, for example, Hare 1952: 81–5, 145, 154–5; 1963b: 246–7; 1981: 17–18. Cf. Foot 1958a, 1958b.

we are familiar (cf. Brandt 1959: 163–6; Armstrong 1978: II, 41). Moreover, (2) makes the conditions for synonymy very difficult to satisfy. Few statements are impossible to doubt. Some logical truths may be impossible to doubt. The paradigm cases of analytic truth may also be impossible to doubt. 'Are bachelors men who have never been married?' may ask a genuinely closed question. But almost any question worth asking is open in Moore's sense. This feature of (2) makes the case for (3) very strong, but at the cost of virtually bankrupting the notion of synonymy. For while it is probably true that no moral term is synonymous with any nonmoral term in Moore's sense, it is also true that very few terms are synonymous in this sense. Certainly, few if any terms from one discipline will be synonymous with terms from other disciplines.[7] The traditional theory of meaning makes synonymy a very difficult condition to satisfy.

This is why it is probably a mistake to begrudge Moore (3). It is true that the failure of synonymy between 'good' and any nonmoral term does not follow from the failure of synonymy between 'good' and 'pleasant', 'desired', or 'approved'. But Moore does not claim that the general failure of synonymy follows from the cases he considers. Rather, he claims, not implausibly, that the cases he considers illustrate how one can always sensibly doubt that goodness is the same as some proposed nonmoral property. Given (2), we must conclude that moral and nonmoral terms cannot be synonymous. If we wish to dispute (5) on the basis of (3), we had better dispute the theories of meaning and synonymy underlying (2).

The semantic thesis requires the success of the synonymy and meaning implication arguments. The synonymy and meaning implication arguments are valid. Moreover, (1) and (3) (and their analogues in the meaning implication argument) are plausible. If we are to resist the semantic thesis, we must question (2) (and its analogue in the meaning implication argument) and the theories of meaning and synonymy on which it rests.

I have indicated some reason to doubt (2) and hence to be skepti-

---

7 Moore does think that moral terms are synonymous with other moral terms. For instance, he thinks that the term 'good' is synonymous with 'ought to exist for its own sake' and 'has intrinsic value', and that 'right' is synonymous with 'causes good results'; see Moore 1903: viii, 146–7; 1912: 42. I rather doubt, however, that 'right' is synonymous with 'causes good results'; at least, I doubt that this is true in Moore's theory of synonymy. Cf. Ross 1930: 8.

cal of the semantic thesis. But partly because some might still accept (2), I want to accept the synonymy and meaning implication arguments for the sake of argument. These arguments establish the semantic thesis. The semantic thesis and the logical thesis establish the is/ought thesis. I want to see what consequences for moral realism follow from the supposition that there is an is/ought gap.

As I indicated at the beginning of this chapter, it seems to be a common view that the existence of an is/ought gap would undermine or otherwise discredit moral realism or the objectivity of ethics. Some reasons for this view have been explicitly argued; others require reconstruction. The following are three possible reasons for this view.

3. A THREAT OF SKEPTICISM

First, one might think that the is/ought thesis undermines moral realism on epistemological grounds. Moral realism and moral skepticism are compatible; we might just have no cognitive access to moral facts. But, as I have noted, belief in moral realism would be seriously compromised if there were good reason to believe that we could not justify our moral beliefs. For this reason, moral realism seems to require that there be evidential relations between moral and nonmoral beliefs. I have defended a coherentist moral epistemology, and coherentism requires that there be evidential relations between moral and nonmoral beliefs. But the is/ought thesis establishes that no moral conclusion can be derived from exclusively nonmoral premises (and vice versa), and this may seem to undermine the sort of evidential relations between moral and nonmoral beliefs required by moral realism and coherentism.

4. A THREAT OF NIHILISM

Second, one might think that the is/ought thesis undermines moral realism on metaphysical grounds. As a cognitivist thesis, moral realism is committed to the existence of moral facts. But, someone might argue, a set of claims cannot be fact-stating if none of its members is deducible from other, recognizably fact-stating disciplines. Because, by the is/ought thesis, no moral claim is deducible from nonmoral fact-stating claims, moral claims cannot be fact-stating. Therefore, moral nihilism is true and any cognitivist thesis

155

such as moral realism must be false. This argument is one way of reconstructing the reasoning of those who infer the existence of a fact/value gap that is a factual/nonfactual gap directly from the existence of an is/ought gap.[8]

5. NATURALISM AND NONNATURALISM

Third, one might think that the is/ought thesis undermines moral realism by undermining ethical naturalism. Moore thought that the is/ought thesis, in particular, the semantic thesis undermines ethical naturalism and, for that matter, ethical supernaturalism; he concluded that moral facts and properties are sui generis. Subsequent philosophers accepted Moore's rejection of naturalism and supernaturalism but found his commitment to nonnaturalism unacceptable. They concluded that there are no moral facts or properties and accepted some form of noncognitivism. Let me explain this argumentative strategy in more detail.

In 2.4 I briefly distinguished three views about the nature of the moral realist's moral facts and properties: ethical naturalism, ethical supernaturalism, and nonnaturalism. Naturalism and supernaturalism both deny the nonnaturalist's claim that moral facts and properties are sui generis; each claims that moral facts consist in some other, familiar kinds of facts. The ethical naturalist claims that moral facts and properties are natural (i.e., natural and social scientific) facts and properties; the supernaturalist claims that moral facts and properties are supernatural facts and properties. In order to understand the implications, real or alleged, of the is/ought thesis for naturalism and nonnaturalism, we must examine the metaphysical commitments of ethical naturalism in greater detail (most of my claims about naturalism apply mutatis mutandis to ethical supernaturalism).

Ethical naturalism claims that moral facts are nothing more than familiar facts about the natural, including social, world. I shall gloss this as the claim that moral facts *are* natural and social scientific

---

8 For instance, this reconstructs the reasoning of those who argue from the is/ought thesis to the assimilation of moral judgments and noncognitive moods such as the imperative mood. Sometimes this appears to be Hare's reasoning (see, e.g., 1963a: 2). At other times, as we have seen, Hare appears to argue for the is/ought thesis and against moral realism from a prior assimilation of moral judgments and prescriptions (e.g., Hare 1952: 28–9; cf. 6.1).

(e.g., social, psychological, economic, and biological) facts. To understand the import of this claim, we should distinguish between the 'is' of *identity* and the 'is' of *constitution*. Because 'are' can represent the 'is' of identity or the 'is' of constitution, naturalism can be construed as claiming either that moral facts and properties are identical with natural and social scientific facts and properties or that moral facts and properties are constituted by, but not identical with, natural and social scientific facts and properties.

The claim that moral properties are identical with natural and social scientific properties should and will be understood not as the absurd claim that distinct properties are nonetheless identical, but as the claim that moral terms and certain natural and social scientific terms designate or express the same properties (i.e., refer to the same properties in all possible worlds).[9] Understood as an identity claim, naturalism implies that moral properties and natural (i.e., natural and social scientific) properties are necessarily identical (Kripke 1971, 1980: 97–105; Wiggins 1980: 109–11, 214–15). Naturalistic identity claims should be construed on the model of other common identity claims, such as water = H_2O, temperature = mean kinetic molecular energy, light = electromagnetic radiation, pain = C-fiber firing.

If moral properties are identical with natural properties, they are constituted by natural properties. Identity implies constitution, but not vice versa. Moral properties can *be* natural properties, though, even if they are not identical with natural properties. F can be G even if the property (or properties) designated by 'F' is not (or are not) the same as that (or those) designated by 'G'. If G actually composes or realizes F, but F can be, or could have been, realized differently, then G constitutes, but is not identical with, F. For

9 Cf. Frankena 1939: 58; Kripke 1971, 1980: 97–105, 128–44. Although these property identities require both moral and nonmoral (e.g., natural or social scientific) predicates or general tems, neither predicate or term need correspond to a natural kind from the point of view of the discipline from which the predicate comes. In particular, moral properties could be identical with natural properties, even if there is no natural predicate that designates a natural kind from the point of view of, say, the natural sciences, so long as there is a natural predicate that is *constructible* (e.g., by operations of conjunction and disjunction) from predicates that do designate natural kinds from the point of view of the natural sciences. I shall later express some doubts about the existence of such identities. My point here is only to clarify the notion of property identity to which I appeal at this point: It does not require the existence of two predicates, each of which represents a natural kind from the point of view of the discipline from which it comes.

157

example, a table is constituted by, but not identical with, a particular arrangement of microphysical particles, since the table could survive certain changes in its particles or their arrangement. Similarly, moral properties are constituted by, but not identical with, natural properties if, though actually constituted or realized by natural properties, moral properties can be or could have been realized by properties not studied by the natural or social sciences. Moral properties may well be constituted by natural properties; they may be nothing over and above organized combinations of natural and social scientific properties. But if moral properties, though actually constituted by natural properties, could have been realized by some properties that are not natural – say, by supernatural properties of a divine being – then moral properties are not necessarily natural properties. Though constituted by natural properties, moral properties, on this counterfactual assumption, cannot be identical with natural properties.[10]

Moreover, the multiple realizability of moral facts and properties may provide another reason for resisting the identification of moral and natural properties. A plausible claim about a variety of property types and tokens (properties and property instances) is that they could have been realized in a variety of different ways. Functionalist theories of mind, for example, are based partly on this kind of claim about the one-many relationship between mental states and physical systems (e.g., Putnam 1975a: 418; Dennett 1978: xiv–xvi; Boyd 1980). A similar claim seems plausible about moral properties. For example, both the property of injustice and particular instances of injustice, in whatever social and economic conditions they are actually realized, could have been realized by a variety of somewhat different configurations of social and economic properties and property instances. Moral properties could have been realized by an indefinite and perhaps infinite number of sets of natural properties. If we deny that identity is a relation that can hold between relata

10 Of course, we shall not accept this counterfactual assumption, even though we agree that theism is possible, if we accept theological objectivism – the claim that if God were to exist, she would command all and only good or morally correct actions *because* these actions are good or right prior to and independently of God's will and because God herself is good. For if theological objectivism is true, we will not think that moral properties consist in properties of divine will even in those worlds in which God exists and commands all and only morally correct actions. So ethical naturalism, construed (even) as an identity thesis, is not undermined by God's possible existence if theological objectivism is true.

158

that are indefinitely or infinitely disjunctive – say, because we insist that identity holds only between genuine properties and we deny that disjunctive properties are genuine properties (cf. Armstrong 1978: II, 19–23) – then the multiple realizability of moral properties provides us with a reason for resisting the identification of moral and natural properties.

Similar reasoning applies to materialist and nonmaterialist versions of ethical naturalism. Materialism claims that all facts and properties – including natural and social scientific facts and properties – are organized combinations of physical facts and properties. If moral facts and properties were identical with these natural facts and properties, and these natural facts and properties were identical with certain organized combinations of physical facts and properties, then, because identity is transitive, moral facts and properties would have to be identical with certain configurations of physical facts and properties. But even if natural facts and properties, and thus moral facts and properties, are constituted by organized combinations of physical facts and properties, the natural and hence the moral facts and properties could have been realized both nonphysically and in an indefinite or infinite variety of physical ways. (Similar claims apply, mutatis mutandis, to nonmaterialist naturalism.) We have at least as much reason, then, and perhaps more, to resist the identification of moral facts and properties with organized combinations of physical (or, for that matter, nonphysical) facts and properties as we do to resist the identification of moral facts and properties with natural facts and properties.

There is perhaps some reason, then, to construe ethical naturalism (or, for that matter, ethical supernaturalism) as a claim about the constitution rather than the identity of moral facts and properties. Moral facts and properties, so construed, are constituted, composed, or realized by organized combinations of natural and social scientific facts and properties. The former are, then, in a certain sense nothing over and above the latter. This naturalist claim should be understood on the model of other common constitution claims: for instance, tables are constituted by certain combinations of microphysical particles, large scale social events such as wars and elections are constituted by enormously complex combinations of smaller scale social events and processes, biological processes such as photosynthesis are composed of physical events causally and temporally related in certain ways.

159

Although I think these are reasons to prefer the constitution to the identity construal of ethical naturalism, I shall not distinguish between these two construals of naturalism unless my argument requires me to.

Ethical naturalists often claim that moral facts and properties *supervene* on natural facts and properties. The supervenience of moral facts and properties on natural facts and properties follows from, but does not establish, ethical naturalism. I construe supervenience as a nomological or lawlike relation between, say, properties such that one property F (the supervening property) supervenes on another property or configuration of properties G (the base property or properties) just in case it is a law that if something is G, it is F.[11] One consequence of supervenience is that two things cannot differ in their supervening properties without differing in their base properties. Supervenience, so construed, does not imply naturalism (or supernaturalism), because supervening properties need be neither identical with nor constituted by base properties.[12] Naturalists claim that moral properties supervene on natural properties *because* moral properties are constituted by natural properties.

Because we can distinguish nomological relations that hold necessarily and those that hold contingently, in particular, only in the actual world and relevantly similar possible worlds, we can distinguish two kinds of supervenience: *strong* and *weak*. Ethical naturalism implies both strong and weak supervenience. With strong supervenience, base properties *necessitate* their supervening properties. Once the base properties are fixed, the supervening properties are thereby determined. Any world qualitatively identical with the ac-

---

11 Cf. Sidgwick 1907: 379–80; Moore 1922: 260–1; Broad 1930: 223; Ross 1930: 79, 89, 115, 155; Davidson 1970: 214; Blackburn 1971: 105–16; 1984: 182–7; Kim 1978, 1979, 1984a. Davidson, Blackburn, and Kim are the only ones here who use the term 'supervenience', but all assert a similar nomological relation to hold between properties of one kind and properties of another kind. Noncognitivists such as Hare often assert a similar relation to hold not between moral *properties* and nonmoral properties but between moral *judgments* and nonmoral properties; see Hare 1952: 80–1, 131, 145, 153–5, 176–7; 1981: 7. Hare's claim seems reducible to a constraint of consistency on the grounds of moral judgments.

12 For instance, epiphenomenalists can claim that mental states, though neither identical with nor constituted by physical states, supervene on physical states. Similarly, nonnaturalists can claim – Moore, Broad, and Ross did claim – that moral facts and properties, though nonnatural, supervene on natural facts and properties. (This claim needs to be, and will be, qualified in certain ways; see 6.6.)

tual world in respect of base properties must instantiate qualitatively identical supervening properties. Thus, for example, assuming materialism is true, any world qualitatively identical to the actual world at the microphysical level (including, of course, the *arrangement* of microphysical particles) must realize exactly the same set of supervening (e.g., chemical, biological, social, psychological) properties, including moral properties. But it is often difficult to identify a strong supervenience base, because it is often difficult to be sure a set of base properties includes all the properties required literally to necessitate a set of supervening properties. So we often settle for identifying the weak supervenience base. Weak supervenience states a contingent relation; weak base properties are *sufficient only in the circumstances* for their supervening properties. A set of properties F strongly supervenes on a set of properties G just in case G necessitates F. But if, even though G is sufficient in actual circumstances to produce F and would also produce F in relevantly similar counterfactual circumstances, the properties causally connected with G could have been different enough for G to produce H rather than F, then F only weakly supervenes upon G.

A nonmoral example might help illustrate the difference between strong and weak supervenience. Functionalists in the philosophy of mind claim that although C-fiber firings in the brain are sufficient in the circumstances to produce human pain, we could have had C-fiber firings without pain if enough other properties of human organisms and their relations to their environment had been different. Functionalists, therefore, should claim that human pain supervenes weakly, but not strongly, on C-fiber firings.

Similarly, certain social and economic conditions may be sufficient in our world (and nearby possible worlds) to cause social injustice, even if there are possible societies sufficiently different from our own in certain respects that these social and economic conditions would not constitute injustice. Injustice, then, supervenes weakly, but not strongly, on these social and economic conditions. Thus, there may always be a set of natural properties on which moral properties strongly supervene, even if we can only identify those natural properties on which moral properties weakly supervene.

I shall speak merely of supervenience where the distinction between weak and strong supervenience is not important.

161

As we have seen, moral realism is itself neutral between naturalism and nonnaturalism. But many think that moral realism nonetheless depends on naturalism in a certain way. They think this because they regard nonnaturalism as absurd. For whatever reason, nonnaturalism has been treated much less seriously than other forms of ontological pluralism, such as dualist theories of mind. The rejection of nonnaturalism makes moral realism depend on the success of naturalism (or supernaturalism).

This explains the third way in which the is/ought thesis can be thought to undermine moral realism. It is a common belief that the is/ought thesis, in particular, the semantic thesis, undermines the possibility of ethical naturalism (and, for that matter, of ethical supernaturalism). Moore's open-question argument is designed to show not just failure of synonymy between moral and natural (indeed, nonmoral) terms but failure of identity between moral and natural (indeed, nonmoral) properties. Relying on the failure of meaning implication between moral and nonmoral terms, one can construct a similar claim against the naturalist claim that moral properties, though nonidentical with natural properties, are constituted or realized by natural properties.

As we shall see, the argument against naturalism (and supernaturalism) depends on the claims that synonymy is a test of property identity and that meaning implication is a test of constitution or necessitation. Let *the semantic test of properties* represent these claims.[13] The motivation for the semantic test of properties lies, I think, in the philosophical tradition that views all necessary truths as analytic truths or truths by virtue of meaning. Both identity and constitution claims make intensional claims; identical properties are necessarily identical, and base properties/states/facts necessitate the properties/states/facts that they realize. If all necessity is analytic, we should expect the terms that designate or express the same property to be synonymous and constitutional supervening terms to be part of the meaning of constitutional base terms.[14] The semantic test of properties allows us to use the conclusions of the synonymy and meaning

13 The semantic *test* of properties can be distinguished from the semantic *theory* of properties. The latter view maintains that properties *are* meanings; see, for example, Armstrong 1978.
14 See, e.g., Lewis 1946: 65, 150–1; Carnap 1956: 1, 16, 19, 233–4, 242–3, 246. Cf. Putnam 1970: 305–6; 1973b: 119–20; 1975b; Schwartz 1977: 14–15, 18; Salmon 1982: 9–14, 153n.

implication arguments to formulate an *antinaturalist argument* that both nonnaturalists and noncognitivists accept.[15]

1. There are no meaning implications between moral and nonmoral, e.g., natural, terms.
2. Therefore, no moral term is synonymous with any nonmoral, e.g., natural, term.
3. Meaning determines intension: (a) terms express or designate the same property just in case they are synonymous, and (b) a pair of terms 'F' and 'G' stand for properties F and G such that G necessitates F just in case it is part of the meaning of 'G' that G things are F.
4. Therefore, moral properties are not identical with any nonmoral, e.g., natural, properties.
5. Therefore, moral properties or facts are not constituted by any nonmoral, e.g., natural, properties or facts.
6. Therefore, if moral terms express facts or properties, they must express nonnatural facts or properties that are sui generis, i.e., facts or properties that are neither identical with nor constituted by any nonmoral, e.g., natural, properties or facts.

Philosophers earlier in this century, such as Moore, Prichard, Ross, and Broad, accepted the argument for (6), thought that moral terms do express properties and facts, and so accepted nonnaturalism. Noncognitivists accept the argument for (6) but regard nonnaturalism as absurd or mysterious; they conclude that moral terms, though meaningful, do not express properties or state facts. Rather, moral terms have some noncognitive meaning (cf. Brandt 1959: 203–5, 214; Hancock 1974: 96–7). The noncognitivist conclusion, of course, is inconsistent with moral realism.

6. NATURALISM AND NONNATURALISM RECONSIDERED

I want to consider these three arguments against moral realism in reverse order, starting with the more traditional argumentative strategy I just described. The third argument combines the semantic thesis and the semantic test of properties to undermine ethical naturalism (and, for that matter, ethical supernaturalism). The antinaturalist argument appears valid. And although I raised some questions about the semantic thesis in 6.2, I agreed to concede that thesis for the sake of argument. So, we are to assume that (1) is true.

15 See Moore 1903: 10, 15–17; Ayer 1946: 104–5; Hare 1952: 81–5, 145, 154–5; 1963b: 246–7; 1981: 17–18 (see 6.1 for qualifications about Hare); Blackburn 1971: 105–16; 1984: 182–7, 221.

This leaves only premise (3) to question. Although I shall raise questions about (3) shortly, let us see what follows by conceding it. If we concede (3), we must concede (6). (6) requires the rejection of both naturalism and supernaturalism. In particular, (6) makes moral realism depend on the truth of nonnaturalism. Noncognitivists reject nonnaturalism as absurd or mysterious. Is this rejection justified? Nonnaturalism is supposed to be absurd, because sui generis (i.e., ontologically independent) facts and properties are supposed to be mysterious. Nonnaturalism would make moral facts and properties queer compared to natural facts and properties.

But this cannot be right. If we concede (3), we must concede (6) and the dependence of moral realism on nonnaturalism. But this should not worry the moral realist, because a kind of nonnaturalism will then be equally true about any other discipline; that is, the facts and properties of every discipline will be ontologically independent and, hence, sui generis. In 6.2 I claimed that if there is failure of synonymy and meaning implication between moral and nonmoral, for instance, natural, terms, then this is part of a quite general phenomenon. Synonymy and meaning implication are just as hard to establish between terms of any two disciplines. 'Water' and 'H$_2$O', 'temperature' and 'mean kinetic molecular energy', 'light' and 'electromagnetic radiation', 'pain' and 'C-fiber firing', 'table x' and 'microphysical particles a, b, c . . . organized in such and such a way', 'World War I' and 'events x, y, z . . . causally and temporally connected in such and such a way' are all pairs of terms between which neither synonymy nor meaning implication obtains. It is simply false that any speaker's criteria of application for one term of such a pair must contain his criteria of application for the other term of that pair as a proper subset. So, by (3), neither water and H$_2$O, nor temperature and mean kinetic molecular energy, nor light and electromagnetic radiation, nor human pain and C-fiber firing can be property identities. Tables cannot be constituted by arrangements of microphysical particles, and world wars cannot be constituted by social, political, and economic events. But these identity and constitution claims are just the kind of claims that chemistry, commonsense physical theory, neuropsychology, and history make. If (3) is correct, we must regard the properties/facts/states/events referred to by the terms of any discipline as sui generis or ontologically independent (cf. Putnam 1981:207). Any monistic ontological view must be false, and whatever connections there are between facts and proper-

164

ties of different disciplines must be purely contingent. Different kinds of facts and properties can weakly but not strongly supervene upon one another.[16]

So, if we accept (3), moral realism is committed to nonnaturalism. But this gives us no special complaint against moral realism. In particular, it gives us no reason to question the parity of moral realism with realism about the natural and social sciences, since these disciplines will be equally sui generis.

Of course, we can maintain moral realism by maintaining naturalism (or supernaturalism) if we give up (3). Property identity and constitution claims of the kind just mentioned have been an important part of extremely successful research programs in the natural and social sciences.[17] The a priori failure of standard claims in the natural and social sciences may lead us to question the semantic test of properties upon which the refutation of naturalism depends.

Perhaps we should question the philosophical tradition that motivates the semantic test of properties. Analyticity and necessity are distinct properties (cf. Kripke 1971: 84–5, 89, 1980: 34–9; Putnam 1973b: 130). Necessity is a *metaphysical* (modal) notion; the claim that something is necessary is the claim that things could not have been otherwise in certain respects. This characterization is episte-

16 Nonaturalists such as Moore, Broad, and Ross, however, defend the strong supervenience of moral properties on nonmoral properties. In his reply to critics Moore writes: "I should never have thought of suggesting that goodness was 'non-natural,' unless I had supposed that it was 'derivative' in the sense that, whenever a thing is good (in the sense in question) its goodness (in Mr. Broad's words) 'depends on the presence of certain non-ethical characteristics' possessed by the thing in question: I have always supposed that it did so 'depend,' in the sense that, if a thing is good (in my sense), then that it is so *follows* from the fact that it possesses certain natural intrinsic properties, which are such that from the fact that it is good it does *not follow* conversely that it has those properties" (1942: 588). Here Moore seems to be embracing the strong supervenience of moral properties on natural properties while denying ethical naturalism, at least construed as an identity claim. But it is quite unclear why Moore and others should hold this combination of views. If synonymy is a test of property identity and is so because all necessity is analytic, then meaning implication should also be a test of constitution and strong supervenience. So this combination of nonnaturalism and strong supervenience is inconsistent with the advocacy of the antinaturalist argument, as I have explained and motivated that argument. But perhaps this should not be too surprising, since the nonnaturalists did not distinguish between identity and constitution, or articulate clearly the argument against property identity, or see that this argument could be extended to constitution and strong supervenience claims.
17 Could the success of the sciences depend only on the sort of contingent nomological relations involved in weak supervenience?

165

mologically neutral; in particular, necessary truths are not character-ized as a priori. Analyticity, on the other hand, appears to be a *linguistic* or *semantic* notion; a claim that a statement is analytic appears to be a claim about language or the meaning of words. As such, analyticity is not epistemologically neutral; analytic truths are based on language and not experience and so are a priori, not a posteriori. Because the properties of analyticity and necessity are distinct in this way, we require some deep argument to connect them as the semantic test of properties does.

Philosophers of language, such as Saul Kripke (1980) and Hilary Putnam (1973a, 1973b, 1975b), have argued recently that we cannot maintain both the traditional theory of meaning according to which the meaning of a term is the set of properties that any speaker competent with the term associates with the term and the semantic test of properties according to which meaning determines inten-sion. If they are right and we accept the traditional theory of mean-ing that underlies the semantic thesis – and, hence, (1) – we must reject the semantic test of properties that underlies (3). If we reject (3), then synonymy is neither a necessary nor a sufficient condition for property identity, and meaning implication is neither a neces-sary nor a sufficient condition for either constitution or strong su-pervenience.[18] But this means that the semantic thesis has no bear-ing on naturalism (or supernaturalism). Even if the semantic thesis is true, nothing about the legitimacy of naturalism in ethics or elsewhere follows. The naturalist can concede that there are neither synonymies nor meaning implications between moral and non-moral, for instance, natural, terms and still maintain that moral facts and properties are identical with, or constituted by, natural and social scientific facts and properties. The naturalist's identity or constitution claims can be construed as expressing synthetic moral necessities.[19]

So, even if there is an is/ought gap, it does not commit moral realism to an absurd form of nonnaturalism. If there is an is/ought gap and we accept both the traditional theory of meaning underly-ing the semantic thesis and the semantic test of properties, then

18 Cf. Kripke 1971: 89; 1980: 128, 132–3, 138; Putnam 1970: 305–6; 1981: 84–5, 206–8, 1983: 53–5, 291; Fodor 1974; Hellman and Thompson 1975; Boyd 1980.
19 Cf. Klagge 1984; Adams 1981 defends the comparable claim for ethical super-naturalism.

nonnaturalism will be true but not absurd. A more attractive alternative is to accept the is/ought thesis and the traditional theory of meaning underlying the semantic thesis, if only for the sake of argument, and reject the semantic test of properties. This allows us to defend ethical naturalism (or, for that matter, ethical supernaturalism) even if there is an is/ought gap.

7. NIHILISM RECONSIDERED

The second argument also purports to undermine moral realism. It alleges that the fact, which the is/ought thesis ensures, that moral claims cannot be deduced from premises that are nonmoral and clearly fact-stating shows that moral claims cannot be fact-stating.

But this kind of argument proves too much. It could be used to show that no claims are, or could be, fact-stating. Philosophers of science concerned with intertheoretic reduction have long claimed that propositions in one scientific discipline cannot be deduced from propositions belonging to other scientific disciplines without the addition of bridge premises that nomologically connect possession of properties picked out by the discipline being reduced and properties picked out by the reducing discipline (cf. Nagel 1949, 1961: 343, 353–4; Fodor 1974; Kim 1978). A classic illustration of this claim is the inability to deduce the laws of thermodynamics from the laws of statistical mechanics without the aid of bridge premises, such as the Boyle-Charles law, which state lawlike relations between kinetic molecular energy and temperature. This observation can be generalized into the thesis that no proposition from a given discipline can be deduced from propositions all of which belong to other disciplines, without the aid of bridge premises. Moreover, defenders of the semantic thesis must recognize that these bridge premises are synthetic, not analytic. This shows that the is/ought thesis is structurally no different from various is/is gaps (e.g., between thermodynamics and other disciplines). Because every discipline is such that its propositions cannot be deduced only from other, clearly fact-stating disciplines, acceptance of the second argument would require us to deny that any discipline is fact-stating. I regard this as a reductio of the second argument. The fact that we treat is/is gaps as inferential gaps between fact-stating claims shows that the is/ought thesis provides no reason to deny that moral claims are fact-stating.

167

8. SKEPTICISM RECONSIDERED

The first argument we considered claims that the is/ought thesis undermines moral realism by supporting moral skepticism. The is/ought thesis may seem to undermine the possibility of the sort of evidential relations between moral and nonmoral beliefs required by moral realism and a coherence theory of justification in ethics. But this appearance is mistaken; the is/ought thesis does not undermine the possibility of evidential relations between moral and nonmoral beliefs. The is/ought thesis shows the need for moral bridge premises in the derivation of moral conclusions from nonmoral premises. This fact hardly demonstrates the impossibility of evidential relations between moral and nonmoral beliefs. First, it does not foreclose the possibility of deductive inferences between moral and nonmoral beliefs; indeed, it explains how they are possible. Deductive relations between moral and nonmoral statements are possible in the presence of moral bridge premises. Nor, as we have seen, is this fact peculiar to the inferential relations between moral and nonmoral statements. For instance, biological statements cannot be deduced from statements of particle physics (or any other discipline) without the addition of bridge premises identifying, or at least nomologically connecting, the possession of certain physical properties and the possession of certain biological properties. This is/is gap does not undermine the possibility of evidential relations between physical and biological beliefs. A belief that a certain physical state obtains is evidence for the belief that a certain biological state obtains, given justified belief in the appropriate bridge premises. Similarly, belief that some fact under a nonmoral description obtains is evidence that a certain moral fact obtains, given justified belief in the relevant moral bridge premises. To use our previous, highly simplified, example, the nonmoral belief that Spike could maximize pleasure by keeping his promise to Malcolm is evidence of Spike's moral obligation to keep his promise to Malcolm, given justified belief in the hedonistic utilitarian moral bridge premise that one has an obligation to do that action which maximizes pleasure. There may be grounds *independent* of the is/ought thesis for doubting that belief in moral bridge premises can be justified, and so for doubting that moral bridge premises can be fact-stating, but the is/ought thesis does not support such doubts. Moreover, I have already addressed a number of these independent grounds for doubt.

Belief in premises introduced to bridge either is/ought or is/is gaps is justified just in case that belief coheres in the appropriate way with other beliefs we hold.

Second, the is/ought thesis is defended with respect to deductive inference only. Whatever proponents of the is/ought thesis may have thought, they have never *argued for* the claim that there are no good nondeductive arguments from exclusively nonmoral premises to moral conclusions (or vice versa). Thus, the is/ought thesis leaves open the possibility not only of deductive inferences between moral and nonmoral statements in the presence of bridge premises but also the possibility of good nondeductive inferences between moral and nonmoral statements with, and perhaps without, the benefit of bridge premises. Partly because I do not pretend to know or be able to specify the canons of good nondeductive inference, I am not sure about the existence of good nondeductive inferences between moral and nonmoral statements without the aid of bridge premises. We should be cautious here, but the is/ought thesis, as typically formulated and defended, certainly does not preclude the existence of such inferences.

I assume that, whatever its exact specification, inference to the best explanation is a legitimate nondeductive inference pattern (cf. Harman 1965; 1973: 130–41, 149, 155–61). A belief is justified to some degree, according to this inference pattern, if its truth is the best explanation, given certain background assumptions, of other claims that are taken to be true. For example, in light of physical and optical theories that cohere with other theoretical and observational beliefs we hold, we may conclude with strong nondeductive warrant from a belief that there is a vapor trail in the cloud chamber that a proton passed through the cloud chamber. Now, given only *nonmoral* background assumptions, for example, that moral realism is true and that the appraisers in question are fully rational and fully informed, the moral fact that torturing kittens is wrong may provide the best explanation of the nonmoral fact that appraisers unanimously agree that pouring gasoline over a kitten and igniting it is wrong. Of course, one may question the background assumptions in either explanation. I have argued that moral realism is plausible; I have defended and will defend this claim against antirealist rebuttals. The present point is that the is/ought thesis does not undermine this explanation. (For more on moral explanation, see 7.3.)

But nothing of importance to moral realism depends on the availability of good nondeductive inferences between moral and nonmoral statements without the benefit of bridge premises. The preceding paragraph's nondeductive argument for the physical conclusion about protons helped itself to, among other things, background physical theories about microphysical particles and their behavior in supersaturated atmospheres. There is no reason to deprive nondeductive arguments for moral conclusions of similar help. In the light of moral theories about our responsibilities to animals, which cohere well with our other moral and nonmoral beliefs, we may conclude with strong nondeductive warrant from the fact that Malcolm and Vera poured gasoline over a kitten and ignited it that they did something wrong.

The is/ought thesis, therefore, does not support moral skepticism. Even if there is an is/ought gap, there may be evidential relations between moral and nonmoral beliefs. In particular, the is/ought thesis allows deductive inference between moral and nonmoral beliefs in the presence of belief in moral bridge premises and nondeductive inferences between moral and nonmoral beliefs with, and perhaps without, belief in moral bridge premises.

9. CONCLUSION

The truth or plausibility of moral realism does not require, as many assume it does, the falsity of the is/ought thesis. One may raise doubts about the existence of an is/ought gap, in particular, about the semantic thesis, but the moral realist can concede the is/ought thesis. Even if there is an is/ought gap, no antirealist consequences follow. Consideration of analogous is/is gaps shows that nonnaturalism need not make moral realism queer, that ethical naturalism (or, for that matter, ethical supernaturalism) is defensible, that there can be moral facts, and that there can be evidential relations between moral and nonmoral beliefs as coherentism requires.

7

A posteriori objections to moral realism

My case for moral realism depends on coherentism and the plausibility of belief in moral realism itself and in the reliability of considered moral beliefs. Chapter 6 considered rebuttals to these metaphysical and epistemological claims based on the existence of an is/ ought gap. My main concern in that chapter was to defend the *intelligibility* of the realist's metaphysical and epistemological claims against certain attacks. But even if moral realism makes intelligible metaphysical and epistemological claims that are initially plausible, there may nonetheless be good empirical reasons for rejecting these claims. In this chapter I consider a posteriori rebuttals to my case for moral realism. There are two kinds of argument I shall consider: one metaphysical, one epistemological. Although there have been many proponents of both kinds of argument, we can focus discussion by considering recent and perspicuous formulations of these arguments by J. L. Mackie (1977: chap. 1) and Gilbert Harman (1977: 3–23). Mackie's metaphysical argument claims that the moral realist's account of moral facts and properties, though intelligible, is queer or mysterious compared to the metaphysical commitments of recognizably realist disciplines such as the natural or social sciences. His epistemological argument claims there is no plausible methodology or theory of justification that a moral realist can hold. In particular, Mackie thinks that there are good a posteriori objections to intuitionism, and although he does not, we can construct a posteriori objections to a coherence theory of justification in ethics by appeal to Harman's argument for the observational immunity of moral theories and Mackie's argument from moral relativity or diversity. Harman claims that moral beliefs are not part of a coherent system of belief, because appeal to moral facts is nonexplanatory, whereas Mackie claims that moral beliefs are not part of a coherent system of belief, because the best explanation of moral

171

disagreement is the falsity of all moral beliefs. These a posteriori objections can be made from a variety of metaphysical or ontological standpoints. But the most common setting for such objections is against a materialist or physicalist backdrop.

1. METAPHYSICAL COMMITMENTS

The a posteriori metaphysical objection to moral realism claims that its metaphysical commitments are "queer" compared with those of recognizably realist disciplines such as the natural or social sciences. As Mackie puts it, "If there were objective values, then they would be entities or qualities of a very strange sort, utterly different from anything else in the universe" (1977: 38).

Objectively or intrinsically prescriptive moral facts are supposed to be especially queer or mysterious (1977: 40–1). But, I argued in Chapter 3, the moral realist can concede this; neither the motivational force nor the rationality of moral considerations is a conceptual truth about morality. The realist should reject this internalist assumption. Rather, whether a moral fact or its recognition motivates or provides reason for action depends, as the externalist claims, on the content of morality, a substantive theory of rationality or reasons for action, and a number of (possibly contingent) facts about agents and the world. Nor, as we have seen (3.4–3.13) and will see (8.6), does the truth of externalism prevent our providing a strong justification of the rationality of moral demands.

Although some of the special appeal of Mackie's metaphysical queerness objection derives from this internalist assumption, it applies to externalist versions of moral realism as well. Even if we deny that moral facts need to be intrinsically prescriptive, we may still wonder whether the realist's account of moral facts and properties is queer or mysterious.

The generic worry that the argument for metaphysical queerness expresses is that objective moral facts and properties would have to be so different from facts and properties with which we are familiar, and for which we think we have evidence, that although we can conceive of the existence of moral facts and properties, we have good a posteriori reason to doubt their existence and so to reject moral realism. This generic worry does not depend on any particular ontological assumptions. Anyone might have this worry, so long as the metaphysical commitments of moral realism seem queer

172

when compared with a base of acceptable metaphysical commitments, whatever they might be. For example, a psychological dualist can think moral realism metaphysically queer if its commitments seem strange compared with the commitments of either mental or material substance. By far the more common form this metaphysical worry takes, however, involves materialist ontological assumptions. On this view, moral realism is metaphysically unacceptable, because moral facts and properties cannot be accommodated within a materialist or physicalist world view and so must be strangely sui generis (Mackie 1977: 38–42; Putnam 1981: 211; Field 1982: 562; Harman 1982: 569).

In assessing both generic and materialist forms of this objection, we should ask ourselves what the appropriate reaction would be to a demonstration of the metaphysical queerness of moral realism. If the metaphysical commitments of moral realism turned out to be quite unlike the metaphysical commitments of any other discipline that we regard as realist, would we be justified in rejecting moral realism? Of course, opponents of moral realism think so, but I am less sure. Granted, the case for moral realism would not be as strong in this event as it would be were the metaphysical commitments of moral realism more familiar. But whether we would actually be justified in rejecting moral realism is another matter and would depend on some further issues. First, we would need to know how similar the metaphysical commitments of recognizably realist disciplines are. Only if these are similar to each other and yet quite different from those of moral realism would moral realism's metaphysical queerness be a serious objection to it. Also, we would have to decide just how strong the presumption in favor of moral realism is. For if we accept the evidence for moral realism (Chapters 2–4), it is open to us to accept the metaphysical queerness of moral realism as the (perhaps unhappy) truth about morality. Moreover, our reaction may be affected by our assessment of moral realism's consequences. If, as I argued, rejection of moral realism would undermine the nature of existing normative practices and beliefs, then the metaphysical queerness of moral realism may seem a small price to pay to preserve these normative practices and beliefs. I am not claiming that the presumption in favor of moral realism could not be overturned on a posteriori metaphysical grounds. I am claiming only that we could not determine the appropriate reaction to the

173

success of this metaphysical argument until we determined, among other things, the strength of the presumption in favor of moral realism. Fortunately, it is not necessary to make fine determinations of this sort. For the metaphysical commitments of moral realism are not unlike those of recognizably realist disciplines and can be accommodated within a materialist ontology.

The generic a posteriori metaphysical objection to moral realism assumes that moral facts and properties would have to be sui generis, that is, ontologically independent of those facts and properties, whichever they are, with which we are familiar and for which we believe we have evidence. The standard defense of this assumption appeals to the is/ought thesis, in particular, the semantic thesis and the semantic test of properties. These claims constitute the antinaturalist argument that purports to show that moral facts and properties can be neither identical with nor constituted by natural facts and properties (or, for that matter, supernatural facts and properties). If moral facts and properties are sui generis, aren't they queer?

But in order to establish that the metaphysical commitments of moral realism are queer when compared with those of recognizably realist disciplines, the antirealist must be able to show that moral facts and properties *alone* are sui generis. But this is just what Chapter 6 argued the antinaturalist argument could not demonstrate. The is/ought thesis and the semantic test of properties imply that moral facts and properties are sui generis, but similar considerations show that every discipline is sui generis. The existence of is/is gaps (e.g., between biology and other disciplines) and the semantic test of properties show that facts and properties in one discipline (e.g., biology) are neither identical with nor constituted by facts and properties in other disciplines we regard as objective. On these grounds, it follows that every discipline is sui generis. The connections between facts and properties of different disciplines can only be contingent. Facts and properties in one discipline can weakly but not strongly supervene on facts and properties in other disciplines (cf. 6.5–6.6).

This shows that the standard grounds for construing moral facts and properties as sui generis are equally reasons for construing any objective fact or property as sui generis. Since the queerness argument is supposed to express a *comparative* worry about the metaphysical commitments of moral realism, moral realism cannot be metaphysically queer on these grounds.

174

As we saw in Chapter 6, the realist is not committed to nonnaturalism. Indeed, just because the standard reason for saddling moral realism with nonnaturalism can be generalized so as to yield the conclusion that every discipline is sui generis, some would view the previous argument as a reductio of the semantic test of properties. If we reject the semantic test of properties, as I suggested we could (6.6), then the is/ought thesis erects no barrier to the ethical naturalist's claim that moral facts and properties are natural facts and properties (or, for that matter, to the ethical supernaturalist's claim that moral facts and properties are supernatural facts and properties).

Now, someone could think that the ethical naturalist's claim, though intelligible, is still queer compared with the metaphysical commitments of other recognizably realist disciplines. Mackie queries how moral facts and properties could be ontologically dependent on natural facts and properties.

Another way of bringing out this queerness is to ask about anything that is supposed to have some objective moral quality, how this is linked with its natural features. What is the connection between the natural fact that an action is a case of deliberate cruelty – say, causing pain just for fun – and the moral fact that it is wrong? It cannot be an entailment, a logical or semantic necessity. Yet it is not merely that the two features occur together. The wrongness must somehow be 'consequential' or 'supervenient'; it is wrong because it is a piece of deliberate cruelty. But just what *in the world* is signified by this 'because'? (1977: 41)

If supervenience is construed as a nomological or lawlike relation (6.5–6.6), then the ethical naturalist will claim that moral facts and properties supervene on natural (i.e., natural and social scientific) facts and properties. According to the naturalist, moral facts and properties both weakly and strongly supervene on natural facts and properties. Moral facts and properties strongly supervene on natural facts and properties because some sets of natural properties necessitate certain sets of moral properties. Because he rejects a semantic test of properties, the ethical naturalist denies that this necessary relation represents either logical or conceptual necessity; instead, it represents metaphysical necessity or necessity a posteriori. Which moral properties strongly supervene on which natural properties is determined differently by different moral theories, just as, say, which economic properties strongly supervene on which social and psychological properties is determined differently by different economic theories.

175

But, as we noted (6.5), it will often be difficult, even assuming a particular moral theory, to identify the strong supervenience base of natural properties of a given set of moral properties. This is because it is often difficult to identify those natural properties that literally necessitate a set of moral properties. It is easier to identify the weak supervenience base for a set of moral properties, which is the set of natural properties sufficient in the circumstances for those moral properties. Thus, for example, we are much more likely to be able to identify social and economic conditions that in the actual world (and nearby possible worlds) constitute injustice than we are to be able to identify social and economic conditions that would constitute injustice in any possible society. And as with strong supervenience, just which moral properties weakly supervene on which natural properties is determined differently by different moral theories.

Because supervenience is a purely nomological relation, it is compatible with a wide variety of views about what other metaphysical relations hold between the relata. The ethical naturalist claims that moral facts and properties supervene upon natural facts and properties, because moral facts and properties *are* natural facts and properties. Different naturalistic claims can be distinguished by distinguishing different ways of construing the claim that moral properties are natural properties. As we have seen (6.5), we can distinguish between the 'is' of identity and the 'is' of constitution. If 'are' represents the 'is' of identity, then moral properties are natural properties, because they are identical with natural properties. Because the ethical naturalist rejects the semantic test of properties, the failure of synonymy between moral and natural terms does not interfere with the theoretical identification of moral and natural properties. There is nothing metaphysically queer about an ethical naturalist's identification of moral and natural properties. So construed, ethical naturalism requires theoretical identifications of moral and natural properties similar to other familiar theoretical identifications, for instance, water = H_2O, temperature = mean kinetic molecular energy, light = electromagnetic radiation. Hedonistic utilitarianism, for example, can be construed as making one such naturalistic claim; it claims that rightness = the maximization of pleasure.

The ethical naturalist must claim that moral properties are realized by natural properties, but, as we also saw (6.5), there may be some reason for the naturalist to resist the identification of moral and natural properties. For a moral property to be identical with a natural property, they must be necessarily identical. But it may seem that moral properties, even though actually realized by natural properties, could have been realized by properties that are not natural, for instance, supernatural properties. If so, moral properties are not necessarily natural properties and so cannot be identical with natural properties. Moreover, the fact that moral properties can be realized by an indefinite and perhaps infinite number of combinations of natural properties provides another reason for resisting the identification of moral and natural properties, if we assume that identity is a relation that cannot hold between relata that are indefinitely or infinitely disjunctive.

Moral properties can be natural properties, as the naturalist maintains, even if moral properties are not identical with natural properties. The ethical naturalist can appeal to the 'is' of constitution. Ethical naturalism, on this construal, claims that moral properties are constituted, composed, or realized by different combinations of natural and social scientific properties. Moral properties are nothing over and above organized configurations of natural properties. Moreover, these constitution claims do not guarantee reductive definitions for moral terms. Because she rejects the semantic test of properties, the ethical naturalist can claim that moral properties are constituted by natural properties, even if there are no meaning implications between natural and moral terms.

The ethical naturalist's appeal to the constitution of moral facts by natural facts is not metaphysically queer. This relation of constitution, composition, or realization is quite familiar. Tables are constituted by certain arrangements of microphysical particles; biological processes such as photosynthesis are constituted by physical and chemical events causally related in certain ways; psychological states are constituted by certain arrangements of brain states; and large scale social events such as wars and elections are constituted by enormously complex sets of smaller scale social and political events causally and temporally related in certain ways.

None of the metaphysical commitments of the ethical naturalist seems unusual compared with those of recognizably realist disciplines. Moral facts and properties are constituted by, and so supervene upon, natural (i.e., natural and social scientific) facts and properties. Determination of just which natural facts and properties

177

constitute which moral facts and properties is a matter of substantive moral theory, just as which natural facts and properties constitute which economic facts and properties is a matter of substantive economic theory. (See, for example, my discussion of the metaphysical implications of objective utilitarianism in 8.5.)

Some will claim that the metaphysical queerness of moral realism arises only in trying to give an account of realism's metaphysical commitments on materialist or physicalist assumptions. Moral facts and properties, although intelligible, cannot be accommodated within a materialist ontological world view, and we have good a posteriori evidence for the truth of materialism (cf. Putnam 1981: 211; Field 1982: 562; Harman 1982: 569).

The moral realist's response to this objection should be fairly clear by now. A materialist account of moral facts and properties should be no harder to give than is a materialist account of other supervenient facts and properties. Materialism is a monistic ontological view that claims all facts and properties are physical. Physical properties are basic properties of matter, and physical facts are the possession by particulars of physical properties. If materialism is true, higher-order facts and properties, such as chemical, biological, social, psychological, and economic facts and properties, must be physical facts and properties – in particular, organized combinations of physical facts and properties. Since we can distinguish between the 'is' of identity and the 'is' of constitution, we can distinguish two versions of materialism: identity materialism and constitutional materialism. There are what should by now be familiar reasons to prefer constitutional to identity materialism. If materialism is only contingently true, then higher-order properties, though actually physical properties, could have been realized nonphysically. If so, these higher-order properties are not necessarily physical properties and so cannot be identical with physical properties. Moreover, higher-order properties and property instances could have been realized in a variety of different physical ways. If we deny that identity is a relation that can hold between relata that are indefinitely or infinitely disjunctive, the multiple realizability of these higher-order properties provides reason to deny that they are identical with physical properties. Thus a materialist may prefer to claim that higher-order properties are constituted by, but not identical with, organized combinations of physical properties. On this view, higher-order properties are in some sense nothing over and above organized configurations of physical properties. Different kinds of higher-order properties are different kinds of configurations of physical properties that hang together explanatorily.

A materialist version of ethical naturalism will make the same claims about moral facts and properties; moral facts and properties are just one kind of higher-order fact and property. If the higher-order natural and social scientific facts and properties that constitute moral facts and properties are themselves constituted by organized combinations of physical facts and properties, then, by the transitivity of constitution, moral facts and properties are also constituted by organized combinations of physical facts and properties. So, if materialism is true, moral facts and properties are constituted by, but not identical with, organized combinations of physical facts and properties. They are organized combinations of physical facts and properties that hang together explanatorily.

A materialist version of ethical naturalism follows from the truth of materialism, as do materialist versions of other higher-order properties, and the metaphysical commitments of this version of ethical naturalism are no stranger than those of materialist versions of any other higher-order properties. But, of course, these metaphysical claims aid substantive moral investigation no more than they aid substantive investigation in any other higher-order discipline. For, although the truth of materialism assures us that there is some configuration of physical properties by which any higher-order property is realized, this gives us no idea which configurations of physical properties these are. Indeed, it may be practically, if not theoretically, impossible to identify the physical realization of many, if not all, higher-order properties. Because different kinds of higher-order properties figure in different lawlike and explanatory relations, it should not be surprising if we could not identify the set and organization of physical properties that realize some moral property, say, injustice. This should be no more surprising than our inability to state the set and organization of physical properties that realize some economic property, say, inflation. A higher-order property can support interesting generalizations and so be explanatory. But because higher-order properties can be, and could have been, realized by an indefinite number of sets and configurations of physical properties, the particular combinations and organizations of physical properties that in fact realize this higher-order property need figure in no interesting generalizations and certainly not in

179

those in which the higher-order property figures (cf. Fodor 1974; Garfinkel 1981: chap. 2; 7.3). The metaphysical commitments of moral realism, therefore, do not become queer on materialist assumptions. Materialist versions of ethical naturalism represent moral facts and properties as being, like other higher-order facts and properties, constituted by, and so supervenient on, organized combinations of physical facts and properties.

2. EPISTEMOLOGICAL COMMITMENTS

In addition to his metaphysical complaint about "what in the world" a moral fact would be, Mackie lodges an epistemological complaint about how we could know when a moral fact obtains (1977: 38, 41). We may know that certain natural facts or facts under a nonmoral description obtain, but how would we know or go about finding out whether these natural facts realize any moral facts and, if so, which? Mackie claims that we could gain this kind of moral knowledge only if we had special faculties of moral perception of the sort that some versions of intuitionism ensure: "Correspondingly, if we were aware of them [objective values], it would have to be by some special faculty of moral perception or intuition, utterly different from our ordinary ways of knowing everything else" (1977: 38). But, Mackie claims, we have good a posteriori grounds for believing that no such faculties exist. Therefore, barring the cognitive inaccessibility of moral facts, moral realism must be false.

The belief that moral realism is committed to an intuitionist epistemology rests, in Mackie's case, on the unnecessary metaphysical assumption that moral facts would have to be sui generis. Only if moral facts were metaphysically queer sorts of facts would we need some such special faculty for cognitive access to them. As we have seen (5.3), even this is not clear. The belief that intuitionism is committed to the existence of special faculties of moral perception probably rests on a mistaken view of the status of perceptual belief in a foundationalist epistemology; intuitionism need only claim that some moral beliefs are self-evident. In any case, moral realism is not committed to nonnaturalism; moral facts can be natural facts. This eliminates any need for special faculties of moral perception. Of course, a moral realist could still embrace an intuitionist epistemology. But I have argued at length that the realist should reject intuitionist and other foundationalist epistemologies and defend a coher-

180

ence theory of justification in ethics. Belief that a set of natural facts realizes some particular moral fact is justified just in case it coheres in the appropriate way with our other beliefs, both moral and nonmoral. Chapter 6 explained how inferential relations between moral and nonmoral beliefs were possible. Deductive and nondeductive inferences between moral and nonmoral beliefs are possible given belief in the appropriate moral bridge premises. We have reason to regard these inferences as sound or good just in case we have reason to regard the premises – in particular, the moral bridge premises – as true, and, of course, we have reason for this if the moral bridge premises cohere in the appropriate way with our other beliefs, both moral and nonmoral. Coherentism thus makes moral methodology, like other methodologies, highly theory-dependent by making good inferences depend on background bodies of coherent theory.

This appeal to coherentism raises another a posteriori worry about moral realism. For although Chapter 6 explains how moral realism and coherentism are compossible, someone might argue that none of our moral beliefs does in fact form part of an appropriately coherent system of beliefs. In particular, one might argue, coherence is primarily an explanatory relation, and although there might have been explanatory relations between moral and nonmoral beliefs, there are none of the sort required to establish the coherence of moral beliefs. We can construct two arguments for this antirealist claim. The first relies on Harman's claim that moral facts are not needed in and, indeed, are completely irrelevant to, the explanation of nonmoral facts. The second relies on Mackie's claim that the nonexistence of moral facts is the best explanation of the nonmoral fact of pervasive moral disagreement.

As with the a posteriori metaphysical objection, we may wonder just what this epistemological objection would show even if it were well grounded. No doubt the success of Harman's or Mackie's argument would make moral realism less plausible than it would otherwise be. But would the success of either argument warrant the rejection of moral realism? Perhaps moral beliefs do not provide explanatory support for nonmoral beliefs, or perhaps certain nonmoral beliefs provide explanatory support for nihilism. Moral beliefs (together with the appropriate nonmoral beliefs) could still form a belief system that was internally coherent. Whether this

181

would be sufficient reason for maintaining belief in moral realism might depend on the strength of the presumption in favor of moral realism and on the consequences of rejecting moral realism and adopting some form of antirealism. As before, I do not claim that an a posteriori argument could not overturn the case for moral realism. I claim only that the appropriate reaction to the success of such an argument would depend in part on the other successes and failures of moral realism. Fortunately, we do not need to decide this issue, since the moral realist can account for the explanatory power of moral facts and the nature of moral disagreement.

3. MORAL EXPLANATION

Harman accepts coherentism's claim that the coherence of our moral beliefs would be evidence of their truth. Scientific beliefs are coherent with our other beliefs, because scientific facts are needed to explain other facts, in particular, our observations. Moral beliefs would be coherent with our other beliefs, according to Harman, if, and only if, moral facts were needed to explain nonmoral facts such as the occurrence of the moral judgments we make. But, he claims, this is the basic problem with ethics – its immunity from observational testing (1977: vii–viii, 9, 11, 130; 1986). *Even if there were moral facts,* they would be "completely irrelevant" to the explanation of any nonmoral phenomenon (1977: 7).

Harman himself thinks that the "basic problem with ethics" can be met by adopting the appropriate "naturalistic reduction" of moral claims to psychological facts about how an impartial appraiser would react to various situations (1977: 13–23, 41–52; 1986: 62, 66–7). However, I doubt that this "reduction" is necessary to meet or solve the problem, and I doubt that it is a solution that should appeal to the moral realist.[1]

Harman presupposes that an a posteriori defense of moral realism requires that moral facts be explanatory of nonmoral facts. However, it is not clear that this should be a necessary condition on a defense of moral realism.[2] We can concede that coherence is primarily an explanatory relation. But it is not clear that moral facts need

---

1 Harman joins his brand of naturalism with a form of moral relativism (see 3.5–3.6), which any robust form of moral realism should reject.
2 Nagel (1980: 114n) rejects this as a necessary condition on a defense of moral realism, but he does not explain why. Also see McDowell 1985: 118.

explain *non*moral facts in order for our moral beliefs to be coherent. Harman argues that even if there were moral facts, they would not explain any nonmoral facts and concludes that even if there were moral facts, they would be nonexplanatory. From this it follows that moral beliefs are not coherent and, hence, not justified. But if there were moral facts, they could be explanatory without explaining nonmoral facts; they could and would explain other *moral* facts. For instance, the truth of a particular moral theory would explain the rightness or wrongness of particular action types and tokens.

Someone might reply that this kind of explanatory power cannot be evidential, because many kinds of facts, including supernatural or magical facts, are such that *if they existed,* some of them would be needed to explain others. But the realist need not accept the parity of moral facts and supernatural or magical facts. She can claim that within the class of facts that would be explanatory of their own kind, we need to distinguish between facts that are consistent with our other beliefs and those that are not. What is objectionable about magical facts, the moral realist can claim, is that they are incompatible with natural facts. Appeals to magical and natural facts provide competing explanations of the same phenomena. Our evidence for these natural facts undermines belief in magical facts. But moral facts are not, or at least we have not yet seen any argument establishing that they are, incompatible with natural facts. If, as I shall argue in the next section, the explanation of nonmoral facts about disagreement does not require nihilism, then the coherence of our moral beliefs with each other can be evidential.

I do not concede Harman's claim that moral facts are irrelevant to the explanation of nonmoral facts. I only claim that an a posteriori defense of moral realism does not obviously require that moral facts explain nonmoral facts in order for them to be explanatory.

In fact, moral facts do seem explanatory of nonmoral facts. Sometimes Harman argues that moral facts are nonexplanatory because moral beliefs are immune to observational testing (1977: vii, 4). But, as we have seen (5.9), this claim is false. Moral beliefs, like scientific beliefs, can be observationally tested, but, again like scientific beliefs, only in a holistic or theory-dependent manner. Just as a scientific theory has observational consequences only when conjoined with auxiliary scientific principles, so, too, moral principles have observational consequences but only when conjoined with auxiliary moral principles. As in an earlier example, my moral principle that it is good people who keep their promises when doing so involves great personal sacrifice has no observational implications by itself. But when I conjoin it with my independent moral belief that Zenobia is a good person, I can obtain the observational prediction that Zenobia will keep her promise to Zelda even at great personal sacrifice. My independent moral belief that Barney is thoroughly rotten, together with my moral principle, leads me to expect that Barney will not suffer the personal hardship needed to keep his promise to Bonny. The difficulties surrounding the interpretation of predictive results (success or failure) raise interesting questions about theory confirmation (discussed briefly in 5.9), but I see no special difficulties here for the testing of moral claims. It seems simply false, therefore, that moral beliefs are immune from observational testing.

Perhaps moral beliefs have observational consequences in this way and still fail to cohere with nonmoral beliefs. Harman argues that moral facts would be nonexplanatory, because even if there were moral facts, they would, in contrast with scientific facts, be completely irrelevant to the *explanation* of nonmoral facts.

This, too, seems false. I have argued that (evidence-independent) moral facts are needed to explain various nonmoral facts about the way in which we make moral judgments and argue and deliberate in moral matters (2.5–2.8). Doesn't this show that moral facts explain nonmoral facts? Harman must be interested in a still narrower class of explananda. (Perhaps he thinks that my explananda in Chapter 2 are too philosophical.) He claims that moral facts are irrelevant to the explanation of why we make the moral judgments we do, while scientific facts are needed to explain the observational judgments we make. Although this focus on the occurrence of moral judgments may unfairly restrict the class of explananda, and so may prejudice Harman's case against moral explanation, let us look more closely at his claim that moral facts are irrelevant to the explanation of the moral judgments we make.

Harman attempts to illustrate this claim by comparing two cases. In the first case a scientist performs an experiment in which she observes a vapor trail in a cloud chamber and makes the judgment 'there goes a proton'. In the second case someone, call him Spike, comes upon children setting a cat on fire and makes the judgment 'those children are wicked'. Harman claims that the assumption that there was a proton in the cloud chamber is needed to explain the scientist's judgment, but that the assumption that the children's act was wrong or wicked is irrelevant to the explanation of Spike's judgment.

The observation of an event can provide observational evidence for or against a scientific theory in the sense that the truth of that observation can be relevant to a reasonable explanation of why that observation was made. A moral observation does not seem, in the same sense, to be observational evidence for or against any moral theory, since the truth or falsity of the moral observation seems to be completely irrelevant to any reasonable explanation of why that observation was made. The fact that the observation of the event was made at the time it was made is evidence not only about the observer but about the physical facts. The fact that you made a particular moral observation when you did does not seem to be evidence about moral facts, only evidence about you and your moral sensibility. (1977: 7)

The idea here seems to be that in the explanation of moral judgments we need make no reference to moral *facts*, only to nonmoral facts and the appraiser's moral *beliefs* (also see 1986: 62).

But Harman fails to demonstrate any explanatory disanalogy between the scientific and moral cases. If we make no assumptions about the truth of Spike's moral judgment and theoretical commitments, then it is true that we can provide a certain kind of explanation of Spike's moral judgment by appeal to his "psychological set" alone. Spike judged that the children were doing something wrong, because he believed both that they were needlessly setting a cat on fire and that pointless cruelty is wrong. This explanation contains no commitment to moral facts, only commitment to Spike's beliefs or psychological set. But if we make no assumptions about the truth of the scientist's observational judgment and theoretical commitments, then it is equally true that we can provide a kind of explanation of her judgment by appeal to her psychological set alone. The scientist judged that a proton was passing through the cloud chamber, because she believed, among other things, both that there was a vapor trail in the cloud chamber and a scientific theory about the behavior and observational consequences of protons in supersaturated atmospheres. This explanation contains no commitment to protons (or cloud chambers), only commitments to the scientist's beliefs or psychological set. Both putative explanations are by appeal to psychological set *alone;* just as the explanation of Spike's judgment mentions his moral beliefs, rather than moral facts, so, too, both explanations mention only nonmoral beliefs, not nonmoral facts. There seems, therefore, to be nothing peculiar about moral explanations here. Explanations in terms of psychological set alone are as available and, it seems, as plausible in the scientific case as in the moral case.

However, purely psychological explanations typically seem inadequate. We want an explanation of why the person, whose psychology is being invoked, holds the beliefs that he does. Why does the scientist believe there was a vapor trail in the cloud chamber, and why does she hold the microphysical theory that she does? An adequate explanation of this may begin by referring to other features of her psychological set and to the cultural and institutional influences on her acceptance of the microphysical theory (e.g., her training). But unless we regard her training as in some way mistaken, the explanation of these things is likely to refer, eventually and in part, to the existence of microphysical particles and laws governing their behavior and to people's recognition and transmission of these facts. Similarly, the initial explanation of Spike's judgment in terms of psychological set alone leaves unexplained, among other things, why Spike believes that pointless cruelty is wrong. If we are to explain this, we must go beyond his psychological set and look to facts. We may, no doubt, mention facts about Spike's moral education and other psychological influences. But we need to explain these influences, and unless we regard this education as mistaken or in some way biased, its explanation is likely to refer, eventually and in part, to moral facts, their recognition and transmission. (Remember, Harman grants us that there are moral facts; his position is that *even if there were moral facts,* they would be completely irrelevant to the explanation of anything. So there can be no objection to this talk about the truth of Spike's moral beliefs or of those of his educators.) In order to reject explanations in terms of psychological set alone, therefore, we must assume the truth of a number of background beliefs. If we assume the truth of enough of the scientist's theoretical beliefs (e.g., about microphysics and the normality of the test conditions), then the existence of a proton in the cloud chamber may well help to explain her judgment. But equally, if we assume the truth of enough of Spike's moral beliefs, then the wrongness of the children's act may well help to explain his judgment.

Harman's own discussion centers on the explanation of the occurrence of moral judgments. But there are other nonmoral explananda for which we might offer moral explanations. Consider the events that are potential objects of moral assessment or judgment. We often explain people's actions by appeal to moral features of their character, and, of course, these facts in turn help explain our assessments both of their character and of their actions. For example, we explain a good deal of Caligula's behavior, such as his execution of innocent people, by appeal to his cruelty, and the fact that he had this character vice explains, in large part, our opinion of him and his actions. According to popular accounts (but see, e.g., Fehrenbacher 1981: 238–40, 259–60), it is the fact that Lincoln was a fair and just man that explains his opposition to slavery and, non-coincidentally, the high regard in which he is held today. Moreover, we often explain social facts and events, as well as individuals' actions, by appeal to moral facts about social and legal institutions. We think that political vices (e.g., social injustice) sometimes cause, and so help explain, instability, protest movements, and revolutions; and we think that the political virtues of a society's laws and institutions (e.g., its social justice) can help explain its stability. Thus, we might cite the injustice of slavery as part of the explanation of its demise or the injustice of the South African political and legal system as the cause of its instability and of protest against apartheid. So, too, we might cite the political virtues of a constitutional democracy incorporating a separation of powers and individual rights as part of the explanation of the stability of the U.S. government. Exactly how good these moral explanations are is an empirical matter that will vary from case to case, but they all sound familiar and promising; the appeal to moral facts they involve does not seem "completely irrelevant."

In explaining people's moral judgments of other people and actions, we will often appeal (correctly) to, among other things, the appraiser's moral beliefs. The questions then are whether this shows anything peculiar about the explanation of moral judgments and whether appeal to psychological set alone is adequate. I have suggested that the answer to both questions is no. Now, the moral explanations of individual actions and social events that I just presented do not even mention anyone's moral beliefs. What is wrong with them?

Someone might suggest that we could also explain these events by referring only to nonmoral facts and people's beliefs, especially their moral beliefs, and not to moral facts (cf. Quinn 1986: 529–30). We can explain people's actions by citing their circumstances, their beliefs about their circumstances, and their collateral beliefs and desires. Thus, we might explain Caligula's behavior by appeal to

187

his insensitivity to others' pain or to his political agenda. We might explain Lincoln's behavior by appeal to the nature and consequences of slavery and his moral assessment of these facts. We might try to explain social events by appeal to the circumstances, beliefs, and desires of the actors involved. Thus, we might explain the demise of slavery in this way by appeal to social and psychological facts about slavery and the relevant people's (e.g., slaves' and abolitionists') *beliefs* that slavery is wrong, without having to mention the fact that it was wrong. And we might explain the instability in South Africa and protests against apartheid by appeal to the social and economic conditions in South Africa together with the *beliefs* of black South Africans and their white sympathizers that these conditions are unjust.

What should we make of this reply? First, it is unclear what the force of this response is, even if it is true. As we have seen, Harman claims that appeal to moral facts is always "completely irrelevant" explanatorily. What does the *availability* of such explanations in terms of nonmoral fact and moral belief show about the legitimacy or relevance of the moral explanations of the same events? Their availability, by itself, does not seem to undermine the moral explanations, much less does it show them to be completely irrelevant.

Second, we might claim, as before, that if we can avoid reference to moral facts by appeal to moral beliefs, then we can equally avoid reference to any facts and give our explanations in terms of psychological set alone. And we noted above in our discussion of the explanation of moral judgments that explanations in terms of psychological set alone are a perfectly general possibility, not restricted to events for which we might initially offer moral explanations, and that, moreover, they seem typically to be explanatorily inadequate.

Third, there are cases where a certain kind of fact can explain events, where an agent's belief in that fact could not possibly provide an explanation of the events in question, since the agent does not recognize the fact. Consider the case of Zach and Zenobia. Zach is being unfaithful to Zenobia, but Zenobia does not realize this. Nonetheless, Zach's infidelity manifests itself in his relations with Zenobia: He is quick to find fault with her, he is more distant, and he spends less time with her. Zenobia subconsciously responds to these changes in Zach's behavior: She has trouble sleeping; she finds it difficult to concentrate at work; her job performance slips a little. Now, we would naturally cite Zach's affair as at least part of the explanation of both Zach's own behavior and the changes in Zenobia's behavior. But, of course, we could not cite Zenobia's belief that Zach is having an affair as even a possible explanation of the changes in her behavior. And if Zenobia begins to reflect on these and other changes in the appropriate way, she may come to believe that Zach is having an affair. If so, the fact that Zach is having an affair will be part of the explanation of Zenobia's coming to believe this to be the case.

In a similar way, there will be cases where the causal efficacy and explanatory power of moral facts precede their recognition (cf. Railton 1986). Because, perhaps, of prevailing ideology I may regard my society as basically just, but its laws and institutions are, in fact, unjust. In particular, they deprive members of my class of significant social goods and opportunities in a systematic, if ideologically disguised, way. Though still under the belief that my society is basically just and that people are responsible for their own social positions, I begin to feel (unreflective) resentment about my own social position. I also begin to sympathize with other disadvantaged members of my class as I get to know them and their circumstances. In time, I begin to reflect on this resentment and sympathy and to examine the comparative social position of people in my class and its explanation. This reflection eventually produces the belief that my society is fundamentally unjust, and this in turn leads me to engage in social protest of various kinds. Here, social injustice seems to explain both the feelings I experienced before acquiring a belief in the injustice of my society and, of course, the development of this belief. So even if there is nothing wrong with citing my moral beliefs as part of the explanation of my subsequent protest activities, this belief cannot explain my early nonmoral psychological changes or the change in my moral consciousness.

Thus, even where we could offer an explanation of individuals' actions or social events that mentioned only moral beliefs, not moral facts, moral explanations also exist. Moreover, moral explanations of many such events seem superior to nonmoral explanations by appeal to people's beliefs. Is there, then, anything wrong with these moral explanations?

Harman's claim is that appeal to moral facts is "completely irrelevant" to explaining any nonmoral events (1977: 7). The examples we discussed certainly suggest a different conclusion. We might be able to resolve this issue more satisfactorily if we could formulate criteria of explanatory relevance. Nicholas Sturgeon has suggested a counterfactual test of explanatory relevance (1984: 65). On this suggestion, the test for whether a fact is explanatorily relevant is whether the explanandum *would* have occurred just as it did even if the putatively explanatory fact had not obtained. If the explanandum would have so occurred, then the fact may not be explanatorily relevant; if it would not have so occurred, then the fact is explanatorily relevant.

This counterfactual test of explanatory relevance calls for some comments. First, notice that the test does not ask, concerning the explanatory relevance of some fact, whether – if enough other facts had been different – the explanandum would have occurred without the putatively explanatory fact obtaining. Very little would satisfy *this* test; rather, the test assumes that in these counterfactual situations we hold other facts about the situation as fixed as is possible. Second, as Sturgeon notes (1984: 75–6), there are other qualifications on use of this test. For instance, situations of causal overdetermination pose certain difficulties for the straightforward application of the first half of the test. Fortunately, none of the examples Sturgeon or I use seems to introduce such problems (contrast Quinn 1986: 536–7).

But by this test our moral explanations do appear relevant, for we think that the explananda would not have occurred as they did if the moral facts had not obtained. Caligula would not have slaughtered innocent people if he had not been cruel; nor would we regard him as depraved if he had not been. Black South Africans and white sympathizers would not protest apartheid as they do if South African society were not racially unjust.[3]

3 Someone might deny this counterfactual claim and hold that a moral explanation of black South African protest is inappropriate because black protest can and should be explained in terms of blacks' self-interest. Two replies seem in order, however. The first reply is to insist on the relevance of injustice in the explanation of black protest. In the explanation of black protest by appeal to the injustice of apartheid, and more generally in the explanation of individual and social resistance and protest by appeal to injustices, it seems reasonable to suppose that the injustice of the harms suffered by victims of the injustice plays an important role in the explanation of their resistance and protest. Presumably, the nature of black protest reflects not just the fact that blacks are harmed under apartheid, but also the fact that these harms are *wrongs* and, hence, *illegitimate*. Perhaps blacks would protest merely to advance their interests, but surely the intensity of their protest is due in part to the fact that they are protecting their legitimate interests against wrongful interference. (Of course, some will try to capture the force of this reply by appeal

Perhaps Harman thinks we should understand these counterfactual claims differently. Perhaps he thinks we should leave all the nonmoral facts the same and vary only the moral facts when asking whether these nonmoral explananda would have occurred as they did if the moral facts had not obtained (cf. Sturgeon 1984: 69). Would black South Africans (or white sympathizers) protest if all social, political, and legal institutions were as they now are but there was no racial injustice in South Africa?

Of course, this proposal can be seen to be absurd when its implications are spelled out. The supposition of this counterfactual question is impossible. The ethical naturalist claims that moral facts are constituted by, and so supervene on, natural facts. It is just such social, political, and legal arrangements that constitute South Africa's racial injustice. It is impossible that these natural facts should remain as they are but that racial injustice should fail to exist.

Harman seems to think that moral facts are nonexplanatory *even if* they supervene on natural facts. He allows that the natural facts on which injustice supervenes help explain the social events in question, but he rejects the explanatory power of injustice, because he insists that the *injustice* of these natural facts adds nothing to this explanation (1986: 62–4). Now, this would be true of moral *epiphenomenalism,* but it does not seem to be true of ethical naturalism. The ethical naturalist claims that moral facts not only supervene on, but actually consist in, natural facts. Because the natural facts, which Harman concedes help explain South African instability and protest against apartheid, are what constitute the racial injustice of apartheid, their explanatory power ensures the explanatory power of the injustice that they realize.[4]

to blacks' *perception* of the legitimacy of their interests and the illegitimacy of the harms apartheid inflicts. But this is just another attempt to replace moral explanations by appeal to explanations in terms of psychological set, and I have already argued against the adequacy of this strategy.) The second reply is to appeal to the explanation of *white* protest of apartheid. There is simply no reason to expect that the normal case of white protest can be adequately explained by appeal to whites' self-interest.

4 Harman's strategy of adopting naturalistic "reductions" appears to concede as much (1977: 13–4; 1986: 64–7), although his own version of naturalism is quite different from the kind I am talking about (see note 1). Moreover, as Sturgeon points out (1986b: 72–4), Harman's reductionist strategy seems to hold the explanatory power of moral facts hostage to our possession of a full-blown moral theory. I don't think we need know any of the naturalistic bases of the moral facts we offer in explanation, much less do we need a full-blown naturalistic reduction of all moral claims, in order for these moral explanations to be legitimate.

But wouldn't appeal to moral facts be dispensable in favor of appeal to the natural facts that constitute putatively explanatory moral facts?

Of course, moral explanations might prove *practically* indispensable, since it might often be extremely difficult to identify all those lower-order facts that actually constitute some moral fact that seems explanatorily relevant. But this form of indispensability must be qualified. In particular, two qualifications are in order. First, moral explanations are much more likely to be necessary in this way vis-à-vis physical explanations than vis-à-vis explanations in social, economic, and psychological terms. For – and this is the second point – if we could never or only rarely identify the natural and social scientific facts that constitute the putatively explanatory moral facts, we should be unable to construct and assess moral theories or even to engage in moral reform. For in order to know, say, what social and political institutions to protest against and what social and political reforms to favor, we must have some idea what social, economic, and legal facts realize, say, racial injustice. So there are limits to the claim that we cannot identify any non-moral facts in which moral facts consist, and, of course, this practical need for moral explanations does not show that moral explanations are not eliminable in principle.

Can we do better by moral explanations? Can we defend the legitimacy of moral explanations even in cases where we can or could identify the nonmoral facts in which the moral explanans consist and on which they supervene?

In many cases we will start off using moral explanations, as in the case of explaining South African instability and protest against apartheid by appeal to the racial injustice in South Africa. *By relying on moral theory* about the nature and causes of social and, in particular, racial injustice, we may later begin to cite as explanatory factors the social, political, and economic structures in which this injustice consists.

First among several things to be noticed is that even if, contrary to fact (see the rest of this section), these subsequent explanations couched in nonmoral (e.g., social and economic) vocabulary were to supplant the original moral explanations, this would still seem to provide explanatory support for moral realism. For if it is reliance on moral theory that reliably leads us to our preferred explanatory categories, then this seems to be evidence for the truth of the moral claims. Of course, it is an empirical question to what extent moral theory plays this methodological role. But I think there is good empirical evidence that often, as in my example, moral theory does play this role.

Second, if the moral facts initially cited really consist in the social facts that are subsequently cited, then it would seem that the explanatory power of these moral facts is vindicated even if we could and did ultimately accept only those explanations couched in nonmoral (e.g., social and economic) terms (cf. Sturgeon 1984: 62). For then, although I might use no moral terminology, I would cite facts that *are* moral facts. The situation would be a bit like the one in which I explain various things by appeal to the physical and functional nature of objects that humans use to sit on, without ever using the *word* 'chair'. None of this would seem to show that chair is not an explanatory category (contrast Quinn 1986: 537–9). Similarly, even if we had an ability to avoid moral vocabulary in favor of nonmoral vocabulary, this would not show that moral categories were nonexplanatory.

Third, as these points suggest, explanations by constituting facts and by constituted facts need not compete; an explanation by constituting facts typically *supplements,* rather than supplants, explanation by constituted facts. Explanation of why my ice-cream cone drips onto my trousers by appeal to the temperature of the room is supplemented, not replaced or defeated, by an explanation in terms of the mean kinetic molecular energies of the atmosphere of this room and of the ice cream. Moral facts, too, can be explanatory even if explanation by appeal to the natural facts that constitute these moral facts adds to the moral explanation.

These are all reasons to respect moral explanations even if moral facts and properties are identical with nonmoral facts and properties. But we can, I think, offer even stronger arguments for the legitimacy of moral explanations. The arguments I have in mind are general ones that, if correct, will show many higher-order explanations to be irreducible to lower-order explanations. The arguments apply to explanations involving, as both explanans and explananda, either types or tokens, although, of course, it need only work at one of these levels in order to establish the explanatory power of moral facts. These arguments exploit the difference between identity and constitution claims and the consequent sense in which it is true that constituted facts are (after all) something over and above their

193

bases. And, of course, it is this construal of the relation between many higher-order facts and lower-order facts, and, in particular, between moral and nonmoral facts, that I have been defending (cf. 6.5–6.6 and 7.1). The arguments will focus on the general case, but since I have explained and defended this construal of the relationship between moral facts and properties and their lower-order bases, the arguments should apply to moral explanations.

Because our interest in explanation is typically an interest in understanding past events or predicting future events, we are interested in explanations that support counterfactual generalizations about both explanans and explananda (types or tokens). But although there may be interesting generalizations about an explanandum and higher-order explanans, there may be many fewer interesting generalizations about the explanandum and those facts that compose the higher-order explanans. For instance, there are interesting generalizations about people's mental states and their subsequent actions. But even if materialism is true and each mental state is constituted by neural states of the person organized in a certain way, it does not follow that there are as many interesting generalizations about people's neural states and their subsequent behavior. Certainly, even if each neural state of a person is realized in some set of microphysical (e.g., atomic) states, it does not follow that there are many interesting generalizations about people's microphysical states and their behavior. This is largely because human mental states (both types and tokens) can be and could have been realized in so many different ways. As a result, the arrangements of physical states that constitute these mental states need represent no "natural kind" from the point of view of neurophysiology or microphysics. There may be no "projectible" kind of neurostate or microphysical state corresponding to mental state types or even tokens. Thus, in such cases explanans at the level of the higher-order fact will generalize better than those at the lower level, and this will secure higher-order explanans a distinct and, it would seem, privileged explanatory role. If so, psychological explanation of behavior will not be eliminable in favor of neurophysiological explanation, even if psychological states are all in fact constituted by neurophysiological states. We might put this point by saying that explanation of behavior may well have to cite *structural, rather than compositional,* facts. (Cf. Fodor 1974; Boyd 1980; Garfinkel 1981: chap. 2; and 7.1.)

These considerations apply to moral explanations as well. The particular arrangements of natural facts that could realize explanatory moral facts (types or tokens) may in many cases represent no natural kind from the point of view of economics, social theory, or nutritional theory, and certainly not from the point of view of microphysics. If so, moral explanans will generalize better than would explanans in terms of the lower-order facts that constitute these moral facts. For example, racial oppression in South Africa consists in various particular social, economic, and legal restrictions present in South African society. Now, it seems better to cite racial oppression as a cause of political instability and social protest in South Africa than the particular social, economic, and political restrictions, precisely because there would still have been racial oppression and instability and protest under somewhat different social, economic, and legal restrictions, and the only thing this large set of alternate possible social, economic, and legal bases of oppression have in common is that they realize racial oppression (it is very unlikely that there is a natural – nonmoral – social category that corresponds to this set). In such cases, moral explanations will occupy a distinct and privileged explanatory role.

We establish a similar conclusion about the necessity and irreducibility of moral explanation if we can establish the thesis that causation itself is often structural and not (simply) compositional.

Assume that we begin by considering some world w^1 in which we explain some fact or event E by appeal to some higher-order fact or event H, and that we (correctly) think that H caused E (since we think this sort of explanation is causal). (H and E can be either types or tokens.) Now, H is constituted by, but not identical with, some set of lower-order facts or events L^1; this is at least in part because, although actually constituted by L^1, H could have been realized (in other worlds) by any of a very large number of somewhat different configurations of lower-order facts $L^2, L^3, \ldots L^n$. Now we might also think that we could explain E by appeal to L^1. If this is right, we might ask if H is explanatorily eliminable in favor of L^1. I think not. For in other worlds, otherwise as similar to w^1 as possible, in which H is constituted by one of these alternate L bases, H and E will also occur, and it will also be correct to say that H causes E and so explains E. This implies that H's causal power is neither equivalent to, nor derived from, L^1's causal power (contrast Kim 1984b). It is also true that E would have occurred when and as it did even if L^1 had not occurred. This counterfactual fact may encourage us to

195

claim not just that H's causal power cannot be reduced to that of L^1, but that H and not L^1 is the cause of E – that the cause of E is the structural fact H, not the compositional fact L^1. (Or we might distinguish structural and compositional *aspects* of the same facts or events and claim that the causal powers of facts or events often hold in virtue of their structural, rather than compositional, aspects.) I am less sure that this stronger conclusion is justified, since this might be represented as a case of causal overdetermination, and such cases, as we noted, pose problems for the straightforward application of our earlier test of causal relevance. If E is causally overdetermined, we cannot conclude from the fact that E would have occurred even if a putative cause C^1 had not occurred, that C^1 is not a cause of E. But we certainly can conclude that L^1 does not possess the same explanatory range as H does. So explanatory appeal to H cannot be reduced or replaced without loss by explanatory appeal to L^1. Indeed, this fact about explanatory range is a reason for preferring higher explanatory categories in such cases.

For example, we might explain China's adoption of the one-child policy (E) at least in part by appeal to the fact that the rate of population growth before adoption of the policy was constraining needed capital investment and modernization (H) (modernization needed to provide a certain quality of life). Now, of course, H consisted in, among other things, a certain specific birthrate, which in turn consisted in the births at certain times and places of various Lis, Wangs, Xiaos, Gaos, and so on (L^1). But, of course, there are alternate L bases (e.g., sets of different births) that would realize the same H and, indeed, the same demographic facts. So H's causing E cannot be analyzed as L^1's causing E. And so it is better to cite H than L^1 here, not just because citing L^1 would be so difficult and cumbersome (although, of course, it would be), but because we still would have had E and H even if the birthrate and set of births had been different in certain ways. This may show that it is the structural fact of a certain birthrate and its social importance, rather than the compositional fact about the births of particular Lis, Wangs, Xiaos, Gaos, and so on, at particular times and places, that caused (in part) and so explains (in part) China's adoption of the one-child policy; it certainly shows that appeal to the structural cause of China's one-child policy has greater explanatory range than appeal to its compositional cause.

Similar considerations seem to apply to the moral case. If causally relevant and explanatory moral facts such as racial oppression could have been realized by different social, economic, and legal conditions, then the causal efficacy and, hence, explanatory power of oppression cannot be derived from or reduced to the causal efficacy of the particular social, economic, and legal conditions in which that oppression in fact consisted.

This argument seems to establish the causal and, hence, explanatory irreducibility of higher-order facts – including moral facts – to lower-order facts that constitute, but are not identical with, those higher-order facts.

The truth of ethical naturalism, therefore, cannot undermine moral realism on explanatory grounds. Nonmoral explanations of facts for which we do have moral explanations may not always be available. Their availability would supplement, rather than supplant, moral explanations. Indeed, moral explanations seem irreducible to explanations in terms of the natural facts in which those moral facts consist. And if, contrary to fact, ethical naturalism explained why moral explanations were dispensable, we would then have all the evidence for moral realism we could want.

So, although it is not clear that an a posteriori defense of moral realism need make moral facts explanatory of nonmoral facts, there is every reason to believe that moral facts can be and are explanatory of nonmoral facts.

4. MORAL DISAGREEMENT

Someone might think that moral facts have appropriate explanatory power and still think that our moral beliefs are, as a matter of fact, insufficiently coherent with our nonmoral beliefs. For even if moral facts can and do have some explanatory role, it may still be true that the best explanation of nonmoral facts about moral disagreement requires the truth of nihilism and the falsity of moral realism. If there were objective moral facts to be discovered, one would expect convergence of moral belief at least over time. But, the antirealist might claim, disagreement in ethics is pervasive – more pervasive than it is in the natural or social sciences. Indeed, moral disputes are so pervasive and so intractable that the best explanation of this kind of disagreement is that there are no moral facts.

Of course, this kind of argument from disagreement or diversity now bears a heavy burden. For if this argument is to justify reject-

197

ing moral realism, it must defeat both the presumption in favor of moral realism and the evidence for moral realism provided by the explanatory power of moral facts. It will not be sufficient that nihilism be *an* explanation of the existence and nature of moral disagreement; it must *clearly be the best* explanation.

The argument from moral diversity or disagreement has been a popular and philosophically influential source of moral skepticism.[5] Mackie's "argument from relativity" is the most perspicuous formulation of the argument from disagreement, so I shall focus on it.

The argument from relativity has as its premise the well-known variation in moral codes from one society to another and from one period to another, and also the differences in moral beliefs between different groups and classes within a complex community. Such variation is in itself merely a truth of descriptive morality, a fact of anthropology which entails neither first order nor second order ethical views. Yet it may indirectly support second order subjectivism: radical differences between first order moral judgments make it difficult to treat those judgements as apprehensions of objective truths. (1977: 36)

As Mackie recognizes, disagreement does not entail nihilism; we do not infer from the fact that there are disagreements in the natural or social sciences that these disciplines do not concern matters of objective fact. Nor, from the fact that there is a specific dispute in some discipline, do we make what might seem to be the more modest inference that there is no fact of the matter on the particular issue in question. For example, no one concluded from the apparently quite deep disagreement among astronomers a short while ago about the existence of black holes that there was no fact of the matter concerning the existence of black holes. The argument from disagreement must claim that disagreement in ethics is somehow more fundamental than disagreement in other disciplines. Mackie's claim seems to be that realism about a discipline requires that its disputes be resolvable and that although scientific disputes do seem resolvable, many moral disputes do not. For this reason, the best explanation of the facts about moral disagreement requires the rejection of moral realism.

5 It is hard to document the extent of this argument's influence. Philosophical proponents include Sextus Empiricus *PH* I. 148–63, III. 179–82, 198–218, 232–5, *AM* XI. 68–77; Westermarck 1932: chap. 5; Stevenson 1937, 1948a, 1948b; Nowell-Smith 1957: 48–51; B. Williams 1975, 1985: chaps. 8–9; Mackie 1977: 36–8; and Wong 1984. Nonphilosophical proponents include sociologists and anthropologists such as Benedict 1934, Sumner 1940, and Herskovits 1948.

I think the moral realist should question the premises of this formulation of the argument from disagreement. Does realism about a discipline require that its disputes be resolvable? Certainly, realism about a discipline does not require that all actual cognizers eventually reach agreement. It could be reasonable to expect agreement on a set of facts only if all cognizers were fully informed and fully rational and had sufficient time for deliberation. Thus, if realism about a discipline requires that its disputes be resolvable, this must mean that its disputes must be resolvable *in principle*.

Does realism about a discipline require that its disputes be resolvable even in principle? I think that a realist should resist the assumption that it ought to be possible, in practice or even in principle, to get *any* cognizer to hold true beliefs. All of our beliefs are revisable, at least in principle, and dialectical investigation of our beliefs can identify explanatory tensions in our beliefs and force more or less drastic revision in them if it is carried out thoroughly. In this way, coherentist reasoning can, at least in principle, identify and correct significant and substantial error. But as we have seen (2.8 and 5.7), no theory of justification adequate to the task of accounting for justified but fallible belief (e.g., in an external world) can preclude the possibility of *systematic* error. We cannot demonstrate, and should not be expected to be able to demonstrate, the success of evolutionary theory to someone who holds systematically mistaken observational beliefs about the behavior and adaptation of different species. We cannot defend, and should not be expected to be able to defend, historical hypotheses to someone who holds no true psychological generalizations about human behavior. Similarly, there may be people with such hopelessly and systematically mistaken moral beliefs that we cannot, and should not be expected to be able to, convince them of true moral claims. Because the argument from disagreement alleges that the moral realist cannot adequately explain the nature of moral disagreement, we are entitled to see what could be said about moral disagreement and its resolvability *on realist assumptions*. And, as in these nonmoral cases, we can imagine people whose initial starting points are so badly mistaken that there should be no expectation of convincing them of the truth. We can imagine people whose view of themselves and others is so distorted by, say, self-concern or an inability to represent vividly the consequences of their actions that all of their considered moral beliefs will be badly mistaken. Even though these beliefs are revisable, the fact that they are systematically mistaken means that there may be no basis for correcting their errors.

Although this is, I think, a possibility, and one that demonstrates that the realist need not believe it possible, even in principle, to convince any cognizer of true moral claims, it does not undermine the argument from disagreement. For although a nonskeptical realist need not assume that any and every moral dispute is resolvable even in principle, he cannot treat every serious disagreement as one between interlocutors at least one of whom is systematically mistaken. I lose my claim to justified belief the more I simply dismiss opponents as systematically mistaken. It is incumbent on the moral realist, therefore, to claim that *most* moral disputes are resolvable at least in principle.

Is this claim plausible? Mackie supposes that the realist will defend it by trying to explain away apparent moral disagreements as the application by interlocutors of shared moral principles under different empirical conditions (1977: 37). This is the familiar idea that people who live in different social, economic, and environmental conditions might apply the same moral principle to justify quite different policies. An economically underdeveloped country might think that in a society in its economic condition distributive inequalities provide incentives that benefit everyone and that this justifies such inequalities. A more economically advanced country might oppose distributive inequalities on the ground that in societies at its level of affluence distributive inequalities are divisive and so work to everyone's disadvantage. The economically underdeveloped society thinks it should promote certain distributive inequalities, whereas the economically more developed society thinks it should oppose distributive inequalities. This might look like a moral disagreement, but the fact is that the disagreement is only apparent. The one society thinks that inequalities are justified *in economically backward conditions,* while the other society thinks that inequalities are unjustified *in economically favorable conditions.* Not only is there no disagreement here; a common moral principle seems to justify both beliefs. Since this sort of disagreement is only apparent, it poses no problem for the moral realist.

Mackie finds this realist explanation of moral disagreement inadequate for two reasons. First, this explanation of moral disputes commits the moral realist to treating many moral facts as contingent. The apparently conflicting moral beliefs of apparent disputants can only be contingently true, because their compatibility depends on contingent facts about their different environments. Necessity can attach only to the shared moral principles that underlie their apparent disagreement (1977: 37).

It is not entirely clear how this fact about a realist account of apparent disputes is supposed to constitute an objection to moral realism. Mackie seems to assume that the moral realist cannot accept this kind of contingency and is committed to defending the necessity of moral facts. But why?

It cannot be Mackie's view that moral facts are necessary, since he thinks that no moral statements are true (1977: 39–40). But if Mackie can reject completely belief in the necessity of moral truths, why can't the realist, if she needs to, deny that all moral truths are necessary? Perhaps Mackie thinks that the realist, but not he, is committed to defending common beliefs about morality and that it is a common belief about morality that moral truths are necessary.[6]

But there are several problems with this argument. Although my defense of coherentism commits me to the general reliability of considered moral beliefs, it does not commit me to the reliability of common nonmoral, second-order beliefs about morality. (See 2.5.) Moreover, I see no reason to think that belief in the necessity of moral truths is a common belief about morality, and, even if it were, there would be good reason to reject it. The ethical naturalist claims that moral facts are constituted by, and thus supervene on, natural and social scientific facts such as economic, social, and psychological facts. The naturalist, therefore, ought to accept happily the claim that "if things had been otherwise [in certain respects], quite different sorts of actions would have been right" (1977: 37). The contingency of many moral facts is, I think, a happy, rather than an untoward, consequence of the realist's explanation of apparent moral disagreement.

So, the realist's explanation of apparent moral disagreement commits him to the contingency of some moral facts. But this is a perfectly acceptable commitment, since many moral facts are contingent. Moreover, as Mackie recognizes, the realist's explanation of apparent disagreement allows him to treat some moral facts as necessary. Also, how many moral facts the realist must regard as contin-

6 I am told by Nick Sturgeon that Mackie confirmed this interpretation in a talk he gave at Cornell University in the spring of 1980.

gent depends, in part, on how often the realist seeks to explain moral disagreement away as only apparent moral disagreement.

This brings us to Mackie's second reason for finding the realist explanation of apparent moral disagreement inadequate. Mackie seems to assume that the realist must offer this explanation as a general account of moral disputes, and he points out, quite rightly, that not all putative disagreements are merely apparent (1977: 38). People do disagree about what is right or wrong in a particular set of circumstances, and the realist must be able to explain why most genuine disputes are resolvable at least in principle.

But the realist can plausibly explain this; Mackie is wrong to restrict the realist to explaining moral disputes away as only apparent. We already noted that it is only *most* genuine disputes that a realist must regard as resolvable in principle. Some interlocutors may be so systematically mistaken that although our dispute with them concerns a matter of objective fact, we cannot, and should not be expected to be able to, convince them of true claims. Other genuine moral disputes are also in a certain sense not resolvable even in principle. For even a moral realist can maintain that some genuine moral disputes have no uniquely correct answers. Moral ties are possible, and considerations, each of which is objectively valuable, may be incommensurable. Disputes over moral ties and incommensurable values are resolvable in principle only in the sense that it ought to be possible in principle to show interlocutors who are not systematically mistaken that their dispute has no unique resolution. Of course, there are limits on how often we may construe disputes as tied or incommensurable and still plausibly defend the existence of objective moral facts and true moral propositions.

The moral realist can plausibly maintain that most moral disputes are genuine, have a unique solution, and can be resolved at least in principle. First, many genuine moral disagreements depend on disagreements over the nonmoral facts. Of these, some depend on culpable ignorance of fact and others do not.

Often, at least one disputant culpably fails to assess the nonmoral facts correctly by being insufficiently imaginative in weighing the consequences for various people of different actions or policies. Culpable failure to be sufficiently imaginative may result from negligence (e.g., laziness), prejudice, self-interest, or social ideology. This sort of error is especially important in moral disputes, since thought experiments, as opposed to actual tests, play such an important part in the assessment of moral theories. Thought experiments play a larger role in moral methodology than they do in scientific methodology, both because it is often (correctly) regarded as immoral to assess moral theories by realizing the relevant counterfactuals, and because the desired test conditions for moral theories are often harder to produce (e.g., the experiments would involve too many variables to control for and the subjects would not always want to cooperate). Because moral disputes that depend on this kind of culpable ignorance of nonmoral fact turn on nonmoral issues that are supposed to be resolvable at least in principle, these moral disputes should themselves be resolvable at least in principle.

Other genuine moral disputes depend on reasonable (nonculpable) but nonetheless resolvable disagreements over the nonmoral facts. The correct answers to controversial moral questions often turn on nonmoral issues about which reasonable disagreement is possible and about which no one may know the answer. Moral disagreement can turn on nonmoral disagreement over such questions as 'What (re)distribution of goods would make the worst-off representative person in a society best-off?', 'Would public ownership of the means of production in the United States lead to an increase or decrease in the average standard of living?', 'What are the most important social determinants of personality?', 'What kind of life would Vera's severely mentally retarded child lead (if she brought her pregnancy to term and raised the child), and how would caring for him affect Vera and her family?', 'How malleable is human nature?', 'Which, if any, religious claims are true?', and 'If there is a god, how should its will be ascertained? (e.g., should scripture be read literally?)'. However difficult and controversial these issues are, disputes about them are supposed to be resolvable at least in principle. Insofar as moral disputes turn on such issues, they too are resolvable in principle.

Other genuine moral disputes do not depend on nonmoral disagreement; they represent antecedent moral disagreement. Mackie's discussion of how moral realism will explain apparent moral disagreement shows that he regards moral disagreement as resolvable if, and only if, there is *antecedent* agreement on general moral principles. But this assumption reflects a one-way view of moral justification, according to which moral principles can justify particular moral judgments but not vice versa, that our defense of a coherence theory of justification entitles us to reject. As coherentism insists, justification consists in *mutual* support between moral principles and judgments about particular cases. Agreement about general moral principles may be exploited to resolve (genuine) disagreement about particular moral cases, and agreement about particular moral cases may be exploited to resolve disagreement about general moral principles. Since no one's moral beliefs are entirely consistent, much less maximally coherent, considerations of coherence force each of us to revise our moral beliefs in particular ways. Ideally, we make trade-offs among the various levels of generality of belief in such a way as to maximize initial commitment, overall consistency, explanatory power, and so on. The fact that we disagree about some moral issues at the beginning of this process of adjustment gives no compelling reason to suppose that this process of adjustment will not, in the limit, resolve our disagreement (cf. 5.9). Indeed, the nihilist is committed to claiming that there is often no resolution of competing moral claims even in principle. But this is just one claim about what the results of a systematic dialectical moral inquiry among different interlocutors would be, which must stand alongside various nonskeptical claims about what the results would be, and enjoys no privileged a priori position in relation to its competitors (cf. Dworkin 1986: 85–6). As coherentists and realists about other things, we assume that this kind of coherentist reasoning is in principle capable of resolving quite deep antecedent disagreement in the natural sciences, the social sciences, and philosophy itself. There seems no reason to deny that most moral errors are not also resolvable at least in principle by coherentist reasoning. Certainly, given the burden of proof that the argument from disagreement must bear at this stage of the dialectic, the fact that the realist cannot produce a proof of her claim that most moral error is in principle correctable by coherentist reasoning gives us no reason to doubt this claim.

What of the diachronic character of the argument from disagreement? Does the fact that there seems to have been so little convergence of moral belief over time support the claim that many moral disputes are unresolvable? I do not think these questions raise any difficulties that we have not already addressed, but perhaps they focus issues in a certain way.

We need to distinguish, in our assessments of the amount of current moral consensus and of the prospects for convergence, between two levels of moral thought: (1) popular moral thought, and (2) reflective moral theory. Of course, according to a coherentist moral epistemology, levels (1) and (2) are connected; (2) begins with (1) and is in this respect at least continuous with (1). But coherentism also allows the dialectical investigation of our moral beliefs to force significant revision in those beliefs, and in this way (2) can come to diverge significantly from (1). This difference is important because the prospect of persistent disagreement at level (1) would seem much less troublesome if the prospects for agreement at level (2) were good or if there were plausible realist explanations for why agreement at level (2) should be hard to secure.

There certainly are realist explanations for why there is less convergence to date at level (1) than some might have expected there to be. Moral thinking, as we noted, is subject to various distorting influences such as particular conceptions of self-interest, prejudice, and other forms of social ideology. Because the subject matter of ethics concerns, among other things, the appropriate distribution of the benefits and burdens of social and personal interaction, these distorting influences often afflict moral thinking more than scientific thinking; it is just such issues on which these distorting mechanisms are most likely to operate. (I would not want to underestimate the extent to which such influences have distorted, say, social scientists' claims about the social and economic consequences of particular public policies or psychologists' and biologists' claims about the nature and hereditability of intelligence. But these are the sorts of exceptions that prove the rule, and they also help the realist explain the persistence of moral disputes.) And these sources of distortion are hardy perennials.

There are other realist explanations for why agreement should be hard to secure at both levels.

As others have suggested (e.g., Parfit 1984: 453–4), secular moral theory (level [2]) is in some ways a comparatively underdeveloped area of inquiry. In part, this reflects the influence of religious beliefs on both levels (1) and (2). This is not to say there have not been secular moralists since at least the Greeks, that religious ethics should not be taken seriously, that religious moralists do not make secularly acceptable moral claims, or that secular ethics is incompatible with theism. But it is certainly true that specifically religious doctrines and commitments have at many points shaped and constrained moral thinking. In some periods and places religious constraints on secular moral theory have been direct, taking the form of institutional censorship or sanctions. In other periods and places re-

205

ligious doctrines and commitments have constrained secular moral theory indirectly by affecting level (1). Religious commitments and doctrines have shaped what many people, and not just conscious adherents to these commitments and doctrines, take to be serious moral possibilities (think, for example, about Christian influences on popular views of sexual morality). And this sort of influence is important, since moral progress requires moral debate, and moral debate requires moral imagination. Moreover, insofar as such doctrines and commitments are not rationally defensible but must be held, if at all, as articles of faith, they have not just exerted disproportionate influence on the shape of moral thought but have actually distorted it. For the enterprise of moral theory is simply the attempt to find a rationally defensible system of moral beliefs. Moreover, it is a fundamental moral commitment that in morality's allocation of the benefits and burdens of social and personal interaction, the imposition of burdens on some requires rational justification in order to be morally legitimate. Specifically religious influences on ethics, therefore, have hindered moral progress at both levels (1) and (2), insofar as they have either infected moral thought with nonrational elements or artificially restricted people's moral imaginations. Science was not able to develop properly under similar religious constraints and did not really take off until, among other things, these constraints were largely shed. Perhaps moral thought would benefit from similar autonomy.

In any case, however much it may be due to religious influences, systematic, secular moral theory is a relatively underdeveloped area of inquiry. There are, of course, a number of figures in the history of philosophy who have developed fairly systematic, secular (or secularly acceptable) moral and political theories, many of which are powerful and attractive theories. But notice two things:

First, these figures sum to a very small total (they could perhaps be counted on two or three hands). The number of people who have worked full time to produce systematic moral theories does not even begin to compare with the number of those who have worked full time on theoretical issues in the natural sciences. Although, of course, there have been professional politicians and political strategists for a long time, the idea of a class of people devoting most of their time to the study of issues of moral and political theory is a comparatively recent one. Perhaps more progress is to be hoped for in ethics when systematic moral theory has flourished longer. These considerations provide a realistic explanation of why there has not yet been the right sort of convergence of moral opinion, as well as some reason to be cautiously optimistic about the prospects for convergence at least at level (2) (cf. 4.7).

Second, the theories that have been developed have, with a few exceptions (e.g., Locke and Bentham), had very little and certainly imperfect impact on level (1). Lay persons are typically willing to defer to theorists or theoretical debate on matters scientific, but they seem largely uninterested in profiting from theoretical work that has been done in moral or political theory. (Public debates over abortion, affirmative action, and constitutional litigation concerning civil rights spring to mind.) Of course, it is not surprising that lay persons do not familiarize themselves with all of the philosophical details of existing moral theories. A certain amount of ignorance of theory is necessary if there are to be lay persons; this is as true in ethics as in science. But most lay persons, even those with strong moral sensibilities, seem largely unaware of, or uninterested in, even the outlines of theoretical work in ethics. Nor do I think that this popular ignorance of, or indifference to, moral theory can be justified by appeal to the state of theoretical disagreement in ethics or by appeal to an individual's obligation, as a moral agent, to decide matters for herself. Certainly, an individual's moral views can profit from exposure to ethical theory, even if, indeed, perhaps especially when, theoretical issues are in dispute. And one need not abdicate one's moral agency by consulting others who have thought systematically about the moral issues that concern one. Indeed, moral responsibility would seem to demand that one's moral decision be as informed as possible, and this would seem to argue in favor of consulting moral theory both when moral theory speaks unequivocally and when there is theoretical disagreement (4.7).

This makes one wonder how, if at all, the appropriate development in level (2) might affect level (1). Current popular neglect of the moral theory that is available might encourage skepticism about the effect that the development of moral theory might have on popular moral thought. But if this neglect is due in part to the comparatively underdeveloped state of moral theory, perhaps its development would encourage greater interest in, and respect for, the resources of moral theory. True, such development (with its demands on intellectual resources) may itself presuppose a greater

207

interest in moral theory or moral issues. But marginally greater interest in certain moral issues could spur marginally greater interest in moral theory, which could spur moderately greater allocation of intellectual resources toward moral theory, which in turn could spur further interest in moral issues, and so on.

In any event, the prospects for the appropriate kind of convergence at level (2), given the appropriate development of systematic moral theory, would be sufficient reassurance to the moral realist. The fact, if it would be a fact, that the appropriate sort of convergence at level (2) would not produce similar convergence at level (1) should trouble us no more than the fact that agreement among biologists on some form of evolutionary theory does not secure the agreement of all lay persons (e.g., certain fundamentalist Christians).

Moreover, there are realist explanations for not expecting convergence in ethics, at level (1) or level (2), even over fairly long periods of time. To believe that there are moral facts and that moral knowledge is possible, as the realist does, involves no commitment to thinking that moral knowledge is easy to acquire. Insofar as particular moral disputes depend on complex nonmoral issues about economics, social theory, human nature, and the rationality of religious belief that have themselves been the subject of persistent diachronic dispute, realists should expect to find persistent moral disagreement at level (1). And insofar as these persistent nonmoral disputes are themselves intellectually legitimate (e.g., are not to be explained as the product of some distorting mechanism), realists should expect to find persistent moral disagreement at level (2). That is, there are persistent nonmoral disputes that not only provide the realist with replies by analogy (respectable company to keep) but are, in fact, largely responsible for the persistence of many moral disputes.

Finally, it seems false to the facts to suppose there has been no significant convergence of moral belief or moral progress over time, even at level (1). Most people no longer think that slavery, racial discrimination, rape, or child abuse is acceptable. Even those who still engage in these activities typically pay lip service to the wrongness of these activities and conceal the real nature of their activities from others and often themselves. Cultures or individuals who do not even pay lip service to these moral claims are rare, and we will typically be able to explain their moral beliefs as the product

208

of various religious, ideological, or psychological distorting mechanisms. This will seem especially appropriate here, since the relevant changes in moral consciousness have all been changes in the same direction. That is, with each of these practices, in almost all cases where people's moral attitudes toward the practice have undergone informed and reflective change, they have changed in the same way (with these practices, from approval to disapproval and not the other way around). When changes in moral consciousness exhibit this sort of pattern, this is further reason to view the changes as progress (cf. Slote 1971). Of course, in viewing these changes in moral consciousness as progress and cultural or individual deviations as mistakes, I am relying at least in part on current moral views. But how could assessments of progress in ethics or the sciences be anything other than theory-dependent in this way? Surely, the sort of realism I have been defending is entitled to appeal to this kind of moral convergence as (defeasible) evidence of moral progress.

So nihilism is not clearly the best explanation of the nature of moral disagreement. The moral realist need only claim that *most genuine* moral disputes are *in principle* resolvable. Not all apparent moral disputes are genuine; some merely reflect the application of antecedently shared moral principles in different circumstances. Not every genuine moral dispute is even in principle resolvable, since some interlocutors may be so systematically mistaken in their moral beliefs that it is not possible to convince them of true claims. Moreover, moral ties are possible and some objective values or magnitudes may be incommensurable. Of those genuine moral disputes that moral realism is committed to regarding as resolvable in principle, some depend on disagreement over nonmoral issues, and others depend on antecedent disagreement over moral issues. Since nonmoral disagreement, whether culpable or not, is ex hypothesi resolvable in principle, moral disagreement that depends on nonmoral disagreement must itself be resolvable at least in principle. Finally, there seems no good reason to deny that genuine moral disputes (among interlocutors who are not systematically morally mistaken) that depend on antecedent moral disagreement are resolvable at least in principle on the basis of coherentist reasoning. These resources allow the realist a plausible account of the nature and significance of synchronic and diachronic moral disagreement.

5. CONCLUSION

A posteriori objections to my defense of moral realism are not compelling. The metaphysical and epistemological commitments of moral realism are not only intelligible, but plausible. Moral realism is not metaphysically queer. Moral facts and properties are no more sui generis than are the facts and properties of other higher-order disciplines. Ethical naturalism claims that moral facts and properties are constituted by, and so supervene on, natural and social scientific facts and properties. If materialism is true and these natural facts and properties are just organized combinations of physical facts and properties, then moral facts and properties will themselves be constituted by, and so supervene on, organized combinations of physical facts and properties. Nor is moral realism epistemologically queer. Moral realism should be combined with a coherentist moral epistemology. Those explanatory relations between moral and nonmoral beliefs that coherentism requires are not undermined on a posteriori grounds. Moral facts fulfill whatever explanatory obligation an a posteriori defense of moral realism imposes, and there is good reason to believe that most genuine moral disagreements are resolvable at least in principle on the basis of coherentist reasoning about moral and nonmoral issues.

8

Objective utilitarianism

My defense of moral realism is now near completion. We have seen reasons to want to defend moral realism. Various features of moral inquiry presuppose or are naturally explained by a realist form of cognitivism (2.5–2.8); the practical or action-guiding character of morality supports moral realism (Chapter 3); and moral realism's practical implications seem superior to those of many antirealist theories (Chapter 4). These considerations create a presumption in favor of moral realism and place the burden of proof on the antirealist.

Antirealist rebuttals typically depend on mistaken assumptions about the metaphysical and epistemological commitments of moral realism; it is often assumed that the moral realist's metaphysical and epistemological commitments are quite different from those of recognizably realist disciplines such as the natural or social sciences. These assumptions are mistaken either about the commitments of moral realism or about those of other, recognizably realist disciplines. Those genuine metaphysical and epistemological commitments of moral realism are, indeed, parallel to the genuine metaphysical and epistemological commitments of other realist disciplines.

An intuitionist moral epistemology is no less and no more plausible than foundationalism is in general (5.3); neither moral nor nonmoral beliefs can be self-evident (5.5). Moral realism, like other kinds of realism, can and should be combined with a coherence theory of justification (5.6–5.9). A moral belief's coherence with, among other things, considered moral beliefs will be evidence of its objective truth. Neither moral realism nor a coherence theory of justification in ethics is undermined by the existence of an is/ought gap. Even if there is an is/ought gap, consideration of analogous is/is gaps (e.g., between biology and other scientific disciplines) demonstrates that no antirealist or anticoherentist consequences follow (6.6–6.8). Nonnaturalism need not be a queer doctrine; ethical naturalism (or, for that matter, ethical supernaturalism) can be defended; there can be moral facts and evidential relations between moral and

211

nonmoral beliefs. Moreover, moral realism is not undermined on a posteriori grounds. The moral realist's metaphysical commitments are familiar and plausible. The ethical naturalist, for example, claims that moral properties are constituted by, and so supervene on, natural and social scientific properties (7.1). Moral properties, like other higher-order properties, can be accommodated, if necessary, within a materialist world view. The moral realist's epistemological commitments are also plausible. Moral facts are explanatory (7.3), and the nature of moral disagreement is explainable on realist assumptions (7.4).

Indeed, not only is moral realism defensible against these antirealist rebuttals, consideration of them actually provides further support for moral realism. Insofar as moral facts are explanatory, we have additional evidence for moral realism. Moreover, this style of defense provides cumulative support for moral realism. I have defended moral realism against antirealist rebuttals by explaining how moral realism can help itself to the kinds of metaphysical and epistemological claims that we think (or at least ought to think) are available to realism about the natural and social sciences and commonsense physical theory. The frequency and significance of such parallels between ethics and these other areas of inquiry suggest that ethics is or can be every bit as objective as these recognizably realist disciplines. These considerations, together with the support for moral realism offered in Chapters 2–4, show that moral realism is not just defensible, but quite plausible.

My case for moral realism requires the truth of no one moral theory; the metaphysical and epistemological commitments of moral realism could be met by a wide variety of substantive moral theories. Divine command theories as well as deontological and teleological theories of every shape and size must be viewed as candidate specifications of the moral facts.

A number of moral theories, however, may satisfy the candidacy requirements equally well without being equally good candidates. Different moral theories have different implications for the nature of moral facts, the decidability of moral disputes, and the justification of morality, and for our considered moral beliefs. A coherence theory of justification tells us we should accept that moral theory whose implications, here and elsewhere, are most plausible. We should accept the theory that provides the most systematic account of all of our beliefs, both moral and nonmoral. A coherentist epistemology makes a full-blown defense of any moral theory a long and difficult task, since such a defense requires not only that the theory in question be shown to be coherent with our other beliefs, but also that it be shown to be *more* coherent with our beliefs than other moral theories are.

Of course, I cannot here attempt a full-blown defense of any moral theory. But I do want to present, discuss, and partially defend a kind of utilitarian moral theory. There are good reasons for including substantive moral theory in my discussion of moral realism. First, my case for moral realism required relatively abstract metaphysical and epistemological commitments. Examination of this moral theory will illustrate the kinds of specific metaphysical and epistemological commitments that substantive moral theories bring. Examination of this theory will also illustrate how a coherentist moral epistemology is to be applied. Because there is no decision procedure for when a nondeductive inference is good or when an explanation is acceptable, we were able to say little that was both general and informative about the kind of reasoning a coherentist epistemology implies. But because I regard this kind of utilitarian theory as plausible, and not simply as illustrative, I shall argue that it is more plausible than standard objections to utilitarianism would lead us to believe. In particular, I shall argue that this version of utilitarianism is more coherent with our considered moral beliefs than opponents of utilitarianism allow. Defense of this moral theory, therefore, will also illustrate the kind of coherentist moral reasoning to which, I have argued, moral realism is committed. It will turn out, in fact, that realist metaethical commitments and coherentist epistemological commitments contribute significantly to the defense of this kind of utilitarian moral theory. If successful, the arguments of this chapter should show a version of utilitarianism to provide a plausible model of the sort of moral theory a realist metaethics supports.

1. TELEOLOGICAL ETHICS AND UTILITARIANISM

The moral theory I want to develop is a kind of teleological moral theory. Teleological moral theories, unlike deontological and other nonteleological moral theories, hold rightness or justifiedness to be some positive function of goodness. Teleological theorists have often taken this function to be the maximizing function; rightness consists in maximal goodness. That is, something is right, justified,

213

or obligatory just in case it realizes the most value possible in the circumstances. But not every teleologist has construed, or need construe, rightness as maximal goodness. J. S. Mill held the rightness of an action to consist (roughly) in the value of praising or blaming that action (1861: chap. V, para. 14), and other teleologists have proposed other, nonmaximizing conceptions of the appropriate function from value into rightness or obligation.[1] I have sympathies with some of these nonmaximizing accounts of the relation between the right and the good, and there may be some issues about which it would be important for the teleologist to decide between the more traditional account of rightness as maximal goodness and one or another of these nonmaximizing accounts. But, for present purposes, no harm is done by thinking of teleological ethics as claiming that rightness is maximal value.[2]

1 Slote (1985: chaps. 3, 5) suggests we construe consequentialist or teleological moral theories as claiming only that comparative moral assessments be sensitive to, and track differences in, the value that the objects of moral assessment realize. Although I cannot explore Slote's interesting proposals here, I think his broad construal of teleology may make it difficult to distinguish teleological and deontological moral theories. For teleological theories, in his view, need have no theory of rightness or obligation, and teleological and nonteleological theories are usually distinguished by their contrasting theories of the right.
2 The traditional teleological theory claims that an act is right if, and only if, it maximizes the good and that it is wrong if, and only if, it is not right. Some people think that such a theory of right or obligation is too demanding and, in particular, that it fails to distinguish between supererogation and obligation. Mill's theory of obligation is different from the traditional teleological theory in a way that seems to avoid this objection. According to Mill an act, say, is wrong if, and only if, some kind of censure, blame, or punishment (as opposed, say, to praise or indifference) would be the best attitude we might take toward it. Mill can then say it is not always wrong to fail to do the best action and that supererogatory acts are those with very good consequences whose omission is not wrong. Although the traditional teleologist must treat all suboptimific acts as wrong, he can nonetheless recognize a comparable distinction by distinguishing between the rightness or wrongness of some act x and the rightness of praising or blaming x. The commonsense distinction among (1) the obligatory, (2) the permissible, and (3) the supererogatory can be reconstructed, on this view, as a distinction among (1a) acts whose omission is blameworthy, (2a) acts whose performance is not blameworthy, and (3a) acts that are praiseworthy. The traditional account may seem a bit paradoxical (since it must treat most actions – including most of those in categories [2a] and [3a] – as wrong), but it nonetheless promises to recognize moral distinctions comparable to those of common sense. I raise these issues here not to try to settle them but to indicate what this issue within teleological ethics about the exact relation between the right and the good might involve. The fact that the traditional account promises to be able to recognize moral distinctions comparable to those of commonsense morality and the less traditional teleological theories is the reason why it should do no harm here to think of teleological theories in the traditional way.

214

It is sometimes claimed that teleological theories must also specify goodness independently of rightness, with the result that a moral theory is nonteleological just in case it denies that rightness is maximal goodness or its specification of goodness relies on claims about rightness (cf. Rawls 1971: 24–5, 30–1; Frankena 1973: 14–7). Although I could, for my purposes, accept this account of teleological and nonteleological theories, we should, I think, question it. Teleological and nonteleological theories can be distinguished along traditional lines if a theory is teleological just in case it holds rightness to consist in maximal goodness. This weaker construal of teleology is sufficient to distinguish between teleological and nonteleological theories, although it allows the goodness of states of affairs to be determined by considerations of moral permissibility or acceptability. As long as rightness (i.e., all-things-considered permissibility or obligation) is *maximal* goodness, rightness and goodness will be distinct properties, no matter how goodness is conceived. We can fairly demand of teleological theories that they treat rightness and goodness as distinct properties, without requiring that they make rightness and goodness independent of each other. So I shall assume that what distinguishes teleological and nonteleological moral theories is that the former, unlike the latter, hold rightness to consist in maximal goodness.

We can now make several important points about teleological moral theories, so construed. First, we can distinguish between teleological and consequentialist moral theories; the latter are, on a certain construal, just a special case of the former. Consequentialism is usually understood as the claim that actions and other objects of moral assessment are right or justified just in case their *causal consequences* have more intrinsic value than alternative actions, etc. (cf. B. Williams 1973a: 79, 83–4; 1985: 76–7). This is a special case of the teleologist's claim that actions and other objects of moral assessment are right or justified just in case they *realize* more intrinsic value than alternative actions, and so forth. Consequentialism, so construed, is only a special case of the teleological claim, because, unlike the teleological view, consequentialism treats the objects of moral assessment as bearers only of extrinsic value. The teleologist, on the other hand, allows that objects of moral assessment, such as actions, might have intrinsic value and that their intrinsic value counts toward the rightness or justifiedness of those objects of assessment. If, however, the consequences whose intrin-

215

sic value consequentialism seeks to maximize include *conceptual* as well as causal consequences, then consequentialism can treat actions, motives, and the like as intrinsically valuable. So construed, consequentialism and teleology would be equivalent (cf. Scheffler 1982: 1n, 2n).

Second, this characterization of teleology does not require teleological theories to provide reductive theories of goodness or value. Teleological theories may define rightness in terms of goodness and goodness in terms of moral properties such as fairness or respect for persons. The resulting theory need be neither circular nor deontological. It would be circular, as we have seen, to identify rightness with goodness and then to identify goodness with rightness. But we can define rightness (i.e., all-things-considered permissibility or obligation) in terms of goodness and goodness in terms of still other moral properties without circularity (contrast Frankena 1973: 14). Indeed, as we have seen, since the teleologist defines rightness as *maximal* goodness, she can give an account of the good that relies on the acceptability of certain states of affairs without identifying rightness and goodness.

Third, this characterization of teleology allows for a plurality of objects of moral assessment. Utilitarianism and other teleological theories have traditionally been concerned with the assessment of the rightness of actions. But actions need not and should not be the teleologist's only objects of moral assessment.[3] The teleologist can and should assess motives, rules, and institutions as well as actions. These, too, the teleologist will assess by the value they realize.

Fourth, as we shall see at greater length later in this chapter, teleological theories can be construed as *standards* or *criteria of rightness* or as *decision procedures*. A standard or criterion of rightness explains what makes an action or motive right or justified; a decision procedure provides a method of deliberation. Teleological theories do provide criteria of rightness, but need not provide decision procedures.[4] Just as an agent may best secure her own happiness not by always seeking her own happiness but by pursuing certain activities for their own sake (the so-called paradox of egoism), so, too, an

3 Cf. Bentham 1823: VII, 13; Mill 1861: II, 17; Sidgwick 1907: 428; Adams 1976; Sen 1979a.
4 Cf. Butler 1736: par. 8; 1749: sermon XII, par. 31; Mill 1861: II, 16 and 19; 1873: 100; 1881: bk. VI, chap. xii, sec. 7; Sidgwick 1907: 405–6, 413, 431–3, 489–90; Moore 1903: 162–4; Bales 1971; Railton 1984: 140–6, 152–3; Parfit 1984: 24–9.

agent may act best not as the result of deliberating about how to do so or acting out of benevolence but by reasoning in "nonutilitarian" ways or acting on "nonutilitarian" (nonbeneficent) motives. Finally, different teleological theories result from different specifications of the good. Utilitarian theories are teleological theories with a welfarist theory of value. Utilitarianism claims that human (or sentient) welfare or happiness is what is of value. As a teleological theory, utilitarianism claims that actions, motives, institutions, for example, are right or justified just in case they realize as much human welfare as any available alternative action, motive, institution, or the like (i.e., just in case they *maximize welfare*). Of course, different conceptions of welfare are possible and different conceptions of utilitarianism result from these different conceptions of the good. Traditional versions of utilitarianism construe welfare as either pleasure or preference satisfaction.[5] My own version of utilitarianism, however, relies on quite different claims about the nature of value and human welfare.

2. OBJECTIVISM ABOUT VALUE

Theories of value, as I shall understand them, are theories of *intrinsic value:* They make claims about what things (e.g., actions, states, events) are valuable in themselves, necessarily valuable, or valuable whatever else might be true. Intrinsic goods are to be contrasted with things that are *extrinsically valuable* and things that are *necessary conditions* of realizing intrinsic value. Something is extrinsically valuable if it is instrumentally valuable, valuable as a means, or causally produces (either directly or indirectly) intrinsic goods. In most theories of value, many things that have value will have *only* extrinsic value. Thus, according to the hedonist, since the only thing having intrinsic value is the simple, qualitative mental state of pleasure, all other things, including all nonmental items (e.g., actions, activities, institutions, policies) can have only extrinsic value. In some theories of value, certain things, for example, certain sorts of activities, can be *both* intrinsically and extrinsically valuable. Something is a necessary condition of realizing intrinsic value if without that thing there could literally be no intrinsic value. Finally, something may

5 If Berger 1984 is correct, J. S. Mill is an important exception to this general tendency. According to Berger, Mill defends a version of objective utilitarianism not unlike the theory I defend here.

217

be a necessary condition either of realizing any intrinsic good or of realizing some particular intrinsic good. Thus, if knowledge is the one and only intrinsic good, then (at least according to internalist conceptions of knowledge) justified belief is a necessary condition of realizing any value. Whereas if knowledge is only one among many intrinsic goods, then justified belief (again, on internalist assumptions about knowledge) will be a necessary condition of realizing only this component of value.

Since theories of value are theories of intrinsic value, they have implications about the value of actual and counterfactual states of affairs, lives, activities, actions, and so on. Coherentism implies that we decide among theories of value by seeing which theory coheres better with our other beliefs, including, importantly, our other beliefs about value. We must rely on our experience and imagination in constructing thought experiments to assess the value of different kinds of things (cf. Mill 1861: II, 5–6; Moore 1903: 91, 187; 1912: 24, 27–8, 102). We test or assess theories of value, then, by comparing their implications about these actual and counter-factual cases with our own independent assessments of the cases.

Insofar as our question in these thought experiments concerns someone's life or activities, it is: (1) Is X's life or activity valuable, and, if so, (roughly) how valuable? Question (1) needs to be distin-guished from distinct, even if sometimes related, questions such as: (2) Should X be allowed to pursue this kind of life or activity? (3) Does X regard her life or activity as valuable? (4) Do we share X's goals? X's life or activity can be lacking in value without our being justified in interfering with her; X can regard her life or activity as more, or as less, valuable than it is; and we can fail to share X's goals without thinking her life or activity is any less valuable than ours.

If a theory has counterintuitive implications, then this is prima facie evidence against the theory. But if we decide that this coun-terintuitive implication of the theory is a more or less isolated phe-nomenon and that the theory accounts for a great many of our par-ticular value judgments, and especially if it seems to explain more of our value judgments better than alternative theories, then this initial evidence against the theory will be overridden and we should revise the particular value judgment that conflicts with the theory. In assess-ing theories of value, we seek the theory that is in "reflective equilib-rium" with our other beliefs (cf. 3.11 and 5.8–5.9).

A theory of value is *personal* if it recognizes as intrinsically valuable things that are valuable only insofar as they contribute to the value of people's lives (or, more broadly, the lives of sentient beings); a theory of value is *purely personal* if it recognizes only such goods to be of value. Thus, any theory that recognizes pleasurable sensation as an intrinsic good is a personal theory of value, and hedonism is a purely personal theory of value, since it claims that the one and only intrinsically good thing is pleasurable sensation. A theory of value is *impersonal* if it recognizes as intrinsically valuable things that are valuable independently of their contribution to the value of anyone's life; a theory of value is *purely impersonal* if it recognizes only such goods to be of value. Thus, the theory that beauty is an intrinsic good, such that a world containing beautiful works of art is valuable even if there are no beings in this world whose lives they enrich, is an impersonal theory of value, and the theory that beauty is the one and only intrinsic good is a purely impersonal theory of value. A theory of value is *mixed* if it is pluralistic and has both personal and impersonal components. Thus, a theory that says beauty and pleasure are the only two intrinsic goods is a mixed theory of value.

Moore held a mixed theory of value; he thought beauty is intrinsically valuable (1903: 83–4). But I think that many of us find impersonal theories of value hard to accept. Even if we don't accept Sidgwick's claim that something must make some contribution to human (or sentient) *consciousness* to be of intrinsic value (1907: 113), it seems hard to believe that things might be of intrinsic value that made no contribution whatsoever to anyone's well-being (cf. 1907: 10n). I am assuming, therefore, that if we perform Moore's thought experiment carefully and compare the world containing beauty – in which beautiful objects are created by random processes and so do not result from the creative processes of intelligent beings and in which no one ever has seen, and no one ever will see, these objects and appreciate their beauty – with the world that is otherwise similar but contains no beauty, we will not see any difference in value between these worlds.

But even if we reject the claim that beauty is intrinsically valuable, there may be another kind of impersonal theory of value that deserves our attention. A problem with Moore's theory is that it posits as intrinsic goods things that might exist quite apart from sentient beings. But a theory of value might be impersonal because it posits things that are intrinsically valuable independently of any contribution those things make to human (or sentient) welfare, without assuming that these impersonal goods could exist without the existence of human (or sentient) beings. For example, someone might think that a certain kind of distribution of, say, social and economic goods was intrinsically valuable. For the good of (correct) distribution to be an impersonal good, this distribution would have to be valuable in itself, and *not* because of its effects (causal or conceptual) on the welfare of individuals (cf. Scanlon 1977: 143; Scheffler 1982: 26–32). This impersonal account of the value of distributive justice views the community realizing the correct distribution as a kind of "organic whole," whose value is not exhausted by the total value of the lives of members of such a community, even assuming that an individual's good includes the value of belonging to such a community (cf. Moore 1093: 27–36).

This sort of impersonal theory is intelligible and seems more plausible than the sort of impersonal theory Moore advocates. Nonetheless, I think that even this sort of impersonal theory is less than compelling. We can, and perhaps should, allow that distribution is intrinsically valuable, but we don't need to, and I don't think we should, treat distribution as an impersonal good. If *part of* an individual's good involves essential reference to the welfare of others, say, because it is part of any agent's good to belong to a community in which each member treats others with mutual respect and concern, then what it is for an individual's life to go well will *include* the well-being of others in his community. If so, a certain kind of distributive justice can be intrinsically valuable without being an impersonal good; it will be valuable *because* of how it contributes to the welfare of the individuals in the community. On this view, distribution will be a personal good. I find this personal explanation of the intrinsic value of distribution plausible. I find the impersonal value of distribution harder to understand; it seems to make distribution a kind of impersonal aesthetic value, and, as our criticism of Moore suggests, even aesthetic values seem best viewed as personal goods.

For whatever reasons (these or others), most philosophers have defended purely personal theories of value. Personal theories claim that all intrinsic goods are components of valuable *lives*. But there is great diversity among possible personal goods. We need to distinguish between different kinds of personal theories of value.

Subjective theories of value claim that the components of a valuable life consist in or depend importantly on certain of an individual's psychological states. We can distinguish at least three different versions of subjectivism. *Hedonism* claims that a valuable life literally *consists in* certain psychological states: The one and only intrinsic good is pleasure, which is understood as a simple, qualitative mental state; the one and only thing of intrinsic disvalue is pain, which is understood as another simple, qualitative mental state. *Desire-satisfaction* theories claim that value consists in the satisfaction of one's desires and that disvalue consists in the frustration of one's desires. Although desire-satisfaction theories do not claim that value actually consists in psychological states, they do hold value to depend importantly on people's psychological states. Now desire-satisfaction theories come in two importantly different varieties: *actual* desire-satisfaction theories and *counterfactual* desire-satisfaction theories (3.12). An actual desire-satisfaction theory claims that what is valuable is what would satisfy one's actual desires (and that what is disvaluable is what would frustrate one's actual desires). Because our desires can be inconsistent or based on false beliefs, many proponents of the desire-satisfaction theory prefer a counterfactual desire-satisfaction theory. A counterfactual desire-satisfaction theory claims that what is valuable is what would satisfy one's desires in some preferred epistemic position, for instance, if one's beliefs and desires were consistent and one's desires were based on full (nonevaluative) information.

By contrast with these various forms of subjectivism, *objective* theories of value claim that what is intrinsically valuable neither consists in nor depends importantly on such psychological states. Impersonal theories of value will be objective, and so will personal theories that claim a valuable life consists in the possession of certain character traits, the exercise of certain capacities, and the development of certain relations with others and to the world, and that the value of such a life is independent of the pleasure it contains and whether or not this sort of life is desired or would be desired in some preferred epistemic state.[6]

6 Cf. Scanlon 1975b, 1977, and Kraut 1979. Kraut distinguishes between subjective and objective conceptions of *happiness*. Although I think Kraut is right to find objective components in our conception of happiness, it may be easier to see this distinction as a distinction between different conceptions of *welfare*. For we might think that our criteria for application of the *word* 'happiness' are predominantly subjective, even if we can think of welfare in completely nonsubjective terms. (This is why translation of '*eudaimonia*' by 'happiness' may mislead. 'Happiness' is adequate only if one can simply equate being happy with being well off or having one's life go as well as possible.) I have benefited greatly from Kraut's discussion,

221

A theory of value is *purely subjective,* as both hedonism and the desire-satisfaction theories are, if it contains only subjective components; a theory of value is *purely objective* if it contains only objective components. And, of course, theories of value can be *mixed,* containing both subjective and objective components.

Most of the ancient Greeks (e.g., Homer, Plato, Aristotle, and the Stoics), Mill (on certain readings), and the British idealists (e.g., Green and Bradley) defend different versions of objectivism. But modern philosophical theorizing about the nature of value (especially discussion of utilitarianism) has been dominated by pure subjectivism. Hedonistic utilitarians, such as Bentham and Sidgwick, represent one school of subjectivism. Hume, many twentieth-century utilitarians (e.g., Brandt 1979), and most economists hold one or another version of the desire-satisfaction theory. Moreover, many critics of utilitarianism seem to hold, either implicitly or explicitly, some version of subjectivism (e.g., Rawls 1971: 408–24; Gauthier 1986: chap. 2; cf. B. Williams 1980).

It is hard to explain philosophical preoccupations, but the dominance of subjectivism must be attributable, at least in part, to its

but I must dissent from his conclusion. Kraut presents sufficient reasons for preferring objective conceptions of welfare to subjective conceptions (1979: 177–89); I am indebted to him for the reasons I offer. Kraut himself, however, does not draw this conclusion. Rather, he ultimately rejects objective accounts because he believes both that to accept an objective account we must have a complete and detailed objective theory about which there is not much dispute and that not only is there disagreement about what is objectively valuable but, in fact, no one has ever really offered us a developed theory (1979: 189–97). But these reasons for resisting an objective conception of welfare are poor ones. First, we can be justified in rejecting subjective accounts even if we have no fully worked out objective account. Rejection of subjective accounts will not leave us in a void; we can rely on considered beliefs about objective value even if we do not have a systematic theory to rely on. Nor is there good reason to be skeptical about the existence of a systematic conception of objective welfare. Not only does Aristotle, as Kraut recognizes, offer us one objective conception of welfare; the history of moral philosophy contains a number of objective conceptions. Objective conceptions of welfare can be found in Homer, *The Iliad;* Plato, *Republic* bks. II–IV, VIII–IX; Aristotle, *EN* I, 7, and X; Mill 1859: 10, 53–61; 1861: II, 4–8; Bradley 1876: 79–80, 160–213, 219–25; Green 1883: bks. III and IV; Moore 1903: chap. 6; 1912: 100–8; Nozick 1974: 42–5. And, of course, novelists concerned with moral psychology also provide objective conceptions of welfare. None of these conceptions may be unobjectionable, but they provide us with conceptions that can be compared and used to correct one another. Kraut's complaint about objective conceptions of welfare seems to be no more than an argument from disagreement, and we have found that argument to be wanting (7.4).

simplicity, familiarity, and stability. Subjectivism relies on fairly simple and familiar evaluative ideas. We all know what pleasures and pains are and what it is to have a desire satisfied or frustrated. Other things being equal, we seek pleasure and the satisfaction of our desires and we avoid pain and the frustration of our desires. It is common to think of a happy or good life as one that is pleasant, or in which we have satisfied our deepest desires, and of an unhappy life as one that is painful, or in which our important desires have largely been frustrated. Moreover, subjective theories are socially stable in a certain sense: Those with quite different psychological profiles (i.e., people with quite different sorts of desires and who derive pleasure and pain from quite different sorts of activities) can still agree that the satisfaction of desire is good or that the experiencing of pleasure is good.

By contrast, objective theories seem more metaphysical and perhaps more divisive. Which set of character traits, activities, and relationships should we identify with a valuable life? Must not any such view rest on some implausible essentialist claims about human nature? Moreover, would not such a theory prove socially divisive? Differences in psychological profile just reflect differences in the character traits, activities, and relationships that people value. If value theory is to have any important moral or political implications, won't objectivism involve people in intractable moral and political disagreements?

But it is this very simplicity of subjective theories of value and the metaphysical nature of objective theories of value that make the latter in fact more plausible than the former. Subjective theories of value do not do justice to the complexity of our judgments about welfare and happiness.

We have reason to reject hedonism and other theories of value that make our welfare *consist in* psychological states alone. Some pleasures are valuable, and some, perhaps all, pain is disvaluable. But hedonism is false; pleasure is not the one and only intrinsic good. Familiar thought experiments, involving what we might call disreputable (e.g., sadistic) pleasures, suggest that pleasure per se is not intrinsically good (cf. 8.13). But the more important complaint about hedonism, at least for present purposes, is that pleasure is not the only good. Value cannot consist in psychological states alone. Robert Nozick's experience machine explains why.

Suppose there were an experience machine that would give you any experience you desired. Superduper neuropsychologists could stimulate your brain so that you would think and feel you were writing a great novel, or making a friend, or reading an interesting book. All the time you would be floating in a tank, with electrodes attached to your brain. Should you plug into this machine for life, preprogramming your life's experiences? (1974: 42)

The answer, as Nozick notes, seems clearly to be *no,* at least in part because, as Nozick also notes, each of us wants to *be* a certain kind of person and *do* certain sorts of things and not merely have experiences *as if* he were such a person doing such things (1974: 43–4). This thought experiment shows that a valuable life involves certain character traits, the exercise of certain capacities, and having certain relations with others and to the world and, hence, that value cannot consist in psychological states alone. And this shows that hedonism must be false.

Such considerations, however, do not themselves support objectivism or undermine (pure) subjectivism; in particular, they are perfectly compatible with desire-satisfaction theories of value. For the desire-satisfaction theorist can note that the experience machine does not satisfy its clients' desires to be and do certain things (although it does, ex hypothesi, leave them satisfied). If, and only if, these character traits and activities are valuable independently of their being desired will their value support objectivism.

Although the experience machine does not establish objectivism, there are reasons to think there are character traits and activities that are valuable and whose value is independent of their being desired. I have in mind two main arguments; both appeal to a kind of *explanatory failure* of desire-satisfaction theories of value.

The first explanatory failure of the desire-satisfaction theory parallels an explanatory failure of psychological egoism. A familiar form of psychological egoism claims that an agent engages in activities and personal relations only because of the satisfaction she derives from them. But as Joseph Butler argues, the fact that the agent derives satisfaction from certain activities and relations is evidence *against* psychological egoism, since the satisfaction the agent derives from these activities and relations presupposes that she has desires for these activities and relations (Butler 1749: preface, par. 37; sermon XI, 6). Butler's point is that we cannot make sense of an agent's taking satisfaction in certain activities and relations without positing desires whose object is external to the agent. This claim, though true and important, does not itself strictly undermine psychological egoism, since these desires with external objects might not be basic; these external objects might be desired only as a means of promoting some state of the agent, such as her experiencing of pleasure. Thus, Butler's point is strictly compatible with the psychological hedonist (egoist) claim that the agent's pleasure is the only *basic* or *ultimate* object of desire. Butler's point is nonetheless important because it makes the plausibility of (traditional formulations of) psychological egoism depend on the plausibility of psychological hedonism, and no nontrivial account of psychological hedonism seems plausible. Even if some things external to the agent are desired by her only as a means by which to experience pleasure, there is no reason to believe this is universally true; external objects (e.g., money, another's welfare, knowledge) are sometimes desired for their own sake. In these cases, the psychological egoist has the explanation the wrong way around. It is not that the agent desires external objects for the satisfaction they produce; rather, the agent derives satisfaction from producing these external objects, because she has (basic) desires for these external objects.[7]

A similar problem afflicts desire-satisfaction theories of value. The desire-satisfaction theory says that something is valuable just in case, and because, it would contribute to the satisfaction of actual or counterfactual desires. But as we noted earlier (3.11), this seems to get things just about the opposite way around in many cases; we desire certain sorts of things *because we think these things valuable*. This is true of our preferences for many activities and relations as well as states of the world. It is not that these things are valuable because we desire them; rather, we desire them because we think them valuable.[8]

Desire-satisfaction theories get it *just about* the opposite way

---

7 I am not considering here formulations of psychological egoism which allow external objects to be desired both for their own sakes and for their expected contribution to the agent's own happiness. Cf. Aristotle *EN* 1097a19–1097b22 and Mill 1861: IV, 3–9.

8 Cf. Plato *Euthyphro* 9e–11b; Aristotle *Meta* 1072a29; Mill 1861: II, 4–8, and IV, 3–5 (this reading of Mill requires that we take people's preferences, or at least the preferences of competent judges, to be *evidential, not constitutive,* of the value of the objects of these preferences); Wiggins 1976: 347–8; Platts 1980: 80; Bond 1983: vii, 42–4. Contrast Spinoza (1677: pt. III, proposition 9, Scholium): "It is clear . . . that we do not endeavor, will, seek after or desire because we judge a thing good. On the contrary, we judge a thing to be good because we endeavor, will, seek after and desire it."

around in such cases because such desires presuppose only the *belief* that the object of desire is valuable and not the fact that it is valuable. But this fact about the explanation of desire is important, because it shows that *we presuppose* that some things are valuable independently of their being objects of actual or counterfactual desire.

I say that desire-satisfaction theories get it the wrong way around in *many* cases, because this sort of value-laden explanation may not be required for all desires. We don't seem to need to posit a belief on Alan's part that baklava is more valuable than other desserts in order to explain his preference for baklava. It seems to be enough that Alan likes baklava more than other desserts. Or if we allowed ourselves to be pressed for an explanation of Alan's likings, it would seem to be enough to cite some pleasant qualitative mental states he experiences on eating baklava, and it would not seem necessary to ascribe to him the belief that these qualitative mental states are valuable. Even if there is no need for value-laden explanations of gustatory preferences, this is not true of certain other desires; they require value-laden explanations (cf. Sidgwick 1907: 44–5). At least part of the explanation of my wanting to be a professional philosopher involves my belief that philosophy is a valuable activity; I would not have this desire if I did not think philosophy was a valuable activity. Part of the explanation of my wanting to relieve my neighbor's suffering is that I think pain and suffering are bad; if I were somehow to come to think there was nothing objectionable about pain and suffering, I would probably have little concern about my neighbor's situation.

A great many of our desires are like these and require value-laden explanations. The need for value-laden explanations of many desires shows that we think that desire-satisfaction theories are false.

The second explanatory failure for desire-satisfaction theories surfaces in the attempt to formulate a desire-satisfaction theory that fits our considered evaluative judgments.

We start off with the actual desire-satisfaction theory of value. Something is valuable just in case, insofar as, and because it would produce the object of someone's actual (occurrent or dispositional) desires. But this theory seems inadequate, since it must accord many activities and lives much greater value than they seem to possess. We can imagine lives in which people satisfy their dominant desires and meet self-imposed goals, which we are nonetheless not prepared to regard as especially valuable.

First, there are desires we regard as immoral in certain ways; their satisfaction is not (especially?) valuable. Ludwig is an obsessed and extremely successful Nazi. His primary goal in life is to persecute Jews; he has extirpated all desires not instrumental to the successful pursuit of this goal, and he has formed various subsidiary desires pursuant to this goal. But we do not think his success in satisfying these desires confers value on his life; in fact, satisfaction of his desires may make his life still less valuable than would their frustration. We think not just that Ludwig is missing other valuable activities but that the goal that does guide his life is especially valueless.

Second, there are desires that though perhaps not immoral, nonetheless seem inappropriate or unimportant. Consider Zelda, who, shortly before her death, satisfied her lifelong desire to have the smallest handwriting. This had been Zelda's dominant goal. Though brimming with intellectual, creative, and social capacities, she ignored alternative careers and activities, family, and friends. Of course, she was not frustrated much; she set herself a reasonable schedule for achieving the smallest handwriting, and she satisfied the desires to which this schedule gave rise. Yet we suppose both that Zelda failed to realize important values by allowing her intellectual and creative talents to atrophy and that she focused her energy on an especially unimportant project.

Moreover, desire-satisfaction theories would seem to counsel the cultivation of desires that are most easily satisfiable and the extirpation of desires with more risky objects. Desire-satisfaction theories would have us look favorably upon the lives of Deltas and Epsilons in Aldous Huxley's *Brave New World* (1946). But, of course, we find such lives frightening. We object to the genetic engineering used to restrict artificially the capacities of Deltas and Epsilons, and to the social and psychological training that keeps them from developing capacities that they do have. We do not (in general) increase the value of our lives by lowering our sights, even if by doing so we increase the frequency of our successes.

Nor need such judgments be confined to other people's lives. It is possible to look back at periods in our own lives during which we were satisfying our deepest desires and achieving our goals, decide that those desires and goals were unimportant, and conclude that that part of our lives was not as valuable as we had then supposed. I suppose that this is dramatically demonstrated in the cases of many former alcoholics and drug addicts.

227

In making these judgments about the value of real or imaginary lives and parts of lives, we assume that certain sorts of projects and commitments are worth pursuing and that certain sorts of desires are appropriate to satisfy. We assume that certain sorts of lives and activities are more valuable than others, more or less independently of how the person whose life it is regards her life and her activities. Objectivism is one obvious explanation of our views here. What seems objectionable about many of these cases is that the agent fails to develop appropriate capacities and to enter into appropriate relationships with others. Objectivism can explain these views, since it claims there is a set or range of character traits, activities, and relations that are valuable and whose value is independent of their being objects of actual or counterfactual desire.

But someone might argue that these thought experiments undermine only actual desire-satisfaction theories and so do not establish objectivism. They show a problem with placing evaluative reliance not on the agent's desires but on his *actual* desires. We can avoid these problems, the desire-satisfaction theorist might claim, by making value a direct function of what would satisfy the agent's *counterfactual* desires, that is, the desires the agent would have in some preferred or privileged epistemic state.

How should we characterize this preferred epistemic state of counterfactual desire-satisfaction theory? There might be both motivational and informational constraints upon the subject in this preferred epistemic state (cf. Rawls 1971: 408–24; Brandt 1979; Gauthier 1986: chap. 2).

Counterfactual desire-satisfaction theories typically include informational constraints. Our desires are sensitive to changes in belief, and so desires can be modified by the acquisition of new information. A desire-satisfaction theory might naturally claim that value is determined by what would satisfy the desires of someone who is *fully informed*. Counterfactual desire-satisfaction theories either can relativize value to the desires that would be had by people with all *available* information (what is valuable, then, may change as available information changes) or can define value in terms of the desires that would be had by people with all the information available to people *at the limit of rational inquiry*.

Now, of course, this information must be *nonevaluative* information. The desire-satisfaction theory is offering to explain value in terms of desire – to be the object of (counterfactual) desire is what

228

constitutes being valuable. Therefore, it cannot count only desires based on appropriate evaluative information.

One possible motivational constraint seeks to secure consistency in the subject's desires. We can distinguish the kind of *necessary* inconsistency in desire, which results when the subject both desires x qua F and is averse to x qua F, and *contingent* inconsistency in desire, which results from the fact that, given the way the world is, two desires that are not necessarily inconsistent nonetheless cannot both be satisfied (cf. B. Williams 1965). If I both like and dislike the (same) analytical aspects of philosophical thinking, then my desires are necessarily inconsistent. If I want to be a professional philosopher and want to be a world-class badminton player, and the training and commitment of each is such that I cannot do both, my desires are only contingently inconsistent. Necessarily inconsistent desires are fairly rare, and I see no good reason for the desire-satisfaction theory to eliminate them. They should be recognized, and the desire-satisfaction theory should claim they give rise to conflicts of value. What is, other things being equal, most valuable in such circumstances will, of course, depend on the relative intensities of the two desires. The case of contingently inconsistent desires is somewhat different, since it is possible to be aware of each of the two conflicting desires and yet, because of ignorance of the world, fail to see their practical incompatibility. Often both desires would survive recognition of their practical incompatibility, in which case the desire-satisfaction theory should again recognize conflicts of value. Other times, recognition of a practical conflict among one's desires would lead to the extirpation of one of the conflicting desires. Where this is true, a counterfactual desire-satisfaction theory, precisely because it insists on full information, should recognize only the value of satisfying the desire that would survive.

These are fairly familiar informational and motivational constraints on a counterfactual desire-satisfaction theory. But they seem insufficient, either individually or jointly, to avoid the implausible implications of the actual desire-satisfaction theory. Neither full (nonevaluative) information nor the kind of psychological consistency we might require can ensure either the extirpation of the sort of inappropriate desires we found in Ludwig, Zelda, and the Epsilons or the cultivation of more appropriate desires. Ludwig might be a Nazi whose hatred of Jews is based on false empirical beliefs about the intellectual and affective capacities of Jews, which would be corrected were he to be placed in the ideal epistemic state. And Zelda'a obsession with handwriting might rest on a false belief in the poverty of her other capacities and talents, which also would be corrected if she were to occupy the preferred epistemic state. So we can imagine people otherwise like Ludwig and Zelda whose actual life-style the counterfactual desire-satisfaction theory need not endorse. But Ludwig and Zelda need not be like this. We can also imagine people who have the desires that Ludwig and Zelda actually have, whose desires are not inconsistent (in the relevant sense) and would not be undermined by the acquisition of any genuine nonevaluative information. Such people may be unusual and in some sense psychologically unrealistic, but their description is perfectly coherent. Let's assume that a full characterization of Ludwig and Zelda would show them to be like this. Counterfactual desire-satisfaction theories incorporating only these informational and motivational constraints must, implausibly, confer a great deal of value on the lives of Ludwig and Zelda.

Perhaps all of this just shows that the counterfactual desire-satisfaction theory should incorporate *more* constraints into the preferred epistemic state. What would these additional constraints be? A subject who possessed a variety of social, affective, intellectual, and creative capacities, who recognized herself as such a being, and who desired to exercise such capacities, would never, if properly informed, hold the sorts of desires, commitments, and projects that Ludwig, Zelda, and the Epsilons do. A counterfactual desire-satisfaction theory that builds such conditions into its preferred subject promises a good fit with our considered evaluative judgments.

This response shows that any plausible theory of value can be formulated in desire-satisfaction terms. For any theory about which activities and relationships are valuable, we can formulate another theory of value in terms of the desires that would be had by a subject with certain capacities and certain information that will coincide in its evaluative implications with the original theory of value.

But, of course, this spells defeat, not victory, for the desire-satisfaction theory. For what *explains* the value of the activities that are valuable, on such a view, is our specification of the subject of desire and not the fact that she desires these things; the fact that she desires the things that are valuable simply follows from our specification of her capacities. Appeal to her desires is otiose; we could just appeal to the value of exercising the capacities that we have ascribed to her. Just as the subject's capacities are now specified prior to and independently of her desires, so too the value of exercising such capacities by engaging in certain activities and relationships is independent of these activities' and relationships' being the object of desire. And this is precisely what the objectivist affirms and the desire-satisfaction theory denies.[9]

These arguments show that purely subjective theories of value, both hedonism and various desire-satisfaction theories, are implausible. Value must contain important objective components. This fact can be accommodated either within a purely objective theory or within a mixed theory.

Just which version of objectivism about welfare is correct is a difficult issue, which I cannot argue here. Instead, I want to sketch an objective theory of welfare that I think is plausible, incorporate this theory of value into a teleological moral structure, and explore the implications of the resulting utilitarian moral theory.

A plausible objective conception of welfare must, I think, recognize a number of distinct, even if related, components of human welfare. It should also distinguish among components of human welfare that are intrinsically valuable, goods that are extrinsically valuable, and necessary conditions for human welfare (which may also have a great deal of extrinsic value). I propose to discuss a theory of welfare that counts reflective pursuit and realization of agents' reasonable projects and certain personal and social relationships as the primary components of valuable lives. Freedom, education, and the conditions of basic well-being are among the goods that serve as necessary conditions for these intrinsic goods and that possess extrinsic value as causal contributors to human welfare, so construed.

An objective account of a valuable life will view the exercise of

9 Similar remarks seem to apply to recent attempts by John McDowell and David Wiggins to explain how value can be simultaneously both subjective and objective by appeal to "secondary quality" accounts of value (cf. McDowell 1985 and Wiggins 1987a). Their suggestions are, roughly, that x is valuable just in case x is such as to *merit* approval (McDowell) or x is such as to produce approval in the *appropriate* sort of appraiser (Wiggins). I am not questioning the truth of these claims; of course they are true. Rather, my complaint is that appeal to an appraiser's approval does no significant work in explaining the value of the objects so approved. What does the explanatory work is the account of the meritorious features of the objects that merit approval (and the account of the meritoriousness of these features) and the account of the features of an appraiser that make her an appropriate appraiser (and the account of the appropriateness of these features).

certain capacities as the primary constituents of such a life. I assume, although I cannot develop the idea adequately here, that the assessment of activities and the capacities they exercise will be guided by, among other things, normative conceptions of human nature and ideals of the person (cf. Aristotle *EN* I, 7; Mill 1859: 9; 1861: II, 4–8). These conceptions or ideals will themselves be informed and constrained by empirical study of human cognitive and affective capacities, metaphysical claims about the nature of persons and the conditions of their identity through time, and substantive evaluative views about what sort of things seem valuable and why. Many such ideals prize our rational and social natures; according to such ideals, projects whose pursuit realizes capacities of practical reason, friendship, and community will be especially important, and their importance is more or less independent of anyone's recognition of their value (although, of course, this is not to say that value does not attach to the recognition of their value).

Part of what seems special and valuable about human nature is the capacity for practical reason – the capacity to evaluate courses of action and decide what to do. We realize this capacity in forming, evaluating, revising, and implementing plans and projects. The value of practical reason will in this way constrain the way projects should be formed and pursued. The formation and pursuit of projects should be reflective; an agent's decisions should reflect a concern for her entire self. This requires that she attempt to integrate projects into a coherent life plan, one that realizes the capacities of the kind of being that normative reflection on human nature tells her she is. These constraints will obviously place some constraints on the content of projects as well. Projects that wholly or in large part abdicate the agent's powers of practical reason (as in Zelda's case), even if reached as the result of some (necessarily limited and imperfect) reflection, will be less valuable for that reason. Other constraints on the content of projects must await further specification of the relevant ideal. But if this ideal contains important social aspects, then we should expect to conclude that practical deliberation in the service of projects that impose unnecessary or unjustifiable suffering on others will have comparatively little value, certainly if the same deliberative capacities could be equally well realized in other, socially more constructive ways.

Ideals of the person will in this way constrain the content as well as the formation and pursuit of personal projects. I assume, however, that the appropriate capacities for practical deliberation can be effectively realized in quite different life plans, and so I shall also assume that such constraints are compatible with a certain kind of pluralism about the contents of a valuable life and so do not imply any objectionable form of elitism.[10] Thus, the appropriate set of constraints on a project's value should still leave a wide range of admissible projects the pursuit of which is intrinsically valuable.

If our account of the constituents of a valuable life is even to approach completeness, it must be of some value not just that people reflectively pursue appropriate personal projects but also that these projects and life plans be realized. Realization of such projects must, therefore, also be a component of human welfare.

Another feature of human beings commonly held to be special and valuable is sociality of various kinds. We have social capacities for sympathy, benevolence, love, and friendship whose realization makes our lives better than they would otherwise be. These relationships involve treating others as people whose welfare matters and with concern for the others' own sake. Family relations, friendships, and social relations involving mutual concern and respect exercise these capacities, secure individuals against a variety of misfortunes, and extend their interests in new ways.[11] These are rea-

10 Here and in the previous paragraph I make, without articulating or defending, certain assumptions about both the individuation of deliberative capacities and the comparative significance, in light of the underlying ideal of the person, of different deliberative capacities. For an examination and defense of Aristotle's view on these matters, a view I find attractive, see Irwin 1988: chap. 8, secs. 1–5.

11 I assume these claims will seem plausible for at least two kinds of reasons: We see ourselves as social beings (beings with distinctive social capacities, whose psychological profiles are shaped to a large extent by their relations to others), and we regard lives lived in this way with others as richer than solitary lives. If we allowed ourselves to try to justify these social components in a person's good to someone who did not admit the force of these reasons, we might appeal to ways in which participation in relationships involving concern for the other's own sake can contribute to one's own good. Such relationships make possible reliable forms of cooperation, which allow me to pursue projects and aims I could not have pursued on my own or in ways I could not have pursued on my own. As a special instance of this, such cooperation will be valuable to me insofar as I identify myself with certain projects and aims, and these relationships give me some assurance that others will pursue these projects and aims even when I am unable to. If these relationships are necessary for me to pursue my own good in this way, I have reason to care for others for their own sake, and I should regard their good as part of my own in important ways. At least this is the *kind* of justification I would try to offer in reply to this sort of challenge. It relies on Aristotle *EN* VIII–IX and borrows from Irwin's resourceful interpretation (Irwin 1988: chap. 8, secs. 10–12).

sons to treat personal and social relationships that exhibit appropriate kinds of mutuality of concern as another component of human welfare.

As components of human welfare, pursuit and realization of admissible projects and personal and social relationships exhibiting respect for persons are intrinsically valuable. Actions, motives, and other things that express these values are themselves intrinsically valuable, while actions, motives, and other things that causally contribute to the realization of these values are extrinsically valuable.

This conception of the components of human welfare suggests a number of necessary conditions for welfare and extrinsic goods. First, realization of any one of these three components requires possession of the goods of basic well-being (basic goods). Basic goods are goods required to satisfy at least minimal nutritional, medical, and psychological needs. Second, pursuit of personal projects and pursuit of the appropriate kinds of personal and social relationships requires certain kinds of personal and civic freedoms and opportunities (e.g., freedoms of speech, press, and association and rights of political participation). Third, pursuit of admissible projects requires that agents possess certain abilities. They must be able to compare actual projects with alternative projects, assess the relative importance of actual projects, and formulate subprojects designed to facilitate the realization of larger projects. Such abilities require, and are enhanced by, education. Fourth, although it is actually part of human welfare to have personal and social relationships involving mutual concern and commitment, this kind of respect for persons is also a practical requirement for the realization of many projects. For basic and nonbasic goods that are necessary for the pursuit of most personal projects are typically available only as the result of diachronic cooperative activity. But diachronic cooperative activity is typically available only to, and is certainly enhanced by, participants who treat one another with a certain amount of mutual concern and commitment. This requires that participants in cooperative endeavors respect one another and that social cooperation be conducted on fair terms, to the mutual advantage of participants. Finally, pursuit and realization of many personal projects require, and are enhanced by, varying amounts of nonbasic goods (e.g., philosophers require access to books and time to think and write, painters require access to supplies and similar free time, and carpenters require access to tools and materials).

234

These goods are all literally necessary for, or at least typically enhance significantly, the realization of the intrinsic goods we have recognized.

Of course, alternative actions or motives, say, will typically bear on human welfare in different ways, that is, will affect different aspects of human welfare. So, in a fully developed theory we would have to determine what priority relations, if any, obtain among various intrinsic goods, necessary conditions, and extrinsic goods. In the spirit of this sketch, I shall propose, but not attempt to defend, a rough ordering that seems intuitively appealing. Pursuit of admissible projects and personal and social relationships that respect persons are both typically more important than the actual realization of projects pursued. It is typically more important that one be able to pursue one's projects and that one actually have the appropriate sort of interaction with others than that one actually accomplish specific tasks that one undertakes. (I assume there may be some personal projects whose realization is as important as pursuit of other projects or personal and social relationships, say, because their realization is a condition of pursuing most other projects.) Pursuit of admissible personal projects may seem a somewhat more important part of a valuable life than the appropriate kind of interaction with others, since it seems that we can imagine valuable lives that are comparatively solitary. But priority here is difficult to establish, at least partly because pursuit of admissible projects itself seems to involve certain kinds of personal and social interaction. Respect for others is a condition of admissibility in projects, and many personal projects demand the sort of diachronic cooperation with others that requires, or is greatly enhanced by, treating one's fellow participants with respect. We would do well, perhaps, to regard pursuit of admissible projects and personal and social relationships that involve respect for others as of roughly equal value.

If pursuit of admissible projects and personal and social relationships have priority over the realization of projects, then we can form some idea of the relative importance of the goods that are necessary for, or typically enhance, the realization of intrinsic goods. Since freedom and basic well-being are necessary conditions for the realization of any intrinsic value, they must have priority in any ordering of goods. Education greatly enhances the reflective pursuit and realization of projects and our relations with others, while respect for persons is often necessary for, and greatly enhances, the sort of social cooperation needed to pursue and realize many personal projects. Behind these, in order of importance, are the nonbasic goods needed to pursue and realize specific kinds of projects.

3. OBJECTIVE UTILITARIANISM

This is a very rough account of the probable relations among the various goods involved in this objective conception of welfare. This conception, no doubt, needs to be articulated more fully, and this articulation might reveal further components of human well-being and more specific or additional relations of priority among its components. But its roughness should not affect the purposes to which this conception will be put. If we incorporate such an objective conception of welfare into a teleological moral structure, the result is a weighted pluralist version of objective utilitarianism. In order to distinguish the version of objective utilitarianism I have just sketched from other possible versions of objective utilitarianism, let us refer to it as 'OU'.

Why take OU seriously? Even if something like the objective conception of value that I have sketched seems plausible, why incorporate it into a teleological moral structure? What is the plausibility of such a moral theory?

Later (8.9), I shall argue that OU has certain structural properties that are desirable from a coherentist point of view, but its initial plausibility lies in its apparent ability to accommodate two common and fundamental claims about morality. The first is that morality has to do with human (or, perhaps, sentient) good and harm; morality concerns, at least in large part, the way in which the benefits and burdens of personal and social interaction are to be distributed.[12] The second claim is that the moral point of view requires an impartial concern among different people's welfare; this distribution of benefits and burdens must be impartial. Teleological theories represent this kind of impartiality by claiming that because everyone's welfare matters equally, the right thing to do is to promote human welfare as much as possible.

Of course, none of this represents a knockdown argument for OU or any other teleological moral theory: These two claims are

12 Cf. Foot 1958a, 1958b (indeed, she thinks it is analytically true that morality has to do with human good and harm); Warnock 1971; Mackie 1977: chap. 5; Scanlon 1982: 108–10.

substantive moral claims and thus are revisable; OU may not be the only or best way of trying to accommodate these claims; and there may be other claims that a moral theory should try to accommodate. But these are important beliefs about the content of morality, and, as we shall see, OU represents a vey natural way of accommodating them. This is perhaps reason enough to take OU seriously.

In examining and assessing OU, it is important to remember its teleological aspects as well as its objective conception of welfare. First, OU is intended as a standard or criterion of rightness and not as a decision procedure. That is, OU explains what makes right things right; when, or even whether, people should reason or deliberate by appeal to OU is a matter for further investigation. Second, OU provides a theory of rightness or justification for motives, institutions, policies, and so on, as well as for actions. Motives, institutions, and policies, as well as actions, are justified by the amount of objective welfare they realize.

Insofar as OU does provide a theory of right action, however, it should provide an *act* teleological rather than, say, a rule teleological theory. Rule teleology claims that an action is right just in case it conforms to a rule the general acceptance of which realizes at least as much value as any alternative rule. But rule teleology will justify actions that are not optimific; in particular, it will make actions right that conform to rules that *would* be optimific if generally accepted, but which are *not in fact* generally accepted. But if we assume, as I shall assume, that rightness is determined by the *actual* value realized, then we have no reason to prefer rule teleology to act teleology and, in fact, positive reason to prefer act teleology. Thus, I will construe OU as containing an act teleological theory of right action; an action is right just in case it contributes to human welfare at least as much as any alternative action available to the agent.

This completes my sketch of OU. Investigation of OU's metaphysical, epistemological, and normative implications should bring out its depth and appeal.

4. METAPHYSICAL AND EPISTEMOLOGICAL COMMITMENTS OF OBJECTIVE UTILITARIANISM

The case for moral realism in Chapters 2–7 required relatively abstract metaphysical and epistemological commitments. Different substantive moral theories bring somewhat different metaphysical and epistemological commitments. OU allows us to illustrate the sort of particular metaethical commitments that substantive moral theories bring.

5. OBJECTIVE UTILITARIAN NATURALISM

In Chapters 6 and 7 I argued that the moral realist's metaphysical commitments were similar to, and as plausible as, those of other objective disciplines. Acceptance of the is/ought thesis and the semantic test of properties commits moral realism to nonnaturalism. But a commitment to nonnaturalism for these reasons, we saw, would be no indictment of nonnaturalism, since, for similar reasons, every discipline would be sui generis. A nonnaturalist could accept something like OU. He could claim that moral facts and properties are neither identical with nor constituted by, but nonetheless weakly supervene on, natural and social scientific facts and properties that contribute to the realization of human welfare. If, for instance, certain social and economic relations among individuals (e.g., gross distributive inequality) are sufficient in actual circumstances to instantiate insufficient respect for persons, then a nonnaturalist could claim that, other things being equal, these social and economic relations are wrong.

Although nonnaturalism is a possible version of moral realism, I have suggested that the realist is better advised to defend ethical naturalism. In order to overcome traditional objections, the ethical naturalist need only deny either the traditional theory of meaning underlying the semantic thesis of the is/ought gap or the semantic test of properties. The ethical naturalist can then claim that moral facts and properties are natural facts and properties.

OU claims that goodness is identical with a certain nonreductive, objective conception of human welfare and that rightness is identical with the maximization of welfare, so construed. A naturalistic version of OU implies that these moral facts will consist in natural facts, that is, natural and social scientific facts that contribute to human welfare. Moral facts, according to a naturalistic version of OU, are constituted by those economic, social, psychological, and biological facts that make up and contribute to the pursuit and realization of agents' projects as well as to the development of personal and social relationships involving mutual concern and commitment. Determination of which economic, social, psychological, and biological facts these are will, of course, depend on both empirical research and moral theory.

It follows from a naturalistic version of OU that moral facts and properties both weakly and strongly supervene on economic, social, psychological, and biological facts and properties. According to OU, distributive injustice is intrinsically bad because it is inconsistent with the sort of respect for persons constitutive of admissible projects and of appropriate personal and social relations. Some sets of natural base properties literally necessitate certain moral properties; these moral properties strongly supervene on these natural properties. If distributive injustice strongly supervenes on certain social and economic conditions, then it is literally impossible for these social and economic conditions to obtain without injustice existing. As we have noted, strong supervenience bases are difficult to identify. Although it is hard to know which natural properties literally necessitate injustice, we may be able to identify the weak supervenience base of such moral properties. Moral properties weakly supervene on a set of natural properties if those properties are sufficient in the actual world (and nearby possible worlds) to instantiate those moral properties. For instance, certain social and economic conditions may be sufficient in societies of the sort we are familiar with to cause distributive injustice, even if there are possible societies different from those we are familiar with in enough respects that these social and economic conditions would not cause injustice. According to OU, distributive injustice weakly supervenes on these social and economic conditions.

The truth of materialism guarantees that there are organized combinations of physical facts and properties that contribute to human welfare, and so which moral facts and properties are constituted by and supervene on. According to a naturalistic version of OU, moral facts and properties are constituted by, and so supervene on, higher-order facts and properties, such as social and economic facts and properties, that contribute to human welfare. If, as materialism claims, these higher-order facts and properties are themselves constituted by, and so supervene on, organized configurations of physical facts and properties, then, by the transitivity of constitution and supervenience, moral facts and properties will also be constituted by, and so supervene on, organized combinations of physical facts and properties. And this can be true even if, as seems likely, we will rarely, if ever, have any idea which combinations of physical facts and properties these are (7.1 and 7.3).

6. OBJECTIVE UTILITARIANISM AND THE JUSTIFIABILITY OF MORALITY

In explaining the commitments of moral realism, I defended externalism against internalism (Chapter 3). The concept of morality shows neither that moral considerations motivate nor that they provide reasons for action. Whether a moral fact or its recognition motivates or provides reasons for action depends on a substantive theory of reasons for action, the content of morality, and various facts about agents and the world.

The issue about the rationality or justifiability of moral demands is, as far as I can see, much more interesting than the issue about whether moral considerations motivate. Whether recognition of moral facts motivates seems to be, in any moral theory, a psychological matter depending on the desires agents happen to have (although the moral facts in some moral theories may, as a matter of fact, be more likely to elicit the motivation of agents than they would in other theories).

Whether moral facts provide agents with reason for action depends on what morality requires and on what agents have reason to do. If OU is true, morality requires agents to do that which maximizes human welfare. But, of course, until we know what actions and character traits promote human welfare, we do not know just what OU requires of agents. We can assume, though, that OU will sometimes require agents to benefit others at some cost to themselves. This fact about OU may lead us to ask, 'Do agents have reason to comply with OU's other-regarding demands?'. (Of course, this is a familiar question about the justification of morality, not one peculiar to OU's account of morality.)

The answer depends on what agents have reason to do, and this depends on a substantive theory of reasons for action or rationality. In Chapter 3 we examined two different theories of rationality and their implications for the justifiability of morality (3.12–3.13). Rational egoism claims that an agent has reason to do x just in case, and insofar as, x would contribute to her own interest or welfare; it is an agent relative theory of rationality because it takes an agent's

240

reasons for action to be a direct function of how alternative actions affect *her*. An agent neutral theory denies this; it takes an agent's reasons for action to be a direct function of the value her actions would produce, whether this value accrues to her or not. *Rational altruism* is an agent neutral theory incorporating a purely personal theory of value; it claims that an agent has reason to do x, just in case, and insofar as, x would contribute to people's interest or welfare.

If rational altruism is true, then agents always have reason to do as OU requires, whatever it requires.[13] This would provide a very strong externalist justification of morality. By contrast, many have thought, rational egoism would provide a very weak justification of morality. Does our ability to provide a reasonably strong externalist justification of morality depend on the truth of rational altruism?

In *The Possibility of Altruism*, Nagel argues for rational altruism by analogy with prudence. Just as the interests of an agent's *future* self provide her with reasons for action *now*, so, too, Nagel argues, *others'* interests also provide *the agent* with reasons for action. Failure to recognize temporal neutrality involves temporal dissociation - failure to see the present as just one time among others - and failure to recognize agent neutrality involves person dissociation - failure to recognize oneself as just one person among others. Both kinds of dissociation are cognitive mistakes. The parity of time and person within rationality, therefore, requires rejecting rational egoism and accepting agent neutrality.[14]

But the rational egoist will not be very impressed by this analogy

13 Indeed, Sidgwick *identifies* rational altruism (or, as he calls it, "rational benevolence") with utilitarianism (1907: 385, 418, 498). This reflects Sidgwick's internalism about morality and reasons for action (see Brink 1988a). Of course, this is not my claim; I claim only that rational altruism would justify, or vindicate the rationality of, a utilitarian moral theory.

14 Nagel 1970: 16, 19, 99–100. Although Nagel calls his position 'altruism', and although his appeal to the parity of time and person to reject rational egoism seems to commit him to defending a view I have called 'rational altruism' (see Brink forthcoming), Nagel himself often understands altruism to be only the denial of egoism (or agent relativity); for he has doubts about whether (his) altruism should aggregate people's interests in the manner in which (my) rational altruism does and in which many utilitarian moral theories do (1970 : 133–42). Nonetheless, I shall construe Nagel's argument as an argument for (my) rational altruism, since I think this the natural conclusion of his appeal to the parity of time and person (Brink forthcoming), and since these doubts seem plausible only on the sort of subjectivist assumptions about value that I have argued against (8.2).

with prudence. We saw in Chapter 3 how rational egoism depends on the principle that sacrifice requires compensation (SRC). An agent has reason to make a sacrifice only if she is appropriately compensated for this sacrifice. We also saw that SRC, though not indisputable, has some intuitive support (3.12).[15] But if we accept SRC, we will find prudence and rational altruism importantly disanalogous. For, in the prudential case, a sacrifice of my present interests in favor of my greater future interests is supported by SRC, because these future interests are *mine* – they belong to a future stage of myself – and not simply because these future interests are greater. I am compensated when I sacrifice my present interests for my own future interests. But the interests of other selves, however great, are not (ipso facto) interests of mine; they belong to no stage of me, present or future. Unless there is some connection between my interests and those of others (as, of course, there will in fact often be), I am not compensated when I sacrifice my interests (present or future) for those of others. Justified concern for my future does not itself establish justified concern for others. (cf. Brink forthcoming).

There may be other defenses of rational altruism, but our ability to justify the demands of morality need not be tied to their success. As our discussion of rational egoism (3.12) and our defense of objectivism about value suggest, we can provide a strong defense of the rationality of OU's demands even on rational egoist assumptions.

First, we should notice some of OU's demands. OU will not enjoin great self-sacrifice. OU will not interfere greatly with an agent's important projects and commitments. Often it is difficult to know what would benefit others, and even when one does know, one is often in a poor position to produce those benefits without great cost to oneself. More important, as OU recognizes, special value attaches to people's having and pursuing personal projects and to the development and maintenance of close personal relationships involving mutual concern and commitment. The moral importance of an agent's personal projects and commitments insulates agents from certain other-regarding demands (cf. Sidgwick 1907: 432–4). Of course, OU requires agents to respect other people as persons and to help others realize personal projects and commit-

15 Nagel himself seems to assume something like SRC when he rejects the possibility of "*inter*personal compensation of sacrifice" (1970: 142; my emphasis), which he thinks utilitarianism promises.

ments when this can be done without greater cost to the agent's own personal projects and commitments. But many of these other-regarding obligations can be carried out in ways that are minimally disruptive of the agent's own projects and personal commitments (e.g., by taxation schemes and mutual-aid organizations). So, even if we assume that agents' interests are largely independent, or even competing, many of OU's demands are justifiable on rational egoist grounds.

Just how much of OU is justifiable on egoist grounds, of course, depends on our theory of agent interest or welfare. In fact, we have reason to regard agents' interests as interdependent in significant ways, and this fact greatly strengthens the defense of OU's demands available to rational egoism. In the course of sketching OU, I defended an objective conception of welfare that includes various social components. For pursuit and realization of one's projects to be valuable, these projects must be, among other things, morally acceptable. The pursuit of projects that would impose avoidable hardship upon others is not intrinsically valuable. Moreover, personal and social relationships that involve mutual concern and commitment are *part of* an agent's welfare. An agent's welfare, therefore, is directly related to the welfare of others in certain ways. One is better off when another's welfare is enhanced, and especially when one enhances another's welfare, and, similarly, one suffers when others suffer, and especially when one causes the suffering of others. Not only is the good of others part of an agent's own good, and so intrinsically valuable from the agent's point of view; promoting others' good is extrinsically valuable. Pursuit and realization of many worthwhile personal projects require diachronic social cooperation, which sometimes requires, and is almost always enhanced and facilitated by, fair terms of cooperation. Fair terms of cooperation require that cooperation be conducted on terms of mutual advantage to all participants. In order to pursue her own projects, therefore, an agent is well advised to make sure that others benefit from cooperative endeavors.

Because an agent's welfare depends upon the welfare of others in these ways, an agent has reason to promote the welfare of others. It will be in an agent's interest to develop strong, relatively coarse-grained social dispositions from which she rarely deviates. It would be a mistake to assume that self-regarding and other-regarding components of an agent's good never conflict or that the other-

243

regarding components must always win. But an appropriate objective conception of welfare explains why an agent typically has reason to comply with OU's demands. Indeed, on such a conception of welfare, an egoist can plausibly claim that agents always have *some* reason to benefit others, even if they do not always have *conclusive* reason to benefit others.[16]

It might be claimed against any such egoist justification of morality that the egoist cannot justify *moral* demands, because morality requires not just that we perform the actions it demands of us but also that we fulfill its demands out of a sense of duty and not because doing so contributes to our own interests. The egoist might question the Kantian assumption underlying this objection.[17] But the safer and stronger reply is that rational egoism is compatible with *this* Kantian claim. This Kantian claim represents a claim about moral *motivation*. But rational egoism is a theory about the grounds of reasons for action, not a theory of motivation or of how agents do reason or should reason. So rational egoism places no constraints on the kind of motivation that duty may require; it says only that if an agent is to have reason to do her duty, whatever that may require, then doing so must contribute to her own good. And we have seen how the rational egoist can insist that a rational agent have intrinsic concern for things other than herself; both the paradox of egoism and objective theories of welfare explain how acting out of concern for things other than oneself (e.g., the moral law) can contribute to the agent's own good.

Thus, OU affords a strong externalist justification of morality even on rational egoist assumptions. It is not clear that we should expect any more than this from either a moral theory or a theory of rationality. The fact that we regard the question 'Why be moral?' as often both pressing and difficult to answer is evidence that moral considerations, though important practical considerations, need not

16 My view of how an objective conception of welfare underwrites an egoist account of the justifiability of morality's other-regarding demands might be compared with what I take to be similar views in Plato, Aristotle, Bradley, and Green. Cf. Plato, *Republic* II–IV and VII–IX (see Irwin 1977: chap. 7); Aristotle, *EN* I.7, VIII–IX, and *Pol.* I.2 (see Irwin 1981: 214–21; 1985, 1988: chaps. 8, 9); Bradley 1876: 79–80, 160–213, 219–25; and Green 1883: 192, 199–202, 210–14, 248–9.

17 Cf. Foot 1972a: 164. Foot considers this objection to her rejection of the Kantian claim that duty provides an agent with reason for action independently of his desires or purposes. Her response, unlike mine, is to reject the Kantian assumption about duty underlying the objection.

always control our practical deliberations. (Some of these issues are pursued further in 8.17.)

7. OBJECTIVE UTILITARIAN EXPLANATIONS

In addressing a posteriori epistemological objections to moral realism, I argued that whatever the explanatory commitments of moral realism, moral facts can and do figure in the explanation of nonmoral facts. We often explain an individual's actions and our assessment of that individual's character by appeal to moral properties of his character. For instance, Lincoln's opposition to slavery is due, according to popular accounts, at least in part to his decency and fair-mindedness. Moreover, we often explain certain social events as due in part to facts of political morality. For instance, it is the racial injustice of South African society that explains why black South Africans (and white sympathizers) protest against their government.

Now these moral explanations are straightforward causal explanations within extensional contexts; in particular, these explanations invoke no propositional attitudes. For this reason, we might expect the claim that a moral explanation makes to remain true and explanatory when the correct analysis of the moral fact cited in the explanation is substituted for the moral fact originally cited. That is, if an explanandum occurs in virtue of a moral fact, then we might expect the facts in virtue of which that moral fact holds to explain the explanandum as well. I say that we might expect this, because there is some controversy over whether explanatory contexts are transparent or opaque and over what sorts of substitutions opacity precludes. (If the argument of 7.3 is correct, we should not expect counterfactual transparency in explanatory contexts; moral [and other explanatory higher-order] facts will be explanatory in counterfactual situations in which the lower-order facts they consist in do not obtain.) But consider similar substitutions in nonmoral cases. The temperature of the room explains, in part, why my ice-cream cone melts onto my trousers if I do not eat it fast enough. But the heat of the room just is a certain mean kinetic energy of the molecules in the room. We expect and find that we can also explain the melting of my ice-cream cone by appeal to the mean kinetic energy of the molecules in the room. It is this sort of case that motivates the expectation about the kind of substitution in explana-

245

tory contexts that I mentioned. But since this substitution principle may be controversial, perhaps we should claim not that failure of substitutivity counts against a proposed analysis of the moral facts but only that substitutional success provides some support for a proposed analysis of the moral facts.

OU's analysis of moral facts seems to confirm the explanatory power of moral facts. OU will claim, roughly, that racial injustice in South Africa consists in those social, political, and legal arrangements whereby the objective welfare of black members of the community is arbitrarily frustrated. Blacks are denied the freedom necessary to pursue and realize personal projects and personal and social relationships of certain sorts, and they are denied nonbasic and sometimes basic goods necessary to pursuit and realization of their projects. These social facts, like the moral facts they realize, explain at least in part why black South Africans (and their sympathizers) are protesting and why they are protesting what they are protesting. Lincoln's fairness, according to OU, consists, roughly, in his respecting other people as persons who have an interest in the pursuit and realization of personal projects and in the development of personal and social relationships involving mutual concern and commitment. Such facts about Lincoln's character, like the fairness in his character that they realize, seem to explain at least in part why he opposed the institution of slavery.

OU's substitutional success in explanatory contexts provides only limited support for it, both because of the controversial nature of substitution in explanatory contexts and because OU's account of the moral facts involved in these moral explanations is not peculiar to OU. Nonetheless, OU is helped, not undermined, by the moral explanations which it supports.

8. OBJECTIVE UTILITARIANISM AND MORAL DISAGREEMENT

Common sense and attention to the argument from disagreement tell us that moral disputes can be extremely difficult to resolve. In 7.4 we saw how the nature of moral disagreement could be explained on realist assumptions. OU helps explain how many moral disputes that are in principle resolvable are nonetheless so difficult to resolve, even under favorable conditions.

First, some apparent moral disputes will be only apparent; in these cases "disputants" apply similar moral principles in different circumstances to justify different policies. Although these may look like real disputes, the interlocutors are ascribing different moral properties to different action types. For example, people both in economically backward and in economically advanced societies might appeal to OU to determine distributional policies. People in economically backward conditions (c_1) might (correctly) use OU to justify certain distributive inequalities, if, say, these inequalities would be to the benefit of all members of the community, while people in economically favorable conditions (c_2) might (correctly) use OU to justify distributive equality, if, say, inequalities in these conditions would benefit only some participants in social and economic cooperation. Although someone might be misled into thinking there is a moral disagreement between these two societies about distribution policy, there is in fact no disagreement. One society thinks inequalities are justified in c_1, while the other thinks that inequalities are unjustified in c_2. There is no disagreement here; indeed, OU explains how both moral beliefs can be true.

Of course, not everyone accepts OU. Some hold no moral theory (only considered moral beliefs), and some hold nonutilitarian moral theories. But, of course, this sort of antecedent disagreement over OU should no more lead us to doubt that OU is objectively true or false than should disputes about the hereditability of intelligence or about the origins of World War I lead us to doubt that these issues concern matters of objective fact. The most a realist need concede about such disputes is that most of them are resolvable at least in principle (7.4). Since no one's actual beliefs even approximate ideal coherence, the fact that people actually disagree provides very little reason for thinking that disagreement will persist in the limit of coherentist inquiry. So long as there is, as there always is, some significant initial agreement, we have reason to pursue coherentist reasoning with those with whom we disagree in the expectation that our dispute is resolvable at least in principle, that is, in the limit of inquiry. Of course, the most we will ever do is *improve* the coherence of our beliefs. I shall not pretend to establish that OU is the moral theory on which cognizers would converge in the limit of coherentist inquiry. But I shall try to show that it is coherent – indeed, more coherent than is usually thought. I shall argue not only that OU can respond to many of the standard objections to utilitarianism but that it coheres well with many of our considered moral beliefs. And, of course, even if my argument fails to convince, this will not show that the dispute over OU is in principle unresolvable.

Some antecedent moral disagreement may be within, rather than about, OU. That is, some moral disputes may reflect disagreement not over objective utilitarianism but over the exact components of human welfare, the conditions necessary for human welfare, or the priority relations among these components and conditions. Someone might claim that pursuit and realization of admissible personal projects and the development and maintenance of personal and social relationships involving mutual concern and commitment do not exhaust the components of a valuable life, or that I have misidentified the priority relations among these components and their necessary conditions. Indeed, I insisted that my account of OU is underdeveloped and at best only approximately true. But such disagreements give us no reason to suppose that these issues about the nature of human welfare are not resolvable, at least in principle, by reasoning that appeals to full information, experience, imagination, and our considered beliefs about what sorts of things are, or could be, valuable or desirable. Disputants can be more or less reasonably mistaken about the correct conception of human welfare.

People might agree on a conception of OU, apply it correctly, and still disagree. Because right and wrong, according to OU, depend on facts about what contributes to human welfare, and these facts depend at least in part on complex and controversial issues in empirical disciplines such as nutrition theory, economics, social theory, and psychology, even disputants who agree on OU and are well informed can disagree about right and wrong.

And, of course, persistent disagreement with some (at least possible) interlocutors should not be taken to undermine belief in OU. Extremely harsh environmental or social conditions, for example, could so distort a person's moral beliefs or beliefs about a person's own interests as to make it impossible, even in principle, to convince him of true claims. (See 7.4.) Extremely harsh environmental conditions could produce interpersonal antagonisms that make it psychologically impossible for people in such conditions to see the intrinsic and extrinsic benefits of social cooperation. False social ideology could also block acceptance of OU (that is, even if it were true). Some social theorists believe that particular modes of social and economic organization create dominating and dominated classes.

Dominating classes can develop a mistaken conception of their interests and use their social power to develop and maintain a social and cultural ideology that reinforces a mistaken conception of, among other things, appropriate terms of social cooperation. If this ideology is pervasive enough, members of either class in such a society may be psychologically unable to accept a moral theory, like OU, that requires agents to maximize human welfare and recognizes obligations of mutual respect and concern.

9. THE IMPORTANCE OF UNIFIED MORAL THEORIES

This completes my study of OU's metaphysical and epistemological implications. Any substantive moral theory will bring more or less plausible commitments of this kind. OU's commitments here may not be uniquely plausible, but they are plausible enough to merit consideration of OU's overall coherence.

Despite OU's ability to accommodate the belief that the moral point of view involves an impartial concern for human welfare and to illustrate the commitments of moral realism, many will find OU insupportable. Utilitarianism has been the object of much criticism, most of which is thought to undermine all forms of consequentialism or teleology. I shall consider four types of criticism. First, it is argued that utilitarianism is incoherent or self-defeating because it presupposes an ability to compare the consequences of different actions for the welfare of different people.[18] Second, utilitarianism is often criticized for making moral mistakes. It is alleged that utilitarianism has a crude theory of value[19] and that it fails to accommodate the extent of our obligations,[20] the existence of moral and political rights,[21] and the demands of distributive justice.[22] Third, it is claimed that utilitarianism's impartiality does not recognize the importance of the agent's personal point of view.[23] Finally, the

18 Robbins 1935; Donagan 1977: 199–205; cf. Schneewind 1977: 141–2, 146.
19 Rawls 1971: 30; B. Williams 1973a: 105; Dworkin 1976: 234–8, 1978: 275–7.
20 Ross 1930: 22, 34–5, 38; Baier 1958: 203–4; Rawls 1971: 572–3; Fried 1978: 2, 169.
21 Rawls 1971: 209–11; Dworkin 1970, 1984; Nozick 1974: 28–9; Gewirth 1978: 200, 296; Fried 1978: 81–105; Lyons 1982.
22 Rawls 1958, 1971; Nozick 1974: 150–64; Gewirth 1978: 200, 296; B. Williams 1973a: 137.
23 B. Williams 1973a: 82, 97–118; 1976a; 1976b; Rawls 1982: 180–1; Fried 1978: 2, 34, 114; Lomasky 1983; Nagel 1979b: 205; 1980: 108, 119–20, 127, 131, 135; Scheffler 1982.

second and third problems for utilitarianism are often thought to follow from its failure to recognize the separateness of persons.[24] As I have noted, although these objections have been directed at traditional subjective versions of utilitarianism, they have been thought to undermine all forms of teleological ethics.[25] Indeed, many have concluded that these kinds of objections reveal the radical pluralism of moral considerations and so undermine the prospect of a *unified* moral theory of the sort utilitarianism typically represents. Unified moral theories relate distinct moral considerations; they explain why things to which we attach moral value are all of moral value and attempt to organize different moral considerations in some fairly systematic order. Based in large part on their criticism of utilitarianism, Thomas Nagel, Bernard Williams, and Charles Taylor all contend that we must abandon the search for a systematic and unified moral theory and recognize a variety of distinct moral considerations that are connected by no common principles.[26]

I think we should be very careful in rejecting unified moral theories such as utilitarianism and in embracing nonunified moral theories. Moral realism implies that some moral claims are true, and a coherence theory of justification in ethics provides strong, but defeasible, reasons for the truth of some unified moral theory. Coherentism makes justification a matter of relations among beliefs; other things being equal, the more interconnections and mutual support among beliefs, the better justified those beliefs are. Coherentism places a premium on systematic explanation. Coherentism, therefore, favors unified moral theories over nonunified or fragmented moral theories. Indeed, coherentism not only favors unified moral theories but also unification between moral theories and our nonmoral beliefs. Insofar as a moral theory explains the connections among moral considerations and arranges them in a systematic fashion, as unified theories do, it makes our beliefs more coherent and better justified. By making moral considerations irreducibly distinct and unrelated, nonunified moral theories have a hard time

24 Nagel 1970: 134, 138, 142; Rawls 1971: 23–4, 27, 29, 187–8, 191; 1974: 17; Nozick 1974: 31–4; B. Williams 1976a: 3; Fried 1978: 33–4, 105, 114.
25 See B. Williams 1973a: 79, 81; Nozick 1974: 28–9; Fried 1978: 2, 8, 104; Scheffler 1982.
26 Nagel 1979a: 134–5; 1980: 108, 119, 135; B. Williams 1979; 1981: ix; 1985: 100–1, 111–13; Taylor 1982. Cf. Moore 1903: 222; 1912: 106; Ross 1930: 18–30; Prichard 1912: 9.

explaining how to resolve moral conflicts and why moral considerations are all *moral* considerations. Why are these disparate things all intrinsic goods or prima facie duties? Nonunified or fragmented moral theories, therefore, leave our moral beliefs less systematic and less coherent.

It is important to recognize the variety of possible unified moral theories. Teleological structure is neither a necessary nor a sufficient condition for a theory's being unified. In fact, the unified-nonunified distinction cuts across the teleological-deontological distinction. Traditional subjective versions of utilitarianism represent one kind of unified theory; they define rightness in terms of goodness and provide a monistic theory of the good in terms of pleasure or desire satisfaction. But unified theories need not be monistic. OU, for example, contains a pluralistic theory of the good, but its intrinsic goods are all represented as components of human welfare. Some teleological theories fail to be unified, because they recognize a plurality of distinct and unrelated goods (e.g., Moore 1903: 25, 147–8, 222; 1912: 72–83, 106). And, whereas many deontological theories appear to be no more than an "unconnected heap" of obligations,[27] deontological theories can be unified. For example, a Kantian moral theory that attempts to explain our obligations in terms of what a rational being *as such* would will may provide the basis for a unified moral theory (Kant 1785: 408, 412, 425–6; 1788: 32; cf. Scanlon 1982: 110–19).

The fact that insofar as a moral theory is unified, it makes our moral beliefs more coherent creates a presumption in favor of unified moral theories. Of course, this presumption could be defeated. If it turned out that all unified moral theories have as many defects as it is claimed utilitarian theories have, and if nonunified theories could account for our considered moral beliefs,[28] then we might be justified in accepting some nonunified moral theory. The *most coherent* set of moral beliefs could be radically pluralistic or fragmented. This is why unified teleological theories such as OU must take the standard objections to utilitarianism seriously.

The possibility that nonunified moral theories might be maxi-

---

27 This phrase and charge derive from Joseph 1931: 67 (quoted in Irwin 1977: 342). Cf. Prichard 1912: 9; 1937: 114, and Ross 1930: 23.
28 I suppose nonunified theories can trivially account for our considered moral beliefs, since any set of considered moral beliefs can count as a nonunified moral "theory."

mally coherent might lead some to doubt moral realism. The unification or promise of unification in other disciplines, such as the natural sciences, seems to be one mark of their objectivity. But this is the wrong reaction to this possibility. Only if there were good reason to regard moral theory as so badly fragmented that no general moral claims could be reconciled with our considered moral beliefs might moral realism be threatened. And even in this event, the case for moral realism established in Chapters 2–7 might warrant belief that such a badly fragmented moral theory was objectively true. It is hard to believe, however, that a unified moral theory that required the revision of some considered moral beliefs would not be more reasonable to accept than such a badly fragmented moral theory.

Of course, I do not believe that all unified moral theories are so badly off as to make nonunified moral theories preferable. The standard objections to utilitarianism fail to undermine OU, I shall argue, either because they depend on construing utilitarianism as a decision procedure, or because they assume a subjective conception of welfare. Because OU avoids these commitments, it can respond persuasively to standard objections to utilitarianism. Thus, OU's responses are plausible enough to make it preferable to nonunified moral theories.

10. INTERPERSONAL COMPARISONS OF WELFARE

Against utilitarianism it is often claimed that the interpersonal comparisons of welfare that its application requires are either theoretically or practically impossible. I want first to consider the theoretical impossibility of interpersonal comparisons of welfare. Since traditional versions of utilitarianism conceive of welfare as either pleasure or preference satisfaction, the traditional problem has been whether these interpersonal comparisons of pleasure or preference (utility) are possible. We do make judgments that Bonny was more pleased or has stronger preferences in some area than Barney, and, often, especially when the differences appear to be gross, we are quite confident about such judgments. What reasons are there for thinking that these judgments could not possibly be correct?

Someone might think that interpersonal comparisons of utility are impossible, because of the formal properties of utility functions in social choice theory. If individual utility functions are con-

252

structed on an ordinal basis, then the value we assign to the preference of any individual is defined only relative to her other preferences. This will be true of everyone's individual utility function. Thus, the existence of such utility functions does not seem to provide a basis for comparing the values of the preferences of two different individuals – no common currency has been established (e.g., Luce and Raiffa 1957: 34). But, of course, this does not show interpersonal comparisons of utility to be impossible; at most, it shows them to be impossible only on the basis of certain limited data. Given only ordinal utility functions, we have no basis for comparison.

Any theoretical problem for the interpersonal comparison of welfare would have to be quite general. As I said, the traditional objection has been to interpersonal comparisons of subjective states. But if the problem were confined to the comparison of subjective states, there would be no serious problem for OU, since OU's theory of welfare is objective.[29] Moreover, the problem about interpersonal comparisons of welfare cannot be confined to the comparison of subjective states. The comparison of subjective states would be peculiarly problematic only if there were a theoretical problem about the existence of other minds or our access to them. Indeed, some have diagnosed the worry about interpersonal comparisons of welfare as a worry about the existence of other minds (Little 1957: 54; Sartorius 1975: 29; Hare 1981: 126). But first, a worry about other minds is part of a general skeptical worry and so poses no *special* problem for utilitarianism. Second, a worry about the existence of other minds would contradict the assumption that there are in fact a plurality of individual linear utility functions. Someone might think that the worry about interpersonal comparisons of utility depends on worries not about the existence of, but about the reliability of our access to, other minds. But this transforms the

29 It is true that OU requires maximization of, among other things, pursuit and realization of personal projects, and this will require that we be able to assess the importance of people's projects. Insofar as this assessment requires comparisons of the strength of different people's preferences, its possibility depends on the possibility of interpersonal comparisons of subjective states. As we shall see, there is no motivation for denying this possibility. Moreover, the importance of people's projects is not, according to OU, to be determined solely by subjective criteria. Importance of a project is determined by its relation to other reasonable projects the agent has, its attainability, the value of the capacities that pursuit of that project realizes, and its implications for other components of human welfare. Cf. Scanlon 1975b, 1977.

worry into a practical or epistemological worry (which I shall discuss later in this section and in the next).

These considerations suggest that any theoretical problems about the possibility of making interpersonal comparisons of utility must be problems for making interpersonal comparisons of welfare, however we construe welfare. But notice how general and far reaching such a problem would be. The problem will afflict any moral theory that requires comparisons of persons' welfare, no matter how welfare is construed. The problem will afflict nonutilitarian and even nonteleological moral theories. Rawls's theory of justice will be undermined because it takes primary goods to be the politically relevant constituents and measure of a person's or group's welfare, and the difference principle requires comparisons of different persons' quantities of primary goods such as basic well-being, opportunities, and the conditions of self-respect. Deontological theories that recognize duties of beneficence also require the possibility of comparisons of welfare as part of the determination of where the duties of beneficence lie.

In fact, the implications of a real metaphysical or theoretical impossibility of interpersonal comparisons of welfare would be still more far reaching. If synchronic interpersonal comparisons of welfare are really impossible, then diachronic *intra*personal comparisons of welfare must be impossible too. But this result would undermine any plausible theory of rationality or prudence.

Before we accept results such as these, we need a very firm foundation for believing interpersonal comparisons of welfare to be metaphysically or theoretically impossible. No foundation has been offered. Our common judgments about people's lives and our most plausible moral theories and theories of rationality presuppose the possibility of such comparisons. In defending the metaphysical or theoretical possibility of interpersonal comparisons of welfare in this way, I am not assuming that it is possible, even in principle, to produce a "complete" ranking of the value of alternate possible states of the world (i.e., that there is a unique ranking for each pair of alternatives). Not only are ties possible, but some pairs of alternatives may be incommensurable, either because they realize kinds of value that are incommensurable or because they contain bundles of goods that are incommensurable. All I assume is that partial comparability and something like a "quasi-ordering" of alternatives are possible (cf. Sen 1973: 4–6, 47–76). Thus, I assume that OU can demand that agents maximize value even if there is no unique maximum; in such a case, an agent's obligation would be defined disjunctively.

Someone might give up the metaphysical or theoretical impossibility of interpersonal comparisons of welfare and still maintain that there is a practical problem about making such comparisons. Even if people's lives exhibit different magnitudes of value, we may have no reliable method of measuring these magnitudes.

General epistemological skepticism about the reliability of interpersonal comparisons of welfare cannot be warranted. It cannot be that we are never warranted in making interpersonal comparisons of welfare. If magnitudes of welfare exist and we sometimes make confident judgments about these magnitudes, then there is no reason to deny that we can sometimes make reliable judgments of this sort. Depending on what things have intrinsic or extrinsic value, we will have a variety of means by which to measure value directly or indirectly. According to OU, liberty has great extrinsic value, and liberty can presumably be measured directly by the absence of legal, physical, and perhaps psychological restraints. Pleasure and pain can be measured by a variety of indices (e.g., introspective reports and nonlinguistic behavior). Basic well-being can be measured by a variety of nutritional, medical, and psychological criteria. Respect for persons can be measured (in a way that relies on moral theory, of course) by a variety of social, psychological, and economic indices. Many questions about the appropriate methods of measurement, of course, can be best addressed only after one has fully articulated the components and conditions of human welfare. There is no reason, however, to claim that we cannot now make some highly accurate comparisons of the welfare of different individuals or groups.

But even if some interpersonal comparisons of welfare can be made reliably or accurately, it would be disingenuous to claim that we are generally reliable at making interpersonal comparisons of welfare or at estimating the total, long-run consequences of alternative actions and policies with a high degree of accuracy. The causal mechanisms involved in many of these counterfactual situations are numerous and complex, our time is frequently limited, our information is also frequently limited, and calculations are often distorted because of prejudice, self-concern, and failure of imagination. For these and other reasons, there must be many cases in which estimates of what would maximize human welfare would be highly unreliable. Any agent who uses utilitarianism as a decision procedure and so always acts with the intention of maximizing welfare (any U-agent), therefore, will frequently fail to maximize welfare. Of course, U-agents can make use of rules of thumb. But these are mere summaries of former prospective and retrospective estimates. Any U-agent must continually scrutinize these rules and depart from them whenever he thinks a new situation is sufficiently different from the previous ones. And, of course, both the estimates embodied in the rules of thumb and those used in departing from rules of thumb are subject to the same sorts of errors as were the estimates that rules of thumb were introduced to avoid. Therefore, rules of thumb will provide little, if any, help in keeping U-agents from failing to maximize welfare. Thus, one might conclude, practical problems about calculating total, long-run consequences and their value show utilitarianism to be self-defeating.

11. CRITERIA OF RIGHTNESS, DECISION PROCEDURES, AND PUBLICITY

The practical problems of reliably estimating total consequences and their value undermine utilitarianism only if utilitarianism is construed as a decision procedure. Although some utilitarians may have taken their theory to offer a *decision procedure*,[30] utilitarianism need not be and typically has not been construed in this way. Utilitarianism need only provide the *criterion* or *standard of rightness*.

Butler, Mill, Sidgwick, Moore, and others have distinguished, in various terms, between moral theories as criteria or standards of rightness and moral theories as decision procedures (see footnote 4). Criteria of rightness supply the property or properties in virtue of which objects of moral assessment, for instance actions, are right or justified. A decision procedure states how agents should deliberate, reason, and make moral decisions. As such, a decision procedure also has implications for the content of a moral agent's motives. Because utilitarianism claims that everyone's happiness matters and that total happiness should be maximized, a utilitarian decision procedure would require, among other things, that agents be disin-

---

30 Bentham (1823: II, 10) seems to be construing utilitarianism as a decision procedure (Berger [1984: 73–7] disputes this). Interestingly, it is almost entirely opponents of utilitarianism who make this assumption.

terestedly benevolent at all times. But utilitarianism can be a standard of rightness without being a decision procedure. Sidgwick makes this point in the following way:

Finally, the doctrine that Universal Happiness is the ultimate *standard* must not be understood to imply that Universal Benevolence is the only right or always the best *motive* of action. For, as we have observed, it is not necessary that the end which gives the criterion of rightness should always be the end at which we consciously aim: and if experience shows that the general happiness will be more satisfactorily obtained if men frequently act from other motives than pure universal philanthropy, it is obvious that these other motives are reasonably to be preferred on Utilitarian principles. (1907: 413)

Sidgwick's point is that because of facts such as our limited abilities to benefit effectively people whom we do not know and the special importance of personal projects and relationships, utility will not be maximized by universal benevolence. Rather, the standard of utilitarianism will be better satisfied if we have special concern for ourselves and those near at hand (1907: 432–4). The practical problems that prevent us from making generally reliable estimates of consequences and their value present similar reasons for believing that agents should deliberate not by attempting to maximize the value of the consequences of their actions but by appealing to rules that are in fact justifiable as contributing to human welfare. Many of these rules may be similar in content to the rules of conventional or commonsense morality. Indeed, this should not be surprising if, as many have suggested, the dictates of commonsense morality can be seen and explained as part of a system of norms whose observance promotes the good of everyone.

These rules will *not* be mere rules of thumb, because they will not function as aids in utilitarian deliberation. Rather, moral rules, on this view, should be appealed to and applied more or less strictly and uncritically in most cases. The complexity of the moral rules that are justifiable on utilitarian grounds, and the strictness with which they should be followed, depends on just how serious and general our inability to estimate consequences and their value is, and this may vary among societies and individuals. It may be that our inabilities as U-agents are so great that we are never justified in departing from a relatively coarse-grained set of moral rules (Moore [1903: 162–4] thought so). It is much more likely, however, that we should set aside the moral rules and deliberate as U-agents in certain unusual circumstances and in cases of conflicts of moral rules.[31] When the application of generally optimific rules would clearly fail to maximize the general welfare (e.g., would produce significant and clearly avoidable suffering), and when moral rules – each with a utilitarian justification – conflict, agents should deliberate as U-agents. (Of course, in some cases of conflict we may be poor U-agents and there may be generally optimific priority rules that should, therefore, be followed.)

It may be useful to emphasize that insofar as it is a theory of right action, this utilitarian account of moral rules is an act utilitarian theory. The rightness of actions is determined by their actual contribution to human welfare. But agents need not and should not deliberate as U-agents. Because of our unreliability as calculators of welfare, we would often be better off acting from "nonutilitarian" motives and rules. Part of our unreliability as U-agents is our frequent inability to discriminate those cases in which the best action would involve departing from established rules. Our motivational and cognitive abilities are such that we could depart from established rules and maximize welfare in this case, only by being such as also to depart from established rules in other cases in which doing so would not maximize welfare. There are good utilitarian reasons, therefore, for acting from sturdy motives and established rules that one knows will sometimes fail to maximize welfare. By acting from optimific motives and in accord with optimific rules, we shall almost certainly perform some wrong actions. But this just shows that the assessment of particular actions is not the most important dimension of assessment for a utilitarian; it may be much more important, from a utilitarian point of view, to possess the right motives than it is to perform right actions. For by acting from optimific motives and in accord with optimific rules, we shall maximize the total value realized by our actions.

Even if agents should typically act from sturdy motives and in accord with established rules, there may nonetheless be good utilitarian reasons for them to deliberate as U-agents in order to avert disaster, adjudicate conflicts among moral rules, and critically assess the value of their moral rules in a "cool hour" when their calculations are less subject to distortion.

31 Cf. Mill 1861: II, 25 (Berger 1984: 66–73, 82–4); Sidgwick 1907: 401, 426, 429, 453, 461; Hare 1976: 31–7; 1980: 171–5, 180–5; 1981: chaps. 2, 3.

Recognition of the distinction between criteria of rightness and decision procedures allows the utilitarian to justify nonutilitarian motives and rules. Utilitarianism does not require people to be U-agents. This implies that practical problems about our unreliability in estimating consequences and their value do not undermine utilitarianism.

But some would reject this defense of utilitarianism on the ground that utilitarianism cannot be maintained as a criterion of rightness rather than as a decision procedure. For a moral theory to provide a standard of right conduct, they would claim, it must be a standard that can be taught and that can serve as a public justification of actions, policies, institutions, and the like.[32] If so, it might seem that utilitarianism cannot distinguish between criteria of rightness and decision procedures so as to justify nonutilitarian motives and uncritical acceptance of a plurality of moral rules. Williams makes this objection as follows:

There is no distinctive place for . . . utilitarianism unless it is, within fairly narrow limits, a doctrine about how one should decide what to do. This is because its distinctive doctrine is about what acts are right, and, especially, for utilitarians, the only distinctive interest or point of the question what acts are right, relates to the situation of deciding to do them. (1973a: 128)

Williams also refers with approval to Rawls's insistence that utilitarianism not violate a publicity condition. Rawls writes:

We should note, then, that utilitarianism, as I have defined it, is the view that the principle of utility is the correct principle for society's public conception of justice. . . . What we want to know is which conception of justice characterizes our considered judgments in reflective equilibrium and best serves as the public moral basis of society. Unless one maintains that this conception is given by the principle of utility, one is not a utilitarian. (1971: 182)

Rawls's objection to the distinction between criteria of rightness and decision procedure rests on his acceptance of the publicity constraint: A theory of justice must be able to serve as a public standard by which citizens can assess and justify social institutions. This constraint can be construed as a conceptual constraint on what can count as a moral theory or, alternatively, as a substantive and revisable moral belief.[33]

32 See Rawls 1971: 133, 177–82, 582; Williams 1973a: 123, 125, 128, 135; Stocker 1976; Donagan 1977: 198–200; and Lomasky 1983: 275, 279. Cf. Medlin 1957.
33 Rawls fairly clearly intends the latter construal of the publicity condition; see Rawls 1971: 130.

Construed as a formal or conceptual claim that would undermine the distinction between criteria of rightness and decision procedures, the publicity constraint simply begs the question against teleological moral theories. Whether the true moral theory should be recognized, taught, or recommended as a decision procedure is itself a practical question the answer to which, the teleologist claims, depends on the intrinsic and extrinsic value this sort of publicity produces. Nor is this separation of *truth* and *acceptance value* peculiar to ethics (cf. Railton 1984: 154–5). Not only do we distinguish the truth and acceptance value of nonmoral claims, but we recognize, as reasonable, claims that certain facts should be suppressed. We may not always think suppression is justified, but we find such claims intelligible and take them seriously. It is conceivable that truth and acceptance value are not separate in the case of *moral* truth, but this needs to be argued.

Of course, it would be difficult to separate moral truth and acceptance value if moral realism were rejected. If moral claims could not be true, but only acceptable, as some noncognitivists claim, or if the truth of moral claims consisted in their acceptability, as some constructivists claim, then moral truth and acceptance value could not be distinguished so as to justify the claim that utilitarianism can be a standard of rightness without being a decision procedure.[34] But, of course, I have been arguing that moral realism is not only defensible but plausible. Moral realism allows us to separate the truth and acceptance value of moral claims as this defense of utilitarianism seems to require. (As we saw in 4.3, this fact illustrates how metaethical and normative issues are not entirely independent and, in particular, how the dispute between moral realism and antirealism can matter morally.)

The publicity constraint, therefore, must be construed as a substantive moral claim. Here, I think, a utilitarian should claim that there is no reason to think that utilitarianism *will* violate the publicity constraint and that, in those counterfactual situations in which it *would,* this constitutes no objection to utilitarianism.

34 Thus, one might wonder whether Smart can reconcile his noncognitivism (1973: 3–8) with his distinction between standards and motives (1973: 51–2) or whether Hare can reconcile his prescriptivism with his distinctions between "the levels of moral thinking" (1981: chaps. 1–3). Moreover, it may be Williams's doubts about moral realism (1965, 1966, 1975) that explain his unwillingness to allow the utilitarian to distinguish criteria of rightness and decision procedures.

In the actual world, utilitarianism satisfies the publicity constraint. Publicity would be violated only if utilitarianism could not be recognized as the standard of rightness and utilitarian reasoning was always inappropriate. But a utilitarian commitment to moral rules that are more than rules of thumb, and to the moral value of motives other than benevolence, is compatible with the recognition that the moral justification for these rules and motives consists in their contribution to human welfare. Moreover, utilitarian assessment is appropriate in some circumstances. Circumstances in which the relevant calculations can be made accurately can limit the application of moral rules and call for utilitarian deliberation; conflicts among moral rules, each of which has a utilitarian justification, can call for utilitarian deliberation; and some agents, in some circumstances, should take the time and effort to assess the consequences of past and continued adherence to a particular set of moral rules. This attitude toward utilitarianism is psychologically possible, does not require an esoteric morality, and so does not offend against the publicity condition.

Of course, there must be possible circumstances, even if they are difficult for us to describe, in which it would be best that most people not even recognize utilitarianism as providing the standard or criterion of right conduct. Under these circumstances, utilitarianism would indeed be an "esoteric morality" (cf. Sidgwick 1907: 489–90). But this is a possibility for any (plausible ?) moral theory. For any moral theory, there are possible circumstances in which its recognition and application would satisfy the theory worse than recognition and application of some alternative theory.[35] The proper response of anyone who, as a theorist, believes the theory in question to be true is to think that in *those* circumstances the true theory should be suppressed and some false theory recognized. Publicity is a plausible, but revisable, substantive moral commitment. A moral theory that violated publicity in the actual world would be less plausible for that

35 Aren't there circumstances in which a Kantian would think publicity should be violated? Imagine people who have hopelessly false beliefs about what a rational being *as such* would will. In such circumstances, agents might better satisfy the Categorical Imperative if they do not always deliberate about how to satisfy it. They might better approximate how rational beings as such would act by acting directly on a particular set of moral rules. In such circumstances, might not a Kantian want to keep the Categorical Imperative from agents (at least as long as agents still acted on these rules out of a sense of duty)? Indeed, we might wonder whether these circumstances are merely possible.

reason. But the fact that there are merely possible circumstances in which a moral theory would require violation of publicity is not a fact peculiar to utilitarianism and is not itself, I think, an objection to utilitarianism or any other moral theory.

So, a defense of utilitarianism and, in particular, OU against the charge of practical incoherence that relies on the distinction between criteria of rightness and decision procedures is not undermined by considerations of publicity. The utilitarian claims that the value of publicity depends on its effects on human welfare. There are possible circumstances in which a utilitarian would and should violate the publicity condition. In normal circumstances, however, there is no reason for a utilitarian to violate publicity.[36]

12. MORAL OBJECTIONS TO UTILITARIANISM

Utilitarianism is often rejected on moral grounds. It is alleged that utilitarianism fails to recognize the moral importance of sources and kinds of pleasure or preference, that utilitarianism is both too lax and too strict in its account of our obligations to others, that utilitarianism cannot account for the existence of moral and political rights, and that utilitarianism cannot accommodate considerations of distributive justice. Many of these charges are held to undermine any teleological theory.

My defense of realism and coherence in ethics gives an important evidential role to considered moral beliefs; it is a serious count against a moral theory if there are large bodies of considered moral beliefs it cannot accommodate. As I have argued, however, the respect that considered moral beliefs deserve does not make them sacred. The dialectical investigation of our moral beliefs can provide us with reason to reject or revise previous moral beliefs and acquire new ones; our postdialectical moral beliefs (that is, the moral beliefs we *would* hold after a full dialectical inquiry) can be significantly different from our predialectical moral beliefs. These objections to utilitarianism, therefore, must show not only that

---

36 Cf. Sidgwick 1907: 489–90; Scheffler 1982: 45–52; Railton 1984: 154–5; and Parfit 1984: 24–51, esp. 40–3. Railton and Scheffler appear to assume that utilitarianism does violate the publicity constraint and argue that this is not so bad. I agree that violation of publicity is not so bad when it is necessary, but I do not agree that it is actually necessary.

utilitarianism fails to accommodate considered moral beliefs but also that this failure is widespread or otherwise defective. I want to outline a defense of OU against these moral objections to utilitarianism. Such objections to OU are not compelling, I shall argue, either because they depend on construing utilitarianism as a decision procedure or because they depend on construing welfare as subjective versions of utilitarianism have construed it. Because OU avoids these commitments, it need do no great violence to our considered moral beliefs on these matters.

13. VALUE

It is often said to be a defect of utilitarianism that it is too indiscriminate in recognizing the value of pleasures or preferences. Surely, not all pleasures or preferences are of value or of equal value (see footnote 19). Against hedonistic utilitarianism it is claimed, for example, that sadistic pleasures are not valuable. Against preference-satisfaction forms of utilitarianism, Dworkin argues that what he calls "external preferences" are not of value. Personal preferences are preferences about how one's own life should go, whereas external preferences are preferences about the lives of others, that is, preferences about what others should do and what goods they should be assigned. Dworkin claims it is a moral defect of utilitarianism to recognize the value of external preferences as well as personal preferences (1976: 234–8, 1978: 275–7).

Subjective utilitarians might claim that their commitments here - when properly understood - are defensible. The hedonistic utilitarian might insist that *insofar* as sadistic pleasures are *pleasures,* they are valuable; however, *insofar* as sadistic pleasures are *sadistic,* they require and produce desires for others' pain, and so have disvalue. Preference-satisfaction forms of utilitarianism might offer a similar reply to Dworkin. *Insofar* as satisfying external preferences *satisfies preferences,* it is valuable; however, *insofar* as satisfying preferences satisfies *external* preferences (of the sort Dworkin has in mind),[37] doing so requires frustrating the preferences of those other than the agent and so has disvalue.

37 Hart (1979: 211–21) argues that it cannot be external preferences per se to which Dworkin objects, since some external preferences, for example, for the welfare of others, ought to have value.

The problem with these subjective utilitarian responses is that, although they can recognize disvalue in sadistic pleasure and (certain) external preferences, they seem to leave it as a contingent matter whether sadistic pleasures or external preferences are right or justified. This is likely to strike us as wrong. Sadistic pleasures and (certain) external preferences *couldn't* be morally justified, no matter how great the sadist's pleasure or how intense the external preference.

But, of course, utilitarian theories that incorporate an objective conception of welfare, as OU does, are not committed to the value of pleasure or preference satisfaction per se. As I have formulated OU, it does recognize the value of pursuing and realizing personal projects, and this fact may seem to let sadistic pleasures and external preferences in the back door. But there are moral constraints on valuable projects; in order for the pursuit or realization of a project to be of value, that project must, among other things, respect other people at least in the minimal sense of not causing significant and avoidable harm. Moreover, personal and social relationships involving mutual concern and respect form an important part of human good, according to OU's theory of value. So, OU is not indiscriminate in the way it distributes value among pleasures and preferences. Certainly, nothing about the structure of a teleological theory commits such theories to be indiscriminate in the way purely subjective versions of utilitarianism seem to be. Nor should this be surprising. These objections focus only on particular conceptions of human welfare incorporated in particular formulations of utilitarianism and so do not affect the teleological or welfarist structure of utilitarianism.

14. OBLIGATIONS TO OTHERS

Utilitarianism is also held to provide a mistaken account of the nature and extent of our obligations to others. Utilitarianism, it is claimed, is both too lax and too strict about these obligations. On the one hand, utilitarianism is too lax, because it implies that agents should disregard obligations they owe to others, for instance, promissory obligations, whenever breach of these obligations promises to have better consequences than observing these obligations (e.g., Ross 1930: 34–5, 38). On the other hand, utilitarianism is too strict, because being impartial among everyone's goods, it requires of agents continual benevolence and self-sacrifice (e.g., Baier 1958: 203–4; Rawls 1971: 572–3; cf. B. Williams 1973a: 93–118). Here, as elsewhere, critics of utilitarianism do not always distinguish clearly between criteria of rightness and decision procedures. These and other moral objections to utilitarianism can be directed at utilitarianism either as a criterion of rightness or as a decision procedure. Utilitarianism is too lax or too strict as a criterion or standard of rightness if it offers a mistaken analysis of our actual obligations to others. It is too lax or too strict as a decision procedure if utilitarian reasoning would tend to produce unjustified breaches of obligation or unjustifiable demands on agents. Because it is difficult to describe cases in which it is clear that we have an obligation to do something that is actually suboptimific, or in which it is clear that we have no obligation to do something that really is optimific, it is easier to make these objections to utilitarianism as a decision procedure. Thus, even if utilitarianism gives the correct account of our actual obligations, utilitarian reasoning leads to unjustified violation of our obligations to others.

But these objections are not compelling. Consider the charge of laxness first. Special obligations, such as promissory obligations, it is plausible to maintain, are threatened by utilitarian *reasoning*. But if we construe utilitarianism, as I have been construing OU, as a criterion of rightness and not as a decision procedure, then utilitarianism will not require utilitarian reasoning and so will not undermine special obligations such as promissory obligations. The institution of promise-keeping is valuable; as long as promissory agreements are kept by and large, such agreements can support reliable mutual expectations and so facilitate cooperation of various kinds. Doubtless there are cases in which – the importance of frustrating people's expectations and the adverse consequences that one's decision has on the institution of promising notwithstanding – welfare would be marginally increased by an agent's violating his promissory agreement and doing something else (with beneficial consequences). But as we noted, the causal sequences initiated by keeping and violating promissory agreements are quite complex; our time, information, and cognitive abilities are limited; and our calculations are subject to various forms of bias and distortion. For these reasons, we are unable to discriminate reliably for cases in which the results of breaking our promises would be marginally better than keeping them. We are cognitively and motivationally such that by utilitarian reasoning we

265

could violate a promise and so maximize welfare in one case, only by being such as to violate promises in cases where this fails to maximize welfare. Therefore, utilitarianism requires us to act from sturdy motives and by direct appeal not to utilitarianism, but to rules of promise-keeping. Of course, we know that acting on these motives and rules will fail to maximize welfare in some cases, but we do not know which cases these are. This is not to say there won't be any cases involving promissory obligations in which agents should act as U-agents and violate promises. Where rules of promise-keeping conflict with other moral rules that have a utilitarian justification or where disastrous consequences would clearly follow from keeping a promise, agents should perhaps attempt to maximize welfare. But such situations do not undermine the utilitarian's account of promissory obligation, since no one thought that promissory obligations are absolute.

Similarly, one will think that utilitarianism requires perpetual self-sacrifice and so is too strict if one construes utilitarianism as a decision procedure. Surely, morality does not require agents to base all of their actions on consideration of how they might promote *everyone's* welfare. But as we saw, there is good reason to deny that a utilitarian decision procedure satisfies the utilitarian standard of rightness. Our ability to provide others with nonbasic goods is limited. Our knowledge of other people's projects is limited, and even if we know what will help them realize their projects, we may not be in a position to help. We can promote more reliably our own welfare and that of family and friends. Such considerations provide a utilitarian justification of the adoption of greater (though by no means exclusive) concern for oneself and those close to one.

Because utilitarianism is a standard of rightness and not a decision procedure, the utilitarian can, and indeed should, deny the appropriateness of utilitarian reasoning in many of an agent's dealings with others. So, even if utilitarian reasoning would produce treatment of others that is clearly immoral, this is no objection to utilitarianism.

Some may think, however, that this defense of utilitarianism gets the right results for the wrong reasons. Is this so? It depends on whether utilitarianism provides the correct standard or criterion of rightness. Does utilitarianism offer a defensible analysis of our actual obligations to others?

Doubts about utilitarian analyses of our actual obligations to others are more difficult to motivate than doubts about utilitarianism as a decision procedure. For although it may be clear that utilitarian reasoning will lead to actions that treat others in clearly immoral ways, it is less clear, say, that promises it would actually be better to break should nonetheless be kept, or that there is no obligation to make the personal sacrifices that would actually produce more good than harm. It is hard to come by cases that are described in enough detail to make it really plausible that it would maximize welfare to break a promise or to act beneficently but in which it is clear we ought not to break the promise or need not act beneficently. Thus, legitimate doubts about the application of a utilitarian decision procedure to interpersonal affairs do not guarantee the legitimacy of doubts about a utilitarian criterion of rightness as an analysis of interpersonal obligations.

Moreover, depending on their theories of welfare, different utilitarian theories will have different implications about interpersonal obligations. OU's objective conception of welfare equips it with a plausible account of the extent of interpersonal obligations. For example, OU can explain the importance of promissory obligations. OU places value on personal and social relationships that respect persons. This requires agents to observe fair terms of social cooperation. And this arguably requires that parties to voluntary agreements keep their agreements except in unusual circumstances where, say, great suffering can be avoided if one party breaches the agreement. Moreover, observance of promissory agreements is essential to the sort of diachronic social cooperation necessary to the pursuit and realization of so many personal projects.

OU also explains why there is a ceiling on the amount of beneficence and self-sacrifice that is morally required of agents. The value of beneficent motivation and action is limited not just by our causal and cognitive infirmities. OU attaches important value to the pursuit and realization of personal projects. As we saw, freedom or autonomy is required for realizing these values. Thus, OU will give high priority to personal autonomy. Moreover, OU attaches great value to the development of close personal relationships involving mutual concern and commitment. A proper concern for one's own projects and the welfare of those close to one, therefore, will limit the amount of beneficence OU requires of agents.

Of course, OU's justification of differential concern for personal projects and relationships should not be exaggerated. OU has some clear (re)distributive implications. Because OU is a teleological theory, it assesses the rightness of an action by its consequences for *everyone's* welfare. This impartiality means that, other things being equal, one person's personal projects and relationships are as valuable as another's. Because freedom and basic well-being are conditions of this kind of value, OU will require that agents in a position to contribute to the freedom and well-being of others without endangering their own should so contribute. But, of course, these obligations can be carried out in ways that are more or less disruptive of an agent's personal projects and relationships. Many agents will, with good reason, assume personal projects whose object is community service. For agents who do not assume such projects, participation in publicly organized forms of mutual aid, such as taxation schemes and public charities, can carry out many of their obligations to others in a way that is minimally disruptive to the pursuit of their personal projects and relationships.

The precise nature of OU's implications for agents' obligations to others deserves much fuller discussion. But it is clear that OU does not require agents to set their own personal projects and relationships aside in the single-minded pursuit of benefiting others. (This point will receive fuller articulation in 8.17–8.18.) Utilitarianism offers a criterion of rightness, not a decision procedure, and so encourages neither infidelity nor perpetual self-sacrifice. Moreover, utilitarianism can provide a plausible account of our actual obligations to others. Even if there are well described cases that seem to impugn traditional subjective versions of utilitarianism as criteria of rightness, OU's objective conception of welfare provides a plausible account of the extent of our obligations to others.[38]

15. RIGHTS

It is also argued that utilitarianism cannot account for the existence of moral and political rights (see footnote 21). Notoriously, writers disagree about what rights we have. Rights are claimed both to assignments of goods and services (positive rights) and to freedom from various kinds of treatment from others (negative rights). However, most people agree that rights exist to protect or guarantee

38 In thinking about the stringency of utilitarian demands, it is also worth remembering that the utilitarian can and will claim that some actions that are wrong, because they fail to maximize welfare, are not blameworthy (such actions may, but need not, result from optimific motives). Cf. footnote 2.

especially important interests. If these interests are to be protected by rights, rights must be moral considerations with a certain dialectical force. Rights must "trump" or defeat claims that we should violate certain interests in order to promote some otherwise valuable goal (Dworkin 1970; 1978: xi; 1984; cf. Nozick 1974: 28–33). If I have a right to x, then I cannot be deprived of x merely on the ground that some desirable goal could be advanced by so depriving me. Rights are not absolute; one right can be defeated by another, weightier right, and a right can be defeated if the consequences of respecting it in those circumstances would be disastrous. But rights are claims that cannot be defeated by mere appeals to the possibility of maximizing utility. Therefore, utilitarianism seems unable to account for the existence of moral and political rights.

A traditional utilitarian can try to accommodate moral and political rights by distinguishing between standards and decision procedures and insisting on the sort of utilitarian commitment to moral rules developed in this chapter. Certain goods and liberties have great extrinsic value; they are the means to the realization of much utility. It is generally best, then, that claims to these goods and liberties be respected. For the usual reasons, we are unreliable calculators, and we would do much more harm than good were we to decide whether to protect these goods and liberties by calculating the consequences of doing so. Therefore, it would be best to regulate our conduct by more or less inflexible rules safeguarding the individual in her title to these goods and liberties. Only in cases of conflicts of rights, or in other suitably unusual circumstances, should agents hold goods and liberties protected by rights accountable to utilitarian calculation.

OU strengthens this traditional utilitarian response by recognizing the greater value of certain interests *within* its theory of value. A plausible set of rights includes positive rights to goods and services essential to basic well-being and negative rights to freedom from harm and from interference in one's pursuit of reasonable projects. OU generates such a set of rights, because freedom and basic well-being are both necessary conditions for the realization of most any kind of value. If basic well-being is essential to the realization of any value, then magnitudes of basic well-being should not be traded one-for-one with magnitudes of other values (e.g., nonbasic goods or realization of projects). In a similar way, considerations of freedom or autonomy should trump promotion of nonbasic goods and

269

the realization of personal projects. Because of the importance of autonomy and basic well-being, any individual's interest in these goods will outweigh the value of large magnitudes of other goods. This means that OU can explain why we have interests in freedom and well-being such that we have a right to such goods vis-à-vis the promotion of other goods.[39]

Of course, one individual's interest in these goods will not trump another's interest in these same goods (here, individuals are holding cards of the same suit). But this doesn't show that neither has a right to such goods; rather, it is a case of rights conflicting. Such conflicts are to be resolved by teleological considerations. We must pay attention to the importance and number of the rights involved and aim at minimizing the weighted total violation of rights.

16. DISTRIBUTIVE JUSTICE

Perhaps the most common complaint about utilitarianism is that it cannot account for considerations of distributive justice.[40] Because utilitarianism is a teleological theory, it is concerned with the *maximization* of total value and not its distribution. It is claimed, for example, that utilitarianism must be indifferent between egalitarian and radically inegalitarian distributions of the same amount of value. In fact, maximization of utility may require radically inegalitarian distributions (see footnote 22).

As with other objections to utilitarianism, "the justice objection" can be pressed against utilitarianism as a decision procedure or as a criterion of rightness. In its former aspect, the justice objection claims that utilitarian *reasoning* produces unjust distributions. In its latter aspect, the justice objection claims that distributions that are (or would be) optimific are (or would be) unjust. Since we think

---

39 Rights to basic well-being, whether positive or negative, are presumably more basic than the right to autonomous action. Basic well-being is a necessary condition for the realization of *any* value, whereas liberty in action is necessary for the pursuit and realization of many but not all projects. If push comes to shove, therefore, positive and negative rights to basic well-being should have priority over rights to liberty in speech and action. Cf. Rawls's distinction between general and special conceptions of justice; Rawls 1971: 62–3, 150–2, 247, 542.

40 Another common complaint is that utilitarianism cannot provide an account of *retributive* justice; see, for example, Ross 1930: 56–64; Carritt 1947: 65. I shall focus on distributive justice; I leave it as an exercise for the reader to construct a utilitarian reply on the basis of a utilitarian account of moral rules and OU's recognition of the importance of autonomy.

some inequalities are justified, it may not be clear that there are inegalitarian distributions that are both genuinely optimific and clearly unjust. So it may not be clear that utilitarianism's criterion of rightness has unjust implications. Perhaps for this reason, the typical form of the justice objection applies to utilitarianism as a decision procedure. Even if distributions that are in fact optimific are just, utilitarian reasoning may nonetheless produce unjust results.

The standard utilitarian reply has been to insist that utilitarianism and the principle of diminishing marginal utility favor equal distributions of goods. The standard antiutilitarian rebuttal has been that diminishing marginal utility is only an approximation. Not all individuals experience diminishing returns at the same rate or point; "pleasure wizards" (Sen 1979a: 357) or "utility black holes" (Lomasky 1982: 272), for whom diminishing returns begin much later, will force inequalities in a utilitarian distribution, and these inequalities will seem morally arbitrary.

A traditional utilitarian might respond by appeal to the need for more or less egalitarian distributional rules. Justifiable deviations from equality are difficult to predict. Utilitarian reasoning would produce more unjustifiable deviations from equality than justifiable ones. So there are good utilitarian reasons to decide distributional questions by appeal to rules of more or less strict equality. (This is not to commit utilitarianism to strict egalitarianism. There may be good reasons for different kinds of utilitarians to recognize somewhat inegalitarian distributional rules. My point here is only that the existence of pleasure wizards does not force deviation from egalitarian distributional rules.) Since utilitarianism is not a decision procedure, the utilitarian can defend himself against the charge that utilitarian reasoning would produce immoral inequalities.

However, is this defense adequate? Is it *only* because of contingent cognitive limitations on our part that utilitarianism produces distributions that satisfy our beliefs about justice? If we were perfectly reliable calculators of utility, wouldn't the existence of pleasure wizards commit utilitarianism to radically unjust distributions? These questions raise worries about the distributional implications of utilitarianism's criterion of rightness.

OU's objective theory of welfare allows defense of its distributional implications. Because traditional subjective versions of utilitarianism recognize only pleasures or preferences to be of value, and all pleasures or preferences to be of equal value, they hold equality of distribution hostage to the principle of diminishing marginal utility. OU, however, does not. As OU's account of rights illustrates, though not itself a component of human welfare, basic well-being is a fundamentally important good. This is because the components of basic well-being are all either necessary conditions for the realization of any value or maximally flexible assets in realizing value. Moreover, the requirements of basic well-being, that is, basic goods such as health, nutrition, shelter, and education, are minimally variable.[41] Therefore, inequalities in basic goods cannot be justified as maximizing the total amount of welfare. It will always be better (i.e., more valuable) to give basic goods to one more person than to increase someone else's supply of nonbasic goods. Moreover, OU's insistence on respect for persons constrains acceptable inequalities in nonbasic goods. In order for pursuit or realization of one's personal projects to be valuable, they must respect the interests of others, and the development and maintenance of personal and social relationships involving mutual concern and commitment are intrinsically valuable. For distributions of goods and services to respect persons, they must express fair terms of social cooperation. Just what constraint this imposes on acceptable distributions is a matter of substantive debate. But fair terms of cooperation presumably must be to the mutual advantage of cooperators, and this presumably excludes gross inequalities in the distribution of nonbasic goods among cooperators. OU's theory of value is thus itself distribution-sensitive (cf. 8.2).

These claims may strike some people as antiutilitarian. Rawls claims that this response to the justice objection is unavailable to the utilitarian; he claims that a distribution-sensitive theory of value disqualifies a moral theory as utilitarian and, indeed, as teleological. "Whereas if the distribution of goods is also counted as a good, perhaps a higher order one, and the theory directs us to produce the most good (including the good of distribution among others), we no longer have a teleological view in the classical sense" (1971: 25). While it may be true that the subjective theories of value incorporated in traditional forms of utilitarianism are not distribution-sensitive, it is simply false that no utilitarian or teleological theory

41 The requirements of basic well-being for the handicapped, of course, will be greater than those of the nonhandicapped. Thus, insofar as OU provides the means for basic well-being, it will be somewhat inegalitarian. But this, I assume, *is* a justifiable deviation from equality.

can be distribution-sensitive (cf. Berger 1984: 213). Teleological theories define rightness in terms of maximal value and differ according to their specifications of value. Utilitarian theories are teleological theories that construe value as welfare or happiness. Even if subjective conceptions of welfare are not distribution-sensitive, there is no reason why other conceptions cannot be. OU's is; it treats distribution as a personal good. Still less is there any reason for thinking that no theory of value could be. Indeed, Rawls concedes the possibility of such a theory. But if we define rightness in terms of maximal goodness, where our conception of goodness is distribution-sensitive, then we have a teleological moral theory that is distribution-sensitive.

Perhaps Rawls thinks that a distribution-sensitive theory of value would violate the teleological constraint that goodness be defined independently of rightness. I have already indicated reasons for thinking that this constraint is too strong; teleological theories need only claim that rightness and goodness are distinct (see 8.1). A distribution-sensitive theory of value need not violate the independence constraint, and certainly need not violate the distinctness constraint. Call a version of utilitarianism whose theory of value is distribution-sensitive *distributive utilitarianism*. Rightness is all-things-considered permissibility or obligation. Distributive utilitarianism defines rightness as maximal goodness and goodness as a function of, among other things, distributional moral properties such as fairness or respect for persons. This way of construing rightness and goodness is not circular and so does not violate the teleological constraint that the good be specifiable independently of the right, and it certainly does not collapse the distinction between the good and the right.

Traditional forms of utilitarianism, therefore, allow a commitment to the importance of distributional considerations in moral reasoning. Moreover, OU's objective conception of welfare is distribution-sensitive and so provides a strong defense of the moral importance of distributional considerations.

17. THE PERSONAL POINT OF VIEW

In a series of papers, Bernard Williams argued that no utilitarian or teleological moral theory can account for the moral significance of "personal integrity" (1973a: 93–118; 1976a; 1976b). More recently,

Samuel Scheffler argued that utilitarianism cannot account for "the natural independence of the agent's point of view" (1982). The claim common to Williams, Scheffler, and others[42] is that the impartiality characteristic of utilitarianism and teleological theories in general cannot account for the moral significance of what I shall call the *personal point of view*.

Williams formulates his version of the claim that utilitarianism cannot accommodate the importance of the personal point of view as a claim about personal integrity. He claims it is a deep commitment to certain personal projects that gives one's life meaning and, hence, integrity. Because utilitarianism assesses the rightness of, say, actions by the consequences of those actions for *everyone's* welfare, Williams claims, utilitarianism requires agents to assume an *impersonal* point of view. This impersonal point of view requires agents to take an impartial attitude toward their own welfare; an agent must view her own projects as no more valuable than those of others. Utilitarianism, therefore, cannot accommodate the *personal* point of view.

> The point is that he [an agent] is identified with his actions as flowing from his projects and attitudes which in some cases he takes seriously at the deepest level, as what his life is about. . . . It is absurd to demand of such a man, when the sums come in from the utility network which the projects of others have in part determined, that he should just step aside from his own project and decision and acknowledge the decision which utilitarian calculation requires. It is to alienate him in a real sense from his action and the source of his action in his own convictions. It is to make him into a channel between the input of everyone's projects, including his own, and an output of optimific decision; but this is to neglect the extent to which *his* actions and *his* decisions have to be seen as the actions and decisions which flow from the projects and attitudes with which he is most closely identified. It is thus, in the most literal sense, an attack on his integrity. (1973a: 116–17)

As Williams and others construe this objection, it is an objection to utilitarianism's requirement that agents *regard* their projects from an impersonal point of view (Williams 1973a: 113, 115–16, 123, 128; Scheffler 1982: 43). So construed, the integrity objection is an objection to utilitarianism as a decision procedure: Utilitarian *reasoning* requires agents to discount their own projects in a way that involves disregard for the personal point of view. If utilitarianism were a

---

42 Cf. Rawls 1982: 180–1; Fried 1978: 2, 34, 114; Nagel 1979b: 205; 1980: 108, 119–20, 127, 131, 135; Lomasky 1983.

decision procedure, it would require everyone to value his projects and commitments impersonally and, hence, impartially. People would be required to act on motives of impartial benevolence and to sacrifice frequently their own projects and commitments in order to maximize total welfare. Utilitarian reasoning cannot recognize the special concern an agent has for his own projects and commitments and so cannot recognize the moral importance of the personal point of view.

But utilitarianism does not require the assumption of the impersonal point of view in normal circumstances. It would require this only if it were a decision procedure. But utilitarianism need provide only a standard or criterion of rightness and not also a decision procedure. As we saw (8.6 and 8.14), there are good utilitarian reasons for agents in normal circumstances to avoid the impersonal point of view and adopt a differential concern for their own projects and the welfare of those close to them. Even in normal circumstances an agent does have an obligation to contribute to the basic well-being of others, but this obligation can be carried out in predictable and minimally intrusive ways that do little violence to his important personal projects and commitments. In normal circumstances, therefore, utilitarianism can justify a limited but nonetheless differential concern for personal projects and so will not require agents to be forever setting aside their own projects and commitments in the impersonal pursuit of welfare maximization (cf. Sidgwick 1907: 432–4; Scheffler 1982: 15; Railton 1984).

Williams anticipates this defense of utilitarianism and claims that it is unacceptable because it would violate the publicity constraint (1973a: 123, 125, 128, 135; cf. 1972: 107). We considered this issue in 8.11, however. There is no clear motivation for making publicity a condition of the truth of a moral theory. Publicity seems to be a reasonable constraint in normal circumstances, but then utilitarianism does not violate publicity in normal circumstances. Utilitarianism makes the value of publicity contingent on various social and psychological factors, but on reflection this commitment seems reasonable.

Someone might wonder whether this defense of utilitarianism adequately answers the worry raised by the personal point of view. Even if utilitarianism does not require agents to adopt a purely impersonal *attitude,* it still *assigns moral value* impersonally.

I am not convinced *this* sort of impersonality is morally objectionable. Is it objectionable for a standard of rightness to be impersonal? Do I care whether value is assigned to projects impersonally, if I am not required to view my own projects impersonally? But let us see what can be said to someone who thinks that the impartiality of a utilitarian standard of rightness undervalues the moral significance of agents' projects and commitments.

If the possession and pursuit of personal projects and commitments that are supposed to be constitutive of personal integrity are so important, then a utilitarian's account of human welfare should recognize this fact. OU's conception of human welfare does. It recognizes the intrinsic value of pursuit and realization of personal projects. OU claims that an action, say, is right just in case it maximizes the appropriately weighted function of, among other things, pursuit and realization of personal projects. Because pursuit and realization of personal projects are dominant components in an agent's good, freedom to formulate and pursue personal projects will trump other less important intrinsic and extrinsic goods. OU will not hold one person's reasonable and important projects hostage to the whims or preferences of others. In this way, OU might claim that it accommodates the moral importance of the personal point of view.[43]

This response may well not satisfy those who think that the impersonal assignment of value undervalues the moral significance of agents' projects. For their objection presumably is not that utilitarianism undervalues projects but that it undervalues *the agent's* projects. Their worry is about the impersonal point of view, and this worry is not assuaged by taking account of the personal point of view, as it were, from the impersonal point of view. Even if utilitarianism can treat autonomy as a dominant good, it must be impartial between the autonomy of different people.

Williams presents an example that illustrates this issue: Jim is a foreign explorer who comes upon a small South American village in which an army captain is about to execute twenty innocent villagers for "purely political" reasons. As an honored visitor, Jim is offered the privilege of shooting one of the twenty villagers. If he does, the other nineteen villagers will be released unharmed (of this, Williams stipulates, there is no doubt). If he does not, the captain will shoot all twenty as planned. No other options are reasonably open to Jim

---

43 OU's position here might be compared with Nozick's "utilitarianism of rights" (1974: 28–30).

(Williams's stipulation, again). Not implausibly, Williams claims that in these circumstances it is clear that Jim would maximize welfare – including, I might add, personal projects – by killing the one villager, and that utilitarianism requires him to do so (1973a: 98–9). (Williams is not explicit about this, but presumably the commitment that utilitarianism requires Jim to abandon here is a moral commitment not to kill innocent people.) Jim's case illustrates what, in this view, is the problem with utilitarianism: It allows the impersonal value of an agent's projects to exhaust their moral significance (cf. Scheffler 1982: 9, 61).

One might accept this criticism of utilitarianism and demand that morality accommodate the personal point of view. One might then reject utilitarianism in favor of a moral theory that incorporates what Scheffler calls "agent-centered prerogatives" (1982: chaps. 2, 3). On such a theory, the moral significance of agents' projects is not exhausted by their impersonal value; an agent's projects have moral significance out of proportion to their impersonal value. Agent-centered prerogatives permit but do not require agents to maximize the good and so would produce what Scheffler calls a "hybrid" moral theory. Rightness, on this hybrid view, is defined disjunctively: An action, say, is right just in case it either maximizes the good or preserves the agent's projects and commitments in the appropriate way.[44] This hybrid theory is superior to utilitarianism, according to Scheffler, because it reflects "the natural independence" of an agent's concern for his own projects and commitments.[45] A hybrid moral theory containing agent-centered prerogatives, therefore, might seem the best way to recognize the importance of the personal point of view.

The utilitarian need not accept this criticism and so need not move to a hybrid moral theory. Impersonal moral theories can assign moral value to the commitments of agents like Jim, but they

44 Scheffler (1982: 17–21) discusses more specific formulations of the second disjunct. In particular, the scope of agent-centered prerogatives does not include just any personal projects or commitments; morally obnoxious projects and commitments receive little or no protection from agent-centered prerogatives.

45 Scheffler 1982: 56, 79, 116. Scheffler seems ambivalent about what conclusion to draw. At times, he explicitly refuses to conclude that his hybrid theory is superior to sophisticated forms of utilitarianism of the sort OU represents (1982: 65, 77). But he does claim that the objection to utilitarianism based on the personal point of view is well founded (1982: 6, 13, 56, 90, 116). If this objection to utilitarianism is well founded, then a hybrid theory that avoids this objection is presumably superior to utilitarianism, other things being equal.

refuse to assign Jim's commitments any special value because they are *his*. Jim's commitments are important, but they are no more important than those of the nineteen villagers whom he could save. In this way, the impersonal point of view is impartial. It is impartiality of this kind that we expect a moral theory to reflect. Nor is this kind of impartiality peculiar to utilitarianism or even to teleological moral theories. Many nonteleological theories recognize duties to forgo one's own good in order to prevent great harm to others. It is, of course, a substantive moral claim that this kind of impartiality is characteristic of the moral point of view, but it is a plausible claim that cannot be rejected lightly. If the claim is correct, then it is no indictment of utilitarianism that it is impersonal.

This defense of utilitarianism does not force us to deny the importance of the personal point of view. The personal point of view is important, and we can recognize this without making morality capture its importance. The worries that the importance of the personal point of view raises can be viewed not as *moral worries* but as *worries about morality*. Our sympathies for Jim need not be moral sympathies. Cases like Jim's can be dilemmatic, if they are dilemmatic, because they raise serious questions about the justification of morality. We can imagine that if Jim is a decent fellow, that is, has the right sort of motives, he may be haunted by doing as utilitarian morality requires and killing an innocent villager. He may experience doubts and serious personal anguish. We may come to wonder whether Jim has reason or enough reason to do as morality requires in these circumstances. These are worries about the justification or supremacy of moral demands, not about the correctness of a utilitarian account of morality.

Two preliminary points should be made about this interpretation of the importance of the personal point of view. First, such an interpretation of the conflict between utilitarianism and the personal point of view assumes that it is a substantive question whether moral considerations provide an agent with reason or sufficient reason for action. An internalist might deny this, claiming that "the concept of morality" makes this conflict inconceivable or unintelligible. It is simply part of the concept of a moral consideration that moral considerations necessarily provide reason or conclusive reason for action (cf. Chapter 3). But as we have seen, there is reason to reject this internalist assumption. The amoralist's challenge to the rationality of moral demands is not only intelligible but de-

278

serves to be taken seriously. Moreover, we have seen, at least in outline (3.7–3.13 and 8.6), how an externalist can provide a strong justification of the rationality of moral demands.

Second, on this interpretation, the worries about utilitarianism that the personal point of view raises can be represented as worries about either the rationality or the supremacy of moral demands. I assume that if something is in one's interest, then one has reason to bring that thing about. Rational egoism claims that one has reason to do x if, and only if, x is in one's own interest. The personal point of view can be seen as representing the interests of the agent. If rational egoism is true, then the worries about utilitarianism that the personal point of view raises can be represented as worries about the *rationality* of morality. Do agents have reason to do as utilitarian morality requires? This question is answered by a substantive theory of human welfare that explains to what extent the demands of utilitarian morality, in particular its demands to benefit others, promote or are constitutive of the moral agent's well-being. As we saw (3.12–3.13 and 8.6), OU's objective conception of human welfare allows a strong justification of utilitarian morality even on rational egoist assumptions; agents typically have rational egoist reasons to do as OU requires. Indeed, because there are both self- and other-regarding components to an agent's good, there may always be *some* rational egoist reason to do as OU requires, even if there is not always *conclusive* rational egoist reason to do so. Later in this section I shall comment on a rational egoist account of the rationality of OU's implications in exceptional circumstances such as Jim's.

Alternatively, if rational egoism is false and agents have reason to do as utilitarian morality requires independently of its contribution to their own well-being, we can represent the worries about utilitarianism that the personal point of view raises as worries about the *supremacy* of moral demands. Because even if rational egoism is false, agents presumably still have prudential reasons for action, among others, one may wonder whether agents have sufficient or conclusive reasons to do as utilitarian morality requires.

I shall not attempt to decide here between these alternative representations of the conflict between utilitarian morality and the personal point of view. Rather, I want to stress what is common to them: Both represent the worries raised by the personal point of view as worries about the justifiability of moral demands rather than as moral worries.

This interpretation of the true conflict between utilitarianism and the personal point of view is confirmed by Williams's claims in "Persons, Character and Morality."

A man who has such a ground project will be required by Utilitarianism to give up what it requires in a given case just if it conflicts with what he is required to do as an impersonal utility-maximizer when all of the causally relevant considerations are in. That is quite an absurd requirement. But the Kantian, who can do rather better than that, still cannot do well enough. For impartial morality, if the conflict really does arise, must be required to win; and that cannot necessarily be a reasonable demand on the agent. There can come a point at which it is quite unreasonable for a man to give up, in the name of the impartial good ordering of the world of moral agents, something which is a condition of his having any interest in being around in the world at all. (1976a: 14)

The fact that Williams here takes Kantian views of morality to be equally guilty of making unreasonable demands on agents supports the claim that the real worry latent in the conflict between utilitarianism and the personal point of view is not the worry *within* morality about which moral theory is correct but the worry *about* morality concerning the rationality or supremacy of moral demands.[46] We can recognize the importance of the personal point of view without granting it *moral* importance.

Indeed, not only *can* we recognize the importance of the personal point of view without granting it moral importance; we *should not* concede it moral importance. Not only is Scheffler's preference for a hybrid moral theory incorporating agent-centered prerogatives unnecessary; hybrid moral theories actually misrepresent the connection between morality and the personal point of view. There are two reasons for this.

First, the impartiality among various persons' goods characteristic of OU and other teleological theories represents important considered beliefs about the nature and demands of morality better than a hybrid moral theory that incorporates the personal point of view into morality. An important moral belief is that the moral perspective is an impartial perspective; moral demands frequently require us to put aside purely personal projects and commitments. One argu-

---

46 Although we arrived at our views separately, I would like to record my agreement on this point with Sarah Conly's suggestive review of Scheffler's book (Conly 1984). Interestingly, this theme is not emphasized in her discussion of Williams (Conly 1983). Although Railton's title (1984) suggests this interpretation of Williams's argument, Railton does not develop this interpretation fully. But see Railton 1984: 163n–164n.

ment for the impartial character of morality parallels Scheffler's own argument against *agent-centered restrictions*. Scheffler distinguishes between his own agent-centered prerogatives, which permit but do not require an agent to maximize the good, and agent-centered restrictions, which do not even permit the agent to maximize the good. Agent-centered restrictions are based on the claim that it is sometimes wrong to maximize the good. Scheffler defends what he calls *the asymmetry thesis:* Although the natural independence of the personal point of view provides a principled rationale for agent-centered prerogatives, there is no principled rationale for agent-centered restrictions (1982: chap. 4, esp. 82–100). In particular, Scheffler argues that a moral theory incorporating agent-centered restrictions does not represent a rational response to the demands utilitarianism places on agents. For example, against Nozick's construal of rights as side constraints (Nozick 1974: 28–30), Scheffler claims, if a violation of a right is a bad thing, then it is rational to want to minimize the violation of rights – even if we must violate one person's rights in order to do this. Similarly, if Jim's projects and commitments are valuable, then so are those of the nineteen villagers whose lives he could save, and it is rational to minimize the violation of people's projects and commitments as utilitarianism instructs Jim to do. But, against Scheffler, if these violations of people's basic projects are of disvalue, their minimization is arguably obligatory and not merely permissible. Moreover, this judgment seems to be confirmed by considered moral beliefs. Regrettable as this kind of situation is, one *ought to* violate one person's right, say, to liberty, if this is necessary to prevent a greater number of equally serious violations of liberty (or some equally weighty right). Also, disagreeable as this is, Jim *ought to* kill the one innocent villager if this is necessary to save nineteen innocent lives. Failure to do what one can to minimize such harms evidences a kind of moral squeamishness that, even if understandable, fails to take sufficiently seriously the harms to others it is in one's power to prevent.[47] Morality appears impartial among people's goods in the way OU and other teleological theories claim.

---

47 After all, it is not as if the utilitarian asks the agent to be *guided by* the suffering of the person to whom, in these circumstances, he must cause harm. If A causes suffering to B in order to prevent still greater harms to C and D, then A is not guided by B's suffering, because his aim is the prevention of other, greater suffering. If there were other, less harmful ways to prevent these greater harms, A would employ those means. Cf. Nagel 1986: 180–3.

Second, if we were to accept the demand that morality accommodate the personal point of view, as Scheffler does, we would find ourselves unable to ask a question that, we have seen, is surely intelligible and legitimate. We would be unable to ask whether the demands of morality are really rational or justifiable. If morality were forced to incorporate the personal point of view, we could not get what are at least apparent conflicts between the demands of morality and the interests of agents. Common sense and philosophical reflection on the demands morality can make lead one to question whether there are always good and sufficient reasons to be moral. Philosophical deliberation about the demands of morality, the nature of an agent's good, and the nature of rationality may vindicate the rationality or supremacy of moral demands. But even if we are able to answer the question 'Why be moral?' we need to be able to formulate the question. If we are to be able to formulate the question about the rationality or supremacy of morality, we must be able to represent what are at least apparent conflicts between the demands of morality and interests of agents. Hybrid moral theories could represent apparent conflicts within morality, but not the conflicts between morality and the agent's interest with which we are familiar.[48] Because we are familiar with these apparent conflicts, it is a virtue of moral theories that are impartial, in the way in which OU is, that they allow, indeed lead one to expect, such conflicts, and it is a defect of hybrid moral theories that they cannot represent such conflicts.

If it is really a worry about the rationality or supremacy of morality that the personal point of view raises, then the personal point of view presents no objection to utilitarian accounts of morality. Indeed, as Williams's later writings testify, the worry about morality that the personal point of view raises is not a worry peculiar to utilitarianism or even to teleological moral theories.

48 It might seem that hybrid theories could represent the conflict between morality and self-interest, because agent-centered prerogatives do not incorporate the personal point of view completely into morality. Scheffler claims that agent-centered prerogatives would not protect morally obnoxious personal projects and commitments (e.g., those of Caligula or Hitler). So hybrid theories leave room for conflict between morality and *these* personal projects and commitments. But I doubt that any plausible theory of agent good would recognize these conflicts as conflicts between morality and self-interest. The objective conception of welfare developed in 8.2, for instance, would not. In any case, the apparent conflicts between morality and self-interest with which we are familiar are not limited to such cases.

The justifiability of morality raises large issues that are independent of the merits of utilitarianism. We already touched on some of these issues (3.7–3.13 and 8.6). We saw that even on rational egoist assumptions, agents will normally have reason to do as OU requires. Of course, not all circumstances are normal. Jim's case illustrates how utilitarianism can sometimes demand a great deal of agents. It is true that if Jim is a decent fellow – having the right sort of motives – he may suffer if he complies with the demand of utilitarian morality that he kill an innocent villager. But surely Jim would suffer just as much, if not more, assuming again that he is a decent fellow, if he refuses to comply with the demands of utilitarian morality. Here too, he may experience doubts and anguish. Indeed, this time he would be haunted not by the death of one innocent villager but by the nineteen innocent lives he could have saved. It is *the situation, not utilitarian morality,* that is hard on Jim. The fact that Jim may be poorly off no matter what he does is one reason the situation is dilemmatic.

Fortunately, these kinds of dilemmas are rare. In normal circumstances, utilitarianism's account of morality is compatible with the moral permissibility of a differential concern for one's own projects and the welfare of those close to one. In some circumstances, an impartial weighting of everyone's good will require agents to sacrifice important personal projects or commitments in order to prevent great harm to, or produce great benefit for, others. This is the sort of demand we expect a moral theory to make. And where the sacrifice demanded of the agent is great, he may typically take consolation in the knowledge that his suffering would be no less were he to resist the demands of morality.

18. THE SEPARATENESS OF PERSONS

The charges that utilitarianism cannot accommodate moral rights, distributive justice, and the personal point of view are often based on the charge that utilitarianism fails to recognize the separateness of persons. Utilitarianism's failure to recognize the separateness of persons is supposed to follow from its decision procedure. Utilitarianism is said to extend the individual or prudential decision procedure to social contexts. (See Sidgwick 1907: 381–2, 418.) Prudential calculations, in a traditional view, should be impartial among different stages of one's life so as to be indifferent among different distributions of the same amount of welfare over the course of one's life. Utilitarianism and teleological theories in general, it is said, apply this same choice principle in social contexts. Just as prudence is indifferent among different distributions of the same amount of welfare across the various stages of an individual's life, so, too, utilitarianism must be indifferent among different distributions of the same amount of welfare among different persons. In effect, utilitarianism treats social groups as big persons and different individuals as different stages in the life of a big person. This, it is said, is to fail to recognize the separateness of persons (see footnote 24).

If the failure to recognize the separateness of persons is indeed a sufficient condition for failure to accommodate rights, justice, and the personal point of view, then my defense of OU's ability to accommodate these things demonstrates that utilitarianism recognizes the separateness of persons. But it may nonetheless be instructive to examine the "separateness objection" to see why it fails.

The separateness objection could be construed as raising the *metaphysical* question of how separate persons *are*, or as raising the *moral* question of how separate persons *should be*. Although it is most natural to construe the separateness objection as a moral objection, it is worthwhile considering the metaphysical construal, because some critics of utilitarianism have written as if utilitarianism violates what is literally constitutive of personal identity (B. Williams 1973a: 116; 1976a: 12; Lomasky 1983: 259, 273). Does utilitarianism require us to violate or otherwise disregard the conditions of personal identity and thus the separateness of persons?

The colorful derivation of utilitarianism as an extension of the prudential decision procedure into social choice situations is misleading. First, I do not see why utilitarian or teleological theories need be motivated by an appeal to prudence. We can be motivated to hold or pursue a utilitarian moral theory because we think such a theory promises to capture important moral beliefs. Many of our moral judgments tell us that morality is concerned with human good and harm (i.e., human welfare). But we also believe that the moral point of view is impartial; it tells us that everyone's welfare matters equally. Now, these are different interpretations of this kind of impartiality. Utilitarianism provides one interpretation. Its reasoning is something like this: Because everyone's welfare matters, but no one's welfare matters more than another's, the correct thing to do is to maximize welfare. Of course, utilitarianism's interpretation of impartiality might prove inadequate. Indeed, this can be seen as the point of the sorts of moral objections to utilitarianism that we have been considering. But I have argued that these objections are not compelling as they stand; whether or not traditional subjective versions of utilitarianism provide an acceptable interpretation of impartiality, OU's interpretation of impartiality can be defended against many standard moral objections. Prudence may imply a kind of temporal impartiality akin to utilitarianism's impartiality among persons. If so, then this shows only that utilitarianism and prudence share a conception of impartiality, not that the motivation for utilitarianism is posterior to that for prudence.

Second, even if the motivation for utilitarianism did depend, as critics claim, on assimilating social choice to prudential choice, this would not demonstrate utilitarianism's failure to recognize the metaphysical distinctness of persons. Utilitarianism recognizes the existence of separate persons, measures their welfare in certain ways, and then adds these magnitudes. Utilitarianism may or may not give the separateness of persons proper moral weight, but it does not fail to recognize that persons are separate.

Sometimes the objection to utilitarianism based on the personal point of view is presented as the claim that in requiring agents to sacrifice their own projects and commitments for the good of others, utilitarianism deprives agents of the constituents of their identity. But this is absurd. By changing my projects, I do not go out of existence. Nor does failure to secure the aim of my projects cause me to go out of existence. Even if we assume that the meaning of Jim's life is lost when he complies with the utilitarian demand to shoot an innocent villager, it is still Jim who suffers. Personal projects and commitments may be important to me, but they are not constitutive of me in this way.[49]

Finally, even if, contrary to fact, utilitarianism could not treat persons as fundamentally distinct, this fact would constitute an objection to utilitarianism only if persons are fundamentally dis-

---

49 If OU expressed a decision procedure and required agents to regard their projects impersonally, then perhaps OU would require of agents a kind of willingness to make uncompensated sacrifices that is incompatible with their possessing personal projects and commitments that are, on some views of personal identity, partly constitutive of personal identity (or of what matters in personal identity) (cf. 3.12). I am not quite sure of this. But, in any case, OU does not express a decision procedure (8.11) and so does not require this sort of attitude in agents (8.17).

tinct. Derek Parfit and others have argued that what really matters in issues about personal identity is the existence of the right sort of causal relations among person-stages, rather than personal identity per se (1984: pt. 3; cf. Shoemaker 1984). Parfit claims that these relations are psychological continuity and connectedness (diachronic retention of such things as memories, intentions, and character traits).[50] These relations, unlike identity, can hold to different degrees. In particular, because psychological connectedness can depreciate greatly over time, the relations between my present self and later stages of myself (person-stages causally continuous with my present and past selves) can resemble the relations between my present self and current stages of other selves, with whom I causally interact, more than is commonly supposed. If so, persons might seem to be less separate than other theories of personal identity would lead us to believe, and it might, therefore, be less of an indictment of utilitarianism if it could be shown that it was unable to treat persons as fundamentally distinct.

So, for example, such "reductionist" theories of personal identity might lead us to question the moral importance of distributional considerations. If we accept the reductionist claims about the similarity between the relations among stages of a single self and the relations among distinct selves, we might conclude that the distribution of goods across lives is no more important than that across stages of a single life and so worry less about OU's distributional implications.

Someone might use these reductionist claims to argue in the opposite direction, however. Since reductionist views of personal identity seem to treat the relations among stages in one life more

---

50 As I understand these two conditions of survival, psychological connectedness is explanatorily prior. The psychological states of two person-stages p_1 and p_2 at times t_1 and t_2 are psychologically connected just in case they are causally related in the appropriate way and are significantly similar. Because the similarity relation involved in psychological connectedness is not exact similarity, psychological connectedness can vary and, in particular, can depreciate over time. Thus, p_1 can be psychologically connected to p_2, and p_2 can be psychologically connected to p_3, but p_3 need not be, and is unlikely to be, as closely connected with p_1 as p_2 is. A series of person-stages p_1 through p_n at times t_1 through t_n is psychologically continuous just in case the members of every pair of temporally contiguous person-stages in this series are psychologically connected. It follows that p_1 and p_n can be psychologically continuous even if they are not psychologically well connected or even connected at all. (Cf. 1984: 204–9.)

like the relations among different lives, one might conclude that the scope of distributive considerations ought to be extended from interpersonal contexts into intrapersonal contexts and not that distributional considerations are less important. This would seem to argue against the kind of temporal neutrality characteristic of rational egoism and prudence in intrapersonal contexts and to require that one be concerned with the way one distributes goods among the stages of one's life (as well as among different lives) and not just with maximizing the total number of goods enjoyed over the course of one's life. This conclusion would mean that an appeal to reductionist accounts of personal identity would provide no defense of OU's distributional implications.

There seem to be two problems with this line of argument. First, it focuses on only half of the reductionist's position. Insofar as (1) the reductionist view brings the relations among stages of a single life closer to the relations among different lives, perhaps it supports (2) extending the scope of distributional considerations into intrapersonal contexts. But (3) the reductionist also brings the relations among different lives closer to those among stages of a single life, and insofar as this is true, it would seem to support (4) reducing the importance of distributional considerations in interpersonal contexts, since the importance of distributional considerations depends on the separateness of the units distributed over. Because the reductionist position implies (3) as well as (1), this would seem to argue for (4) as well as (2), and this should make us worry less about OU's distributional implications. (This is essentially Parfit's own response; see 1984: chap. 15.)

Second, it is not clear that (1) supports (2). (2) would imply that an agent should attach rational significance to her own distant benefits and harms out of proportion to the magnitude of those benefits or harms in order to achieve the appropriate distribution of benefits and burdens across the various stages of her life. But each of the different stages of a life belongs to that life, even if their relation to one another (the reductionist's "relation R") is one that can hold to different degrees. So the rational egoist who accepts SRC can resist the introduction of (independent) distributional considerations, since benefits and harms are equally benefits or harms to her regardless of their temporal location in her life. Thus she is sufficiently compensated for a present sacrifice as long as the later gain is greater than the present sacrifice, and she is insufficiently compensated for such a sacrifice as long as the later gain is less than the present sacrifice (cf. Brink forthcoming).[51]

Of course, there can be no *inter*personal compensation (unless, of course, I benefit from your benefit); so this argument cannot be used to reject distributional considerations in interpersonal contexts. But this does no harm to my defense of OU. First, although I sympathize with the claim that the *rationality* of sacrifice requires compensation, it is not my view that the *morality* of sacrifice requires compensation. The moral point of view is impartial in a way that, I think, provides no a priori guarantee that agents will be compensated for the sacrifices morality demands of them. So if OU does sometimes (morally) require insufficiently compensated sacrifices, this need not, in my view, constitute an insuperable objection to OU. Second, OU, as we saw, is distribution-sensitive (8.16). And third, as far as I can see, we could still rely on (3) to support (4).

These claims obviously raise large issues in philosophy of mind, and about the connection between philosophy of mind and moral philosophy, that I cannot resolve or even fully address here. I wish only to draw attention to some of the assumptions implicit in the separateness objection. It is the burden of the proponent of this objection in its metaphysical form to demonstrate not only that utilitarianism must deny the metaphysical separateness of persons but also that this denial constitutes a defect in utilitarianism. I have explained why utilitarianism is not committed to denying the separateness of persons. Parfit's arguments and the ones I just considered illustrate how the separateness objection could be questioned even if utilitarianism had metaphysical implications, which it clearly does not.

It is more plausible to regard the separateness objection as raising the moral question of how separate persons should be. Proponents of this objection, so construed, must regard it as desirable that persons be more independent of one another than utilitarianism allows. This may be the thought underlying the complaint, frequently made, that utilitarianism must treat persons as mere means and not as ends in themselves.

But OU recognizes as much independence as is desirable, I think.

51 Parfit thinks there are other reductionist objections to rational egoism's temporal neutrality (1984: chap. 14). I discuss these objections and defend rational egoism's compatibility with reductionism in Brink forthcoming.

OU recognizes the importance of autonomy to pursue and realize personal projects and personal relationships. There are good utilitarian reasons for agents to possess and act from a differential concern for their own welfare and the welfare of those close to them. So agents will not have to view their own time and energy as mere resources for the realization of others' pleasures or preferences. Of course, OU limits individual autonomy in important ways. As we have seen, because OU recognizes the importance of basic well-being to the realization of any kind of value and the importance of respect for persons, it will give priority to claims to basic goods and so will be, in effect, distribution-sensitive. This means that no one's conditions for a valuable life (basic goods) can be treated as mere resources for use by others in pursuit of nonbasic goods. Moreover, OU will require sacrifice of some of an agent's projects if such a sacrifice will prevent great harm to others or produce great benefit to others (although, as we have seen, there are certain moral limits on what can count as a great benefit or a great harm to others).

Someone might claim that such restrictions on individual autonomy are still too great and do not make persons sufficiently independent of one another. Nozick, for example, claims that recognition of the separateness of persons implies that no one (who is not herself violating the libertarian rights of others) can ever be required to set her projects aside in order to benefit others or prevent harm to them (1974: 30–3). But surely this is too much independence. It cannot be that we are never justified in asking an agent to set aside personal projects in order, say, to prevent great suffering (cf. Hart 1979: 206–7; Conly 1983: 308–10). This kind of independence cannot be morally important. Indeed, if the sort of objective conception of welfare embodied in OU is correct, an agent's projects cannot be valuable if they fail to show respect for others. Respect for others requires recognition that others matter, and this requires that we recognize their claims to basic well-being and overall welfare in certain ways.

OU promises to represent adequately the moral importance of the separateness of persons. A moral theory should recognize the moral independence of persons insofar as autonomy is valuable; OU does this. But the moral independence of persons is limited, as OU recognizes, by certain distributional considerations.

19. CONCLUSION

This completes my defense of OU against certain standard objections to utilitarianism. I have not canvassed all of the common objections to utilitarianism, and the defense I have offered has been highly programmatic in many respects. But my examination of OU has accomplished its objective. OU helps illustrate the kind of metaphysical and epistemological commitments that substantive moral theories bring, and defense of OU illustrates the nature of coherentist moral reasoning.

OU turns out to be a fairly plausible account of the moral facts. Coherentism creates a presumption in favor of unified moral theories such as OU. OU provides a more coherent account of our moral beliefs than standard objections to utilitarianism would lead one to suppose. Not only does OU provide an interpretation of the claims that morality has to do with human good and harm and that the moral point of view is an impartial one; these standard objections to utilitarianism are not compelling against OU, either because they depend on construing utilitarianism as a decision procedure or because they depend on construing welfare as traditional subjective versions of utilitarianism have construed it. OU provides a criterion of rightness, rather than a decision procedure, and incorporates an objective construal of welfare. These features of OU allow it to respond persuasively to the standard objections. In particular, OU makes reasonable claims about the possibility and reliability of interpersonal comparisons of welfare; it can accommodate our moral beliefs about value, our obligations to others, moral and political rights, and distributive justice; and it allows proper recognition of the personal point of view and the separateness of persons. This is not to say that OU can answer all objections or that it can be defended as uniquely reasonable. But it does represent a plausible normative theory that moral realists (among others) should take seriously.

Appendix 1: Must an infinite regress of justification be vicious?

As we saw in Chapter 5, there are three strategies for incorporating the epistemological requirement that justifying beliefs be justified: (1) All justification is both linear and inferential; (2) although all justification is inferential, it is not all linear; and (3) although all justification is linear, it is not all inferential. Foundationalism represents (3), and the regress argument claims that foundationalism, and it alone, is an acceptable strategy. According to this argument, strategy (1) involves a vicious regress of justification, whereas strategy (2) involves a vicious circle of justification.

We saw that this argument fails. First, foundationalism is not an acceptable strategy; there are no noninferentially justified beliefs (5.5). Second, strategy (2) can be defended. By distinguishing between systematic and contextualist justification, we can see how coherentism can provide the correct account of systematic justification even if circular reasoning is generally inadmissible in contextualist justification (5.6).

It seems, however, to be generally agreed by both foundationalists and coherentists that the case made against strategy (1) by the regress argument is conclusive.[1] I think this conventional wisdom is unfounded. If there is something wrong with (1), it is not what the standard objection alleges.

1. A VIRTUOUS REGRESS

I think it must be concluded that (1) can incorporate the epistemological requirement *as it has been formulated* only at the cost of an infinite and vicious regress. If any justifying belief must itself *be*

---

1 Peirce is the only one I know of who seems to advocate (1). See Peirce 1934: 154–5, 158, 186; cf. Armstrong 1973: 154–5, and Quinton 1973: 122. But see Irwin 1988: chap. 5, sec. 5. Harker (1984) documents and criticizes a number of objec-

justified, then, if, as (1) claims, all justification is inferential and linear, one can be justified in holding a belief p only if one holds and is justified in holding an infinite number of beliefs. We could hold and justify an infinite number of beliefs if we were immortal, but I assume that we do not want the justification of our beliefs to depend on our being immortal.

We should ask, however, if (1)'s problems depend on this particular formulation of the epistemological requirement. Must justifying beliefs be justified, or need they be only *justifiable*? Does one's justification in holding p require more than that one *be able* to justify p? Accepting the more modest epistemological requirement that justifying beliefs be justifiable may affect the case against (1).

Modifying the epistemological requirement means that (1) now implies only that if (some belief) q is to justify one in holding p, one must be able to justify an infinite number of beliefs underlying q. This claim can be interpreted two ways: (1a) A justified cognizer must have the capacity to, or be able to, perform the infinite task of justifying an infinite number of beliefs. Thus, it must be true of someone that she can perform the following task: first justify p, then justify q, then justify r, ... But if (1) is construed as implying (1a), then (1) still involves a vicious regress, because we could do infinitely many things in this way only if we were immortal.

Someone might defend (1a) by appeal to Achilles' ability to pass through an infinite number of points in a finite period of time (cf. Peirce 1934: 154–5). I do not, however, think this capacity of Achilles' realizes a capacity to do an infinite number of things of the sort required in order to satisfy (1a). This is because even if there is a sense in which Achilles does an infinite number of things in a finite period of time, he could not perform just one of those things that is part of his infinite task. By contrast, each part of a justified cognizer's infinite task, namely, the justification of each belief, ought to be a performable action.[2]

Alternatively, (1) can be construed as implying (1b) for any belief that is part of an inferential chain justifying p, a cognizer must be able

tions to (1) but objects to (1) himself because it represents a purely epistemic theory of justification and so is unable to guarantee truth. Of course, I have argued that it is wrong to demand that justification guarantee truth and that, as a result, purely epistemic accounts of justification can explain how evidence is evidence of objective truth (5.7).

2 Peirce apparently rethought the adequacy of this defense between 1868 and 1903; see Peirce 1934: 97, 113.

to justify it. Thus, an infinite number of things must be true of a justified cognizer: It must be true of him that he can justify p by reference to q, it must be true of him that he can justify q by reference to r, it must be true of him that he can justify r by reference to s, ... But what is wrong with this? I do not see what prevents (1b) from being satisfiable, even if there are an infinite number of beliefs, about any one of which it must be true that one can justify it.

One worry about (1b) is not that it requires cognizers to be able to perform an infinite task but that it makes justification too piecemeal. It does not seem sufficient for justification that for any belief one be able to produce its immediate evidential ancestor. One must be able to connect the links in an evidential chain together in certain ways. It is not sufficient that someone be able to cite q in support of p, that she be able to cite r in support of q, that she be able to cite s in support of r, and so forth. She must be able to connect s et al. with p. This objection can take the form of a dilemma. Either (1b) requires only that cognizers be able to make a number of discrete inferential moves, in which case it makes justification too piecemeal, or it requires cognizers to perform an infinite task, in which case it leads to a vicious regress.

The defender of (1), however, might claim that this dilemma is not genuine. If someone not only could justify p, could justify q, could justify r, . . . but also could connect these justificatory links into fairly long chains, wouldn't he be able to justify an infinite number of beliefs without making justification too piecemeal? This justificatory capacity seems to be possible and to steer between the horns of this dilemma.

If so, if we weaken the epistemological requirement to the claim that justifying beliefs be justifiable, and if we construe (1) as requiring only (1b), it seems that (1) can avoid the standard charge that it is committed to a vicious regress.[3]

2. A VIRTUOUS REGRESS AND COHERENTISM

Does this defense of (1) undermine the defense of coherentism in 5.6? It need not. First, I have not claimed that (1) is correct; I have claimed only that the standard reason for rejecting it is not compelling.

3 It should be noted that weakening the epistemological requirement in this way does not affect the case made against foundationalism in 5.5. Beliefs are no more *self-justifiable* than they are *self-justifying*.

Moreover, I think there are at least two grounds on which one might prefer coherentism to strategy (1). The first ground for preferring coherentism is that at least one justificatory chain appears to be circular. There is good reason to suppose that the principle of noncontradiction is presupposed in all justifications, including the justification of the principle of noncontradiction itself.[4] I assume that justification in holding a belief p to be true implies justification in holding not-p to be false. Since anything follows from a contradiction, the failure of the principle of noncontradiction would justify belief in anything and, hence, in nothing. This applies as well to belief in the principle of noncontradiction. We can be justified in believing the principle of noncontradiction only by assuming that it is true. This means that the justification of the principle of noncontradiction must be circular.

The second ground for preferring coherentism to (1) is that, unlike coherentism, (1) may still represent justification as too piecemeal in a certain respect. Strategy (1) can avoid one charge that it is too piecemeal by insisting that cognizers be able to reproduce large segments of the infinite inferential chain, but the linearity of this chain may still leave justification too piecemeal. (1) gives a cognizer's belief p one justifier, namely, belief q; belief q one justifier, namely, belief r; belief r one justifier, namely, belief s; and so on. (1) does not represent how s and r, for example, can both support q. I take this phenomenon of multiple support for a given belief to be one that we want a theory of justification to capture. Coherentism captures this phenomenon insofar as it makes the justification of beliefs a matter of their *mutual* support. (This is why the web-of-belief metaphor is often less misleading for coherentism than the metaphor of a single circle of beliefs arranged in single file.)

Strategy (1) can attempt to capture this phenomenon of multiple support by insisting that every justified belief form a node on several different branches of linear justification. The result would be a set of interlocking justificatory chains, each infinite in length. But now (1) becomes difficult to distinguish from coherentism's claim that justified beliefs form a system of beliefs held together by relations of mutual explanatory support. Even if it could be distinguished from coherentism (e.g., because it requires *infinite* justi-

---

4 Cf. Aristotle (*Meta* IV, chaps. 3 and 4), who argues that the principle of noncontradiction is a presupposition of belief and, indeed, of significant assertion.

ficatory chains), this version of (1) would share a great deal in common with coherentism.

3. CONCLUSION

I conclude that the standard objection to strategy (1) contained in the regress argument fails. An infinite regress of justification need not be vicious. However, this defense of (1) need not undermine coherentism. Although conclusive resolution of the relative merits of (1) and coherentism is beyond the scope of this appendix, one may raise doubts about whether there is a form of strategy (1) that is both distinct from and preferable to coherentism.

Appendix 2: Coherence, internalism, and externalism in epistemology

Chapter 5 defends a coherence theory of justification. I should explain, even if I cannot defend here, how this defense of coherentism bears on the debates between internalism and externalism in epistemology.

We should distinguish between internalism and externalism about both knowledge and justification. *Internalism about knowledge* construes knowledge as requiring justified belief. The traditional analysis of knowledge as justified true belief, for example, represents internalism about knowledge. *Internalism about justification* makes justification a function of properties of a cognizer's beliefs that are internal or accessible to the cognizer himself. Versions of foundationalism that base justification on foundational beliefs that are indubitable, for example, represent internalism about justification. *Externalism about justification,* by contrast, makes justification a natural (e.g., causal) relation between a cognizer's beliefs and the world (see, e.g., Goldman, 1979). A justified cognizer, on this view, need not believe or be aware that this relation obtains. *Externalism about knowledge,* however, rejects justified belief as a requirement for knowledge; it makes knowledge itself consist in some natural (e.g., causal) relation between a cognizer's beliefs and the world (e.g., Goldman 1967, 1976; Armstrong 1973: pt. 3; Nozick 1981: chap. 3).

1. AGAINST EXTERNALISM ABOUT JUSTIFICATION

The failure of foundationalism – in particular, of objective foundationalism (5.5) – explains what is wrong with externalist accounts of justification. Justification cannot be, as the externalist claims, the causal reliability of a cognizer's beliefs or any other such natural relation between a cognizer's beliefs and the world, for this would allow justification to be inaccessible to the cognizer herself. A belief *p* could be true and reliably produced by the cognizer's causal interaction with the facts that *p* represents without the cognizer's holding any beliefs that make it reasonable to hold *p* (cf. Bonjour 1980). The mere fact that certain beliefs *are*, say, reliable does not itself justify a cognizer in holding them. Indeed, although *p* may have been reliably produced, a cognizer's set of beliefs may actually give her reason to doubt or reject *p*. In order for one to be justified in holding *p*, even if *p* has been reliably produced, one must base *p* on second-order beliefs about what kind of belief *p* is and why *p*-type beliefs should be true or reliable. Justified beliefs must be based on beliefs about the nature and reliability of the beliefs whose justification is in question. If so, externalism about justification is unacceptable. About justification, we must be internalists. Coherentism is an internalist theory of justification; it requires justified beliefs to be based on, among other things, second-order beliefs about the nature and reliability of the beliefs whose justification is in question.

2. COHERENTISM AND INTERNALISM AND EXTERNALISM ABOUT KNOWLEDGE

My defense of a coherence theory of justification involves a defense of internalism about justification insofar as it contains an argument against externalism about justification and insofar as coherentism is one form of internalism about justification. But it is itself neutral between internalism and externalism about knowledge. A defense of coherentism explains what the content of an internalist theory of knowledge should include, but it does not itself show that justification is, as the internalist about knowledge claims, necessary for knowledge. Moreover, the externalist, too, can recognize the epistemological importance of coherentism. Although he denies that justification is necessary for knowledge, the externalist can still regard justification as an important epistemological property. He can accept coherentism even if it is not part of his theory of knowledge.

I would like to make two proposals about the role of coherence in the debate between internalism and externalism about knowledge.

297

First, I think it is possible to regard internalism and externalism about knowledge as complementary, rather than competing, theories; each can explicate a different sense of 'know'. In some contexts – especially moral, legal, and philosophical contexts – when we ask about someone's knowledge or claim to knowledge, we are especially interested in her reasons for holding a particular belief and so are especially interested in her justification for holding that belief. If a cognizer is to be said to know that p in these circumstances, it must be reasonable or justified for her to believe that p given the other beliefs she holds or that are available to her. For such contexts, an internalist account of knowledge is required. In other contexts – especially perceptual and other scientific ones – when we are concerned about someone's knowledge or claim to knowledge, we are interested in how reliably she acquires and processes information (e.g., about her environment). If a cognizer is to be said to know that p in these circumstances, her belief that p need only be a reliably produced true belief. In these contexts, I suggest, an externalist account of knowledge is required. I do not suppose it is always easy to distinguish such contexts or that these two sets of contexts are entirely disjoint. But I do think this proposal is worth pursuing if only as a way of accommodating the apparent insights of both internalist and externalist perspectives on knowledge.

Because this proposal recognizes the need for an internalist account of knowledge, Chapter 5's defense of coherentism provides reasons to prefer an internalist theory of knowledge that incorporates a coherence theory of justification. This will be compatible with recognizing the need for an externalist account of knowledge for other contexts.

Second, whether or not internalism and externalism about knowledge can be reconciled as this proposal suggests, coherence can and should play an important part in the theory of knowledge. Considerations of coherence should figure not only in justification but even in an externalist account of knowledge.

Externalist theories of knowledge standardly construe it as something like reliably produced true belief. Many such analyses focus on explicating the reliability of the causal mechanisms involved in perceptual belief production. This focus is important, but we should not overlook many of our inferential belief-formation mechanisms. We acquire and modify many of our beliefs on the basis of other beliefs

298

we hold. An externalist account of this kind of inferential knowledge must explain which such inferential mechanisms are reliable and under what conditions they are reliable. Coherentist reasoning will often prove reliable. In particular, beliefs acquired or modified on the basis of their coherence with other beliefs we hold will be reliably produced if a sufficient number of beliefs contained in our inferential base are approximately true. Thus, adoption of a true theory on the basis of its coherence with observational and auxiliary theoretical beliefs (on the basis of inference to the best explanation) will constitute scientific knowledge, according to the externalist, if a sufficient number of our observational and theoretical beliefs are approximately true. As philosophers, we may want to know if we have good reason to regard our inferential base as sufficiently approximately true. This is a request for justification, and, according to Chapter 5, a coherentist reply is in order.

Not only should coherence play a part in an externalist epistemology; it should also play an important part in an externalist moral epistemology. Belief in a true moral theory accepted on the basis of its coherence with, among other things, considered moral beliefs will count as knowledge, according to the externalist, if a sufficient number of our considered moral beliefs are approximately true. As philosophers, we may want to know if we have good reason to regard such an inferential base as sufficiently approximately true. This too is a request for justification, and, as such, a coherentist reply is in order. Most of this book is part of such a reply. We have reason to believe there are moral facts and true moral propositions (2.6–2.8). We have reason to regard considered moral beliefs as reliable; they have been formed under conditions we have moral and nonmoral reason to regard as reliable (5.7–5.9). And our moral claims appear to be explanatory (7.3).

3. CONCLUSION

My defense of coherentism in Chapter 5 represents a form of internalism about justification and provides reason to reject externalism about justification. By itself, this defense does not decide between internalism and externalism about knowledge. Although coherentism is a theory of justification, the externalist about knowledge can and should incorporate coherence into his epistemology. Moreover, we might view internalism and externalism about knowledge and their respective uses of coherence as complementary rather than competing theories by viewing them as explicating different senses of 'know'.

Appendix 3: The is/ought thesis and intuitionism

One reason many have thought an is/ought thesis is fatal to moral realism is that they have claimed or assumed that foundationalism is true. Foundationalism and the is/ought thesis, many think, force us to choose between intuitionism and antirealism. But intuitionism is absurd: It is implausibly committed to the existence of a special faculty for the perception of moral facts, it is embarrassed by the existence of moral disagreements, and it is committed to the mysterious doctrine of nonnaturalism. Because the is/ought thesis forces us to choose between intuitionism and antirealism, and because intuitionism is absurd, we should reject moral realism and accept some form of noncognitivism.

There are at least three things wrong with this use of the is/ought thesis against moral realism. First, intuitionism is not absurd; it is no less plausible than foundationalism is generally. We saw in 5.3 that intuitionism is not committed to the existence of special faculties of moral perception and that intuitionism need not be embarrassed by the existence of moral disagreement. In Chapter 6 we saw that the is/ought thesis implies nonnaturalism only if the semantic test of properties is true, and we raised doubts about the semantic test of properties. If we reject the semantic test of properties, neither the is/ought thesis nor a foundationalist epistemology requires rejection of ethical naturalism. But even if the semantic test of properties is true, nonnaturalism is not absurd, because in that case the facts and properties of any discipline will be sui generis. So, even if the is/ought thesis and foundationalism established the dependence of moral realism on intuitionism, this would pose no special problems for moral realism.

Second, this use of the is/ought thesis against moral realism requires the truth of foundationalism; it is foundationalism and the is/ought thesis that are held to make moral realism depend on intuitionism. But, of course, we have reason to reject foundationalism (5.5). Not only is foundationalism false; coherentism can be defended. We saw in Chapter 6 how a coherentist moral epistemology can incorporate the is/ought thesis. Moral coherentism can concede that no moral conclusion can be derived from nonmoral premises without the benefit of moral bridge premises and claim that we have reason to regard valid arguments for moral conclusions as sound just in case the premises, including the moral bridge premises, cohere well with our other beliefs, both moral and nonmoral.

Third, this use of the is/ought thesis against moral realism mistakenly assumes that foundationalism and the is/ought thesis imply an intuitionist epistemology. Foundationalism might be true and there might be an is/ought gap without moral justification requiring foundational *moral* beliefs. All our justified moral beliefs might belong to a set of beliefs justified on the basis of *nondeductive* inference from foundational nonmoral beliefs (cf. Locke 1700: I, iii, 1–4, and IV, iii, 18; Lewis 1946; Chisholm 1977: 123–6). Although I did not demonstrate the existence of good nondeductive inferences between moral and nonmoral beliefs in the absence of belief in moral bridge premises, I did offer some reasons for thinking them possible (6.8). At least the is/ought thesis, as typically formulated and defended, does not preclude such a position. So foundationlism and the is/ought thesis do not themselves imply intuitionism.

Thus, moral realism is not undermined by the combination of the is/ought thesis and foundationalism. The realist should reject foundationalism; foundationalism and the is/ought thesis do not themselves imply an intuitionist epistemology; and even if foundationalism and the is/ought thesis did impose an intuitionist epistemology on moral realism, this would not commit the realist to any absurd form of nonnaturalism.

Appendix 4: Rawlsian constructivism

In his writings since *A Theory of Justice,* Rawls has, among other things, made a number of claims about the status and justification of his theory of justice. I would like to consider a possible epistemological objection to moral realism based on Rawls's recent Dewey Lectures, "Kantian Constructivism in Moral Theory" (1980). As we shall see, it is difficult to know whether the Dewey Lectures contain any kind of challenge to moral realism or any metaethical view. If not, we need not worry about Rawls's claims there. But, I shall argue, the Dewey Lectures can be read as containing such a challenge (and are so read by a number of people). If so, Rawls's position merits our attention, not only because of the influence exerted by his views but also because he continues to accept the sort of coherence theory of justification in ethics that I have been defending. These are reasons to explore the bearing of Kantian constructivism on my defense of moral realism.[1]

Since he wrote his article "Outline for a Decision Procedure in Ethics," Rawls has advocated a coherentist moral epistemology according to which moral and political theories are justified on the basis of their coherence with our other beliefs, both moral and nonmoral (1951: 56, 61). A moral theory that is maximally coherent with our other beliefs is in a state that Rawls calls "reflective equilibrium" (1971: 20). In *A Theory of Justice,* Rawls advances two principles of justice and claims that they are in reflective equilibrium. He defends this claim by appeal to a hypothetical social contract and argues that parties in a position satisfying certain informational and motivational criteria, which he calls "the original position," would

---

1 Brink 1987 was written before Rawls's paper "Justice as Fairness: Political Not Metaphysical" (1985) appeared. My analysis here of the Dewey Lectures remains essentially unchanged from Brink 1987; however, I tried here to take into account the complications raised by this later paper. (See section 1 of this appendix.)

choose the following two principles of justice to govern the basic structure of their society:

1. Each person is to have an equal right to the most extensive total system of equal basic liberties compatible with a similar system of liberty for all.
2. Social and economic inequalities are to be arranged so that they are both (a) to the greatest benefit of the least advantaged and (b) attached to offices and positions open to all under fair conditions of equality of opportunity. (1971: 302)

Rawls refers to this conception of justice as "justice as fairness."

Although Rawls claims that theories of the person play an important part in the justification of theories of justice (1971: 258–65, 584) and explores a Kantian interpretation of justice as fairness (1971: 251–7), he does not provide a systematic justification of his use of the original position or the contract device. Instead, he claims only that features of the original position represent various considered judgments about conditions of fairness in choice.

But Rawls's Dewey Lectures do offer a systematic justification of the original position; he argues that a Kantian ideal of the person that conceives of persons as free, equal, rational, and socially cooperative motivates the use of a contract device, underlies the original position, and explains its various features.

There is a wealth of interesting and persuasive argument in Rawls's Dewey Lectures that I will not discuss. Instead, I want to focus on his defense of Kantian constructivism. Someone who had followed the development of Rawls's views to this point might easily have concluded that Rawls had now completed (what we might call) a realist defense of his theory of justice. Rawls claims that his two principles of justice would be chosen by contractors in the original position, and the original position is supposed to represent the constraints of a Kantian ideal of the person. One would have thought that he was claiming that this ideal of the person is true independently of anyone's beliefs or evidence, from which it would follow that Rawls's theory of justice purports to be objectively true. But Rawls resists this interpretation; instead he calls his own position "constructivist." Exactly why he resists the realist interpretation and what constructivism is are not quite clear. I shall argue that on one plausible reading of the Dewey Lectures, Rawls can be understood to claim that this appeal to a Kantian ideal of the person supports an antirealist, constructivist thesis about ethics. Because of the difficulty involved in making sense of all the disparate things Rawls wants to say about the status of justice as fairness, I shall devote a significant portion of the discussion to explaining the credentials of this antirealist interpretation of Kantian constructivism.

On this interpretation, constructivism is or implies an antirealist metaethical view according to which moral truth is constituted by our moral beliefs, in particular, by our ideals of the person. Kantian constructivism is that set of moral truths constituted by a Kantian ideal of the person. And on this interpretation, Rawls justifies Kantian constructivism by appeal to the importance of ideals of the person in framing and justifying moral theories. Because of the importance of ideals of the person in moral theory and the existence of competing ideals of the person, moral facts or truths must be relativized to, or defined in terms of, different ideals of the person. Hence, moral realism is false and constructivism in ethics is true.

But if this interpretation of Kantian constructivism is correct, we can identify a tension in Rawls's epistemological views. For this defense of constructivism requires Rawls, implicitly, to assign to ideals of the person an evidential role incompatible with a coherentist moral epistemology. But a coherence theory of justification in ethics of the sort Rawls himself has advocated allows one to recognize the importance of ideals of the person in moral theory and the existence of competing ideals without conceding any antirealist claims.

But this is to anticipate; we must first see if there is anything to this interpretation of Kantian constructivism.

1. KANTIAN CONSTRUCTIVISM

What is Kantian constructivism? Rawls sometimes distinguishes between constructivism and Kantian constructivism; Kantian constructivism is apparently one kind of constructivist doctrine. The Dewey Lectures represent, among other things, Rawls's recognition of the importance of theories of the person in moral theory and of the way in which his own conception of justice as fairness depends on a Kantian theory of the person. This suggests, as I shall confirm, that constructivism in some way recognizes the importance of theories of the person and incorporates them into moral theory; Kantian constructivism is a constructivist view incorporating a Kantian ideal of the person.

305

Although this gives us some idea of constructivism and Kantian constructivism, and their relation to each other, it leaves many questions unanswered. How does constructivism incorporate theories of the person? Rawls claims that constructivism yields a conception of objectivity in ethics. What view of objectivity is it supposed to imply? How is this conception of objectivity related to other conceptions? Why does recognition of the importance of theories of the person in moral theory imply any conception of objectivity? Unfortunately, Rawls is not as clear about these issues as one would like.

Since constructivist views are usually metaphysical views that contrast with realist views, it would be natural to interpret Kantian constructivism as a form of antirealism about ethics. Indeed, I do think that this is a natural and defensible construal of Kantian constructivism, at least as it occurs in Rawls's Dewey Lectures. However, it is worth comparing this metaphysical construal of Kantian constructivism with two other construals, since Rawls makes a variety of different claims about Kantian constructivism.

For reasons that will become clear, we might call the first construal of constructivism the *political* construal. It relies on Rawls's distinction in "The Independence of Moral Theory" between moral *theory* and moral *philosophy* (1974: 5–7, 21). Moral theory merely articulates given moral conceptions or structures and is not concerned with the truth or plausibility of these conceptions or structures. So moral theory is neutral with respect to the metaphysical, epistemological, and semantic questions about ethics that moral philosophy addresses. Indeed, at the beginning of the Dewey Lectures, Rawls claims that the aim of political philosophy (as well as that of political theory) is "to articulate and make explicit those shared notions and principles thought to be already latent in common sense; or, as is often the case, if common sense is hesitant and uncertain, and doesn't know what to think, to propose to it certain conceptions and principles congenial to its most essential convictions and historical traditions" (1980: 518). On this construal, constructivism represents no more than an articulation of a specific moral and political structure – in particular, a specific theory of the person. Kantian constructivism would then articulate a moral structure based on a Kantian theory of the person. On the political interpretation of constructivism, Rawls would simply be agnostic about the truth or plausibility of a Kantian theory of the person and of the moral structure the theory supports.

306

Rawls does claim that the contractors are agents of construction and that they view themselves as determining, rather than discovering, principles of justice (1980: 524, 564, 568), and this may seem to threaten the metaphysical neutrality (and, hence, a political construal) of constructivism. But such claims hold *within* the social contract device and so should have no metaphysical import. The contract is an analytic device to be used in moral theory and is not intended to represent the way the world is. Just as the disinterestedness of the contractors shows nothing about human motivation, the contractors' view of themselves as agents of construction (if, indeed, they do or should so view themselves) has no implications for the metaethical status of the two principles of justice that result from the contract device. A political construal of constructivism, therefore, would be metaphysically, epistemologically, and semantically neutral and so would presuppose no antirealist metaethical view.

An *epistemological* construal of constructivism results from taking it to represent a coherence theory of justification in ethics. Epistemological constructivism represents recognition of the importance of the theories of the person within a coherentist moral epistemology. Rawls clearly advocates a coherentist moral epistemology (1980: 534). Although an epistemological construal of constructivism could not, of course, be epistemologically agnostic, it could be agnostic about the sort of metaphysical issues about ethics that moral realism and antirealism concern.

Finally, a *metaphysical* construal of constructivism results from taking it to represent an antirealist metaethical view. Recall that constructivism in ethics claims that there are moral facts or truths and that these facts or truths are constituted by our evidence for them. Constructivism in ethics contrasts with moral realism, which claims that there are moral facts and true moral claims that are independent of our beliefs about what these moral facts are (2.3). A constructivist in ethics who accepts a coherence theory of justification, as Rawls does, would be committed to a kind of coherence theory of moral truth according to which a moral belief is true just in case it is part of a reflective equilibrium On this construal, moral facts and truth are constituted by our moral beliefs in reflective equilibrium, in particular, by our ideals of the person; Kantian constructivism refers to those moral facts, including justice as fairness, that are constituted by a Kantian ideal of the person.

Since constructivist views are usually antirealist metaphysical views, it would be natural to regard Kantian constructivism as this kind of antirealist metaethical view. For this reason, there is perhaps presumptive evidence against both political and epistemological construals of Kantian constructivism and in favor of a metaphysical construal.

But matters are not so simple; there are various difficulties for each construal, including the metaphysical construal. Perhaps the most serious difficulty for the metaphysical construal comes from Rawls's article "Justice as Fairness: Political Not Metaphysical" (1985). As the title of the article suggests, Rawls there offers what I have been calling a political conception of justice as fairness. He claims that the task of political philosophy in a democratic society is to find terms of social cooperation that are acceptable to people with different and conflicting conceptions of the good. A political conception pursues this task by drawing "upon basic intuitive ideas that are embedded in the political institutions of a constitutional democratic regime and the public traditions of their interpretation" (1985: 225). Kantian constructivism, so construed, presumably draws on the Kantian ideal of the person, which is supposed to be latent in our political traditions. As a political conception, it remains agnostic about metaethical issues, in particular, about the truth or plausibility of this ideal of the person or the theory of justice which it supports. "Thus, the aim of justice as fairness as a political conception is practical, and not metaphysical or epistemological. That is, it presents itself not as a conception of justice that is true, but one that can serve as a basis of informed and willing political agreement between citizens viewed as free and equal persons" (1985: 230). In particular, the political interpretation of Kantian constructivism makes no antirealist assumptions.

We try, then, to leave aside philosophical controversies whenever possible, and look for ways to avoid philosophy's longstanding problems. Thus, in what I have called "Kantian constructivism," we try to avoid the problem of truth and the controversy between realism and subjectivism about the status of moral and political values. This form of constructivism neither asserts nor denies these doctrines. (1985: 230)

Thus, if we concerned ourselves only with "Justice as Fairness: Political Not Metaphysical," we would take seriously only the political construal of Kantian constructivism and would rightly reject the metaphysical and epistemological construals. And this, of course, would be the end of the moral realist's worries; she would need fear nothing from Rawls.

But we should not be so quick to accept the political interpretation or to reject the metaphysical one. There are, I believe, serious philosophical difficulties for the political conception of justice as fairness. If so, we might look favorably on a reading of the Dewey Lectures that avoided such a conception. Although Rawls's most recent work may be committed to this political conception, the Dewey Lectures need not be. In fact, a metaphysical conception of Kantian constructivism makes better sense of certain features of the Dewey Lectures than a political conception does.

First, the philosophical problem. Presumably, Rawls wants to claim that justice as fairness is the correct conception of justice to govern the basic structure of society, or at least, as he sometimes suggests, the basic structure of a constitutional democracy. That is, justice as fairness is supposed to state terms of social cooperation that *are in fact just*. This task is not fulfilled merely by showing how justice as fairness depends on a Kantian theory of the person; knowing this does not establish that justice as fairness states terms of social cooperation that are in fact just. If Rawls were to claim that this Kantian theory of the person is true or that we have good reason to believe it is true, then the fact that justice as fairness depends on, and draws support from, a Kantian theory of the person would justify justice as fairness. Since the political construal of Kantian constructivism is agnostic about the truth or plausibility of the moral structure built around a Kantian theory of the person, that construal would seem inadequate to Rawls's task. This is so even if the Kantian moral structure is, as Rawls suggests, implicit or latent in our political culture (1980: 517–19; 1985). To establish that justice as fairness states terms of social cooperation for our society that are just, he must claim that the Kantian theory of the person is part of a reflective equilibrium (as the epistemological construal could), that it is true (as a moral realist could), or that its truth consists in its being deeply embedded in our political culture (as the metaphysical construal could).[2] The political construal can make none of these claims.

---

2 Another alternative would be for Rawls to make the normative claim that it is always right for a society to maintain and pursue assumptions that can be ascribed to its political tradition, regardless of the moral content of those assumptions. I assume that it is obvious why this sort of moral and political conservatism renders this alternative unappealing. Moreover, it would certainly not allow Rawls to avoid controversial assumptions.

But perhaps Rawls is not interested in showing that justice as fairness states terms of fair cooperation in a constitutional democracy. After all, he has described the task of political philosophy as that of finding terms of social cooperation, rooted in a society's political traditions, that will secure citizens' willing and informed agreement. Perhaps Rawls thinks that the practical problem of securing agreement on the basic terms of social cooperation comes first.

But surely Rawls's task cannot be to seek terms of agreement with no commitment to the fairness of those terms. We would certainly need a good deal of argument to be convinced that *this* is the appropriate task of political philosophy. After all, what is so great about an agreement, unless we have reason to think that the terms of the agreement, or the positions it was negotiated from, are fair? And a political conception, so understood, could hardly claim the virtue of avoiding contested philosophical issues.

My guess is that Rawls would (and perhaps does) make these claims about the fairness of the initial conditions, but he cannot do *this,* I have been arguing, while remaining agnostic about the truth or plausibility of the ideal of the person on which the specification of these conditions is based.

Although these objections to the political interpretation of Kantian constructivism may *motivate* the search for another plausible interpretation, they are not themselves evidence for one. And I do not see how there can be any other interpretation of "Justice as Fairness: Political Not Metaphysical." But I do think that another interpretation of the Dewey Lectures is possible.

One apparent stumbling block to an alternative interpretation - in particular, a metaphysical interpretation – is that Rawls seems to assert in the Dewey Lectures, as he will later do more clearly in "Justice as Fairness: Political Not Metaphysical," that Kantian constructivism is metaethically agnostic. Near the end of the Dewey Lectures, Rawls writes, "Furthermore, it is important to notice here that no assumptions have been made about a theory of truth. A constructivist view does not require an idealist or verificationist, as opposed to realist, account of truth" (1980: 565). But this denial of a metaphysical construal of Kantian constructivism is only apparent, for the passage continues: "Whatever the nature of truth in the case of general beliefs about human nature and how society works, a constructivist moral doctrine requires a distinct procedure of construction to identify the first principles of justice" (1980: 565). This part of the passage indicates that Rawls claims only that Kantian constructivism does not imply an antirealist theory of truth for certain *nonmoral* propositions. For all that this passage claims, Kantian constructivism may imply moral antirealism. Now, there are two serious difficulties for a political interpretation of the Dewey Lectures. First, there is Rawls's contrast between Kantian constructivism and intuitionism (1980: 557–60, esp. 557).

Since the political construal is metaphysically and epistemologically neutral, it is not a rival of intuitionism and so would not seem to explain Rawls's contrast between Kantian constructivism and intuitionism. The epistemological construal, on the other hand, does provide an explanation of the contrast; a coherence theory of justification in ethics is incompatible with the foundationalist element of intutionalism. But the epistemological construal does not provide the only explanation of this contrast. As Rawls observes, intuitionism also contains a metaphysical component, namely, a realist view about moral facts and truth. Intuitionism claims that we have foundationally justified knowledge of moral facts whose existence and nature are independent of our evidence for them. So the metaphysical construal of Kantian constructivism also explains the contrast between constructivism and intuitionism; constructivism's antirealism is inconsistent with intuitionism's moral realism.

Second, and most importantly, the Dewey Lectures contain a number of metaphysical characterizations of Kantian constructivism, which neither the political nor the epistemological construals can explain. Recall that Rawls devotes the entire third lecture to explaining Kantian constructivism's version of *objectivity*. In understanding its conception of objectivity, we should look not only to the constructivist contrast with realism but also to several passages in which Rawls implies that Kantian constructivism involves an antirealist, constructivist view about the nature of moral facts and truth. For instance, early in the Dewey Lectures, Rawls describes Kantian constructivism as follows: "Kantian constructivism holds that moral objectivity is to be understood in terms of a suitably constructed social point of view that all can accept. Apart from the procedure of constructing principles of justice, there are no moral facts" (1980: 519). Later, he writes:

The parties in the original position do not agree on what the moral facts are, as if there already were such facts. It is not that, being situated impartially, they have a clear and undistorted view of a prior and independent moral order. Rather (for constructivism), there is no such order, and therefore no such facts apart from the procedure of construction as a whole; the facts are identified by the principles that result. (1980: 568)[3]

These seem to be straightforward antirealist claims. According to these passages, Kantian constructivism implies that there are no moral truths independent of, or antecedent to, a full justification of some set of moral principles; moral truth is constituted by the moral principles that result from the investigation.

I think we must conclude that Rawls's various discussions of Kantian constructivism are not fully coherent. A metaphysical construal of Kantian constructivism represents a poor interpretation of Rawls's more recent claims; a political construal is appropriate here. But a political interpretation provides a poor account of Rawls's earlier claims, in particular, of the Dewey Lectures; here, a metaphysical interpretation is more plausible. Indeed, a metaphysical interpretation seems to be the strongest interpretation of the Dewey Lectures. And, as I shall now explain, Rawls's writings contain an argument for Kantian constructivism, metaphysically construed. These are reasons enough for us to take seriously and explore the antirealist metaphysical interpretation of Kantian constructivism.

2. RAWLS'S ARGUMENT FOR CONSTRUCTIVISM

Does Rawls have an argument for constructivist antirealism? He clearly thinks that the way we justify moral theories supports constructivism. Some critics of *A Theory of Justice* seem to assume that a coherence theory of justification in ethics requires constructivism, because coherence could be evidence of truth only if coherence were

3 Someone might try to offer a political reading of the first two sentences of this passage as descriptions of how the contract device looks, as it were, from the inside. I said that a political construal could claim that *the contractors do not view themselves* as discovering moral truth but as creating it. The availability of this reading, however, cannot save Kantian constructivism from antirealism. For (1) the previous passage, the last sentence of this passage, and other passages (listed below) all seem to be straightforward antirealist statements, and (2) as we have seen, a political construal cannot adequately explain Rawls's contrast between Kantian constructivism and intuitionism. Compare: "The search for reasonable grounds for reaching agreement rooted in our conception of ourselves and in our relation to society replaces the search for moral truth interpreted as fixed by a prior and independent order of objects and relations, whether natural or divine, an order apart from how we conceive of ourselves" (1980: 519). Cf. Rawls 1980: 516, 537–8, 551–2, 564, 569.

constitutive of truth. If Rawls were to accept this reasoning, his defense of a coherentist moral epistemology would commit him to constructivism in ethics. (See section 4 of this appendix.) But Rawls's explicit statements about constructivism suggest a different motivation for constructivism. As I have already suggested, he claims that the role of theories of the person in framing and justifying moral theories supports constructivism. "This [Kantian constructivism's] rendering of objectivity implies that, rather than think of the principles of justice as true, it is better to say that they are principles that are reasonable for us, given our conceptions of persons as free, equal, and fully cooperating members of society" (1980: 554).

But why should the importance of theories of the person in moral theory support constructivism? Rawls's reasoning is not transparent, but we can reconstruct it. This reconstruction draws primarily upon "The Independence of Moral Theory" and the Dewey Lectures and requires us to make explicit a distinction, which Rawls implicitly recognizes, within theories of the person between *conceptions* of the person and *ideals* of the person.[4] Conceptions of the person are the province of philosophy of mind, and ideals of the person are the province of moral philosophy. Conceptions of the person provide accounts of the concept of a person, that is, of the nature of synchronic and diachronic personal identity or survival; ideals of the person provide accounts of what kinds of persons we really are, and want or ought to be (8.2). For example, Locke, on one interpretation, offers us a conception of the person according to which diachronic personal identity consists in the continuity of memory from one stage of a person's life to another (1700: II, xxvii; cf. Perry 1975, Shoemaker 1984). Aristotle offers us an ideal of the person in the *Nicomachean Ethics* when he claims that *eudaimonia* consists in the exercise of a certain set of practical and intellectual virtues.

We need make no claim that conceptions and ideals of persons are unrelated. Nor need we claim that conceptions of persons are morally neutral while ideals of the person are morally loaded (although we can and should claim that ideals of the person are *more* morally loaded than conceptions of persons are). However difficult it may be to draw it precisely, the distinction between conceptions and ideals of the person is one of which we have an intuitive grasp.

4 Rawls seems to recognize this distinction; see Rawls 1974: 17, 21; 1980: 534, 571; 1985: 232n. But he typically fails to mark or observe it.

Relying on this distinction, we can reconstruct Rawls's argument from the role of theories of the person in moral theory to constructivism in ethics. In "The Independence of Moral Theory," Rawls claims that standard moral theories embody ideals of the person and that conceptions of the person set feasibility constraints on ideals of the person. A moral theory can be rejected if the ideal of the person that it embodies prizes physical or psychological characteristics whose realization the philosophy of mind can show would violate conditions necessary for personal identity or survival. But, Rawls claims, this feasibility constraint is very weak; all standard moral theories are compatible with the conditions for personal identity or survival laid down by plausible conceptions of the person. Thus, the concept of the person radically underdetermines choice among competing moral theories in the sense that no plausible conception of the person alone provides conclusive evidence for the truth of one moral theory over all others. Rawls concludes that determinacy in theory choice in ethics is possible only if we appeal to the morally more robust ideal of the person (1974: 15–21; cf. Daniels 1979b: 274). In the Dewey Lectures, Rawls develops the role of ideals of the person in moral theory. He claims that ideals of the person play a uniquely important role in the justification of moral theories. "[First] principles of justice must issue from a conception [an ideal] of the person through a suitable representation of that conception [ideal] as illustrated by the procedure of construction in justice as fairness" (1980: 560). In an earlier paper, " A Well-ordered Society," Rawls made this claim more plainly:

When fully articulated, any conception of justice expresses a conception [an ideal] of the person, of the relations between persons, and of the general structure and ends of social cooperation. To accept the principles that represent a conception of justice is at the same time to accept an ideal of the person; and in acting from these principles we realize such an ideal. Let us begin, then, by trying to describe the kind of person we might want to be and the form of society we might wish to live in and to shape our interests and characters. In this way we might arrive at the notion of a well-ordered society. (1979: 6)[5]

There are closer and more important evidential relations between ideals of the person and moral theories than between conceptions of

5 Cf. Rawls 1974: 17–20; 1980: 516–17, 535–6; 1982: 169, 180–1. See also Daniels 1979b, 1980, and Scheffler 1979: 297.
  Someone might resist the claim that Rawls assigns a uniquely important role in

314

the person and moral theories. Ideals of the person thus provide greater determinacy in the choice among competing moral theories than do conceptions of the person. But even ideals of the person in a certain sense underdetermine theory choice in ethics. Rawls's claim is not that particular ideals of the person cannot require particular moral theories, for he clearly thinks that a Kantian ideal of the person that conceives of persons as free, equal, rational, and socially co-operative requires, or makes uniquely reasonable, his two principles of justice.[6] But Rawls does seem to hold that there are competing ideals of the person and that we cannot adjudicate this disagreement (1980: 516–17, 534–5, 537–8, 554; cf. Scheffler 1979: 295–300). Thus, because ideals of the person are themselves underdetermined, ideals of the person may be said to underdetermine theory choice in ethics in the sense that that part of moral philosophy concerned with ideals of the person does not itself provide conclusive evidence for one moral theory over all others. Because of the importance of ideals of the person in moral theory and the underdetermination of ideals of the person, the truth of moral theories must be defined in terms of, or relativized to, those moral beliefs about persons on which such theories depend (evidentially). But this implies that moral facts are evidence-dependent rather than evidence-independent. So moral realism is false and constructivism in ethics is true.[7]

moral theory to ideals of the person by appeal to the public conception of justice in the justification of Rawls's two principles of justice. "The model-conception of the well-ordered society," as well as "the model-conception of the moral person," helps determine the selection of the two principles of justice (1980: 517, 537–8, 555). But even if, contrary to fact, the model-conception of the well-ordered society were independent of the model-conception of the moral person, Rawls's texts make clear the greater importance of the model-conception of the moral person (1971: 584; 1979: 6, 20; 1980: 516–17, 518, 520, 535–6, 547–52, 554, 559–60, 571; 1982: 172; cf. Buchanan 1975; Scanlon 1975a: 171, 178–9; Daniels 1979b; 1980; and Scheffler 1979: 295). In fact, the model-conception of the well-ordered society is not independent of the model-conception of the moral person; the former is heavily influenced by the latter. The well-ordered society, especially the specification of its inhabitants, depends in important ways on the Kantian ideal of persons as free, equal, rational, and socially cooperative (1979: 6, 20; 1980: 519–22, 543–7; 1982: 172).

6 Rawls 1971: 251–65, 584; 1979: 6–7, 19–20; 1980: 516, 519–22, 534–6, 547–52, 554, 559–60, 571; 1982: 169, 172, 180–1. For useful discussions of Rawls's ideal of the person and how it supports his two principles of justice, see Buchanan 1975; Scanlon 1975a; Scheffler 1979.

7 Indeed, since Rawls's argumentative strategy contains an argument for underdetermination, it supports a relativistic version of constructivism (cf. 2.3). Thus, Rawls's argument for constructivism creates a tension with his official agnosticism in the Dewey Lectures between relativism and nonrelativism. Cf. Rawls 1980: 569–70.

3. IDEALS OF THE PERSON AND MORAL REALISM

Does Rawls's argument from the role of ideals of the person in moral theory undermine moral realism and support constructivism in ethics? First, I should say something about the role of underdetermination in Rawls's argument. Rawls, as I reconstruct him, seeks to establish the underdetermination of theory choice in ethics and concludes that there are no moral facts save those that can be defined by different ideals of the person. In this, Rawls's argument may assume that underdetermination implies indeterminacy. Many philosophers have assumed that if a choice among competing claims is genuinely underdetermined by all of the available evidence (both deductive and nondeductive), then there can be no (evidence-independent) fact of the matter as to which of those claims is correct (cf. Quine 1960: chap. 2; 1968). If this were true, then genuine underdetermination in ethics would imply that there are no evidence-independent moral facts and that moral facts must be defined relative to different bodies of evidence, for instance, to different ideals of persons. Of course, because moral realism claims that moral facts are evidence-independent, it denies that underdetermination *implies* indeterminacy. Strictly speaking, all that follows from genuine underdetermination among claims is that there are no grounds for believing that any one of the claims in question (rather than another) is true. So, someone might argue, we ought not to attribute this argument to Rawls, because it presupposes a connection between justification and truth, and hence between underdetermination and indeterminacy, that the realist will deny. But even if the argument did require the implication from underdetermination to indeterminacy, the popularity of this inference pattern would allow us to include it as part of a reconstruction of Rawls's argument for constructivism. Moreover, Rawls's argument does not require the implication from underdetermination to indeterminacy. Although moral realism and genuine underdetermination are *compatible* (we may have no good grounds for distinguishing true and false moral theories), there is little *motivation* for us to believe in the existence of evidence-independent moral facts *if there is good reason* to believe that there is in principle no way to decide among competing moral theories. In this way, the falsity of moral realism and the truth of constructivism in ethics may provide the *best explanation* of genuine underdetermination in ethics.

Someone might think that nihilism, rather than constructivism, was the proper conclusion to draw from the sort of genuine underdetermination for which I claim Rawls argues. Nihilism is also an antirealist thesis. But notice that nihilism is the best explanation of underdetermination only if we have already ruled out the claim of constructivism that moral facts are to be relativized to different sets of coherent belief that include different ideals of the person. I suppose that Rawls or someone impressed by certain cognitivist presuppositions of our normative practices (cf. 2.6–2.8) might think it is unacceptable to conclude simply that there are *no* moral facts; once we deny the existence of evidence-independent moral facts, we must reconstruct the objectivity of moral claims as best we can. The natural way to do this, given underdetermination, is to make the moral facts evidence-dependent, as constructivism does.

Does Rawls's argument provide good reason for thinking that theory choice in ethics is genuinely underdetermined? We can agree that theories of the person play an important role in the justification of moral theories. We can also agree that conceptions of the person underdetermine theory choice in ethics. Perhaps Parfit is right that the conception of the person that we adopt can make some moral theories more plausible than others (1984: chap. 15; cf. 8.18 and Daniels 1979b: 267–9). Even if this is so, I think we should concede that no plausible conception of the person determines theory choice in ethics in the sense that it alone provides conclusive evidence for the truth of one moral theory over all others. We can, with Rawls, conclude that if theories of the person are to determine theory choice in ethics, then ideals of the person had better do the job. But Rawls goes on to claim that even if particular ideals of the person require particular moral theories, there are competing ideals of the person among which we cannot adjudicate. A Kantian ideal may require Rawls's two principles of justice, but there are alternative ideals of the person (e.g., utilitarian and libertarian ideals) that require other moral principles. Since we have no way of deciding among these ideals, Rawls claims, appeal to the ideal of the person cannot determine theory choice in ethics. Because of the importance of ideals of the person in moral theory, theory choice in ethics is therefore underdetermined.

We can deny this underdetermination thesis by resisting Rawls's claim that ideals of the person underdetermine theory choice in ethics. Appeal to the ideal of the person would underdetermine

317

theory choice in ethics if, in addition to the existence of competing ideals, these ideals were unrevisable. But ideals of the person, like other moral beliefs, are revisable, and so we can at least begin to adjudicate among competitors. According to a coherentist moral epistemology, ideals of the person are revisable on the basis of their coherence with empirical (e.g., psychological and social) theories, conceptions of the person, and considered evaluative views about the nature and constituents of a valuable life (8.2). Rawls himself seems to think that there are only a small number of competing ideals of the person. If so, there is good reason to suppose (at least Rawls has given us no reason to doubt) that coherentist reasoning about the support for these ideals can, at least in principle, decide among the competitors. If we accept the sort of holistic epistemology that a coherence theory of justification in ethics represents, we can concede the existence of competing ideals of the person without conceding that appeal to the ideal of the person underdetermines moral theory.

Moreover, we can deny Rawls's conclusion about underdetermination by resisting his tacit assumption that ideals of the person provide the only, or the decisive, support for moral theories. Rawls claims that ideals of the person underdetermine theory choice in ethics and concludes that theory choice in ethics is underdetermined. This conclusion would follow only if ideals of the person provided not only important but exclusive, or necessarily decisive, support for moral theories. But there is little reason (and Rawls has provided none) to suppose that ideals of the person are the only, or the decisive, evidence for moral theories. In fact, according to a coherence theory of justification in ethics, moral theories receive support from nonmoral beliefs about such things as sociology, economics, and psychology (including our observations of people's behavior and social events) and from considered moral beliefs about concrete moral issues as well as from ideals of the person. Indeed, a coherentist moral epistemology should lead us to *expect* that moral theory is underdetermined by appeal to the ideal of the person (or any other subset of our total set of beliefs). If moral theories are justified by their coherence with considered moral beliefs about particular cases and various nonmoral beliefs as well as ideals of the person, then it should come as no surprise that appeal to the ideal of the person does not itself decide between competing moral theories. But precisely because coherence with considered moral beliefs and various nonmoral beliefs is evidential, we can concede that ideals of the person do underdetermine moral theory without concluding that theory choice in ethics is underdetermined.

These two lines of resistance to Rawls's thesis about underdetermination in ethics illustrate a tension in Rawls's epistemological views in the Dewey Lectures that becomes apparent only after his argument for constructivism is fully articulated. A coherence theory of justification in ethics is compatible with an emphasis on the importance of theories of the person, in particular, ideals of the person, in justifying moral theories (8.2). But Rawls's argument for constructivism presupposes a different justificatory role for ideals of the person. The inference from the underdetermination of ideals of the person to the underdetermination of theory choice in ethics presupposes something like an intuitionist epistemology in which ideals of the person play the part of incorrigible foundational moral beliefs. Assigning *this* justificatory role to ideals of the person is incompatible with a coherentist moral epistemology. This intuitionist view about the role of ideals of the person in moral theory represents an implausibly restrictive view of moral justification and conflicts with Rawls's own considered epistemological views. A coherentist epistemology of the sort Rawls himself advocates elsewhere allows one to concede the importance of ideals of the person in moral theory and the existence of competing ideals of the person without conceding that theory choice in ethics is underdetermined. If Rawls's grounds for believing that moral theory is underdetermined are weak, as I have argued they are, then he has provided us with no good reason for denying the existence of evidence-independent moral facts or for believing constructivism.

4. COHERENCE AND REALISM IN ETHICS

Rawls might think that underdetermination is avoided only by giving in to constructivism. Perhaps he believes not that competing ideals of the person cannot be adjudicated among but that they can be adjudicated among only by coherentist reasoning from moral beliefs whose truth is evidence-dependent. Moral principles justified on the basis of the most plausible ideal of the person would then have a constructivist status.

Of course, this argument would beg the question. We expect Rawls to provide an argument for constructivism in ethics; he cannot do this by appealing to constructivism about the truth of particular moral beliefs.

Constructivism in ethics need not presuppose constructivism about particular moral beliefs. One might argue that a coherentist defense of cognitivism commits one to constructivism in ethics. As we have seen, many critics of Rawls's epistemological position in *A Theory of Justice* argue just this. Perhaps Rawls's Dewey Lectures reflect his acceptance of the kind of epistemological argument underlying their criticisms. (Perhaps this is another issue on which Rawls has been influenced by Dworkin 1973.)

Although this kind of argument has been influential, Rawls does not advance it. Indeed, this argument seems quite independent of the one argument Rawls does advance for constructivism, namely, the argument based on the role of theories of the person in moral theory. And, of course, whether or not Rawls accepts the epistemological argument from a coherence theory of justification in ethics to constructivism, we have seen a reason to reject that argument. Moral realists can and should claim that coherentist reasoning is both reliable (Appendix 2) and evidential (5.7–5.9).

5. CONCLUSION

A significant part of my discussion of Rawls's Dewey Lectures has been reconstructive exegesis. Thoughtful readers of Rawls's discussion of constructivism will appreciate the need for this. I despair of reconciling all of Rawls's writings; I claim only that Kantian constructivism, as found in the Dewey Lectures, admits of an antirealist construal and that it is possible to construct an argument for it, so construed. This argument has the following form. Ideals of the person are underdetermined. Hence, appeal to the ideal of the person underdetermines moral theory. Because of the importance of ideals of the person in moral theory, the underdetermination of moral theory by appeal to the ideal of the person implies the underdetermination of moral theory. The best explanation of the underdetermination of moral theory is that there are no evidence-independent moral facts; moral facts and truth must be defined relative to different bodies of evidence, in particular, relative to different moral beliefs about persons (ideals of the person). Hence, moral realism is false and constructivism in ethics is true. If this argument is not Rawls's, perhaps we may be excused for thinking that it is or could be. It is, in any case, an argument with an important bearing on our project. Once this argument is fully articulated, its assessment is more straightforward. Although ideals of the person play a central role in moral epistemology, Rawls's argument commits him to a moral epistemology that is incompatible with the sort of coherence theory of justification in ethics that he has long advocated. A coherence theory of justification in ethics allows us to recognize the importance of ideals of the person in moral theory, and the existence of competing ideals of the person, without conceding the underdetermination of theory choice in ethics or any other antirealist claims. Because ideals of the person are revisable on the basis of coherentist reasoning, there is no reason to deny that there is a uniquely plausible ideal of the person, which, in turn, might determine theory choice in ethics. Moreover, even if ideals of the person do underdetermine theory choice in ethics, a coherence theory of justification in ethics allows us to concede this point without concluding that theory choice in ethics is underdetermined. Despite the importance of ideals of the person in moral theory, moral theories do not depend exclusively or decisively on ideals of the person. Moral theories are justified on the basis of their coherence with all of our beliefs, both moral and nonmoral. Recognition of the importance of ideals of the person in moral theory, therefore, commits us to neither the truth of constructivism nor the falsity of moral realism.

Bibliography

Adams, R. M. 1976. "Motive Utilitarianism." *Journal of Philosophy* 73: 467–81.

1981. "Divine Command Metaethics as Necessary A Posteriori." In P. Helm (ed.), *Divine Commands and Morality*. New York: Oxford University Press.

Aristotle. *Metaphysics. (Meta).*

Nicomachean Ethics (EN).

Politics (Pol).

Posterior Analytics (APo).

Armstrong, D. M. 1968. *A Materialistic Theory of Mind.* Boston: Routledge & Kegan Paul.

1973. *Belief, Truth, and Knowledge.* Cambridge: Cambridge University Press.

1978. *Universals and Scientific Realism.* 2 vols. Cambridge: Cambridge University Press.

Austin, J. L. 1962. *How to Do Things with Words.* Cambridge, Mass.: Harvard University Press.

Ayer, A. J. 1940. *The Foundation of Empirical Knowledge.* New York: Macmillan.

1946. *Language, Truth, and Logic.* 2nd ed. London: Gollancz.

Ayer, A. J. (ed.). 1959. *Logical Positivism.* New York: Free Press.

Baier, K. 1958. *The Moral Point of View.* Ithaca, N.Y.: Cornell University Press.

Bales, R. E. 1971. "Act-Utilitarianism: Account of Right-making Characteristics or Decision-making Procedure?" *American Philosophical Quarterly* 8: 257–65.

Benacerraf, P., and Putnam, H. (eds.). 1983. *Philosophy of Mathematics.* 2d ed. Cambridge: Cambridge University Press.

Benedict, R. 1934. "Anthropology and the Abnormal." *Journal of General Psychology* 10: 59–82.

Bentham, J. 1823. *An Introduction to the Principles of Morals and Legislation.* London: Athlone, 1970.

Berger, F. 1984. *Happiness, Justice, and Freedom.* Los Angeles: University of California Press.

Blackburn, S. 1971. "Moral Realism." In J. Casey (ed.), *Morality and Moral Reasoning.* London: Methuen.

1980. "Truth, Realism, and the Regulation of Theory." *Midwest Studies in Philosophy* 5: 353–71.

1981. "Rule-Following and Moral Realism." In Holtzman and Leich 1981.

1984. *Spreading the Word.* New York: Oxford University Press.

1985. "Errors and the Phenomenology of Value." In Honderich 1985.

Blanshard, B. 1939. *The Nature of Thought,* vol. 2. London: Allen & Unwin.

Block, N. (ed.). 1980. *Readings in Philosophy of Psychology,* vol. 1. Cambridge, Mass.: Harvard University Press.

Bond, E. J. 1983. *Reason and Value.* Cambridge: Cambridge University Press.

Bonjour, L. 1976. "The Coherence Theory of Empirical Knowledge." *Philosophical Studies* 30:281–312.

1980. "Externalist Theories of Empirical Knowledge." *Midwest Studies in Philosophy* 5:53–73.

1986. *The Structure of Empirical Knowledge.* Cambridge, Mass.: Harvard University Press.

Boyd, R. 1980. "Materialism Without Reductionism: What Physicalism Does Not Entail." In Block 1980.

1988. "How to Be a Moral Realist." In G. Sayre-McCord (ed.), *Essays on Moral Realism.* Ithaca, N.Y.: Cornell University Press.

Bradley, F. H. 1876. *Ethical Studies.* New York: Oxford University Press.

1914. *Essays on Truth and Reality.* New York: Oxford University Press.

Brandt, R. B. 1959. *Ethical Theory.* Englewood Cliffs, N.J.: Prentice-Hall.

1979. *A Theory of the Good and the Right.* New York: Oxford University Press.

Brink, D. O. 1984. "Moral Realism and the Sceptical Arguments from Disagreement and Queerness." *Australasian Journal of Philosophy* 62:111–25.

1986a. "Externalist Moral Realism." In Gillespie 1986.

1986b. "Utilitarian Morality and the Personal Point of View." *The Journal of Philosophy* 83:417–38.

1987. "Rawlsian Constructivism in Moral Theory." *Canadian Journal of Philosophy* 17:71–90.

1988a. "Sidgwick's Dualism of Practical Reason." *Australasian Journal of Philosophy* 66:291–307.

1988b. "Moral Realism Defended." In L. Pojman (ed.), *Ethical Theory.* Belmont, Calif.: Wadsworth.

Forthcoming. "Rational Egoism, Self, and Others: A Rationale for Temporal Neutrality and Agent Relativity. " In O. Flanagan and A. Rorty (eds.), [provisionally entitled] *Morality and Character: Essays in Moral Psychology.* Cambridge, Mass.: MIT Press.

Broad, C. D. 1930. *Five Types of Ethical Theory.* Boston: Routledge & Kegan Paul.

Buchanan, A. 1975. "Revisability and Rational Choice." *Canadian Journal of Philosophy* 5:395–408.

Butler, J. 1736. *A Dissertation upon the Nature of Virtue.* Reprinted in S. Darwall (ed.), *Five Sermons.* Indianapolis, Ind.: Hackett, 1983.

1749. *Fifteen Sermons.* Reprinted in S. Darwall (ed.), *Five Sermons.* Indianapolis, Ind.: Hackett, 1983.

Carnap, R. 1956. *Meaning and Necessity.* 2d ed. Chicago: University of Chicago Press.
Carritt, E. F. 1947. *Ethical and Political Thinking.* New York: Oxford University Press.
Carson, T. 1984. *The Status of Morality.* Boston: Reidel.
Chisholm, R. 1977. *The Theory of Knowledge.* 2d ed. Englewood Cliffs, N.J.: Prentice-Hall.
1982. *The Foundations of Knowing.* Minneapolis: University of Minnesota Press.
Clarke, S. 1728. *A Discourse of Natural Religion.* Reprinted in Raphael 1969.
Cohon, R. 1986. "Are External Reasons Impossible?" *Ethics* 96: 545–56.
Conly, S. 1983. "Utilitarianism and Integrity." *The Monist* 66: 298–311.
1984. "Review: Samuel Scheffler, *The Rejection of Consequentialism.*" *Philosophical Review* 93:489–92.
Copp, D. 1984. "Considered Judgments and Moral Justification: Conservatism in Moral Theory." In Copp and Zimmerman 1984.
Copp, D., and Zimmerman, D. (eds.). 1984. *Morality, Reason, and Truth.* Totowa, N.J.: Rowman & Littlefield.
Daniels, N. 1979a. "Wide Reflective Equilibrium and Theory Acceptance in Ethics." *Journal of Philosophy* 76:256–82.
1979b. "Moral Theory and the Plasticity of Persons." *The Monist* 62:265–87.
1980. "Reflective Equilibrium and Archimedian Points." *Canadian Journal of Philosophy* 10:83–103.
Daniels, N. (ed.). 1975. *Reading Rawls.* Oxford: Blackwell.
Darwall, S. 1983. *Impartial Reason.* Ithaca, N.Y.: Cornell University Press.
Davidson, D. 1970. "Mental Events." Reprinted in Davidson 1980.
1980. *Essays on Actions and Events.* New York: Oxford University Press.
Dennett, D. 1978. *Brainstorms.* Cambridge, Mass.: MIT Press.
Descartes, R. 1642. *Meditations.* In *The Philosophical Works of Descartes,* trans. E. S. Haldane and G. R. T. Ross. 2 vols. Cambridge: Cambridge University Press, 1931.
Donagan, A. 1977. *The Theory of Morality.* Chicago: University of Chicago Press.
Duhem, P. 1914. *The Aim and Structure of Physical Theory.* New York: Atheneum, 1981.
Dummett, M. 1963. "Realism." In Dummett 1978.
1972. "Truth." Reprinted in Dummett 1978.
1975. "What Is a Theory of Meaning? (I)." In Guttenplan 1975.
1977. *The Elements of Intuitionism.* New York: Oxford University Press.
1978. *Truth and Other Enigmas.* Cambridge, Mass.: Harvard University Press.
1981. *Frege: Philosophy of Language.* London: Duckworth.
Dworkin, R. 1970. "Taking Rights Seriously." Reprinted in Dworkin 1978.
1973. "The Original Position." Reprinted in Daniels 1975.
1976. "Reverse Discrimination." Reprinted in Dworkin 1978.

325

1978. *Taking Rights Seriously.* London: Duckworth.
1984. "Rights as Trumps." In Waldron 1984.
1986. *Law's Empire.* Cambridge, Mass.: Harvard University Press.
Falk, W. D. 1947. " 'Ought' and Motivation." Reprinted in W. Sellars and J. Hospers (eds.), *Readings in Ethical Theory.* New York: Appleton-Century-Crofts, 1952.
Fehrenbacher, D. 1981. *Slavery, Law, and Politics.* New York: Oxford University Press.
Field, H. 1982. "Realism and Relativism." *Journal of Philosophy* 79:653–67.
Fodor, J. 1974. "Special Sciences or the Disunity of Science as a Working Hypothesis." Reprinted in Block 1980.
Føllesdall, D. 1982. "The Status of Rationality Assumptions in Interpretation and in the Explanation of Action." *Dialectica* 36:301–16.
Foot, P. 1958a. "Moral Arguments." Reprinted in Foot 1978.
1958b. "Moral Beliefs." Reprinted in Foot 1978.
1972a. "Morality as a System of Hypothetical Imperatives." Reprinted in Foot 1978.
1972b. "Reasons for Action and Desire." Reprinted in Foot 1978.
1978. *Virtues and Vices.* Los Angeles: University of California Press.
Foot, P. (ed.). 1967. *Theories of Ethics.* New York: Oxford University Press.
Frankena, W. 1939. "The Naturalistic Fallacy." Reprinted in Foot 1967.
1958. "Obligation and Motivation in Recent Moral Philosophy." Reprinted in K. Goodpaster (ed.), *Perspectives on Morality.* Notre Dame: University of Notre Dame Press, 1976.
1973. *Ethics.* 2d ed. Englewood Cliffs, N.J.: Prentice-Hall.
Frankfurt, H. 1970. *Demons, Dreamers, and Madmen.* Indianapolis, Ind.: Bobbs-Merrill.
Frege, G. 1892. "Sense and Reference." In M. Black and P. Geach (trans.), *Translations from the Philosophical Writings of Gottlob Frege.* Oxford: Blackwell, 1980.
Fried, C. 1978. *Right and Wrong.* Cambridge, Mass.: Harvard University Press.
Garfinkel, A. 1981. *Forms of Explanation.* New Haven, Conn.: Yale University Press.
Gasper, P. 1987. *Intentionality, Reference, and Knowledge: A Defence of Physicalism.* Ph.D. diss., Cornell University.
Gauthier, D. 1967. "Morality and Advantage." Reprinted in Gauthier 1970.
1986. *Morals by Agreement.* New York: Oxford University Press.
Gauthier, D. (ed). 1970. *Morality and Rational Self-Interest.* Englewood Cliffs, N.J.: Prentice-Hall.
Gewirth, A. 1978. *Reason and Morality.* Chicago: University of Chicago Press.
Gillespie, N. (ed.). 1986. *Moral Realism: Proceedings of the 1985 Spindel Conference. The Southern Journal of Philosophy,* Supplement 24.
Goldman, A. 1967. A Causal Theory of Knowing." Reprinted in Pappas and Swain 1978.

1976. "Discrimination and Perceptual Knowledge." Reprinted in Pappas and Swain 1978.

1979. "What Is Justified Belief?" In Pappas 1979.

Goodman, N. 1978. *Ways of Worldmaking*. Indianapolis, Ind.: Hackett.

Green, T. H. 1883. *Prolegomena to Ethics*. New York: Crowell, 1969.

Grice, R. 1967. *The Grounds of Moral Judgement*. Cambridge: Cambridge University Press.

Guttenplan, S. (ed.). 1975. *Mind and Language*. New York: Oxford University Press.

Hancock, R. 1974. *Twentieth Century Ethics*. New York: Columbia University Press.

Hardie, W. F. R. 1980. *Aristotle's Ethical Theory*. 2d ed. New York: Oxford University Press.

Hare, R. M. 1952. *The Language of Morals*. New York: Oxford University Press.

1957. "Nothing Matters." In Hare 1972.

1963a. *Freedom and Reason*. New York: Oxford University Press.

1963b. "Descriptivism." Reprinted in Hudson 1969.

1972. *Applications of Moral Philosophy*. Los Angeles: University of California Press.

1973. "Rawls' Theory of Justice." Reprinted in Daniels 1975.

1976. "Ethical Theory and Utilitarianism." Reprinted in Sen and Williams 1982.

1978. "Justice and Equality." In J. Arthur and W. Shaw (eds.), *Justice and Economic Distribution*. Englewood Cliffs, N.J.: Prentice-Hall.

1980. "Moral Conflicts." In McMurrin 1980.

1981. *Moral Thinking*. New York: Oxford University Press.

Harker, J. 1984. "Can There Be an Infinite Regress of Justified Beliefs?" *Australasian Journal of Philosophy* 62:255–64.

Harman, G. 1965. "Inference to the Best Explanation." *Philosophical Review* 74:88–95.

1973. *Thought*. Princeton, N.J.: Princeton University Press.

1975. "Moral Relativism Defended." *Philosophical Review* 85:3–22.

1977. *The Nature of Morality*. New York: Oxford University Press.

1982. "Metaphysical Realism and Moral Relativism: Reflections on Hilary Putnam's *Reason, Truth, and History*." *Journal of Philosophy* 79:568–75.

1984. "Is There a Single True Morality?" In Copp and Zimmerman 1984.

1986. "Moral Explanations of Natural Facts – Can Moral Claims Be Tested Against Moral Reality?" In Gillespie 1986.

Hart, H. L. A. 1979. "Between Utility and Rights." Reprinted in Hart 1983.

1983. *Essays in Jurisprudence and Philosophy*. New York: Oxford University Press.

Hellman, G., and Thompson, F. 1975. "Physicalism: Ontology, Determination, and Reduction." *Journal of Philosophy* 72:551–64.

327

Herskovits, M. 1948. *Man and His Works*. New York: Knopf.
Hobbes, T. 1651. *Leviathan*, ed. C. B. MacPherson. New York: Penguin, 1968. (Original pagination.)
Holtzman, S., and Leich, C. (eds.). 1981. *Wittgenstein: To Follow a Rule*. Boston: Routledge & Kegan Paul.
Homer. *The Iliad*.
Honderich, T. (ed.). 1985. *Morality and Objectivity*. Boston: Routledge & Kegan Paul.
Horwich, P. 1982a. "Three Forms of Realism." *Synthese* 51:181–201.
    1982b. "Review: Michael Williams, *Groundless Belief.*" *Nous* 16:312–16.
Hudson, W. D. 1967. *Ethical Intuitionism*. New York: Macmillan.
Hudson, W. D. (ed.). 1969. *The Is/Ought Thesis*. New York: Macmillan.
Hume, D. 1739. *A Treatise of Human Nature*, ed. P. H. Nidditch. New York: Oxford University Press, 1978.
    1751. *An Enquiry Concerning the Principles of Morals*. Indianapolis, Ind.: Hackett, 1983.
Huxley, A. 1946. *Brave New World*. 2d ed. New York: Harper & Row.
Irwin, T. H. 1977. *Plato's Moral Theory*. New York: Oxford University Press.
    1981. "Aristotle's Methods of Ethics." In D. O'Meara (ed.), *Studies in Aristotle*. Washington, D.C.: Catholic University of America Press.
    1985. "Aristotle's Conception of Morality." *Proceedings of the Boston Colloquium in Ancient Philosophy* 1:115–43.
    1988. *Aristotle's First Principles*. New York: Oxford University Press.
James, W. 1907. *Pragmatism*. Cambridge, Mass.: Harvard University Press, 1975.
Joachim, H. 1906. *The Nature of Truth*. New York: Oxford University Press.
Joseph, H. 1931. *Some Problems in Ethics*. New York: Oxford University Press.
Kant, I. 1785. *Foundations of the Metaphysic of Morals*. London: Hutchinson, 1956. (Prussian Academy pagination.)
    1788. *Critique of Practical Reason*. Indianapolis, Ind.: Bobbs-Merrill, 1956. (Prussian Academy pagination.)
Kemeny, J., and Oppenheim, P. 1956. "On Reduction." Reprinted in B. Brody (ed.), *Readings in the Philosophy of Science*. Englewood Cliffs, N.J.: Prentice-Hall, 1970.
Kim, J. 1978. "Supervenience and Nomological Incommensurables." *American Philosophical Quarterly* 15:149–56.
    1979. "Causality, Identity, and Supervenience in the Mind-Body Problem." *Midwest Studies in Philosophy* 4:31–49.
    1984a. "Concepts of Supervenience." *Philosophy and Phenomenological Research* 45:153–76.
    1984b. "Epiphenomenal and Supervenient Causation." *Midwest Studies in Philosophy* 9:257–70.
Kitcher, P. 1982. *Abusing Science*. Cambridge, Mass.: MIT Press.

Klagge, J. 1984. "An Alleged Difficulty Concerning Moral Properties." *Mind* 93:370–80.

Kraut, R. 1979. "Two Conceptions of Happiness." *Philosophical Review* 88:176–96.

Kripke, S. 1971. "Identity and Necessity." Reprinted in Schwartz 1977.

1980. *Naming and Necessity*. Cambridge, Mass.: Harvard University Press.

Kuhn, T. 1970. *The Structure of Scientific Revolutions*. 2d ed. Chicago: University of Chicago Press.

Lehrer, K. 1974. *Knowledge*. New York: Oxford University Press.

Lewis, C. I. 1946. *An Analysis of Knowledge and Valuation*. La Salle, Ill.: Open Court.

Little, I. M. D. 1957. *A Critique of Welfare Economics*. New York: Oxford University Press.

Locke, J. 1700. *An Essay Concerning Human Understanding*, ed. P. H. Nidditch. New York: Oxford University Press, 1975.

Lomasky, L. 1983. "A Refutation of Utilitarianism." *Journal of Value Inquiry* 17: 259–79.

Luce, R. D., and Raiffa, H. 1957. *Games and Decisions*. New York: Wiley.

Lyons, D. 1975. "The Nature and Soundness of Contract and Coherence Arguments." In Daniels 1975.

1982. "Utility and Rights." Reprinted in Waldron 1984.

McDowell, J. 1978. "Are Moral Requirements Hypothetical Imperatives?" *Proceedings of the Aristotelean Society*, supp. vol.:13–29.

1979. "Virtue and Reason." *The Monist* 62:331–50.

1985. "Values and Secondary Qualities." In Honderich 1985.

Mackie, J. L. 1977. *Ethics: Inventing Right and Wrong*. New York: Penguin.

1980. *Hume's Moral Theory*. Boston: Routledge & Kegan Paul.

1982. *The Miracle of Theism*. New York: Oxford University Press.

McMurrin, S. (ed.). 1980. *The Tanner Lectures on Human Values I*. Salt Lake City: University of Utah Press.

Medlin, B. 1957. "Ethical Egoism and Ultimate Moral Principles." Reprinted in Gauthier 1970.

Mill, J. S. 1859. *On Liberty*. Indianapolis, Ind.: Hackett, 1978.

1861. *Utilitarianism*. Indianapolis, Ind.: Hackett, 1979.

1873. *Autobiography of John Stuart Mill*. New York: Columbia University Press, 1924.

1881. *A System of Logic*. London: Longmans, 1970.

Moore, G. E. 1903. *Principia Ethica*. Cambridge: Cambridge University Press.

1912. *Ethics*. New York: Oxford University Press.

1922. *Philosophical Studies*. Boston: Routledge & Kegan Paul.

1925. "A Defence of Common Sense." Reprinted in Moore 1959b.

1939. "Proof of an External World." Reprinted in Moore 1959b.

1942. "A Reply to My Critics." In P. Schlipp (ed.), *The Philosophy of G. E. Moore*. La Salle, Ill.: Open Court.

1959a. "Certainty." In Moore 1959b.

1959b. *Philosophical Papers*. London: Allen & Unwin.

Murdoch, I. 1970. *The Sovereignty of the Good*. New York: Schocken.
Nagel, E. 1949. "The Meaning of Reduction in the Natural Sciences." In R. Stauffer (ed.), *Science and Civilization*. Madison: University of Wisconsin Press.
　1961. *The Structure of Science*. Boston: Routledge & Kegan Paul.
Nagel, T. 1970. *The Possibility of Altruism*. Princeton, N.J.: Princeton University Press.
　1979a. "The Fragmentation of Value." Reprinted in Nagel 1979c.
　1979b. "Subjective and Objective." Reprinted in Nagel 1979c.
　1979c. *Mortal Questions*. Cambridge: Cambridge University Press.
　1980. "The Limits of Objectivity." In McMurrin 1980.
　1986. *The View from Nowhere*. New York: Oxford University Press.
Nesbitt, W. 1977. "Categorical Imperatives: A Defense." *Philosophical Review* 86:217–25.
Neurath, O. 1932. "Protocol Sentences." In Ayer 1959.
Nielsen, K. 1963. "Why Should I Be Moral?" Reprinted in P. Taylor (ed.), *Problems of Moral Philosophy*. Belmont, Calif.: Wadsworth, 1978.
Nowell-Smith, P. 1957. *Ethics*. New York: Philosophical Library.
Nozick, R. 1974. *Anarchy, State, and Utopia*. New York: Basic.
　1981. *Philosophical Explanations*. Cambridge, Mass.: Harvard University Press.
Pappas, G. (ed.). 1979. *Justification and Knowledge*. Boston: Reidel.
Pappas, G., and Swain, M. 1978. *Essays on Knowledge and Justification*. Ithaca, N.Y.: Cornell University Press.
Parfit, D. 1984. *Reasons and Persons*. New York: Oxford University Press.
Pastin, M. 1975. "Modest Foundationalism and Self-Warrant." Reprinted in Pappas and Swain 1978.
Peirce, C. S. 1934. *Collected Papers*, vol. 5. Cambridge, Mass.: Harvard University Press.
Perry, J. (ed.). 1975. *Personal Identity*. Los Angeles: University of California Press.
Plato. *Euthyphro*.
　Republic.
Platts, M. 1980. "Moral Realism and the End of Desire." In M. Platts (ed.), *Reference, Truth, and Reality*. Boston: Routledge & Kegan Paul.
Price, R. 1787. *A Review of the Principal Questions in Morals*. Reprinted in Raphael 1969.
Prichard, H. A. 1912. "Does Moral Philosophy Rest on a Mistake?" Reprinted in Prichard 1949.
　1937. "Moral Obligation." Reprinted in Prichard 1949.
　1949. *Moral Obligation*. New York: Oxford University Press.
Prior, A. N. 1949. *Logic and the Basis of Ethics*. New York: Oxford University Press.
　1960. "The Autonomy of Ethics." Reprinted in Prior 1976.
　1976. *Papers in Logic and Ethics*. London: Duckworth.
Putnam, H. 1970. "On Properties." Reprinted in Putnam 1979.
　1973a. "Explanation and Reference." Reprinted in Putnam 1975a.

1973b. "Meaning and Reference." Reprinted in Schwartz 1977.
1974. "The Corroboration of Theories." Reprinted in Putnam 1979.
1975a. *Mind, Language, and Reality: Philosophical Papers*, vol. 2. Cambridge: Cambridge University Press.
1975b. "The Meaning of 'Meaning'." Reprinted in Putnam 1975a.
1976. "Realism and Reason." Reprinted in Putnam 1978.
1978. *Meaning and the Moral Sciences*. Boston: Routledge & Kegan Paul.
1979. *Mathematics, Matter, and Method: Philosophical Papers*, vol. 1. 2d ed. Cambridge: Cambridge University Press.
1981. *Reason, Truth, and History*. Cambridge: Cambridge University Press.
1983. *Realism and Reason: Philosophical Papers*, vol. 3. Cambridge: Cambridge University Press.
Quine, W. V. O. 1951. "Two Dogmas of Empiricism." Reprinted in Quine 1961.
1960. *Word and Object*. Cambridge, Mass.: MIT Press.
1961. *From a Logical Point of View*. New York: Harper & Row.
1968. "Ontological Relativity." In Quine 1969a.
1969a. *Ontological Relativity*. New York: Columbia University Press.
1969b. "Epistemology Naturalized." In Quine 1969a.
1975. "The Nature of Natural Knowledge." In Guttenplan 1975.
Quinn, W. 1986. "Truth and Explanation in Ethics." *Ethics* 96:524–44.
Quinton, A. 1973. *The Nature of Things*. Boston: Routledge & Kegan Paul.
Railton, P. 1984. "Alienation, Consequentialism, and the Demands of Morality." *Philosophy and Public Affairs* 13:134–71.
1986. "Moral Realism." *Philosophical Review* 95:163–207.
Raphael, D. D. (ed.). 1969. *The British Moralists*. 2 vols. New York: Oxford University Press.
Rawls, J. 1951. "Outline for a Decision Procedure in Ethics." Reprinted in Thomson and Dworkin 1968.
1958. "Justice as Fairness." Reprinted in H. Bedeau (ed.), *Justice and Equality*. Englewood Cliffs, N.J.: Prentice-Hall, 1971.
1971. *A Theory of Justice*. Cambridge, Mass.: Harvard University Press.
1974. "The Independence of Moral Theory." *Proceedings of the APA* 48:5–22.
1979. "A Well-ordered Society." In P. Laslett and J. Fishkin (eds.), *Philosophy, Politics, and Society*. 5th series. New Haven, Conn.: Yale University Press.
1980. "Kantian Constructivism in Moral Theory." *Journal of Philosophy* 77: 515–72.
1982. "Social Unity and Primary Goods." In Sen and Williams 1982.
1985. "Justice as Fairness: Political Not Metaphysical." *Philosophy and Public Affairs* 14:223–51.
Reid, T. 1788. *Essays on the Active Powers of Man*. Reprinted in Raphael 1969.
Robbins, L. 1935. *An Essay on the Nature and Significance of Economic Science*. New York: Macmillan.

Rorty, R. 1980. *Philosophy and the Mirror of Nature*. Oxford: Blackwell.
Ross, W. D. 1930. *The Right and the Good*. New York: Oxford University Press.
Russell, B. 1912. *The Problems of Philosophy*. New York: Oxford University Press.
Salmon, N. 1982. *Reference and Essence*. Oxford: Blackwell.
Sartorius, R. 1975. *Individual Conduct and Social Norms*. Encino, Calif.: Dickenson.
Scanlon, T. M. 1975a. "Rawls' Theory of Justice." In Daniels 1975.
    1975b. "Preference and Urgency." *Journal of Philosophy* 72:655–69.
    1977. "Rights, Goals, and Fairness." Reprinted in Waldron 1984.
    1982. "Contractualism and Utilitarianism." In Sen and Williams 1982.
Scheffler, I. 1954. "Justification and Commitment." *Journal of Philosophy* 51:180–90.
Scheffler, S. 1979. "Moral Scepticism and Ideals of the Person." *The Monist* 62:288–303.
    1982. *The Rejection of Consequentialism*. New York: Oxford University Press.
Schlick, M. 1934. "The Foundation of Knowledge." In Ayer 1959.
Schneewind, J. 1977. *Sidgwick's Ethics and Victorian Moral Philosophy*. New York: Oxford University Press.
Schwartz, S. (ed.). 1977. *Naming, Necessity, and Natural Kinds*. Ithaca, N.Y.: Cornell University Press.
Searle, J. R. 1969. *Speech Acts*. Cambridge: Cambridge University Press.
Sellars, W. 1956. "Empiricism and the Philosophy of Mind." Reprinted in Sellars 1963.
    1963. *Science, Perception, and Reality*. Boston: Routledge & Kegan Paul.
Sen, A. 1973. *On Economic Inequality*. Oxford: Clarendon Press.
    1979a. "Utilitarianism and Welfarism." *Journal of Philosophy* 76:463–89.
    1979b. "Equality of What?" Reprinted in Sen 1982.
    1982. *Choice, Welfare, and Measurement*. Oxford: Blackwell.
Sen, A., and Williams, B. (eds.). 1982. *Utilitarianism and Beyond*. Cambridge: Cambridge University Press.
Sextus Empiricus. *Outlines of Pyrrhonism (PH)*.
    Adversus Mathematicos (AM).
Shoemaker, S. 1984. "Personal Identity: A Materialist's Account." In R. Swinburne and S. Shoemaker, *Personal Identity*. Oxford: Blackwell.
Sidgwick, H. 1879. "The Establishment of Ethical First Principles." *Mind* 4:106–11.
    1907. *The Methods of Ethics*. 7th ed. Chicago: University of Chicago Press.
Singer, P. 1974. "Sidgwick and Reflective Equilibrium. *The Monist* 57:490–517.
    1979. *Practical Ethics*. Cambridge: Cambridge University Press.
Slote, M. 1971. "The Rationality of Aesthetic Value Judgments." *Journal of Philosophy* 68:821–39.

1985. *Common-Sense Morality and Consequentialism.* Boston: Routledge & Kegan Paul.
Smart, J. J. C. 1973. "An Outline of a System of Utilitarian Ethics." In Smart and Williams 1973.
1984. *Ethics, Persuasion, and Truth.* Boston: Routledge & Kegan Paul.
Smart, J. J. C., and Williams, B. 1973. *Utilitarianism: For and Against.* Cambridge: Cambridge University Press.
Sober, E. 1982. "Realism and Independence." *Nous* 16:369–85.
Spinoza, B. 1677. *The Ethics,* trans. S. Shirley. Indianapolis, Ind.: Hackett, 1982.
Stevenson, C. L. 1937. "The Emotive Meaning of Ethical Terms." Reprinted in Stevenson 1963.
1944. *Ethics and Language.* New Haven, Conn.: Yale University Press.
1948a. "The Nature of Ethical Disagreement." Reprinted in Stevenson 1963.
1948b. "Meaning: Descriptive and Emotive." Reprinted in Stevenson 1963.
1963. *Facts and Values.* New Haven, Conn.: Yale University Press.
Stocker, M. 1976. "The Schizophrenia of Modern Ethical Theories." *Journal of Philosophy* 73:453–66.
Sturgeon, N. 1984. "Moral Explanations." In Copp and Zimmerman 1984.
1986a. "What Difference Does It Make Whether Moral Realism Is True?" In Gillespie 1986.
1986b. "Harman on Moral Explanations of Natural Facts." In Gillespie 1986.
1987. "Moral Skepticism and Moral Naturalism in Hume's *Treatise.*" Unpublished manuscript.
Sumner, W. G. 1940. *Folkways.* New York: Ginn.
Taylor, C. 1982. "The Diversity of Goods." In Sen and Williams 1982.
Thomson, J., and Dworkin G. (eds.). 1968. *Ethics.* New York: Harper & Row.
Waldron, J. (ed.). 1984. *Theories of Rights.* New York: Oxford University Press.
Warnock, G. 1967. *Contemporary Moral Philosophy.* New York: Macmillan.
1971. *The Object of Morality.* London: Methuen.
Westermarck, E. 1932. *Ethical Relativity.* New York: Humanities Press.
White, M. 1981. *What Is and What Ought to Be Done.* New York: Oxford University Press.
Whiting, J. 1986. "Friends and Future Selves." *Philosophical Review* 95:547–80.
Wiggins, D. 1976. "Truth, Invention, and the Meaning of Life." *Proceedings of the British Academy* 62:331–78.
1980. *Sameness and Substance.* Oxford: Blackwell.
1987a. "A Sensible Subjectivism?" In Wiggins 1987b.
1987b. *Needs, Values, and Truth.* Oxford: Blackwell.
Williams, B. 1965. "Ethical Consistency." Reprinted in Williams 1973b.

1966. "Consistency and Realism." Reprinted in Williams 1973b.
1972. *Morality: An Introduction to Ethics.* New York: Harper & Row.
1973a. "A Critique of Utilitarianism." In Smart and Williams 1973.
1973b. *Problems of the Self.* Cambridge: Cambridge University Press.
1975. "The Truth in Relativism." Reprinted in Williams 1981.
1976a. "Persons, Character, and Morality." Reprinted in Williams 1981.
1976b. "Utilitarianism and Moral Self-Indulgence." Reprinted in Williams 1981.
1979. "Conflicts of Values." Reprinted in Williams 1981.
1980. "Internal and External Reasons." Reprinted in Williams 1981.
1981. *Moral Luck.* Cambridge: Cambridge University Press.
1985. *Ethics and the Limits of Philosophy.* Cambridge, Mass.: Harvard University Press.
Williams, M. 1977. *Groundless Belief.* New Haven, Conn.: Yale University Press.
1980. "Coherence, Justification, and Truth." *Review of Metaphysics* 34:243–72.
1984. "Book Review: Hilary Putnam, *Reason, Truth, and History.*" *Journal of Philosophy* 81:257–61.
Wittgenstein, L. 1969. *On Certainty.* Oxford: Blackwell.
Wong, D. 1984. *Moral Relativity.* Los Angeles: University of California Press.

Index

conservatism, *see* coherentist epistemology
considered moral beliefs, 34, 132–43
constitution, 157–9, 176–7, 193–7
constructivism: ethical, 18–20, 33–4, 80, 139–40; metaphysical, 16–17, 31–5, 106–7, 114, 125
content of moral judgments, 25–9, 87
cooperation, 233–4, 272
Copp, D., 141
criteria of rightness, 216–17, 265–7. See *also* standards of rightness; utilitarianism

Daniels, N., 103, 132, 134, 141, 314, 315, 317
Darwall, S., 39, 40
Davidson, D., 39, 160
decision procedure, 10, 216–17, 265–7. *See also* utilitarianism
deliberative capacities, 232–3
Dennett, D., 158
Descartes, R., 101, 109
desire-satisfaction theories of rationality, 55–7, 62; actual, 69–70; counterfactual, 69–70; and instrumentalism, 63–6; and rational egoism, 67–74
desire-satisfaction theories of utilitarianism, 10; *see also* utilitarianism
desire-satisfaction theories of value, 10, 21, 66–9, 221, 224–31, 263–4; actual, 68, 221, 226–8; counterfactual, 68–9, 221, 228–31
disagreement, moral, 85–6, 110–12, 142–3, 197–209, 246–9; antecedent, 203–4, 247–8; diachronic character of, 204–9, *see also* progress; and ethical theory, 204–9; merely apparent, 200–2, 246–7; and nonmoral disagreement, 202–3, 248
distribution, *see* justice
dogmatism, 94–5
Donagan, A., 249, 259
Duhem, P., 103, 137
Dummett, M., 16, 17, 102, 153
Dworkin, R., 20, 125, 133, 139, 249, 263, 269, 320

egoism: psychological, 67, 224–5; rational, *see* rational egoism
emotivism, 18–19. *See also* noncognitivism

epiphenomenalism, 160, 191
epistemic justification: and circular reasoning, 105, 116, 121, 123–4; contextual and systematic, distinguished, 123–4; diachronic and synchronic, distinguished, 32, 126, 128; and infinite regress, 105, 291–5; and linear reasoning, 123–4; and second-order beliefs, 117–22, 124–5, 127–33; *see also* coherentist epistemology; epistemological requirement; foundationalism; objectivism about justification; regress argument
epistemological requirement, 104–5, 116, 121–2, 291–3
epistemology: externalist, 296–300; internalist, 296–300; and justification, *see* epistemic justification; moral, 3–4, 8–9, 100, 180–2. *See also* coherentist epistemology; considered moral beliefs; disagreement; explanation, moral; theory
esoteric moralities, 87–90, 261–2. *See also* publicity; utilitarianism
ethical egoism, 67
ethical naturalism, *see* naturalism
evaluative method, 64–6, 218. *See also* thought experiments
experience machine, 223–4
expertise, 95–8, 205–9
explanation, moral, 182–97, 245–6; of actions and social events, 187–97; and counterfactual test of relevance, 189–90; and explanatory reduction, 179–80, 191–7; of moral judgments, 184–6; structural nature of, 193–7; in terms of psychological set, 185–8
externalism: in epistemology, 296–300; about morality, 8, 42–3, 49–50, 58–62

Falk, W. D., 38, 39, 43
fallibilism, 94–5
Fehrenbacher, D., 187
Field, H., 173, 178
first-order beliefs, 35, 127
first-order moral issues, 1–2. *See also* independence of metaethics and normative ethics
Fodor, J., 166, 167, 180, 194
Føllesdall, D., 40
Foot, P., 39, 43, 61, 76, 153, 236, 244
form of moral judgments, 25–6, 87
foundationalism, 101–3; and anti-

skeptical argument, *see* antiskeptical argument for foundationalism; groundless, 120–2; hybrid, 119–20; and regress argument, *see* regress argument; rejected, 116–22; subjective and objective versions of, 108–9, 114–15, 117–20. *See also* epistemological requirement; intuitionism; objectivism about justification
Frankena, W., 39, 43, 45, 102, 147, 157, 215, 216
Frankfurt, H., 109
Frege, G., 148
Fried, C., 249, 250, 274

Garfinkel, A., 180, 194
Gasper, P., x, 52
Gauthier, D., 40, 43, 222, 228
Gewirth, A., 249
Goldman, A., 296
Goodman, N., 16
Green, T. H., 222, 244
Grice, R., 39
groundless foundationalism, 120–2
groundless intuitionism, 120

Hancock, R., 163
happiness, 221–2. *See also* utilitarianism; value
Hardie, W. F. R., 103
Hare, R. M., 3, 19, 23, 31, 37, 39, 42, 43, 46, 81, 85, 125, 133, 134, 139, 141, 145, 147, 148, 153, 156, 160, 163, 253, 258, 260
Harker, J., 292
Harman, G., xi, 2, 4, 37–9, 42, 44, 52–77, 103, 169, 171, 173, 178, 180–91
Hart, H. L. A., 263, 289
hedonism, 221, 223–4, 263–4. *See also* utilitarianism; value
Hellman, G., 166
Herskovits, M., 20, 198
Hitler, A., 55–6
Hobbes, T., 47
holism, epistemic, 34, 136–8, 183–4
Homer, 222
Horwich, P., 125
Hudson, W. D., 100, 108
Hume, D., 9, 37, 49, 63–4, 145–6, 222
Huxley, A., 227

idealism, 15
ideals of person, 232–3, 304, 312–21

identity: of persons, 232, 284–8, 313–14; of properties, 157, 176–7
impartiality, 132, 236–7, 274–6, 278, 280–1, 284–5, 288
impersonal theories of value, *see* value
independence of metaethics and normative ethics, 4–5, 21–2, 81–99, 212, 249–52, 260
inference to best explanation, 169
infinite regress, *see* epistemic justification
inquiry, moral, 23–5
instrumental theories of rationality, 63–6. *See also* rationality
integrity, *see* personal point of view
internalism: in epistemology, 296–300; about morality, 8, 37–53, 58–62, 145–6, 172, 278–9; about rationality, 39
interpersonal comparisons of welfare, 252–9
intolerance, 92–4
intrapersonal comparisons of welfare, 254
intuitionism, 2–3, 8, 100, 102–3, 107–13, 180, 301–2; groundless, 120; mathematical, 17, 102; philosophical, 108, 112–13. *See also* foundationalism
intuitions, moral, 109, 133–5
inverse plausibility argument, 75–7
inverted-commas usage, 46–7, 59
Irwin, T. H., x–xi, 43, 103, 112, 233, 244, 291
is/ought thesis, 29–30; and antinaturalist argument, 163–7; and bridge premises, 149, 151, 167; explained, 145–9; internalist version of, 145–6; and intuitionism, 301–2; and logical thesis, 149–51; and meaning implication argument, 153–5; and naturalism and nonnaturalism, 9, 156–67, 174–5, 177; and nihilism, 155–6, 167; plausibility of, 149–55; and semantic thesis, 151–5, 174–5; and skepticism, 155, 168–70; and synonymy argument, 152–5

James, W., 16
Joachim, H., 16, 103, 125
Joseph, H., 251
judgments, considered moral, *see* considered moral beliefs
justice: distributive, 200, 219–20, 270–3, 285–8; retributive, 270

justification: epistemic, *see* epistemic justification; of morality, 27, 46–78, 240–5, 278–83

Kant, I., 50, 57, 63, 70, 251, 261
Kantian constructivism: epistemological conception of, 307, 311; and ideals of person, 304, 312–21; metaphysical conception of, 307–12; political conception of, 306–10. *See also* Rawls, J.
Kantian moral assumptions, 50–2, 54, 57, 63–4, 70, 75–7, 244, 251, 280
Kemeny, J., 151
Kim, J., 160, 167, 195
Kitcher, P., 103, 137
Klagge, J., 166
Kraut, R., 69, 221–2
Kripke, S., 33, 157, 165–6
Kuhn, T., 16, 121, 125

Lehrer, K., 103
Lewis, C. I., 101, 102, 104, 135, 148, 162, 302
Little, I. M. D., 253
Locke, J., 102, 207, 302, 313
logical thesis, *see* is/ought thesis
Lomasky, L., 249, 259, 271, 274, 284
Luce, R. D., 253
Lyons, D., x, 125, 133, 139, 249

McDowell, J., 39, 43, 44, 182, 231
Mackie, J. L., 2, 4, 17, 18, 24, 37–9, 42, 43, 44, 51–77, 81, 100, 108, 146, 171–82, 197–203, 236
Mamet, D., 47
materialism and metaphysics of ethics, 159, 178–80, 239–40
meaning implication, 148, 149, 153–5
meaning implication argument, 153–5
Medlin, B., 39, 80, 89, 259
metaethics, 1–5; *see also* antirealism; disagreement; epistemology; explanation; independence of metaethics and normative ethics; inquiry; is/ought thesis; justification, of morality; moral psychology; naturalism; nonnaturalism; realism; semantics; value
Mill, J. S., 88, 120, 214, 216, 217, 218, 222, 225, 232, 256–8
mistakes: in attitude, 30–1; moral, 29–31
Moore, G. E., 2, 6, 8, 22, 100, 102, 109, 120, 146, 151–4, 160, 162, 165, 216, 218–20, 222, 250, 251, 256–7

moral epistemology, *see* epistemology, moral
moral language, 19, 165–7
moral psychology, 1, 8, 37. *See also* action-guidingness; externalism, about morality; internalism, about morality; justification, of morality; personal point of view; rationality
motivation, *see* action-guidingness; externalism, about morality; internalism, about morality; moral psychology
multiple realizability, 158–9, 177–80, 193–7
Murdoch, I., 39

Nagel, E., 151, 167
Nagel, T., 2, 31, 32, 43, 44, 51–2, 54, 58, 70, 73, 182, 241–2, 250, 274, 281
naturalism, ethical, 9, 22, 91, 156–67, 175–80, 238–40
naturalistic fallacy, 146, 151–4, 156, 162–3
Nesbitt, W., 61
Neurath, O., 103
Nielsen, K., 39, 43
nihilism, 16–17; moral, 18–19, 155–6, 167, 317
noncognitivism, 3–5, 18–19, 26–31, 78–9, 83–7, 162–3
nonnaturalism, 3, 22, 156, 164–5, 174, 238, 301
normative ethics, 1–2, 4
Nowell-Smith, P., 3, 37, 39, 43, 100, 108, 145, 198
Nozick, R., 71, 222–4, 269, 276, 281, 289, 296

objective utilitarianism, *see* utilitarianism
objectivism: about justification, 106–7, 114–16, 125–7, 129; about value, *see* value
objectivity, 5–7, 11, 20
observational beliefs, 34; and considered moral beliefs, 135–9
open-question argument, 151–4, 162–3
Oppenheim, P., 151

Parfit, D., 89, 205, 216, 262, 286–8, 317
parity of ethics and science, 6–7, 11, 135–9, 211–12

338